AUBREY'S BRIEF LIVES

AUBREY'S BRIEF LIVES

Edited from the Original Manuscripts
and with a Life of John Aubrey by

OLIVER LAWSON DICK

Foreword by EDMUND WILSON

ANN ARBOR
THE UNIVERSITY OF MICHIGAN PRESS

To

Sir STEPHEN TALLENTS

FOREWORD *by* EDMUND WILSON

JOHN AUBREY, who flourished between 1626 and 1697, was an English country gentleman of lively intellectual interests but rather infirm character. He was, one suspects, made unsure of himself by an obtuse and obstructive father, and his life became a series of projects that almost invariably ended unsatisfactorily. His education at Oxford was interrupted by the Civil Wars; the estates that he inherited from his father were heavily involved in lawsuits, and he was eventually obliged to sell them all; an attempt to marry resulted in the lady's clapping another suit on him; a collection of biographical material that he had allowed to get into the hands of professional scholars was partly used by them without acknowledgment and partly destroyed or lost. Yet Aubrey was an antiquary of some distinction and a charter member of the Royal Society, and his collection of biographical data turned out to be extremely valuable. As "Aubrey's Brief Lives," it has figured as a source book for historians. Now it has a splendid new edition at the hands of Oliver Lawson Dick.

This edition is, indeed, the first one that has been faithful to Aubrey's text and that has attempted to make a book from his manuscripts. For what Aubrey left was not a book. He loved to compile gossip about famous men and to note their peculiarities, and in pursuit of this information he often went to considerable trouble. It was said of him by one of his friends that he expected to hear of Aubrey's breaking his neck someday as the result of dashing downstairs to get a story from a departing guest. But he did not keep his records in order. He would try to get things down on paper the morning after a convivial evening—"Sot that I am!" is the apologetic cry that is reiterated in his writings—when the people he was visiting were still in bed and he himself was suffering from hangover. He sometimes mixed anecdotes about different people, sometimes wrote the same story several times, and sometimes noted down under a subject's name only a few words or a mere list of dates and facts.

Mr. Lawson Dick has selected from the 426 headings in Aubrey's manuscripts 134 that have something substantial attached to them; he has restored to them the passages expurgated by nineteenth-century editors; he has arranged them alphabetically; and he has written for them an introduction, itself as long as a small book, called "The Life and Times of John Aubrey," which is a masterpiece of its kind—for, using wherever possible the words of Aubrey himself, put together from his scattered writings, Mr. Lawson Dick has succeeded in producing an intimate portrait of his subject embedded in the density of current events. You can see much of the seventeenth century through Aubrey, because he was involved more or less in almost all its activities and interests: social, political, religious, scientific, and literary. And Aubrey's own accounts of his contemporaries and of the men of the preceding period—Boyle, Harvey, Hobbes, Ben Jonson, Marvell, Milton, Monk, Raleigh, Shakespeare, Sidney, Rochester, Wolsey, etc.— take you quite out of the Hall of Monuments of the established reputation and the accepted classic, and into a world where all these celebrities are still alive and kicking or have not long ceased to be so. For Aubrey, they were people one knew or who had been known by people one knew. His own weaknesses and vulnerabilities made him notice what was odd about them, and he had a great sense of the illuminating incident and the characteristic trait— such as Bacon's "delicate, lively, hazel Eie," of which he says Dr. Harvey told him that it was "like the Eie of a viper," and on which Lytton Strachey pounced to exploit it for dramatic effect in "Elizabeth and Essex." But his own more serious interests compelled him to respect what was serious, and he writes about Thomas Hobbes, whom he had known since he (Aubrey) was a child of eight, at what is for him great length.

The whole ferment of the Elizabethan Age and the vigor of the century that followed are still exciting and fresh in this book. I have never read anything else that made me feel in quite the same way what it must have been like to live then, to find oneself part of an England that was venturesome, unsettled, and eager, that was opening new horizons. John Aubrey, not one of its giants, brings its heroes down to human scale. He becomes, with Mr. Lawson Dick's edition, an unmistakable and a manageable classic.

PREFACE

The original material used in this edition has been taken from fifty volumes in the Bodleian Library at Oxford and from sixteen volumes in the libraries of the Wiltshire Archaeological and Natural History Society, The Royal Society, the Corporation of London, and the British Museum. The passages from the original manuscripts that have been included in this edition have been selected on the following plan:

1. Any life that has nothing of intrinsic value to offer has been discarded. The 426 lives which Aubrey wrote vary so considerably in length (one consists of two words, another of twenty-three thousand) that many of them are of no interest whatsoever, consisting either of extracts from books or of mere lists of dates and facts. All that Aubrey has to say of John Holywood, for instance, is "Dr. Pell is positive that his name was Holybushe."

2. In the 134 lives that have been selected, many sentences have been rejected. For Aubrey starts one life as follows: "James Harrington, Esq; the son of . . . Harrington of . . . in the Countie of . . . , by . . . , daughter of Sir . . . Samuel, was borne at . . . (Sir . . . Samuel's house in Northamptonshire) anno . . . ." All sentences like this, which display nothing more than Aubrey's ignorance of a date or a place or the title of a book, have been omitted.

3. The imperfections of Aubrey's copy have been amended in the way that he intended they should be. A choice has been made between the alternative words he jotted down, and the several versions of his favourite stories, which he repeated sometimes as many as seven times, have been collated and a single version produced. As an instance, the two-page life of William and Philip Herbert was assembled from eleven different manuscripts; and this whole edition has been built up, like a jigsaw, until the disconnected pieces have at last resolved themselves into a complete picture.

4. All notes, quotation marks, and other distractions to continuous reading have been excluded from the text, and each life has been prefaced with a paragraph, written by the editor, outlining those facts about the subject which Aubrey has ignored. These are always included in square brackets [ ].

5. Wherever a Latin quotation in the text is not self-explanatory, its translation has been given in square brackets. The word "pounds" has also been substituted throughout for the Latin "libri."

6. Aubrey's many mistakes have been left uncorrected, except in the case of two gross misquotations of famous poems. On the

few occasions when Aubrey has not only left a gap to be filled in later, but has also given the reference from which the fact can be obtained, that fact has been supplied. For instance, in the life of Sir William Petty Aubrey says: "Anno Domini . . . happened that memorable accident and experiment of the reviving Nan Green, which is to be ascribed and attributed to Dr. William Petty, as the first discoverer of life in her, and author of saving her. Vide and insert the material passages in the Tryal, and anatomicall experiment of Nan Green at Oxon: vide the narrative." In the face of such clear instructions, I have felt justified in including seven lines describing the incident from Anthony Wood's "Journal." Nowhere else has such an insertion been made, but on a few occasions the word "some" has been introduced to make good the omission of a figure; and in one place a word which Aubrey uses elsewhere, "denigrating," has been inserted in the life of William Camden to complete a sentence.

7. Aubrey's original spelling has been retained throughout, except that merely artificial tricks of writing (y^t for that, wch for which, m̃ for mm) have been neglected. Aubrey's use of capital letters has also been followed. Wherever possible, his original punctuation has been given, and italics have been used, when necessary, to clarify the meaning.

8. In "The Life and Times of John Aubrey," however, italics have been used merely to distinguish those passages which occur in Aubrey's own handwriting in the manuscripts.

9. Aubrey's use of sign language has been abandoned, and wherever possible this form of shorthand has been translated into words.

10. Lastly, there comes the vexed question of obscenity. In the seventeenth century sex had not yet been singled out as the sin par excellence, it was merely one among many failings, and Aubrey no more thought of concealing it than he dreamed of avoiding the mention of gluttony or drunkenness. After judging his work, therefore, by its general tendency and not by particular details, it has been decided not to bowdlerise it in the slightest degree, but to print it as it was written, without emphasis and without concealment.

CONTENTS

CONTENTS

[x]

CONTENTS

CONTENTS

THE LIFE AND TIMES OF JOHN AUBREY

NOT long after John Aubrey's death, a wise man warned us against treating books like members of the nobility : that is, against learning their titles and bragging afterwards of acquaintance with them. Yet this has been peculiarly Aubrey's fate ; for his reputation is founded almost entirely upon hearsay and the piecemeal quotation of his work by other writers.

The reason for the extraordinary neglect of this man of genius is not hard to find and the fault, it must be admitted, is entirely his own. For Aubrey's love of life was so intense, his curiosity so promiscuous and so insatiable, that he proved quite incapable of completing any work he undertook. Each one was started in a most businesslike and practical fashion, but before long the original plan was always buried beneath the flood of digressions and notes, of horoscopes, letters and stories, which his restless mind seemed powerless to control.

Having decided to write a life, Aubrey selected a page in one of his notebooks and jotted down as quickly as possible everything that he could remember about the character concerned : his friends, his appearance, his actions, his books and his sayings. Any facts or dates that did not occur to him on the spur of the moment were left blank, and as Aubrey was so extremely sociable that he was usually suffering from a hangover when he came to put pen to paper, the number of these omissions was often very large. In the first flush of composition, too, his mind raced so far beyond his pen that he frequently resorted to a sort of involved shorthand and made use of signs instead of words.

He then read over what he had just written and put in any stories that he thought were even vaguely relevant, wrote alternatives to words and phrases, inserted queries, numbered words, sentences and paragraphs for transposition, disarranged everything.

Any facts that occurred to him later were jotted down quite at random, in the margin if there was still room, otherwise on another page or in the middle of another life, often in a different volume, sometimes even in a letter to a friend. And there the text was left, for he rarely made a fair copy of anything that he had written because, as he confessed, he *wanted patience to go through Knotty Studies.*

Even the optimistic author despaired at last of ever reducing his life's work to a manageable shape. *Considering therefore that if I should not finish and publish what I had begun,* he wrote, *My Papers might either perish, or be sold in an Auction, and some body else (as is not uncommon) put his name to my Paines : and not knowing any one that would undertake this Design whilst I live, I have tumultuarily stitcht up what I have many yeares since collected : I hope, hereafter it may be an Incitement to some Ingeniose and publick-spirited young Man, to polish and compleat, what I have delivered rough hewen : For I have not leisure to heighten my Stile.*

[xiii]

Accepting this clear mandate and electing myself the *Ingeniose and publick-spirited young Man*, I have taken Aubrey at his word, and using his manuscripts as if they were my own notes, I have constructed the following book : with the important reservation that I have nowhere departed from the original text, although I have ruthlessly rearranged it.

Of this behaviour Aubrey would have thoroughly approved, for he purposely left his manuscripts in note form. *I know here be several Tautologies,* he wrote to Anthony Wood, when he sent him what the latter rightly called " the foul draught of Mr. Hobbs life," *but I putt them downe thus here, that upon reviewe I should judge where such or such a thing would most aptly stand,* and his considered opinion was that *First Draughts ought to be as rude as those of Paynters, for he that in his first essay will be curious in refining will certainly be unhappy in inventing.*

The present book, in the editor's opinion, approximates as nearly as possible to Aubrey's original intention. During the preparation of this edition, moreover, so much new information about Aubrey himself has come to light, that it is now possible to give a full account of his life. For when he came to write his own biography, Aubrey was overcome by a modesty, which is quite inexplicable when one considers the care with which he preserved even the smallest trivialities about other people. But the three pages on which he did finally jot down a few bare facts about himself were accompanied nonetheless by the instruction, *To be interposed as a sheet of wast paper only in the binding of a booke.*

He was borne, he says, (*longaevous, healthy kindred*) *at Easton Pierse, a Hamlet in the Parish of Kington Saint Michael, in the Hundred of Malmesbury in the Countie of Wilts, his mother's* (*daughter and heir of Mr. Isaac Lyte*) *inheritance, March the* 12 (*St. Gregorie's day*) *A.D.* 1625, *about Sun-riseing, being very weake and like to dye that he was Christned before morning prayer.*

His father, Richard Aubrey, was of the Aubrey's of Herefordshire, a family which had built up a considerable estate on the foundations laid by William Aubrey, *Doctor of Lawes,* a man of some importance at the Court of Queen Elizabeth, *who loved him and was wont to call him ' her little Doctor.'* He was one of the *Delegates for the tryall of Mary, Queen of Scots,* according to John Aubrey, *and was a great Stickler for the saving of her life, which kindnesse was remembered by King James att his comeing-in to England, who asked after him, and probably would have made him Lord Keeper, but he dyed a little before that good opportunity happened. His Majestie sent for his sonnes, and knighted the two eldest, and invited them to Court, which they modestly and perhaps prudently declined. They preferred a Country life.* And in the country the family stayed, slowly enlarging its estates by good management and strategic marriages, until within a generation the Aubreys had so firmly established their place amongst the richer gentry of England that Aubrey's father was three times fined " for not taking the Order of Knighthood at the Coronation of King Charles I." But one less agreeable legacy descended from this worthy to his children : *He engrossed all the witt of the family,* said his great-grandson sadly, *so that none descended from him can pretend to any.*

John Aubrey was born during one of the Golden Ages of history, when *there had been a long serene Calme of Peace, and Men minded nothing but peace and Luxury*. The English Renaissance was at its height, and despite the squalor and the dirt and the barbarity that surrounded the material side of life (and which the modern world, mistaking comfort for civilisation, is too apt to overemphasise) the art of living reached its peak in England during the early years of Charles I's reign. When Erasmus had described, a century before, the things upon which the various nations prided themselves, the Scots their nobility and logical sense, the French their breeding, he said of the English that they " particularly challenge to themselves Beauty, Music and Feasting." And upon these specifically human virtues the nation still prided itself. For it was an aristocratic age, which had no admiration for the Little Man, and its inhabitants were not ashamed to admit that there were many excellencies which were not universally attainable. And loneliness, the plague of modern civilisation (with all its attendant discontents) had still not subdued the mediæval gregariousness of the English people.

But though a true aristocracy existed, it was soundly based on worth, and the social classes, though clearly marked and unquestioningly accepted, were very fluid. Aubrey, besides noting with approval both John Gadbury's saying that *the Heavens are the best Heraulds* and Ben Jonson's remark *the most worthy men have been rokked in mean Cradles*, added on his own account *Poets and Bravos have Punkes to their Mothers*. For the rewards for ability were unlimited, no matter how humble one's circumstances might have been : *The father of Richard Neile, ArchBishop of Yorke, was a Tallow-Chandler in Westminster :* and the newly ennobled were so little ashamed of their mean origins that Aubrey falls severely upon Lord Burghley for his absurd pride. *The true name is Sitsilt,* he says, *and is an ancient Monmouthshire family but now come to be about the degree of yeomanry. 'Tis strange that they should be so vaine as to leave off an old British name for a Romancy one, which I beleeve Mr. Verstegen did putt into their heads, telling his Lordship, in his Booke, that they were derived from the ancient Roman Cecilii.*

The reasons for this sudden blossoming of the spirit were largely religious. The power of the Church had only recently been broken and had not yet been replaced by the tyranny of the State, and the consequent feeling of freedom and infinite opportunity made it a blessed time to live. For the destruction of the Church of Rome brought with it a release from the burden of sin which had weighed down the English spirit in the past, and life became, for a few short generations, not a thing to be put up with, but a gift to be enjoyed with zest. Even more important, the Puritans were still only a religious sect, and their prejudices, so soon to become the accepted opinions of the middle classes, were still looked upon as fanatic delusions ; nor had they yet infected the whole nation with their pernicious idea of the seriousness of work, which has ever since distorted the idea of recreation into mere idleness or games. In the Stuart Century the great mass of the nation still followed Aristotle's rule that " the first principle of all action is leisure," and leisure to the seventeenth-century man was not relaxation, but another form of activity. For the simultaneous discovery of the New Learning and the New World had so fired the imagination that there had emerged a whole society of full grown men and women, to whom Milton could justly say : " Lords and Commons of England—Consider what nation it is whereof ye are : a nation not slow and dull, but of quick, ingenious and piercing spirit ; acute to invent, subtile and sinewy to discourse, not beneath the reach of any point that human capacity can soar to." And it was into this world that John Aubrey was born.

I think I have heard my mother say I had an Ague shortly after I was borne, says Aubrey, taking up his own life again. *1629 : about 3 or 4 years old, I had a grievous Ague : I can remember it. I gott not strength till I was 11 or 12 yeares old ; but had sickenesse of vomiting (the Belly-ake : paine in the side) for 12 houres every fortnight for several yeares, then about monethly, then quarterly, and at last once in halfe a yeare. About 12 it ceased. This Sicknesse nipt my strength in the bud.*

1633 : 8 yeares old, I had an Issue (naturall) in the coronall suture of my head, which continued running till 21. 1634 : October : I had a violent Fever that was like to have carried me off. 'Twas the most dangerous sicknesse that ever I had. About 1639 (or 1640) I had the Measills, but that was nothing : I was hardly Sick.

This catalogue of illnesses marks perhaps the sharpest difference between Aubrey's time and our own. For death was everywhere, and the dozen or so children born to every marriage kept it firmly before each man's eyes : it being as unusual then for a child to live, as it is now for one to die. *Ten children in one Grave ! a dreadful Sight !* lament the tombs,

> *Could Beauty, Youth, or Innocence*
> *Their frail Possessors save*
> *From Death, sweet Babe, a sure Defence*
> *Thoud'st had, and not been hurryed hence*
> *Into the silent Grave.*

> *But mortal Creatures, borne to dye,*
> *To Nature must submit :*
> *When that commands, all must comply,*
> *No Parts can sheild from Destiny,*
> *We then the Stage must quitt.*

To a generation which was ever conscious that man was, as Marcus Aurelius had said, " a pigmy soul carrying a dead body to its grave," there seemed to be some strange comfort in the fact that all nature shared the same doom :

> *Like to the Damask Rose you see,*
> *Or like the Blossome on the Tree,*
> *Or like the dainty Flower of May,*
> *Or like the Morning of the Day,*
> *Or like the Sun, or like the Shade,*
> *Or like the Gourd which Jonas had,*
> *Even so is Man, whose Thread is spun,*
> *Drawn out, and cutt, and so is done.*

[xvi]

> *The Rose withers, the Blossom blasteth,*
> *The Flower fades, the Morning hasteth,*
> *The Sun setts, the Shadow flies,*
> *The Gourd consumes, and Man he dies.*

Out of this constant grief there arose at last the very glorification of death. " What a noble animal is man, splendid in ashes, pompous in the grave," intones Sir Thomas Browne, and Sir Walter Raleigh exults " It is therefore Death alone that can suddenly make man to know himself. He holds a glass before the eyes of the most beautiful and makes them see therein their deformity and rottenness and acknowledge it." This praise of death even made men gloat over the corruption that was only too evident in the shallow graves and gibbetted felons of the time. *It is still accounted undecent for Widows to marry within a yeare (I thinke)*, John Aubrey says, *because in that time the husbands body may be presumed to be rotten.* And in what other century could a man have written of his own child :

> *Christopher Michell's Sonn lyeth here, Richard Michell was his Name,*
> *His Father's Love was so to him, he caus'd to write the same :*
> *He was but 4 Yeares 5 Monetbs old, and then was buryed here,*
> *And of his Body the Wormes did find a Dish of dainty chere.*

But it was not only in childhood that death threatened. The law, not yet having learnt to distinguish between crime and sin, punished both with the utmost savagery, for in the absence of a police force or any method of detection, the few wrongdoers who were caught had to suffer a painful and public death as a sufficient discouragement to others. " The Court doth award that you be drawn upon a hurdle to the place of execution and there shall be hanged by the neck, and, being alive, shall be cut down and your entrails to be taken out of your body, and, you living, the same to be burnt before your eyes, and your head to be cutt off, your body to be divided into four quarters, and head and quarters to be disposed of at the pleasure of the King's Majesty : and the Lord have mercy on your soul ! " The most educated and sensitive men were onlookers at these dreadful spectacles : even the kindly Aubrey reports, *I did see Mr. Chr. Love beheaded on Tower-hill in a delicate cleare day*, although he seems to have had some doubts about the ceremony, for he added, *about half an hour after his Head was struck off, the Clouds gathered blacker and blacker, and all that night and till next noon such terrible Claps of Thunder lightning and Tempest as if the Machine of the World had been dissolving.* Aubrey never deceived himself, however, as to the real reason for his interest in these exhibitions. *Ah ! 'tis the best lechery to see 'em suffer Correction*, observes one of the characters in his play. *Your London Aldermen take great Lechery to see the poor wretches whipt at the Court at Bridewell. Were it not for the Law there were no living*, he decided. *Some would take delight in killing of men.*

The abscence of any sure method of redressing private wrongs, the law being so cumbersome and so corrupt, led to the continuation of the personal feud in the unlighted and unpatrolled streets. *Capt.*

Yarrington dyed at London about March last, Aubrey noted. *The cause of his death was a Beating and throwne into a Tub of Water.* Furthermore, the sword was still a part of everyday dress and this made men, when they were in drink, *verie apt to doe bloudy Mischiefes.* However, we soon become indifferent to the lethal weapons of our own times, and there is no reason to think that the danger of stabbing worried the men of the seventeenth century any more than the prospect of a motoring accident troubles us. In fact, the attitude was remarkably similar. *Edmund Wyld, Esq. had the misfortune to kill a man in London, upon a great provocation, about A.D.* 1644, Aubrey reports, and he himself, despite all his benevolence, was three times in *Danger of Expiration* in this way. *Memorandum,* he jotted down, *St. John's night,* 1673, *in danger of being run through with a sword at Mr. Burges' chamber in the Middle Temple. Quaere the yeare that I lay at Mris. Neve's,* he continued, *for that time I was in great danger of being killed by a drunkard in the street opposite Grayes-Inn gate—a gentleman whom I never sawe before, but (Deo Gratias) one of his companions hindred his thrust.* On the third occasion, though, there was no doubt as to the identity of the culprit. *Danger of being killed by William, Earl of Pembroke, then Lord Herbert, at the Election of Sir William Salkeld for New Sarum,* Aubrey reported bluntly, and ever afterwards his writing took on a peculiarly spiteful tone at any mention of the Herberts. But sometimes even this violence had good results : *After Dr. Lamb was killed in the streets by the Apprentices of London,* Aubrey mentions, *the City was fined* 10,000 *pounds which payd for the Building of the Banquetting house.*

Far more worrying than this occasional violence were the continual outbreaks of the plague in the early years of the century, when the Black Death of the Middle Ages flared into a dying fury before destroying itself finally in the Great Plague of 1665. At the time, there was no reason to suppose that this disaster was the last visit of the scourge that had lain upon the country for so long, and as late as 1680 we find Aubrey making this ominous note : *Mr. Fabian Philips sayes the winter* 1625 *before the Plague was such a mild winter as this : quod* N.B.

As the mediæval plague finally consumed itself with its own violence : *At Petersham the Plague made so great a Destruction, that there survived only five of the Inhabitants :* its place was taken by a new pestilence, syphilis, which had been brought back from the New World by Columbus' crew to rage with dreadful fury in the fresh soil of Europe. For the first outbreak of the disease was so violent, its progress was so rapid and the symptoms so revolting, that even the lepers refused to live beside its victims.

Small-pox, too, raged throughout the land with a dreadful regularity. *The Small-Pox is usually in all great Towns,* says Aubrey complacently, *but it is observed at Taunton in Somersetshire, and at Sherburne in Dorsetshire, that at the one of them every Seventh Year, and at the other every Ninth Year comes a Small-Pox, which the Physitians cannot master.*

Nor was it from disease alone that death threatened, for Aubrey mentions that George Villiers' mother, *the Countesse of Bucks, died of a dropsi and Phisick.* For the medical profession, with neither knowledge nor traditions, was groping its way so unsurely from quackery towards

[xviii]

enlightenment that many people must have come, like Robert Boyle, to "apprehend more from the physician than the disease."

The majority of even the most eminent practitioners were still amateurs, like *Fish, M.D., or so called, who practised Physick and Astrologie, and had a good practise in both, in Convent Garden London,* and each jealously guarded the secrets of his cures from his rivals, so that no advance in the science was possible. And perhaps they were wise to conceal their methods after all, for William Harvey sadly confessed to Aubrey that *after his Booke of the Circulation of the Blood came-out, he fell mightily in his Practize, and 'twas beleeved by the vulgar that he was crack-brained.*

In each generation, therefore, the doctors started from scratch again and, pursuing their own strange remedies, dealt death indiscriminately until they stumbled by chance on a treatment that did less harm than good, and then they concealed the secret until they were able to take it with them to the grave, unless they had previously managed to sell it for a good profit, like that " kinswoman of Sir A. King's which," Robert Hooke noted in his Diary, " had a certain cure for a Leprosy or Scaled head. Shee had £100 per annum of St. Bartholomews hospitall to which she promised to Leave the Receipt."

Very few men were so scientific as Dr. Jacquinto, Physician to Queen Anne, James I's consort, *who went into the Marshes of Essex, where they putt their sheep to cure them of the Rott, where he lived sometime purposely, to goe after the sheep, and observe what plants they did eat : and of those Herbes he made his Medicine for the Consumption, which did great Cures.* The great majority still depended largely on magic for their treatments, and dreams and prayers were considered far more valuable than any research. Dr. Napier, for instance, who *was no Doctor, but a divine (rector Lindfordiensis) and practised Physick, when a Patient, or Quaerent came to him, presently went to his Closet to Pray : It appears by his Papers,* says Aubrey, *that he did converse with the Angel Raphael, who told him if the Patient were curable or incurable ;* and the popularity of this treatment is proved by the fact that *his Knees were horny with frequent Praying.*

That visionary prescriptions were not always to be relied on, however, is shown by a gentlewoman of Aubrey's acquaintance, *who had a beloved Daughter, who had been a long time Ill, and received no benefit from her Physitians. She dream'd that a Friend of hers deceased, told her, that if she gave her Daughter a Drench of Yewgh pounded, she would recover. She gave her the Drench and it killed her, whereupon she grew almost distracted. Her Chamber Maid to Complement her, and to mitigate her Grief, said surely that could not Kill her ; she would adventure to take the same her self ; she did so and died also. This was about the Year* 1670 or 1671, Aubrey concludes, *I knew the Family.* Sometimes, though, this indiscriminate dosing did bear unexpected fruit for medical science : *A woman (I thinke in Italy) endeavoured to poyson her Husband (who was a Dropsicall Man) by boyling a Toade in his Potage ; which cured him : and this was the occasion of finding out the Medicine.* Not altogether unexpectedly all the same, for the therapeutic value of frogs had long been known and Aubrey himself has noted down a proven remedy *To cure the Thrush.* Take a living Frog, he says, *and hold it in a Cloth, that it does not go down into the Childs Mouth ; and putt the Head into the Childs*

Mouth till it is dead ; and then take another Frog. It was little wonder, after treatments like this, if the patients reacted strangely too, like *Oliver Cromwell, when he was so dangerously ill in Scotland of a kind of calenture or high Fever, that he pistolled one or two of his Commanders that came to visit him in his delirious rage.*

To Cure the Tooth-ach, Aubrey jots down elsewhere, *Take a new Nail, and make the Gum bleed with it, and then drive it into an Oak. This did Cure William Neal, Sir William Neal's Son, a very stout Gentleman, when he was almost Mad with the Pain, and had a mind to have Pistoll'd himself.* For in the dreadful days before the discovery of anæsthetics or analgesics, even the simplest treatment was to be feared. *The Duke of Southampton (who was a most lovely Youth) had two fore-teeth, that grew out very unhandsome,* wrote Aubrey about Charles II's son by Barbara Villiers. *His Cruel Mother caused Him to be bound fast in a Chaire, and had them draw'n-out ; which has caused the want of his understanding.* To show that such a disastrous result was not unique, Aubrey mentions another case of which he had personal knowledge. *At Broad-Chalke is a Cottage-Family, that the Generation hath two Thumbes. A poore Womans Daughter in Westminster, being born so, the Mother gott a Carpenter to amputate one of them with his Chizel and Mallet. The Girl was then about seven yeares Old : and was a lovely Child. Immediately after the Thumbe was struck-off : the fright and Convulsion was so extreme ; that she lost her understanding, even her Speech : she lived till seventeen in that Sad condition.* And more serious operations were so rarely successful that Aubrey recorded with especial interest that *a Mariner (1688) of Bristowe having the Stone in his Kidney did adventure the cutting of it : The Surgeon took it out : and the Man recovered. Mr. Cole of Bristowe sent this account to the Royal Societie : I think he sent the stone too.*

One can see, therefore, why Aubrey congratulated himself so strongly on having outwitted death so many times during his childhood, for in this he was more fortunate than his brothers and sisters, none of whom survived infancy, until William was born, in 1643, when John was already an undergraduate at Oxford.

When a Boy, Aubrey was *bred at Eston, an Eremeticall Solitude,* which he much resented. *'Twas a great disadvantage to me in my childhood,* he said later, *to be bred up in a kind of Parke, far from Neighbours and no Child to converse withall : so that I did not speake till late. My father had one to teach me in the house, and I was pent-up in a Roome by my selfe melancholy.* But because of this loneliness, the main lines of his character were laid down very early. *He was very curious,* he says of himself, *his greatest delight to be continually with the artificers that came there (e.g. Joyners, carpenters, coupers, masons) and understood their trades.* So soon appeared that indiscriminate curiosity about other people's business, which was to plague him throughout his life, and already it was combined with a corresponding inability to concentrate upon his own work. *About Priorie St. Maries, and in the Minchin-meadowes there,* he says, *but especially at Brown's-hill which is opposite to the house where, in an unfortunate hour, I drew my first breath, there is infinite variety of plants ; and it would have tempted me to be a botanist had I had leisure, which is a jewell I could never master of.*

This solitary childhood forced Aubrey to rely for companionship on the country people who lived round about, and here he imbibed the second mainstay of his character—superstition. *When I was a child (and so before the Civill Warres)*, he says, *the fashion was for old women and mayds to tell fabulous stories nightimes, of Sprights and walking of Ghosts, &c. This was derived down from mother to daughter, from the Monkish Ballance which upheld Holy Church, for the Divines say, Deny Spirits, you are an Atheist. When the warres came, and with them Liberty of Conscience and Liberty of inquisition, the phantoms vanished. Now children feare no such things, having heard not of them ; and are not checked with such feares.* But Aubrey, in his isolation, was surrounded by these tales. *Our Country-people would talke much of Faeries,* he said. *They swept-up the Harth cleane at night : and did sett their shoes by the fire, and many times should find a threepence in one of them.* In this belief the rustics were not alone, for later in life Aubrey reported that *Mris. Markey (a daughter of Serjeant Hoskyns the Poet) told me, that her mother did use that Custome and had as much money as made her a little Silver-cup of thirtie shillings value. Elias Ashmole sayes : there was in his time, a Piper in Lichfield that did know what Houses were Faiery-ground : and that the Piper had oftentimes seen them.* All Aubrey's early education, in fact, seemed purposely designed to encourage his gullibility, for he points out that *in the old ignorant times, before woomen were Readers, the history was handed down from Mother to daughter : and W. Malmesburiensis pickt up his history from the time of Ven. Bede to his time out of Old Songs : for there was no writer in England from Bede to him. So my Nurse had the History from the Conquest down to Carl I. in Ballad.* And it was upon this unsure foundation that Aubrey's historical knowledge was based, for his later education, still in those days entirely classical, did nothing to counteract the superstitions of his childhood.

A further element of his character, *a strong and early impulse to Antiquitie,* was also present long before he went to school. *I was inclin'd by my Genius, from my Childhood to the Love of Antiquities,* he reports, *and my Fate dropt me in a Country most suitable for such Enquiries.* His taste for historical gossip appeared early too, for he mentions that, *when a Boy, he did ever love to converse with old men, as Living Histories,* and it was particularly to his mother's parents, Isaac and Israel Lyte, that he turned for information. *I was always enquiring of my grandfather of the Old time, the Rood-loft, etc., ceremonies of the Priory, etc.,* he says, and in one of these conversations his grandfather told him a story that sums up the whole difference between the seventeenth century and the twentieth : *My Grand Father Lyte told me that at one Lord Majors shew there was the Representation of the Creation of the World, and writt underneath AND ALL FOR MAN.*

Besides this love of history, Aubrey had developed a practical side. *At* 8, he tells us, *I was a kind of Engineer ; and I fell then to drawing, beginning first with plaine outlines, e.g. in draughts of curtaines. Then at* 9 *(crossed herein by father and schoolmaster) to colours, having no body to instruct me : copied pictures in the parlour in a table booke.*

When he was eight years old, Aubrey *entred into his Grammar at the Latin schoole at Yatton Keynel, in the Church : where the Curate Mr. Hart taught the eldest Boyes, Virgil, Ovid, Cicero etc.,* and where the eldest boys taught the new pupil a lesson in morality. *I was 8 yeares old before I knew what theft was,* he says with understandable bitterness, *scilicet, I had a fine Box top which was stolen from me.* His grandfather Lyte had also studied here as a child, for Aubrey had heard him say that *when he went to Schoole in this Church, in the S. Windowe of the chancell, were severall escutcheons, which a herald that passed by tooke note of : which window,* the future antiquary was quick to note, *is now dammed up with stones, and now no memorie left of them.* The loss of their stained glass made the authorities no more careful of the relics of the past that still survived, however, for Aubrey says, *the fashion then was to save the Ferules of their Bookes with a false cover of Parchment, sc. old Manuscript, which I was too young to understand ; but I was pleased with the Elegancy of the Writing, and the coloured initiall letters. I remember the Rector here (Mr. Wm. Stump, great grand Son of Stump the Cloathier of Malmesbury) had severall Manuscripts of the Abbey. He was a proper Man and a good Fellow, and when He brewed a barrell of Speciall Ale, his use was to stop the bung-hole (under the clay) with a Sheet of Manuscript ; he sayd nothing did it so well ; which me thought did grieve me then to see.* So early did Aubrey come to regret that wanton destruction of antiquities, which was to trouble him till he died.

In the next year, 1634, Aubrey was transferred to a school in the neighbouring parish, which he described as *a mile's fine walke,* although he was careful to point out later to Anthony Wood, *I had then a fine little horse and commonly rode (but this is impertinent) i.e. I was not a vulgar boy and carried not a Satchell at my back. Sed hoc inter nos.* At this new school, *where was the like use of covering of Bookes,* Aubrey *was entred in his Latin Grammar by Mr. R. Latimer, Rector of Leigh de-la-mere, who had an easie way of teaching : and every time we askt leave to goe forth, we had a Latin word from him which at our return we were to tell him again— which in a little while amounted to a good number of Words. 'Twas my unhappiness in halfe a yeare to loose this good Enformer by his death,* Aubrey added, for he was old and *wore a Dudgeon, with a knife, and bodkin, as also my old grandfather Lyte and Alderman Whitson of Bristowe, which I suppose was the common fashion in their young dayes.* But before he died, Robert Latimer was responsible for a meeting which was to influence his young pupil's whole life. *This summer,* Aubrey says, *I remember 'twas in Venison season (July or August) Mr. Thomas Hobbes came into his Native Country to visitt his Friends, and amongst others he came to see his old school-master, Mr. Robert Latimer, at Leigh de-la-mer, where I was then at Schoole in the church. Here was the first place and time that ever I had the honour to see this worthy, learned man, who was then pleased to take notice of me, and the next day visited my relations. His conversation about those times was much about Ben : Jonson, Mr. Ayton, etc. He was then a proper man, briske, and in very good habit : his hayre quite black, and with moist curles. He stayed at Malmsbury and in the neighbourhood a weeke or better. 'Twas the last time that ever he was in Wiltshire.* This friendship, so pleasantly begun between the fifty-five year old philosopher and a *little youth* of eight, was to last for nearly forty years and was only to be broken then by death.

After Robert Latimer's death, Aubrey complains that he was *under severall ignorant rest-in-house teachers,* and for this he lays the blame upon his father, *who was not educated to learning, but to Hawking.* However, in 1638, he was *transplanted to Blandford Schoole in Dorset, to William Sutton, B.D., who was ill-natured,* and although Aubrey refers proudly to the fact that *Blandford was the most eminent Schoole for the education of Gentlemen in the West of England,* his solitary upbringing left him at a sad disadvantage with the other boys. *I was like a Bird that was gott-out of his cage amongst the free Citizens of the aire,* he complained. *'Twas the first time I knew the world, and the wickedness of Boies. The boies mockt me, and abused me, that were stronger then my selfe ; so I was faine to make friendship as a strong line to protections.* Amongst his tormentors seem to have been Walter and Tom Raleigh, the great Sir Walter's grand-nephews, for although Aubrey admits that they had *excellent tuneable voices, and playd their parts well on the violl,* he summed them up as *ingeniose, but all proud and quarrelsome.*

Here, he says, *I recovered my health, and gott my Latin and Greeke best of any of my contemporaries. Our Usher, Thomas Stephens, a very good and ingeniose person, by whom I reap't much information, had (by chance) a Cowper's Dictionary, which I had never seen before. I was then in Terence. Perceiving his method, I read all in the booke where Terence was, and then Cicero—which was the way by which I gott my Latin. 'Twas a wonderfull helpe to my phansie, my reading of Ovid's Metamorphy in English by Sandys, which made me understand the Latin the better. Also, I mett accidentally a booke of my Mothers, Lord Bacon's Essaies, which first opened my Under-standing as to Moralls (for Tullie's Offices was too crabbed for my young yeares) and the excellence of the Style, or Hints and transitions.* It seems from this that Aubrey was still a rather serious child, and he confirms that *he cared not for play, but on play-dayes he gave himselfe to Drawing and Painting,* or to visiting *the shop, and furnaces of Old Harding, the only Country-glasse-painter, that ever I knew.*

His curiosity about other people's business continued unabated, and this appetite was whetted by the periodic holidays that he spent with Alderman Whitson of Bristol, who besides being his godfather and step-grandfather, was also the owner of the Mayflower. *I was wont (I remember) much to lament with my selfe that I lived not in a City, e.g. Bristoll, where I might have accesse to watchmakers, locksmiths, etc.,* he said, for it seems that he *did not very much care for Grammar : appre-hension enough,* he explains, *but memorie not tenacious. So that then a promis-ing morne enough of an inventive and philosophicall head. My witt was alwaies working, but not adroict for verse,* he added, a fact which might perhaps be traced to the extraordinary licence allowed to schoolboys in those days, for he mentions that *at Curry-Yeovill in Somersetshire, where there is a How schole in the Church, they have annually a Barrel of good Ale brought into the church ; and that night they have the priviledge to breake open their Masters Cellar-dore.* The summing up of his schooldays concludes : *Mild of spirit ; mightily susceptible of Fascination. My Idea very cleer ; Phansie like a Mirrour, pure chrystal water which the least wind does disorder and unsmooth. Never riotous or prodigall ; but (as Sir E. Leech said) Sloath and carelessnesse are equivalent to all other vices.*

On the second of May, 1642, at the age of sixteen, Aubrey was entered as a gentleman-commoner at Trinity College, Oxford ; and here at last he was to find his proper element, despite the harshness of the discipline, which he was quick to note. *At Oxford (and I doe*

*believe the like at Cambridge) the Rod was frequently used by the Tutors
and Deanes on his pupills, till Bachelaurs of Arts ; even gentlemen-Com-
moners,* he reported. *One Doctor I knew right well (Dr. Hannibal Potter,
Trin. Coll. Oxon) that whipt his scholar with his Sword by his side when he
came to take his leave of him to goe to the Innes of Court.* For though the
undergraduates were younger in those days (the second Duke of
Buckingham was a Master of Arts by the time he was fourteen)
they were expected to be more serious, and organised games played
no part in their education. Castiglione's instruction " to joyne learny-
ing with cumlie exercise " was still obeyed and our modern games were
not looked on as " cumlie " : football, in fact, " is to be put in per-
petual silence," being " nothing but beastly fury and extreme violence."
The " Courtly exercises and Gentlemanlike pastimes " which " young
men should use and delight in " were listed as follows by Queen
Elizabeth's tutor, Roger Ascham : " to ride comely : to run fair
at tilt or ring : to play at all weapons : to shoot fair in bow, or surely
in gun : to vault lustily : to run : to leap : to wrestle : to swim :
to dance comely : to sing, and play of instruments cunningly : to
hawk : to hunt : to play at tennis : " these were the pastimes for
" a Courtly Gentleman to use." None of them, you will notice,
fostered the team spirit, but what was lost in co-operative virtues was
more than made up for in individuality : for the men of the past were
above all individuals, even to the point of eccentricity, and from this
variety sprang the great strength of the nation.

In Aubrey's day the false distinction had not yet been drawn
between work, regarded as drudgery, and play, regarded as a good
time, and educated men naturally sought their recreation in the study,
rather than on the golf-course. For in the seventeenth century learning
was part of the joy of life, just as much as drinking or love-making,
and it was just as often overdone. John Evelyn, writing on the death
of his five-year-old son, said : " So insatiable were his Desires of
Knowledge, that upon a Time hearing one discourse of Terence
and Plautus, and being told (upon his Enquiry concerning these
Authors) that the Books were too difficult for him, he wept for very
Grief, and would hardly be pacified," and Aubrey mentions that
*Lord Ellesmere was so hard a Student, that in three or 4 yeares time he was
not out of the House : Edward Brerewood, too, went not out of the College
gates in a good while, nor (I thinke) out of his Chamber, but was in his slip-
shoes, and wore out his Gowne and cloathes on the bord and benches of his
chamber, but profited in knowledge exceedingly.* Even when they reached
years of discretion, the men of the Renaissance seemed unable to
moderate their studies. *Laurence Rooke was a temperate man and of a
strong constitution,* says Aubrey, *but tooke his sicknesse of which he dyed
by setting up often for Astronomicall Observations,* while *Michaell Dary,
Mathematician and a Gunner of the Tower (by profession a Tobacco-cutter)
an admirable Algebrician,* came to grief rather like Francis Bacon, for
with writing in the frostie weather his fingers rotted and gangraened.

Lookt through Logique and some Ethiques, says Aubrey of his own
studies, for he had now graduated from the Classics to the Humanities ;
and then comes a most pregnant note : 1642, *Religio Medici printed,
which first opened my understanding.* For at this time learning suddenly

[xxiv]

took a great leap forward, upon the unexpected recognition that *the British language is as copious in expressing congruous Termes of Art as the Greeke : or any language whatsoever.* English had, indeed, reached complete fluency a century before, but it had continued to develop so fast that, even for the Stuarts, the language of the Elizabethans had become antiquated : *Henry, the last Earle of Cumberland, was,* according to Aubrey, *an ingeniose Gentleman for those times and writt a Poeme in English upon the Psalmes, and very well, but the language being now something out of fashion, like Sir Philip Sidney's, they will not print it.* But when James I authorised a new translation of the Bible in 1604, he unwittingly caused the English language to crystallise at its very peak, and gave to it a permanence that it had never enjoyed before ; and as soon as the constant change in the tongue slowed down to a manageable rate, learned works came more and more to be written in English, instead of Latin. The result was that for the first time the new printing presses began to affect the whole nation : not wholly for good, as Aubrey shows, for already the first blow had been struck at the imaginative faculty, which was finally to be smothered under the flood of precise newspaper information in our own time. *Before Printing, Old-wives Tales were ingeniose,* he says regretfully, *and since Printing came in fashion, till a little before the Civill-warres, the ordinary sort of People were not taught to reade. Now-a-dayes Bookes are common, and most of the poor people understand letters ; and the many good Bookes, and variety of Turnes of Affaires, have putt all the old Fables out of doors : and the divine art of Printing and Gunpowder have frighted away Robin-goodfellow and the Fayries.*

Another abandonment of the Classics was to have even more far-reaching results. *All old accounts are in numerall letters,* Aubrey says. *Even to my remembrance, when I was a youth, Gentlemen's Bayliffs in the Country used no other, e.g. i. ii. iii. iiii. v. vi. vii. viii. ix. x. xi. etc : and to this day in the accounts of the Exchecquer. And the Shopkeepers in my Grandfathers times used to reckon with Counters : which is the best and surest way : and is still used by the French.* But now, at last, these Roman numerals were abandoned and the bonds that had confined science for two thousand years were broken. For without mathematics there could be no theory, and the Greeks and Romans had been limited to practical matters, simply because their numerals, though sufficient for counting, were useless for calculating. But while Europe was covered by the Dark Ages, the Arabs had made what is probably the greatest single discovery in the history of thought, the invention of a symbol for nought, and the adoption of the Arabic numerals at the time of the Renaissance opened up a whole new world of thought, which the men of the seventeenth century explored with voluptuous delight.

For *the Mathematicks* was the most popular of all studies during the Stuart Century, and *it was Edmund Gunter who, with his Booke of the Quadrant, Sector and Crosse-staffe did open men's understandings and made young men in love with that Studie. Before, the Mathematicall Sciences were lock't up in the Greeke and Latin tongues and there lay untoucht, kept safe in some libraries. After Mr. Gunter published his Booke, these Sciences sprang up amain, more and more to that height it is at now* (1690).

[xxv]

Soldiers, sailors, courtiers, clerics, all devoted themselves to this intoxicating study, and many a young man was, like Henry Gellibrand, *good for little a great while, till at last it happened accidentally, that he heard a Geometrie Lecture. He was so taken with it, that immediately he fell to studying it, and quickly made great progresse in it. The fine Diall over Trinity Colledge Library is of his owne doeing.* This *dialling*, however, was so comparatively easy and other tricks so impressive and so common, that Thomas Hobbes felt obliged to issue a warning : " Not every one that brings from beyond seas a new Gin, or other jaunty devise, is therefore a Philosopher," he said, " for if you reckon that way, not only Apothecaries and Gardiners, but many other sorts of Workmen will put-in for, and get the Prize." Unabashed, however, some of Aubrey's friends persisted in their unorthodox ways, like Seth Ward, Bishop of Salisbury, who *when he was President of Trinity College, Oxon, did draw his Geometricall Schemes with black, red, yellow, green and blew Inke to avoid the perplexity of A, B, C, etc.,* and William Oughtred, who achieved undying fame with his invention of the multiplication sign, which, he said, *came into my head, as if infused by a Divine Genius.* And the controversies that raged over *Arithmeticall Problemes* reached such a pitch of emotion (particularly when Hobbes thought that he had squared the circle and Dr. Wallis knew that he had not) that poor Aubrey was driven to the conclusion : *sure their Mercuries are in □ or opposition. Ludolph van Keulen, who had been first, by Profession, a Fencing-Master ; but becomeing deafe, betooke himselfe to the studie of the Mathematiques wherin he became famous and wrote a learned booke in 4to of the Proportion of the Diameter of a Circle to the Peripherie, carried the* obsession even further, for *on his Monument (according to his last Will) is engraved the Proportion abovesayd.*

The excitement caused by this serious study is not so surprising when one recalls that Professor Trevelyan has said, " every reader had in some sort to be a student, for apart from poetry and the stage, there was hardly any literature that was not serious. . . . Not newspapers and novels but ballads and songs were hawked about by Autolycus and his comrades to satisfy the common appetite in the city street and on the village green." For the host of adult infants, for whom our magazines and films now cater, had not yet appeared, and the Bible held undisputed sway over the minds of men. " If there had been newspapers, magazines and novels," Professor Trevelyan continues, " to compete with the Bible in manor-house, farm and cottage, there would have been no Puritan revolution."

The result of this monopolising of men's minds by the Scriptures was not long in coming ; the battle of ideas mounted in violence until *the first brush occurred between the Earl of Northampton and Lord Brooke, near Banbury, which was the latter end of July, or the beginning of August,* 1642. *But now Bellona thundered, and as a cleare skie is sometimes suddenly overstretched with a dismall Cloud and thunder, so was this Serene Peace by the Civill Warres through the Factions of those times.*

The outbreak of the Great Rebellion was the more depressing because of the long peace that had preceded it. As far back as living memory could reach, since the fires of Smithfield had died out on Queen Mary's death eighty-four years before, the country of England had

[xxvi]

been at quiet within itself, and for the first time in history a man could have lived out his whole life in peace. England had been involved in wars, it is true, but none had touched her shores, and the fighting on the continent had really increased the tranquillity of this country, by drawing off the more bellicose of her sons into the service of some foreign prince. But now the wars which had plagued England ever since the Romans left broke out again, and the mercenary ruffians who made up the continental armies of those days were to transfer their attentions to this prosperous land. No wonder William Oughtred cried out that he was " daunted and broken with these disastrous times." For the people of England had been so long unused to violence that the results of the conflict were unusually severe ; *The Lady Jordan being at Cirencester, when it was besieged (Anno aetatis* 75°) *was so terrified with the Shooting, that her understanding was so spoyled, that She became a tiny-child, that they made Babies for her to play withall.*

Though the causes of the war were largely intellectual (and Aubrey mentions in the life of Thomas May that *Mr. Decretz was present at the debate at their parting before Sir Richard Fanshawe went to the King, where both Camps were most rigorously banded*) the rebellion gave an excuse for private grudges and family quarrels to flare up into unexampled savagery. Henry Martin sat as one of Charles' judges, because of an insult delivered by the King many years before, and even Sir John Danvers, *a great friend of the King's partie and a Patron to distressed and cashiered Cavaliers,* abandoned his principles to spite his family. *To revenge himselfe of his sister, the Lady Gargrave,* explains Aubrey, *and to ingratiate himselfe more with the Protector to null his brother, Earl of Danby's, Will, he contrary to his owne naturall inclination, did sitt in the High Court of Justice at the King's Triall.*

In these circumstances the savagery of man, about which our ancestors shared none of our perfectionist illusions had full play. *On this Oake,* says Aubrey in his *Naturall Historie of Wiltshire, Sir Francis Dodington hung up thirteen after quarter. He made a Sonn hang his Father or e contra.* And this bestiality was to continue for half a decade, until *the King was beaten out of the field.*

The result of *the first brush* on Aubrey was immediate. *In August following,* he reports, *my father sent for me home, for feare.* But it was not only Aubrey's life that was interrupted : the very continuity of English culture was broken. *When I was a little Boy (before the Civill Warres)* Aubrey was to repeat over and over again in talking of the vanished customs and beliefs of the so-recent past, for a whole way of life disappeared in the convulsion ; a way of life which Aubrey has crystallised in a single sentence : *When I was a Boy every Gentleman almost kept a Harper in his house : and some of them could versifie.* But now the harpers were no more, for it was the life of the rich which suffered annihilation first ; a life which could be traced back as far as history would reach. *After the comeing in of the Goths, the Roman Games and Cirques, were turned into Tilts and Turnaments. Tilting breath'd its last when King Charles I^st left London. The Tilt-yard was where the Guard-house is now, opposite to White-hall. In those dayes all Gentlemen of a thousand pounds per annum kept a Horse or Horses for a Man at Arms.*

It was not only the rich who were to suffer, though, and as soon

[xxvii]

as the whole people was involved, the customs and beliefs of the past collapsed before the storm. *When I was a Boy (before the Civill-warres),* Aubrey says again, *I heard 'em tell that in the old time, they used to put a Penny in the dead persons mouth to give to St. Peter : and I thinke that they did doe so in Wales and in the North Country ;* and in Yorkshire, too, *in the Countrey churches, at Christmas in the Holy-daies after Prayers, they will dance in the Church, and as they doe dance, they cry (or sing) Yole, Yole, Yole.* For, as Aubrey explains, *in the Infancy of the Christian Religion it was expedient to plough (as they say) with the heifer of the Gentiles, i.e. to insinuate with them. and to let them continue and use their old Ethnick Festivals which they new named with Christian names, e.g. Floralia, they turnd to the Feast of St. Philip and Jacob, etc, the Saturnalia into Christmas. Had they donne otherwise, they could not have gain'd so many Proselytes or established their Doctrine so well, and in so short a time. The Gentiles would not perfectly relinquish all their Idols ; so, they were persuaded to turne the Image of Jupiter with his thunderbolt to Christ crucifixus, and Venus and Cupid into the Madonna and her Babe, which Mr. Th. Hobbes sayth was prudently donne.* But now these links with Imperial Rome, which had survived first the coming of the Catholic Church and then the Reformation, were finally destroyed ; and many native myths perished at the same time. *It was a Custome for some people that were more curious then ordinary to sitt all night in their church porch of their Parish on Midsomer-eve ; and they should see the apparitions of those that should die in the parish that yeare come and knock at the dore.* As these regional customs vanished under the stress of war, uniformity began to spread across the land, until at last even the shepherds of Aubrey's native Wiltshire were affected : *Their Habit (I believe) is that of the Roman or Arcadian Shepherds too,* he says, *sc. a long white Cloake with a very deep cape, which comes downe half way their backs, made of the locks of the Sheep ; their Armature was a Sheep Crooke, a Sling, a Scrip, their Tar-box, a Pipe (or Flute) and their Dog. But since* 1671 *they are grown so luxurious as to neglect their ancient warme, and usefull fashion, and goe à la mode.* Every one of these changes was resented by Aubrey as a personal blow, until he was sadly led to conclude that *the Civill Warres comeing on have putt out all these Rites, or customs quite out of fashion. Warres doe not only extinguish Religion and Lawes : but Superstitition ; and no Suffimen is a great fugator of Phantosmes, than Gun-powder.*

By far the worst result of the Rebellion for an antiquary like Aubrey was the acquisition of power by the Puritans, those Philistines whom he despised so much and who, in their turn, despised his kind. Speaking of Robert Sanderson, Lord Bishop of Lincoln, he says scornfully that *the very Parliamentarians reverenced him for his Learning and his vertue : so that he alwayes kept his living.* The accidental destruction of antiquities had been bad enough in the past, for the wanton use of the monastical manuscripts, which he had witnessed as a child, still preyed upon his mind. *In my grandFather's dayes, the Manuscripts flew about like Butter-flies,* he repeated sadly. *All Musick bookes, Account-bookes, Copie bookes, etc, were covered with old Manuscripts, as wee cover them now with blew Paper, or Marbled Paper. And the Glovers at Malmesbury made great Havock of them, and Gloves were wrapt up no doubt in many good pieces of Antiquity. Before the late Warres a World of rare Manuscripts*

*perished here about ; for within half a dozen miles of Easton-Piers were the
Abbey of Malmesbury, where it may be presumed the Library was as well
furnished with choice Copies, as most Libraries of England : Broadstock-
Priory, Stenley-Abbey, Farleigh-Abbey, Bath-Abbey and Cyrencester Abbey.
One may also perceive by the Binding of old Bookes how the old Manuscripts
went to wrack in those dayes.* About 1647, I went to see Parson Stump out
of curiosity to see his Manuscripts, *whereof I had seen some in my Child-hood ;
but by that time they were lost and disperst ; His sonns were gunners and
souldiers, and scoured their gunnes with them.* But at least this destruction
had been due to ignorance, and not to policy. The Puritans, on the
other hand, knew what they were doing and destroyed on purpose
and on principle. *My old cosen Parson Whitney told me that in the Visitation of Oxford in Edward VI's time they burned Mathematical bookes for
Conjuring bookes, and, if the Greeke Professor had not accidentally come
along, the Greeke Testament had been thrown into the fire for a Conjuring booke
too.* This had happened during the only reign in which the Puritans
had so far held power, but since then any form of unnecessary destruction had been discouraged : *Neer Dunnington Castle was an Oake,
under which Sir Jeofry Chaucer was wont to sit, called Chaucer's oake, which
was cutt downe, tempore Caroli I^mi,* Aubrey says, *and so it was, that . . . was
called into the Starre chamber and was fined for it. Judge Richardson harangued
against him long, and like an orator, had topiques from the Druides, etc.*

It was against idolatry, however, that the fury of the Puritans was
chiefly turned and, long before the Civil War, untoward incidents had
begun to occur again. *In St. Edmunds Church at Salisbury were curious
painted Glasse-windowes (especially in the Chancell) where there was one
Window (I think the East window) of such exquisite worke, that Gundamour
the Spanish Ambassadeur did offer some hundreds of Pounds for it, if it might
have been bought. In one of the Windowes was the Picture of God the Father,
like an Old Man (as the fashion then was) which much offended Mr. Shervill,
the Recorder, who out of Zeale came, and brake some of these Windowes about*
1631 ; *and clambering upon one of the Pews (to be able to reach high enough)
fell downe and brake his Legg ; but that did not excuse him for being question'd
in the Starre-chamber for it, and had a great Fine layd upon which I thinke
did undoe him.* But soon the Star Chamber was abolished, and the
Puritans, having achieved power, set about their iconoclasm with such
a will that Aubrey noted sadly : *But what Mr. Shervill left undonne, the
Soldiers since have gonne through with, that there is not a piece of glass-painting
left.* And as the war continued, the merchants of London put the
whole thing on a proper business footing, for Aubrey mentions that
*at Croydon in Surrey in the Rebellion, one Bleese was hir'd, for half a Crown
per Day, to break the painted Glass-Windows, which were formerly fine.*

When the glass was finished, the zealots turned their attention
to the altars and the statues, the vestments, painted tombs and organs,
until Aubrey could write of Corston : *In the Church nothing to be found,
the modern zeale has been a reforming here, as hereabout.* For at nearby
Slaughterford, he had noted : *Here is a prettie small Church, the most
miserably handled that ever I saw, the very barres are taken out of the windowes
by the fanatique rage of the late times ; here have been two good South windowes,
and the doores are gone and the paving, and it serves for any use, viz. Weavers.
The Font has gone to make a trough.*

Having gutted the churches, the Parliamentarians then turned their attention to the buildings themselves. Churches *were pulled-downe to the ground, that the Enemie might not shelter themselves against the Garrison ;* castles, like Dunnington, which had been *Sir Geoffrey Chaucer's, a noble seate and strong castle, which was held by the King,* were *dismanteled ; tuneable Bells were converted into Ordinance ;* and many houses were burnt. The destruction in fact was so widespread, that it led Aubrey, though he was only eighteen, to make his first practical antiquarian move : *I gott Mr. Hesketh, Mr. Dobson's man, a Priest, to drawe the Ruines of Osney, 2 or 3 wayes before 'twas pulled down,* he says. *Now the very foundation is digged up.* And thirty years later, one of these drawings, the only record of the Abbey, was to be reproduced in Dugdale's " Monasticon," with the following inscription : " The Noble Ruines of this Fabrick were drawn from a love to Antiquity, while yet a Youth at Oxford, and (which was not a little lucky) but a short time before they were entirely destroyed in the Civil War, secured now and as it were revived, are dedicated to Posterity, by John Aubrey of Easton Piers in the Country of Wilts, Esq."

In February, 1643, Aubrey says, *with much adoe I gott my father to lett me to beloved Oxon againe, then a Garrison pro Rege,* and a very different place from the University which he had left a few short months before. For the Court had come to Oxford in the preceding November, taking the colleges for its lodgings and driving the older dons, like Dr. Kettell of Aubrey's own college, into a premature grave.

Like Aubrey, most of the scholars had left Oxford on the outbreak of the war. The few who had remained were, according to one don, " debauched by bearing Armes, and doing the Duties belonging to Soldiers, as Watching, Warding, and sitting in Tipling-Houses for whole Nights together." So the atmosphere of the city cannot have been conducive to work, especially for someone so easily distracted as Aubrey. First, there was the King to be seen : *When I was a Freshman at Oxford,* Aubrey says, *I was wont to go to Christ Church to see King Charles I. at Supper : Where I once heard him say, that as he was Hawking in Scotland, he rode into a Quarry, and found the Covey of Partridge falling upon the Hawk : and I do remember this expression further, viz. and I will swear upon the Book 'tis true. When I came to my Chamber, I told this Story to my Tutor : said he, That Covey was London.* And then there was the Court itself, which in those days was particularly fascinating for a young scholar. For at Court, as Professor Trevelyan has pointed out, " the gentleman of England learnt not only the intrigues of love and politics, but music and poetry, and a taste for scholarship and the arts, seeds which they took back to their rural homes to plant there." For " the mediaeval distinction between the learned clerk and the barbarous fighting baron was coming to an end, blending in the ideal of the all-accomplished ' gentleman '." In this ideal, the Stuart sovereigns led the way, although at their real " business as King " they were to prove either woefully incompetent' or grossly corrupt. James I, indeed, was so much of a scholar that he was moved to say on his first visit to the Bodleian Library at Oxford : " If I were not a King, I would be a University man ; and if it were so that I must be a prisoner, if I might have my wish, I would desire to have no other prison than that Library, and to be chained together with so many good Authors and dead Masters." Charles, his son, *that great Antiquary,* was also the finest connoisseur of painting in his realm and the first Englishman to value paintings as art, instead of simply as likenesses or curios. King Charles II was of a more practical bent, but though he dabbled in chemistry, he achieved little of worth : *He had a Mathematicall genius,* Aubrey admitted, *but wanted early education.* Of James II, that lamentable monarch, however, Aubrey could find nothing better to say than that *he was acquainted fully with the State of our Naval Power, and knew as much, if not more than the meanest Sailor ;* and his consort was distinguished by a single feat : *Colonel Popham's great tankard, the Dutches Y : dranke it (almost) off at a draught.*

Even during these troublous times, the Court was still the cultural centre of the nation, and the circle of poets and playwrights that usually clustered round the King, was augmented by the very fact of the war. Many men were in the same case as John Cleveland, the Cambridge poet, who, *being turned out of his Fellowship for a malignant, came to Oxford, where the King's Army was, and was much caressed by them.* And it was while the King was in residence at Christ Church that William Cartwright, the dramatist, was buried in the cathedral there at the early age of thirty-two. *Pitty 'tis so famous a bard should lye without an Inscription,* Aubrey thought, for his contemporaries had expected great things from him : *'Tis not to be forgott that King Charles 1st. dropt a teare at the newes of his death.* In view of this sensibility, it is astounding to find that the manners of the Court were so foul. For in the next reign, Anthony Wood was to write : " To give a further character of the court, though they were neat and gay in their apparell, yet they were very nasty and beastly, leaving at their departure their excrements in every corner, in chimneys, studies, cole-houses, cellars. Rude, rough, whoremongers ; vaine, empty, careless." With this attack Aubrey was in full agreement for he himself pointed out that it was the lascivious King Charles II, and not the elegant Charles I, who *was the Patterne of Courtesie, and first brought good Manners into Fashion in England,* and in 1670 he said, *Till this time the Court itself was unpolished and unmannered. King James's Court was so far from being civill to woemen, that the Ladies, nay the Queen herself, could hardly pass by the King's apartment without receiving some Affront.*

Amidst all these excitements, calamity overtook John Aubrey. *In Aprill I fell sick of the Small pox at Trinity College,* he said, but as usual fate softened the blow for him. *William Radford, my good friend and old acquaintance and fellow collegiate, was so kind as to come to me every day and spend severall houres, or I think melancholy would have spoyled a scurvy Antiquary.* This illness was to mean the end of Aubrey's University career, all the same, for he goes on to say, *when I recovered, after Trinity weeke, my father sent for me into the Country again : where I conversed with none but servants and rustiques and soldiers quartred, to my great griefe, for in those dayes fathers were not acquainted with their children. It was a most sad life to me, then in the prime of my youth, not to have the benefit of an ingeniose Conversation and scarce any good bookes—almost a consumption.* For a library was not yet considered to be an essential part of a gentleman's home : in fact, Lord Herbert of Cherbury was considered almost eccentric because *he had two Libraries, one at London, the other at Montgomery.*

The war itself seems to have made little stir in Wiltshire, and it must have been a great relief when *Major John Morgan fell sick of a malignant fever as he was marching with the King's Army into the West, and was brought to my fathers at Broad Chalke, where he was lodged secretly in a garret.* But though the war provided few diversions, it made the country round about even more unbearable. *Surely this tract of land enclines people to zeale,* exclaimed Aubrey despairingly. *Heretofore nothing but religious houses, now nothing but Quakers and Fanatiqs. A sourewood country,* he decided, *inclines people to contemplation, so that the Bible and ease (for it is all upon dayry grasing, or clothing) setts their witts a running and reforming.* And certainly the description which Aubrey left of his neighbours is most unprepossessing. *In North-wiltshire,* he said, *(a dirty, claeyy Country) they speak (I mean the Indigenies, or Aborigines only) drawning ; they are Phlegmatiq ; Skins pale and livid ; slow, and dull, heavy of Spirit : here about is but little Tillage, or hard labour, they only milk the Cowes and make Cheese. They feed chiefly on Milke meates. which cooles their Braines too much, and hurts their Inventions. These Circumstances make them Melancholy, contemplative, and malicious : by consequence whereof more Lawsuites come out of North Wilts, at least double to the Southern Parts. And by the same reason they are generally more apt to be Fanatiques : (In Malmesbury Hundred, &c.—wett, clayy parts : Here have ever been reputed Witches). Their persons are generally plump and foggy : gallipot Eies, and some black : but they are generally handsome enough. On the Downes (sc. the South part) where 'tis all upon Tillage, or Shepherds : and labour hard, their flesh is hard, their bodies strong : being weary after their hard labour, they have not leisure to reade, and contemplate of Religion, but goe to Bed to their rest, to rise betimes the next morning to their labour. I remember (upon the foresayd reason) that Capt. John Graunt did say, it was observed that there were no Anchor Smyths Fanaticks : for it is a mighty laborious trade : and they must drinke strong drinke to keep up their Spirits : so they never troubled their Heads with curious Notions of Religion.*

To add to the miseries of his exile in the country, Aubrey got on extremely badly with his father, who had no sympathy at all with his son's newfangled learning. *My studies (geometry) were on horse back,* Aubrey confessed, *and in the house of office : (my father discouraged me).* For the relations between parents and children were very rigid in those days and the following passage, which Aubrey wrote in 1670, is plainly autobiographical. *From the time of Erasmus till about 20 years past, the learning was downright Pedantry,* he said. *The conversation and habitts of those times were as stiff and starcht as their bands and square beards : and Gravity was then taken for Wisdome. The very Doctors of those days were but old boies, when quibles past for wit, even in the pulpitts. The Gentry and the Citizens had little learning of any kind, and their way of breeding up their children was suitable to the rest : for wheras ones child should be ones nearest Friend, and the time of growing-up should be most indulged, they were as severe to their children as their schoolmaster ; and their Schoolmasters, as masters of the House of correction. The child perfectly loathed the sight of his parents, as the slave his Torturor. Gentlemen of 30 or 40 years old, fitt for any employment in the common wealth, were to stand like great mutes and fools bare headed before their Parents ; and the Daughters (grown woemen) were to stand at the Cupboards side during the whole time of the proud mothers visitt, unless (as the fashion was) 'twas desired that leave (forsooth) should be given to them to kneele upon cushions brought them by the servingman, after they had done sufficient Penance standing. The boys (growne young fellows) had their forheads turned up, and stiffened with spittle : they were to stand mannerly forsooth, thus, the foretop ordered as before, one hand at the band-string, the other on the breech or codpiece. The Gentlewoemen then had pro-digious fannes, as is to be seen in old pictures, like that instrument which is used to drive Feathers : it had a handle at least half a yard long ; with these the daughters were corrected oftentimes. (Sir Edw : Coke, Lord Chief Justice, rode the circuit with such a fan : Mr. Dugdale sawe it, who told me of it. The Earl of Manchester used also a Fan.) But fathers and mothers slash't their daughters in the time of that Besome discipline when they were perfect woemen.*

No wonder, therefore, that Aubrey was depressed, and it was with obvious regret that he looked back upon the golden past, when *the Holy-mawle hung behind the Church dore, which when the father was seaventie the sonne might fetch to knock his father in the head, as effoete, & of no more use. This sad life I did lead in the country till 1646,* he said, *at which time I gott (with much adoe) leave of my father to let me goe to the Middle Temple, April the 6th, 1646. But my fathers sicknesse, and businesse, never permitted me to make any settlement to my studie.* Not that Aubrey had ever had any idea of making the Law his profession : the progres-sion from University to the Temple was part of the normal education of a gentleman in those days, for only after a threefold training in the Classics, the Humanities and the Law was a man considered competent to manage his estates.

24 June following, Aubrey records, *Oxon was surrendred, and then came to London many of the King's party, with whom I grew acquainted (many of them I knew before). I loved not debauches,* he was careful to explain, *but their martiall conversation was not so fitt for the Muses.*

As the Civil War dragged slowly on towards its close, the happiest period of Aubrey's life was dawning, for he announces : *Novemb. 6, I returned to Trinity College in Oxon again to my great joy ; was much made of by the Fellowes ; had their learned conversation, lookt on bookes, musique. Here and at Middle Temple (off and on) I (for the most part) enjoyd the greatest felicity of my life (ingeniose youths, like Rosebudds, imbibe the morning dew) till Dec. 1648 (Christmas Eve's eve) I was sent for from Oxon home again to my sick father, who never recovered. Where I was engaged to looke after his country businesse and solicite a lawe-suite,* and also incidentally to continue his delvings into the past, for within a month of his return, he had stumbled upon the greatest discovery of his life time.

Salisbury-plaines, and Stonehenge I had known from eight years old, he says, *but I never saw the Countrey about Marleborough, till Christmas 1648 : being then invited to the Lord Francis Seymour's, by the Honourable Mr. Charles Seymour (then of Allington near Chippenham, since Lord Seymour) with whom I had the honour to be intimately acquainted, and whose Friendship I ought to mention with a profound respect to his memorie.*

The morrow after Twelf day, Mr. Charles Seymour and Sir William Button of Tokenham (a most parkely ground, and a Romancy-place) Baronet, mett with their packs of Hounds at the Greyweathers. These Downes looke *as if they were Sow'n with great Stones, very thicke ; and in a dusky evening they looke like a flock of Sheep : from whence it takes its name.* One might *fancy it to have been the Scene where the Giants fought with stones against the Gods.* 'Twas here that our Game began : *and the Chase led us (at length) through the Village of Aubury, into the Closes there : where I was wonderfully surprised at the sight of those vast stones, of which I had never heard before ;* as also at the mighty Banke and graffe *(ditch) about it.* I observed *in the Inclosures some segments of rude circles, made with these stones, whence I concluded, they had been in old time complete.* I left my Company a while, *entertaining myself with a more delightfull indagation : and then (steered by the cry of the Hounds) overtooke the company, and went with them to Kynnet, where was a good Hunting dinner provided.* Our Repast was cheerfull ; *which, being ended, we remounted, and beate over the Downes with our Grey-hounds. In this Afternoon's diversion I happened to see* Wensditch *and an old Camp, and two or three sepulchres.* The evening put a period to our sport, *he con-cluded, and we returned to the Castle at Marleborough, where we were nobly entertained.*

Aubrey was rightly proud of his discovery, for Avebury had been completely ignored before. *It is very strange,* he thought, *that so eminent an Antiquitie should lye so long unregarded by our Chorographers.* And if Aubrey had not come upon it thus, by chance, it is possible that it would have gone unregarded for ever, for the villagers were even then engaged in breaking up the stones to build new houses.

One month later, with the execution of King Charles and the setting up of the Commonwealth, the break with the past was com-pleted. And by a strange chance, in that·very year, the modern world was born. For the idea of progress, a conception which differentiates modern civilisation from everything that has preceded it, appeared quite suddenly, and mankind, abandoning its idea of a static world, was to become increasingly familiar with the idea of development and gradual change. *Till about the yeare* 1649, Aubrey says, *when Experimental Philosophy was first cultivated by a Club at Oxford, 'twas held a strange presumption for a Man to attempt an Innovation in Learnings ; and not to be good Manners, to be more knowing than his Neighbours and Forefathers ; even to attempt an improvement in Husbandry (though it succeeded with profit) was look'd upon with an ill Eie. Their Neighbours did scorne to follow it, though not to doe it, was to their own Detriment. 'Twas held a Sin to make a Scrutinie into the Waies of Nature ; Whereas it is certainly a profound part of Religion to glorify God in his Workes : and to take no notice at all of what is dayly offered before our Eyes is grosse Stupidity.*

The overwhelming importance of this change of attitude cannot be exaggerated, for this freeing of the mind was to cause a violent bound forward in every branch of thought. *In those times, to have had an inventive and enquiring Witt, was accounted Affectation,* Aubrey concludes, *which censure the famous Dr. William Harvey could not escape for his admirable Discovery of the Circulation of the Blood.*

But it was not only the mind of England which had changed : the very face of the country altered as the mighty forests that had covered the island since time immemorial were consumed by the ironworks, until Shakespeare's Arden and *the Forests and Parks of Clarendon* were converted into the arable that we know to-day. *In England till even now since the resprit of these Warres, there were so many Forests, Chases, and Parkes, as were not to be match'd in any Kingdome. These were Vivaries for Beastes (the design of their Lords being to preserve Game) where they were safe not only by the Pale, or Wall ; but under the Protection of many severe Laws : as if they had been naturaliz'd, enfranchis'd, and Citizens of our Commonwealth.* It was not always in this tone that Aubrey spoke of animals, however. *At Fausby (near Daintre) in Northamptonshire,* he said on another occasion, *a Raven did build her Nest on the Leads between the Tower and the Steeple. The oldest Peoples Grandfathers here, did never remember, but that this Raven yearly made her Nest here ; and in the late Civil warre, the Soldiers killed her. I am sorry for the Tragical end of this old Church-Bird, that lived in so many changes of Government and Relegion.*

It is always hard for us to visualise the material life of our ancestors ; to remember that Queen Elizabeth, in her jewelled dresses, had to walk through her palaces on straw-covered floors. But it is on their tables that the widest difference is noticeable, and as Aubrey describes the new foods that had come into England, it is almost impossible to imagine what the people lived on before. For it was Sir Walter Raleigh, more famous for his introduction of tobacco, who brought from the New World the potato, which was immediately impugned for erotic tendencies by the Elizabethans. *Cherries,* according to Aubrey, *were first brought into Kent tempore H. viii, who being in Flanders, and likeing the Cherries, ordered his Gardener, brought them hence and propagated them in England ;* and it was not until Queen Elizabeth's time that that most English of plants, *Hoppes,* became common in Kent. Aubrey states that *about the 15th of Henry VIIIth divers things were newly brought into England, whereupon the Rythme was made*

> *Greeke, Heresie, Turkey-cocks, and Beer,*
> *Came into England all in a yeare.*

England itself remained amazingly regional, mainly because of the difficulties of transport. *The Marquesse Hamilton (that was beheaded),* Aubrey reports, *was a great Lover of Carpes, and was at great expense (but unsuccessfull) to Carry Carpes into Scotland from England in barrells : but their Noses did still gangrene, being bobb'd against the barrell,* and until someone thought of carrying the spawn, rather than the fish themselves, people in the outlying parts of the country had to content themselves with whatever nature provided, for there were no fishmongers inland and so, *by reason of the fasting dayes, all gentlemen's howses had anciently Fishponds, and fish in the motes about the howse.*

Within living memory, even, vast changes had taken place in the nation's diet. *Carrets,* says Aubrey, *were first sown at Beckington in Somersetshire. Some very old Man there (in 1668) did remember their first bringing thither,* and not only did *Mr. Alexander James, Alderman of Bristoll,* tell him that *when he was a Boy, all the Turnips, that they had there, did come from Wales,* but *the Mother of Mr. John Ashe remembred when all the Cabbages were brought from Holland. She was eighty yeares old, and upwards when she died.*

Agriculture, too, was improving, and Aubrey notes : *Limeing of ground began about* 1590 *or some time after the use of Tobacco, by Sir Walter Raleigh,* and it was Sir Richard Weston who *brought the first Clovergrass, about* 1645, *out of Brabant or Flandrs ; at which time he also brought over the Contrivance of Locks, Turnpikes, and tumbling Boyes for Rivers,* while *Sir Isaac Wake was the first that planted Pines and Firres in England.*

Even tabby cats were once newfangled novelties. *W. Laud, A. B. Cant. was a great lover of Catts,* Aubrey reports, *He was presented with some Cyprus-catts, i.e. our Tabby-catts, which were sold, at first for 5 pounds a piece : this was about* 1637, *or* 1638. The fashion thus started resulted in a change which Aubrey strongly resented. *I doe well remember,* he says crossly, *that the common English Catt, was white with some blewish piednesse : sc. a gallipot blew. The race or breed of them are now almost lost.* But another change in the animal population of England at this time would probably not have aroused his anger had he noticed it and recognised its implications, for during Aubrey's lifetime the modern brown rat wiped out and replaced the mediæval black rat, and it was this mediæval rat which had been the carrier of the plague-flea.

Strange flowers, too, were reaching English shores. *Jessamines came into England with Mary, the Queen-Mother,* he says, *and Laurel. was first brought over by Alethea, Countesse of Arundell, grandmother to this Duke of Norfolke.* For *the Pleasure and Use of Gardens were unknown to our great Grandfathers : they were contented with Pot-herbs : and did mind chiefly their Stables. But in the time of King Charles II^d Gardening was much improved, and became common ;* so common in fact that Aubrey could write in 1691, *especially since about* 1683, *there have been exotick Plants brought into England, no lesse than seven thousand.*

But to return to Aubrey's life : for the first three years of the Commonwealth he tried to alleviate the misery of his *sad life in the country,* by toying with the idea of travel abroad. *William Harvey, my she cosen Montague's physitian and friend, proved very communicative and willing to instruct any that were modest and respectfull to him and in order to my Journey, gave me, i.e. dictated to me, what to see, what company to keepe, what Bookes to read, how to manage my Studies : in short, he bid me goe to the Fountain head, and read Aristotle, Cicero, Avicenna, and did call the Neoteriques shitt-breeches.* These plans came to maturity in 1651, Aubrey continued, *when I made my will and settled my Estate on Trustees, intending to have seen the Antiquities of Rome and Italy, and then to have returned and maried, but my mother, to my inexpressible griefe and ruine, hindred this designe, which was the procatratique cause of my ruine.*

His mother's importunities were no doubt caused by the illness of his father, who died at last in 1652, unregretted by his son, who ungratefully mentioned only that he was left *debts* 1800 *pounds,* and ignored the estates in Wiltshire, Surrey, Monmouth, Brecknock, Hereford and Kent which also came to him, albeit they were well entangled with law suits.

Now that he was free from his father's disapproving gaze and

[xxxvi]

master of his own purse, Aubrey embarked wholeheartedly on a career of dilletantism. His estates were left to look after themselves while he led the life of a wealthy young squire in London, which even under *the English Attila, Oliver,* was more congenial than the lonely farms of Wiltshire. For the condition of England *during Oliver's Triumphant Usurpation* is best summed up by an inn-sign near Oxford which, at the beginning of the Commonwealth, had been altered to read " This was the King's Head." And as Aubrey sought out *the merry men in the reigne of the Saintes,* he discovered that the main result of the Commonwealth was an increase in concealment and hypocrisy, rather than a change of heart. The Presbyterians, as Anthony Wood was quick to notice, " would not goe to ale-houses or taverns, but send for their liquors to their respective chambers and tiple it there. Some would goe in publick ; but then, if overtaken, they were so cunning as to dissemble it in their way home by a lame leg or that some suddaine paine there had taken them." A more unexpected result of Puritanism, however, was that " Dr. John Owen, the Deane of Christ Church, when Vice-Chancellor, had as much powder in his haire that would discharg eight cannons," as well as " cambric band with larg costly band-strings, velvet jacket, his breeches set round at knee with ribbons, pointed, Spanish leather boots with Cambrig tops, etc. And all this was in opposition to a prelaticall cut."

The death of his father had started Aubrey on a depressing train of thought, and after considering long and seriously what he was best fitted to do in life, he had to answer : *Truly nothing : only Umbrages. If ever I had been good for anything, 'twould have been a Painter, I could fancy a thing so strongly and had so cleare an idaea of it,* but to become a good painter would have been a laborious business, and so Aubrey decided that his real purpose in life was to be *a wheatstone* and to strike ideas from other people and sharpen their wits for work. He was not long, however, in finding his proper bent, for he mentions that *he began to enter into pocket memorandum bookes, philosophical and anti-quarian remarques, Anno Domini* 1654, *at Llantrithid.*

In 1655, Aubrey says, *there was published by Mr. Web a Booke intituled Stonehenge-restored (but writt by Mr. Inigo Jones) which I read with great delight. There is a great deale of Learning in it : but having compared his Scheme with the Monument it self, I found he had not dealt fairly : but had made a Lesbian's rule, which is conformed to the stone ; that is, he framed the monument to his own Hypothesis, which is much differing from the Thing it self. This gave me an edge to make more researches ; and a farther oppor-tunity was, that my honoured and faithfull Friend Colonell James Long of Draycot, since Baronet, was wont to spend a weeke or two every Autumne at Aubury in Hawking, where several times I have had the happiness to accom-pany him. I should now be both Orator and Soldier to give this honoured friend of mine, a Gentleman absolute in all numbers, his due Character,* said Aubrey, and therefore limited himself to giving a mere list of Sir James's capabilities. *In the Civill Warres, Colonel of Horse in Sir Francis Dodington's Brigade. Maried a most elegant Beautie and Witt. Good sword-man ; horseman ; admirable extempore Orator pro Harangue ; Great Memorie ; great Historian and Romanceer ; great Falkoner and for Horsemanship ; for Insects ; exceeding curious and searching long since, in naturall things.* And to show that he was not alone in appreciating his friend's charms, Aubrey mentions that *Oliver Protector, hawking at Hownslowe-heath, discoursing with him, fell in love with his company, and commanded him to weare his sword, and to meete him a Hawking, which made the strict Cavaliers look on him with an evill eye.*

Our Sport was very good, and in a Romantick countrey, Aubrey continues, *sc. the Prospects noble and vast, the Downes stock't with numerous Flocks of Sheep, the Turfe rich and fragrant with Thyme and Burnet. Nor are the Nut-brown Shepherdesses without their graces. But the flight of the Falcon was but a parenthesis to the Colonell's facetious discourse, who was tam Marti quam Mercurio ; and the Muses did accompany him with his Hawkes and Spanniels.* Unfortunately Aubrey was so entertained by his friend's conversation that he never committed his arguments to paper, and so Inigo Jones went unrefuted.

Undaunted by his failure even to complete a pamphlet, Aubrey at once embarked on a much more elaborate task. *I am the first that ever made an Essay of this Kind for Wiltshire (and for ought I know in the Nation) having begun it in Ano 1656,* he said, and the work he was planning was indeed new. He had undertaken to write *The Naturall Historie of Wiltshire,* and although it was never published, he did in fact bring it nearer to completion than any of his other books.

The mere chapter headings show the vast scope of the work, for they range from *Air, Springs Medicinall, Rivers, Earths, Mineralls, Stones, Plantes, Beastes, Fishes, Birds, Insects and Reptiles, Men and Women,* to *Things Praeternatural, e.g. Witchcraft, Phantomes, &c.,* and *the Number of Attornies every 30 yeares since H. viii.* And there are numerous diversions into subjects like *The History of Cloathing and Cloathiers of Wilts, Faires and Markets : Their Rise and Decay,* and *Of the Grandure of he Herberts, Earles of Pembroke.*

In this book, Aubrey put forward many new theories, some absurd, some endorsed by time. *If you let fall a stone into the water,* he said, *immediately it makes a little Circle, then another bigger without that, and so forth, till it touches at the Bank, and then it recoiles in a little Circle, which generates other bigger Circles ; so sounds move by Sphaeres, in the same manner, which though obvious enough, I doe not remember to have seen in any Booke ;* and this observation he counterbalanced by suggesting that it rains more often when the moon is full because *her Vicinity to the Earth gradually depresseth our amosphere.* This last idea is typical of the seventeenth century for, intoxicated by the possibilities of the scientific method, men were apt to put far more faith in it than it warranted. Aubrey measured the height of Salisbury spire by barometric pressure, for instance, and got the result to the nearest inch, and he says *to find the Proportion of the Downes of this Countrey to the Vales, I did divide Speeds Mappe of Wiltshire with a paire of Cizars, according to the respective Hundreds of Downes and Vale : And I weighed them in a Curious Ballance of a Goldsmith.*

On the whole, however, his observations were accurate and his deductions good. He noticed that the ground rose with age and also that the Roman remains at Silchester, though they were deep underground, were visible from a height, in the grass. Aubrey was the first archeologist that England had produced, and he devoted himself to all the ramifications of that study : geology, heraldry, palaeography, numismatics and comparative architecture : but being the first in the field, he was offered little help by his predecessors. *I have often times wish't for a Mappe of England coloured according to the colours of the Earth : with markes of the Fossils and Minerals,* he said, and he regretted that no one had ever found time to write *a Historie of the Weather.* His study of these archeological remains, too, caused his fertile brain to throw out various ideas which were far in advance of his time. *That the World is much older, then is commonly supposed,* he said, *any man may be induced to believe from the finding Fossils so many Foot deep in the Earth,* and he foreshadowed the theory of evolution when he saw *(to use the Heralds terme) that Fishes are of the elder House.*

The work also contained a less learned side, which was so entertaining that John Ray felt obliged to issue a warning. " I think (if you can give me leave to be free with you)," he wrote to Aubrey, " that you are a little inclinable to credit strange relations. I have found men that are not skilfull in the history of nature very credulous, and apt to impose upon themselves and others, and therefore dare not give a firm assent to anything they report upon their own authority, but are ever suspicious that they may either be deceived themselves, or delight to teratologize (pardon ye word) and to make shew of knowing strange things."

Luckily Aubrey ignored this well meant advice and left in the " strange relations," which nowadays provide the main interest of the work. Such complete irrelevancies as *the best way of dressing a Carpe* find their way into the *Naturall Historie,* besides a most useful hint for the cellar : *Dead Men's bones burn't to ashes and putt into drinke doe intoxicate exceedingly.* Then, too, he was ready with a most efficacious cure for anyone who happened to bang his head : *A Fellow in North-Wales, shrowding of a Tree fell downe on his head, and his Braine being turned, lay for dead : A Mason being thereby, advised that he should have a good strong coffin made, and his feete to come to the end of it, and his head not to touch the other end by two inches : He layeth the Man in the Coffin on a Table-board, and then with a huge Axe, gave a sound Knock at the feet, to turne by that contrary motion his braine right againe. After the blow was given the fellow gave a groane and spake : and he recovered.*

A whole treasure trove of words lies jumbled up together in this book. *In North Wilts,* Aubrey says, *the Milke mayds sing as shrill and cleare as any Swallow sitting on a Berne,* and the next minute he is telling us how *some Cow-stealers will make a hole in a hott loafe newly drawne out of the oven, and put it on an Oxes-horn for a convenient time, and then they can turn their softened hornes the contrary way : So that the owner cannot sweare to his own beast. Not long before the King's restauration, a fellow was hang'd at Tyburn for this Trick, and sayd, that he had never come thither, if he had not heard this Trick spoken of in a Sermon. Thought he, I will try this Trick.* After this salutary warning against the dangers of church-going, Aubrey flies off at a tangent again to report that *Isaac Selfe, a wealthy Cloathier of Milsham, died in the ninety second yeare of his Age, leaving behind him a numerous offspring ; viz. eighty and three in number,* and this reminds him that *Mr. Bonham's wife had two Children at one birth, the first time ; and he being troubled at it, travelled : and was absent seven yeares. After his returne he got his wife with Child : and she was delivered of seven Children at one Birth.* What the moral of this story was, Aubrey omits to say, but he added that *Dr. Wm. Harvey (Author of the Circulation of the Bloud) told me that one Mr. Palmer's Wife in Kent did beare a Child every day for five daies together,* a tale which was capped by *Mris. Hine the Vicar's-wife of Kington St. Michael (a very able Midwife)* who informed Aubrey that *Mris. Kath. H—— (who was brought to bed at Dorchester) (Dorset) was delivered first of a Sonne (now liveing and the Heir) and afterwards for eight daies together, every day another Child : Some whereof had heads, and Armes, and no lower parts ; others had lower, but no upper-parts : but she never had any Child afterwards.* Nor was this all, for *the said Mris. Hine did tell a storie (about 1649) which was confidently averred ; that about Westerly, or Alderly, or that way in Glocestershire, there were two Children born in the grave.* Refusing to be outdone in this vein, William Harvey countered with the story of *a certain Knight in Kent, who having gott his Wives Mayd with Child, sent her to London to lie-in under pretence of seeing her friends : She was brought to bed there about Michaelmas ; and after some convenient time she returned to her Lady : She found herselfe not well, and in December following, she fell in labour again, and was delivered of another Child.* It is unlikely that this untoward incident caused her neighbours much surprise, for when Mary Waterman, half an hour after bearing a normal child, *was delivered of a Monstrous-birth, haveing two Heades the one opposite to the other,* the seventeenth century coped with the matter with exemplary efficiency. *About four o Clock in the after-Noon the same day,* Aubrey records, *it was christened, by the name of Martha and Mary, having two pretty faces, and lived till fryday next.* And then he says, *I will whilst 'tis in my mind insert this Remarque, viz—about 1620 one Ricketts of Newberye. a Practictioner in Physick was excellent at the Curing Children with swoln heads, and small legges : and the Disease being new, and without a name, He being so famous for the cure of it, they called the Disease the Ricketts : as the King's Evill from the King's cureing of it with his Touch ; and now 'tis good sport to see how they vex their Lexicons, and fetch it from the Greek* Ρᾰχις, *the back bone.*

It was no wonder, therefore, that when he presented a fair copy of this work to the Royal Society, it *gave them two or three dayes Entertainment, which they were pleased to like.* But though it circulated widely amongst his friends, and despite its hopeful dedication *to the Right Honourable Thomas Earle of Pembroke, my singular good Lord,* the *Naturall Historie* was never published ; indeed it was never finished, for although Aubrey did his part, his *Advice to the Painter or Graver* was not carried out, and the list of the illustrations he desired went unnoticed, as he half suspected it would. *If these views were well donn,* he had said, *they would make a glorious Volume by itselfe, and like enough it might take well in the World. It were an inconsiderable charge to these Persons of Qualitie : and it would remaine to Posterity, when their Families are gonn, and their Buildings ruin'd by time, or Fire, as we have seen that stupendous Fabrick of Paul's Church, not a stone left on a stone, and lives now onely in Mr. Hollar's Etchings in Sir William Dugdale's History of Pauls. I am not displeased with this Thought as a Desideratum,* he concluded, *but I doe never expect to see it donn : so few men have the hearts to doe publique good : to give 3, 4, or 5 pounds for a Copper Plate.*

It says a great deal for Aubrey's power of concentration that he was able to proceed as far with this work as he did, for in 1656 he also began *his chargeable and taedious Lawesuite about the Entaile in Brecknock-shire and Monmouthshire, which lands,* he said rather hopefully, *now of right belong to me.* For his great-grandfather, the *little Doctor* of Queen Elizabeth's Court, had entailed *the Brecon estate on the Issue male of his eldest son, and in defailer, to skip the* 2ᵈ *son (for whom he had well provided, and had married a good fortune) and to come to the third. Edward the eldest had seaven Sonnes : and his eldest son Sir Will had also seaven sonnes ; and so I am heyre, being the* 18*th man in Remainder, which putts me in mind of* Dr. Donne :

> *For what doeth it availe*
> *To be twentieth man in an Entaile ?*

The tortuous descent of this land was further complicated by the fact that William Aubrey's executor *ran away into Ireland and cosened all the Legatees.* So Aubrey cannot really have been surprised when he lost the case. *It cost me* 1200 *pounds,* he noted sadly all the same, adding *this yeare, and the last, was a strange year to me, and full of Contradictions :— scilicet Love and Law-suites.*

For Aubrey's affairs were rapidly becoming desperate. *Then Debts and Law-suites,* he says, *opus et usus, borrowing of money and perpetuall riding,* which itself was not without complications, for he lists a whole chapter of accidents. *On Monday after Easter weeke,* he reports, *my uncle's nag ranne away with me, and gave me a very dangerous fall. Just before it I had an Impulse of the Briar under which I rode, which tickled him, at the Gap at the upper end of Bery Lane. Deo gratias !* Then (*I thinke*) June 14, *I had a fall at Epsam, and brake one of my ribbes and was afrayd it might cause an Apostumation,* and good antiquary that he was, he religiously preserved among his papers William Harvey's prescription for that treatment. *March or Aprill,* he wrote a few years later, *like to break my neck in Ely Minster, and the next day, riding a gallop there, my horse tumbled over and over, and yet (I thanke God) no hurt.* The next time, however, he was not to be so fortunate, for *Munday after Christmas, was in danger to be spoiled by my horse, and the same day received laesio in Testiculo which was like to have been fatall :* but was not : and ever afterwards he rode quietly.

To my prayse, he said, *I had wonderfull credit in the countrey for money. Sold Manor of Bushelton in Herefordshire to Dr. T. Willis. Sold Manor of Stratford in the same county to Herbert, Lord Bishop of Hereford.* And so began the dissipation of his estates, so recently inherited, so soon to be squandered.

In 1659, Aubrey started a second work relating to Wiltshire, which was intended to form part of a County History of England. *At a Meeting of Gentlemen at the Devizes for choosing of Knights of the Shire in March* 1659, he said, *it was wish'd by some that this County (wherein are many observable Antiquities) was survey'd, in Imitation of Mr. Dugdale's Illustration of Warwickshire ; but it being too great a Task for one Man, Mr. William Yorke (Councellor at Law, and a Lover of this Kind of Learning) advis'd to have the Labour divided ; he himself would undertake the Middle Division, I would undertake the North ; T. Gore, Esq. Jeffrey Daniel,*

Esq. and Sir John Ernely, would be Assistants. And so *An Essay towards the Description of the North Division of Wiltshire* was begun with high hopes, and was soon illustrated with armorial shields elaborately emblazoned and with facsimiles of old deeds and seals. But once again Aubrey malingered and the work stopped just short of completion. *This good design vanished in fumo Tabaci, and was never thought of since,* he said hopelessly eleven years later. However he would not admit final defeat. *I have since that occasionally made this following Collection, which perhaps may sometime or other fall into some Antiquary's Hands, to make a handsom Work of it.* I am heartily sorry, he continued, *I did not set down the Antiquities of these parts sooner, for since the Time aforesaid* (1659) *many Things are irrecoverably lost.*

In former Daies the Churches and great Howses hereabouts did so abound with Monuments and Things remarquable that it would have deterred an Antiquarie from undertakeing it, he said. *But as Pythagoras did guesse at the vastnesse of Hercules Stature by the Length of his Foote, so amongst these Ruines are Remaines enough left for a Man to give a Guesse what noble Buildings &c. were made by the Piety, Charity and Magnanimity of our Fore-fathers.*

And as in Prospects, wee are there pleased most Where something keepes the Eie from being lost And leaves us roome to guesse ; So here the Eie and Mind is no lesse affected with these stately Ruines, then they would have been when standing and entire. They breed in generous Minds a Kind of Pittie : and sett the Thoughts a-worke to make out their Magnifice as they were when in Perfection. But it was not only in buildings that Aubrey was interested, although he was so learned in architectural history : the countryside through which he wandered in search of his material entranced him quite as much. *This is a very noble seate,* he says of Down Ampney House, *and situated with great convenience for pleasure and profitt. By this house runnes a fine brooke, which waters these gallant meadowes on the west sides, where depasture a great number of cattle :—30 milk-mayds singing.* And as he rode through Garesdon, he could not help recalling that *one Mody was a foote-man to King Henry the eighth who, falling from his horse as he was hawkeing (I think on Harneslow-heath) fell with his head in to mudde, with which, being fatt and heavie, he had been suffocated to death had he not been timely relieved by his footman Mody, for which service, after the dissolution of the Abbies, he gave him the manour of Garesdon.* After a regretful sigh at the easy preferment of the past, Aubrey's attention was distracted by a whip in a coat of arms, and the story he ferreted out was that *the Issue male of this Family being all extinct, except a brother who was a White-fryer, the Pope granted a Dispensation of his Vowes, and that he should quitt his Convent and marry to continue the name of the Family : which accordingly he did : and in such cases, the Brother that so departs, is to runne the Gauntlet as the Soldiers doe it, that is; all the fryers putt them selves into two rankes, having every one a Paenitentiall whip in his hand, and the dispensed fryer runnes through, every one giving him a lash.*

In the autumn of 1659, Aubrey was once again in London and was taking part in the debates at James Harrington's club, the Rota, where the principles of Republican government were debated and rotation by balloting was advocated as the cure of all its ills. *The Doctrine was very takeing,* Aubrey admitted, *and the more because, as to human foresight, there was no possibility of the King's returne.* It must be remembered that the prime of Aubrey's youth and early manhood had coincided with the period of the Commonwealth and it seems clear from the vehemence of his defence of Milton's politics, that he had himself become a theoretical Republican. *Whatever he wrote against Monarchie,* Aubrey said, *was out of no animosity to the King's person, or owt of any faction or interest, but out of a pure Zeale to the Liberty of Mankind, which he thought would be greater under a fre state than under a Monarchiall goverment. His being so conversant in Livy and the Roman authors, and the greatness he saw donne by the Roman commonwealth, and the vertue of their great Commanders induc't him to.* And there could be no doubt that the prestige of England had increased under the Protectorate. Then too Aubrey had mixed constantly with the leaders of the Republic : *I heard Oliver Cromwell Protector tell the Lord Arundell of Wardour at Dinner at Hampton-Court 1657, that He had been in all the Counties of England, and that the Devonshire Husbandry was the best.* His membership of the Rota was, therefore, merely the logical outcome of his Republican leanings, but *in February 1660, upon the unexpected turne upon Generall Monke's comeing-in, all these aerie modells vanished,* and Aubrey was soon on the other side, involved in the thick of the negotiations for the restoration of the King. Thomas Mariett, who *every day was tampering with George Monk,* stayed with Aubrey during the parleying, and once again Aubrey's laziness caused him regret. *Every night late,* he said, *I had an account of all these Transactions in bed, which like a Sott as I was, I did not, while fresh in Memorie, committ to writing.* But he did find time to inform Thomas Hobbes of what was in the wind and to advise him to come to London at once, so as *to redintegrate his favour with his Majesty,* as soon as the King arrived.

Aubrey grew quite lyrical over the King's restoration, when it was accomplished, and it was left to Anthony Wood to see the ugly side of the business. The divines hurriedly putting on " the most prelaticall garbe that could be " did not escape his jaundiced eye and he watched with scorn while those " that bore the faces of demure Saints, would now and then put out a wanton (in plaine terms, a baudy) expression, and, as occasion served, a pretty little Oath." But even he had to admit that " after the King came in I never heard of any that were troubled in conscience or that hung himself, as in Oliver's time, when nothing but praying and preaching was used." For there was no doubt that life under the Commonwealth had been an appalling strain ; and Aubrey says in his life of Wenceslas Hollar, *I remember he told me that when he first came into England (which was a serene time of Peace) that the people, both poore and rich, did looke cheerfully, but at his return, he found the Countenances of the people all changed, melancholy, spight-full, as if bewitched.*

When the excitements of the King's homecoming had begun to pall, Aubrey *accompanied A. Ettrick into Ireland for a moneth ; and returning were like to be ship-wrackt at Holyhead, but no hurt donne.* Despite this narrow escape, Aubrey came back from his holiday refreshed in spirit and bubbling over with ideas for work—for other people to carry out. *From N. Wales I went into Ireland,* he wrote to Thomas Hobbes, *where I saw the manner of living of the natives, scorning industry and luxury, contenting themselves only with things necessary. That kingdom is in a very great distemper, and hath need of your advice to settle it ; the animosities between the English and the Irish are very great, and will ere long, I am confident, break into war. Your brother I heare is well, whom I intend to see on Monday next, and shall with him sacrifice to your health in a glasse of sack.*

But Hobbes would not rise to this bait, although on another occasion Aubrey was more successful. *It was I.A.,* he says proudly, *that did putt Mr. Hobbes upon writing his Treatise De Legibus, which is bound up with his Rhetorique that one cannot find it but by chance ; no mention of it in the first Title.* Aubrey had learnt from his previous failure that a direct suggestion was not of much avail, and so this time he used a more roundabout way to achieve his desire. *In 1644 I sayd to him ; Me thinkes 'tis pitty that you that have such a cleare reason and working head did never take into consideration the learning of the Lawes ; and I endeavoured to perswade him to it. To which he was unwilling, telling me that 'twas a long, taedious, and difficult taske and he doubted he should not have dayes enough to left to doe it. Now all men will give the old Gent that right as to acknowledge he is rare for Definitions, and the Lawyers building on old-fashioned Maximes (some right, some wrong) must need fall into severall Paralogismes, for grand practisers have not the leisure to be analytiques. Upon this consideration I was earnest with him to consider these things. I then presented him the Lord Chancellor Bacon's Elements of the Lawe (a thin quarto) in order thereunto and to drawe him on ; which he was pleased to accept, and perused ; and the next time I came to him he showed me therein two cleare Paralogismes in the 2nd page (one, I well remember, was in page 2) which I am heartily sorry are now out of my remembrance. I desponded, for his reasons, that he should make any further attempt towards this Designe ; but afterwards, it seemes, in the Countrey he writt his Treatise De Legibus. He drives on, in this, the King's Prerogative high. Judge Hales, who is no great Courtier, has read it and much mislikes it, and is his enemy. Judge Vaughan has perused it and very much commends it, but is afraid to license it for feare of giving displeasure.* Which explains very well the lack of any mention on the title page.

Although none of Aubrey's works had yet been published, they had circulated widely amongst his friends and, founded upon the good word of Izaak Walton and Sir Thomas Browne, of Thomas Hobbes and John Locke, of Isaac Newton, Edmund Halley, Robert Boyle and Christopher Wren, of Samuel Butler and John Dryden, David Loggan and Nicholas Mercator, Wenceslas Hollar, Sir William Davenant, Edmund Waller, Andrew Marvell, John Evelyn and Sir William Dugdale, Aubrey's reputation as an antiquary was so well established by 1662, that he was nominated as one of the Original Fellows of the Royal Society, an honour of which he was justifiably proud.

The ninety-eight Original Fellows were chosen rather for their interest in science, than for their skill as scientists, and they included many of Aubrey's closest friends ; there were poets like Denham and Dryden and Waller, Evelyn the diarist, Ashmole of Museum fame, Glisson the doctor, Christopher Wren the architect, as well as scientists proper like Hooke and Robert Boyle. Bishops, soldiers and courtiers made up the number, and fourteen peers, including the Duke of Buckingham and the Marquess of Dorchester, were also members : while to complete the roll, King Charles II " was pleased to offer himselfe to be entered one of the Society."

The Royal Society " for the promoting of Physico-Mathematicall-Experimentall Learning " had developed from that small *Philosophicall Clubbe* at Oxford, which has been mentioned before and which had been transferred to London about 1658. *They mett*, says Aubrey, *at the Bull-head Taverne in Cheapside, till it grew to big for a Clubb. The first beginning of the Royal Society (where they putt discourse in paper and brought it to use) was in the Chamber of William Ball, Esqr., eldest son of Sir Peter Ball of Devon, in the Middle Temple. They had meetings at Taverns before, but 'twas here where it formally and in good earnest sett up : and so they came to Gresham Colledge parlour.*

The importance of this foundation cannot be over-emphasised. For the specialist was not yet born, and in the childhood of science it was still possible, as Aubrey has shown in his *Naturall Historie of Wiltshire,* to produce a new intellectual value without having to acquire skill and without troubling to acquaint oneself with a great deal of accumulated knowledge. *I have heard Sr Will Davenant say,* Aubrey noted, *that Witt did seem to be the easiest thing in the World, for when it is delivered, it appeares so naturall, that every one thinks he could have sayd the same : this of his, may also be applied to Inventions and Discoveries.*

The existing body of knowledge about trade and the sciences was so small in the seventeenth century that some of their discoveries do seem childishly simple. *Sir Paul Neale sayd, that in the Bishoprick of Durham is a Coalery, which by reason of the dampes ther did so frequently kill the Workemen (sometimes three or four in a Moneth) that he could make little or nothing out of it. It happened one time, that the workemen being merry with drink fell to play with fire-brands, and to throwe live-coales at one another by the head of the Pitt, where they usually have fires. It fortuned that a fire-brand fell into the bottome of the Pitt : where at there proceeded such a noise as if it had been a Gun : they likeing the Sport, threw down more fire-brands and there followed the like noise, for severall times, and at length it ceased. They went to work after, and were free from Damps, so having by good chance found out this Experiment, they doe now every morning throw-down some Coales, and they work as securely as in any other Mines.* But these improvements were not always accidental : *Before I leave this Towne,* Aubrey wrote of his friend Robert Hooke, *I will gett of him a catalogue of what he hath wrote ; and as much of his Inventions as I can. But they are many hundreds ; he believes not fewer than a thousand.* Nor were his other friends less ingenious : ruled copy books, mathematical symbols, even drogues (*Memorandum Dr. Wilkins his notion of an Umbrella-like invention for retarding a ship when shee drives in a storme*), were invented by Aubrey's immediate circle, but perhaps the most fruitful suggestion of all was made by Sir Edward Ford, who *writt no Books, but two or three Pamphletts of a sheet or so. One was an ingeniose proposall of a publique Banke, as I remember, for the easy raysing of money and to avoyd the griping Usurers and to promote trade.* Aubrey himself was not behindhand in these matters : *Let a Ginne bee invented,* he said, *to shatter out Corne by jogging in stead of soweing or setting, the one being too wastfull, the other too troublesome and taking up too much time : and that the soweing and harroweing may bee but one and the same labour :* and besides this invention, he was working out a phonetic alphabet with Andrew Paschall (*which some persons looke upon as a Whim wham : but if it be so, the learned Verstergen was also liable to that severe censure)* ; and was also engaged in experiments with Francis Potter *to cure diseases, etc. by Transfusion of Bloud out of one man into another*.

Under these conditions, the Royal Society, with its regular Wednesday meetings, for the first time systematised scientific learning by allowing for the free interchange of ideas and the comparing of research, and this was all that was needed to produce the modern world. For, as H. G. Wells has said : " The main difference of modern scientific research from that of the Middle Ages, the secret of its immense successes, lies in its collective character, in the fact that every fruitful experiment is published, every new discovery of relationship explained."

A few months after the incorporation of the Royal Society, Aubrey says, *King Charles IId discoursing one morning with my Lord Brouncker and Dr. Charleton concerning Stoneheng, they told his Majestie, what they had heard me say concerning Aubury, sc. that it did as much excell of Stoneheng as a Cathedral does a Parish Church. His Majestie admired that none of our Chorographers had taken notice of it : and commanded Dr. Charleton to bring me to him the next morning. I brought with me a draught of it donne by memorie only : but well enough resembling it, with which his Majestie was pleased : gave me his hand to kisse, and commanded me to waite on him at Marleborough, when he went to Bath with the Queen (which was about a fortnight after) which I did : and the next day, when the Court were on their Journey, his Majestie left the Queen and diverted to Aubury, where I shewed him that stupendious Antiquity, with a view whereof, He and his Royal Highness the Duke of Yorke were very well pleased. His Majestie then commanded me to write a Description of it, and present it to him : and the Duke of Yorke commanded me to give an account of the Old Camps and Barrows on the Plaines.*

As his Majestie departed from Aubury to overtake the Queen he cast his eie on Silbury-hill, about a mile off : which he had the curiosity to see, and walkt up to the top of it, with the Duke of Yorke, Dr. Charleton and I attending them, Aubrey continued proudly, and later he added this note, which reflects on the oddly public life of Royalty in those days. *When I had the honour to waite on King Charles and the Duke of Yorke to the top of Silbury-hill, his Royal Highnesse happened to cast his Eye on some of these small Snailes, not much bigger, or no bigger than small Pinnes-heads, on the Turfe of the Hill. He was surprised with the novelty ; and commanded me to pick some up ; which I did about a dozen or more, immediately ; for they are in great abundance. The next Morning as he was abed with his Dutches at Bath, He told her of it : and sent Dr. Charleton to me for them to shew Her as a Rarity.*

In September following (1663) *I survey'd that old Monument of Aubury with a plaine table, and afterwards tooke a Review of Stonehenge, and then, I composed this following Discourse in obedience to his Majesties command : and presented it to Him : which he commanded me to put in print.* This last command Aubrey ignored, despite the fact that his book was dedicated *to King Charles by His Majestie's most loyale and obedient Subject John Aubrey.* The thoroughness with which he had carried out the survey is proved by the fact that his plan of Stonehenge shows certain depressions in the ground which have since disappeared : *His Majestie*

[xlvi]

commanded me to digge at the bottom of the stones marked with the fig. 1, *to try if I could find any human bones,* he said, *but I did not doe it.* Because of his plan, these depressions, which are now known as "Aubrey Holes," were excavated and located in 1921, and sure enough they were found to contain cremated remains, possibly of human sacrifices.

There have been several Books writt by learned men concerning Stoneheng, he continued, *much differing from one another, some affirming one thing, some another. Now I come in the Rear of all by comparative Arguments to give a clear evidence these monuments were Pagan Temples ; which was not made-out before : and have also, with humble submission to better judgements, offered a probability, that they were Temples of the Druids.*

When a traveller rides along by the Ruines of a Monastery, Aubrey says, *he knows by the manner of building, sc., Chapell, Cloysters, &c., that it was a Convent, but of what Order, sc., Benedictine, Dominican, &c., it was, he cannot tell by the bare View. So it is clear that all the Monuments, which I have here recounted were Temples. Now my presumption is, That the Druids being the most eminent Priests, or Order of Priests, among the Britaines ; 'tis odds, but that these ancient monuments, sc. Aubury, Stonehenge, Kerrig, Druidd &c., were Temples of the Priests of the most eminent Order, viz. Druids, and it is strongly to be presumed that Aubury, Stonehenge, &c., are as ancient as those times. This Inquiry, I must confess, is a grodeing in the Dark ; but although I have not brought it into a clear light ; yet I can affirm that I have brought it from an utter darkness to a thin mist, and have gonne further in this Essay than any one before me. These Antiquities are so exceeding old that no Bookes doe reach them, so that there is no Way to retrive them but by comparative antiquitie, which I have writt upon the spott, from the Monuments themselves. Historia quoquo modo scripta, bona est* [In whatever way history is written, it is good] ; *and though this be writt, as I rode, a gallop ; yet the novelty of it, and the faithfulness of the delivery, may make some amends for the uncorrectness of the Stile. The first draught,* he concludes, *was worn out with time and handling ; and now, methinkes, after many years lying dormant, I come abroad like the Ghost of one of these Druids.* He felt sufficiently human, nonetheless, to preface the work with *A digression to obviate the scornfull smile,* for he was convinced that people would assume that he was interested in this monument only because it bore the same name as himself.

In the following year, Aubrey realised his lifelong desire to travel on the continent. He had made ambitious plans to see *the Loyer, and the country of Brittany, and that about Geneva,* and after receiving Thomas Hobbes' best "wishes for your safety and the continuance of your health, which is not to be despaired of in one that can temper himselfe from excesses, and especially in fruit, as you can," he set out. But as so often happens with one's fondest ambitions, the trip did not quite come up to his expectations. *June 11, landed at Calais,* he recorded. *In August following had a terrible fit of the Spleen, and Piles, at Orleans. I returned in October. Then Joan Sumner.*

The ominous ring of this last note proved fully justified, for poor Aubrey was as unfortunate in his dealings with women, as he was incompetent with money. Since he had left Oxford, he had often been on the point of getting married, but always at the last moment he was foiled. *My Mother fell from her horse and brake her arme the last day of April* (1649 *or* 50) *when I was suitor to Mris. Jane Codrington,* he wrote, and never mentioned the lady's name again. Probably because in 1651 : *about the* 16 *or* 18 *of April, I saw that incomparable good conditioned Gentlewoman, Mris. M. Wiseman, with whom at first sight I was in love—haeret lateri* [the deadly arrow sticks fast in the side], and indeed the wound did seem more permanent than usual for five years later he was still attached to her, however insecurely, for he notes : 1656. *This Yeare, and the last, was a strange year to me, and full of Contradictions :— scilicet Love (M.W.) and Lawe-suites.* One of these *Contradictions* must have come from M.W., for in the next year he received a double blow, to his heart and his pocket : 1657 : *Novemb.* 27, *obiit Domina Katherina Ryves, with whom I was to marry ; to my great Losse* (2000 *pounds or more, besides counting care of her brother,* 1000 *pounds per annum*). Nothing daunted, however, he tried again : 1665, *November* 1 ; *I made my first address (in an ill howre) to Joane Sumner,* and the catastrophe which then unrolled was to put a stop to his matrimonial adventures for ever.

1666 : he said : *this yeare all my business and affaires ran Kim Kam. Nothing tooke effect, as if I had been under an ill tongue. Treacheries and Enmities in abundance against me.* And an entry in the Salisbury Diocesan Registry this year shows how near he came to taking the fatal step. " Awbry, John, of Easton Pierse," it runs, " and Mris. Joane Sumner of Sutton Benger, sp. Bondmen, William Browne of Sarum, tailor, and Joseph Gwynne of Easton Pierse, yeoman April 11th."

1667 : *December :* he continued, *arrested in Chancery lane, At Mrs. Sumner's suite.*

1668 : *Febr.* 24 *a.m. about* 8 *or* 9, *Triall with her at Sarum. Victory and* 600 *pounds dammage, though divelish Opposition against me.*

1668 : *July* 26, *was arrested by Peter Gale's malicious contrivance, the day before I was to goe to Winton for my* 2ᵈ *Triall, but it did not retain me above* 2 *howres ; but did not then goe to Triall.*

1669 : *March* 5, *was my Triall at Winton, from* 8 *to* 9, *the Judge being exceedingly made against me, by my Lady Hungerford. With much adoe, gott the Moiety of Sarum verdict, viz.* 300 *pounds.*

Joan Sumner's decision to go to law with John Aubrey, instead of to the altar, was the coup de grâce to his tottering affairs, and with a sudden crash all his tangled estates tumbled about his ears. *Sold Easton-Pierse, and the farme at Broad Chalke,* he noted sadly, for his mother's family, *the Lytes, had Easton Piers in Lease and in Inheritance* 249 *years : sc. from Henry* 6th. *Lost* 500 *pounds*+200 *pounds*+*goods*+ *timber,* he continued, and the result was that *in* 1669 *and* 1670 *I sold all my Estates in Wilts. Absconded as a banished man. I was in as much affliction as a mortall could bee, and never quiet till all was gone, and I wholly caste myselfe on God's providence. Never quiett, nor anything of happiness till divested of all,* 1670, 1671, he repeats, *at what time Providence raysed me unexpectedly good Friends.*

For when all was sold, he found relief at last, and his next entry reads : *From* 1670, *to this very day (I thanke God) I have enjoyed a happy delitescency,* a statement which is rather belied by the succeeding paragraph, 1671 : *danger of Arrests.*

During this crisis, a meeting had taken place which was to give purpose to the remaining years of Aubrey's life and was also to provide him with the immortality which he so much desired. For on Thursday, 31st August, 1667, Anthony Wood entered in his accounts :—" Spent with Mr. John Aubrey of Wilts, at Mother Web's and the Meremaid Tavern, 3s. 8d.", and it was not until nearly thirty years later that he returned to his Journal to make a fuller and more famous entry : " Aug. 31 S.," he then wrote, " John Aubrey of Easton-Piers in the parish of Kingston S. Michael in Wiltsh. was in Oxon. with Edward Forest, a Book-seller living against Alls. Coll., to buy books. He then saw lying on the stall *Notitia Academiae Oxoniensis* ; and asking who the Author of that book was, he answer'd the report was that one Mr. Anthony Wood of Merton Coll. was the Author, but was not. Whereupon Mr. Aubrey, a pretender to Antiquities, having been contemporary to A. Wood's elder brother in Trin. Coll. and well acquainted with him, he thought that he might be as well acquainted with A. W. himself. Whereupon repairing to his Lodgings, and telling him who he was, he got into his acquaintance, talk'd to him about his studies, and offer'd him what assistance he could make, in order to the completion of the work that he was in hand with. Mr. Aubrey was then in a sparkish Garb, came to town with his Man and two Horses, spent high and flung out A. W. at all recknings. But his estate of 700 pounds per an. being afterwards sold, and he reserving nothing of it to himself, liv'd afterwards in a very sorry condition, and at length made shift to rub out by hanging on Edmund Wyld Esq. living in Blomesbury, near London, on James Bertie Earl of Abendon, whose first wife was related to him, and on Sir John Aubrey, his kinsman, living sometimes in Glamorganshire, and sometimes at Borstall neare Brill in Bucks. He was a shiftless person, roving and magotie-headed, and sometimes little better than crased. And being exceedingly credulous, would stuff his many letters to A. W. with fooleries, and misinformations, which sometimes would guid him into the pathes of error."

As can be seen from the tone of this entry, Anthony Wood was an impossible man to get on with. An Oxford don, vain, touchy, spiteful and lacking in every social grace, he was impertinent to his superiors, rude to his equals, overbearing to his juniors, ungrateful to his benefactors and unbearable to his family. The Warden of his own college he described as " the very Lol-poop of the University, a most lascivious person, a great haunter of women's company and a common Fornicator," and the Warden's wife he despised for putting " the College to unnecessary charges, and very frivolous expences, among which was a very larg Looking-Glass, for her to see hir ugly face, and body to the middle, and perhaps lower." He quarrelled with John Fell, the great Dean of Christ Church, who at his own expense was publishing Wood's life work. He quarrelled with his fellow dons : " Mr. Roger Brent and I playing at cards, he fell out with me, called me all to nought and struck me. He looked like a rogue, like a whoring rascall, like a whoring rogue."

The resultant unpopularity only increased his fury and loneliness until everything enraged him : " Mr. Davis looked red and jolly, as if he had been at a fish supper at C.C.C., and afterwards drinking—

as he had been : " and a friend's criticism of his book was met with the comment : " the words as ugly as his face."

But the climax was reached with his family, for it seems that his sister-in-law at last could stand no more. " Cold meat, cold entertainment, cold reception, cold clownish woman," Wood noted in his Journal after one meal, and at last, on Easter Day, 1670, " the melancholy, malitious and peevish woman slighted me and rose in the middle of dinner from the table. My brother Kit asked me whether I would be godfather and give a piece of plate to the childe in her belly. She said that she ' would first see it rot, etc.' with an envious eye and teeth." After which scene he " was dismist from his usual and constant diet by the rudeness and barbarity of a brutish woman " and " was put to his shifts. This disaster A.W. look'd upon as the first and greatest misery of his life. It made him exceedingly melancholy and more retir'd." But he soon justified this isolation to himself. " He is so great an Admirer of a solitary and retired Life," he says in the preface to one of his works, " that he frequents no Assemblies of the said University, hath no companion in Bed or at Board, in his Studies, Walks or Journies, nor holds Communication with any, unless with some, and those very few, of generous and noble Spirits, that have in some measure been Promoters and Encouragers of this Work : And indeed all things considered he is but a degree different from an Ascetick, as spending all or most of his time, whether by Day or Night, in Reading, Writing, and Divine Contemplation."

Such was his own view, but the truth of the matter was that Anthony Wood had been born in the wrong century. Suspicious, lonely, intolerant, envious, mean, he found himself isolated in that supremely social age : squeamish, disapproving and obsessed with sex, he was revolted by the coarseness of the physical life around him : spiteful, snobbish and pretentious, he flaunted his lack of social graces in the face of all, until his pompousness and prudery finally cut him off entirely from the life around him. And though he continued to look on himself as " a universal Lover of Mankind," he was forced at length to admit that he was " as 'twere Dead to the World, and utterly unknown in Person to the generality of the Scholars in Oxon." " As to the Author himself," he finally confessed, " he is a Person who delights to converse more with the Dead, than with the Living " ; for being so ill at ease in his own times, he was at last driven to seek refuge in the past, for only there could he show the affection, which he was unable to give to his contemporaries. " Sweet chucks," he wrote, " beat not the bones of the buried : when he breathed, he was a man." But even the dead were not spared his malignity, unless they had been long dead : " March 31. F. died Ann, Duchess of York," he reported. " She died with eating and drinking ; died fast and fustie ; salacious ; lecherous."

And so it says a great deal for Aubrey's charm that, after twenty-five years of friendship, Anthony Wood should merely call him " roving and magotie-headed," an accusation, moreover, which was not altogether without justification, as we shall see.

That this was not Anthony Wood's original view is shown by the following letter, dated soon after the first meeting. " You may

[1]

remember when you were at Oxon," he wrote to Aubrey on 11th November, 1667, " that you promised upon my enquirie &c., to obtained some intelligence concerning Dr. Joh: Hoskyns sometimes of New Coll : of his birth death and buriall, his bookes that he wrote and that might be worthie memorie of him. If you please to informe me as soone as you can, I shall take it for a verie great favour from your hands. 'Tis probable you might upon recollection informe me also of others that were Oxford men. The which, if you at your leisure can, you would alwaies oblige me to be, Sir, your most humble servant Anth: Woode." And a few months later he again assured him, " I am glad I have such a friend as you to stir in my business. I would by noe means have put you to this trouble, could I have reposed confidence in any other."

Anthony Wood, at Dean Fell's suggestion, intended to follow up his " Historia et Antiquitates Universitatis Oxoniensis," with an even more elaborate work entitled " Athenae Oxoniensis : An Exact History of all the Writers and Bishops who have had their Education in the most ancient and famous University of Oxford from the Fifteenth Year of King Henry the Seventh Dom. 1500, to the end of the Year 1690." But he soon found that his unpopularity was a great hindrance to him in gathering the information that he needed ; and for this work, Aubrey's popularity and wide acquaintanceship were ideal. The offer of help, therefore, Wood accepted with alacrity, but Aubrey responded with such a will that Wood's tone soon changed towards him. For exactly four years after his original letter he was writing to Aubrey in this peremptory tone. " Allington is not far from you. If you have occasion to goe that way, pray see whether Mr. Nich. Fuller, the Critick have an Epitaph there. If not take the day and year of his buriall out of the Register. I have heard he died there. If you cannot goe, employ your brother and I shall be gratefull to him. If not buried there, perhaps at Salisbury, where he was prebend. He died about 1626."

As time went on the commands became ever more direct. " Quaere more of Mr. Aubrew," Wood jotted down on his notes and sometimes one of these formidable lists of queries has survived. " 1. Epitaph of Francis Potter ; if none, then the day and yeare where buried.—2. Titles of Dr. Pettie's books published, where borne (Rumney in Hampshire, quaere.)—3. When Dr. John Godolphin died, where he died and where buried ; quaere the bookseller that sold his books.—4. Title of books that John Davyes of Kidwelly translated.—7. Register of S. Pancrass Church.—8. Which daughter and heir of Carew Raleigh was married to Sir John Ellwes.—9. To send to Olor Iscanus to answer my letters.—10. To put John Dugdale in mind of John Davenport.—11. Mr. Hook for the Christian name of . . . Oliver, glass paynter.—12. What is said of Father Simons in his collections.—13. Dr. Walter Charlton, who he succeeded ?—14. My letters to be returned.—15. Where Mr. Robert Boyle lived and died."

Faced with a list like this in an age when there were no books of reference to turn to, Aubrey set about gathering his information as best he could. Sometimes his friends helped him, but though Izaak

Walton wrote part of the life of Ben Jonson and Sir Thomas Browne contributed to John Dee's biography, they could not always be relied on, as that blank page shows which is headed *John Dryden, Esq. Poet Laureate. He will write it for me himselfe.* For as Aubrey was well acquainted with all the great figures of his time, it was mainly with the previous generation that he needed help, which meant that he had to appeal to his seniors for information, and his seniors were by now growing very old. *The Lives of John Dee, Dr. Nepier, Sir William Dugdale, William Lilly, Elias Ashmole, Esq.,* he informed Anthony Wood, *Mr. Ashmole has and will doe them himself ; as he told me, but nowe he seems to faile.*

At other times, his information came in a far more roundabout way. Dr. Bathurst was able to tell him about Lucius Cary, Lord Falkland, because *a mayd that lived with my Lord lived with his father :* nor was this backstairs method neglected by Aubrey himself : *Jack Sydenham was wont to carry me in his armes : a graceful servant,* he said, recalling his childhood, *he gave me this account :* and stone cutters and tradesmen were often pressed into use. Sermons, too, provided some amusing stories and contributed largely to the lives of the Great Earl of Cork, his daughter Mary, Countess of Warwick, and Colonel Charles Cavendish. Then again, church registers were searched, sometimes in vain, it is true : *My brother Tom searched the Register of Wilton from the beginning and talk't with old men. Philip Massinger was not buried there :* but at other times with unexpected results. *When I searched the Register of the Parish of St. Saviours, Southwark in* 1670, *for the Obit of that eminent Dramatick Poet Mr. John Fletcher,* Aubrey wrote to Anthony Wood, *the Parish-Clerk, aged above* 80, *told me that he was his Taylor, and that Mr. Fletcher staying for a Suit of Cloaths before he retired into the Country in the great Plague,* 1625, *Death stopped his Journey and laid him low here.*

Tombstones were scanned for dates, and often proved fallible, for though Aubrey noticed that there was something wrong about the following : *Pray for the soul of Constantine Darrel Esq. who died Anno Domini* 1400 *and his wife, who died Anno Domini* 1495 *:* he had no way of checking on Spenser's epitaph in Westminster Abbey, which, being forty-two years in error over his birth and three years over his death, made him eighty-six at his death, instead of forty-seven. Nevertheless tombstones had to be depended on for these facts, and often they yielded more : *Ellenor, wife of Sir John Denham was a beautiful woman,* he reported, *as appears by her Monument at Egham.* And every now and then he stumbled upon a veritable gold mine : *Did I tell you,* he wrote excitedly, *that I have met with old Mr. Beeston who knew all the old English Poets, whose lives I am taking from him : his father was Master of the Playhouse.* And although *Mr. Dryeden calles him the Chronicle of the Stage,* Aubrey had a virtual monopoly of his information, for he concludes *the more to be admired—he was not a company keeper ; lived in Shoreditch ; would not be debauched ; and if invited to Court, was in pain.*

His fellow historians looked askance at some of these methods. *In my last I gave you some Memoirs of Cardinall Morton,* Aubrey wrote to Anthony Wood, *and that the Tradicion of the Countrey people in Dorset, when I was a Schooleboy there at Blandford, was that he was a Shoemaker's son of Bere : but Sir William Dugdale sayes ' by no means I must putt in writing Heare-Sayes.'* Despite this warning, the most fruitful source of all turned out to be casual conversation, and as Aubrey's taste for gossip was rather undiscriminating, mistakes would keep creeping in and were savagely resented by Anthony Wood, who made no allowances. *I remember,* Aubrey wrote apologetically after one such rebuke, *Sam. Butler (Hudibras) one time at the Tavern sayd, that 'twas this Earl of Dorset's father that translated the Comoedie called the Cid. writt by Corneille. Me thinkes he should not be mistaken : but the world is mighty apt to it you see.* And later he was to protest : *I heard an old Lawyer of the Middle Temple, 1646, who was Sir Edward Coke's country-man, say that he was born to 300 pounds land per annum, and I have heard some of his country say again that he was borne but to 40 per pounds per annum. What shall one beleeve?*

What indeed ? For when Aubrey asked Randall Isaacson a simple question about his father, he was answered with this fantastic rigmarole : " My father died in St. Cathrin Coleman's parrish London, About the 7° of December, 1654, which is neare 34 yeares after my grandfather's death. I Calculate from the tyme of his Birth to my Grandfather's Death to bee 39 yeares : ad the 34 yeares after my Grandfather's death to the 39 before : 39+34 makes 73. years his age— which all the familie agree that hee was seaventy three yeares of age when hee died, soe that he was borne in anno 1581. Borne in anno 1581, dyed aged 73, makes 1654 the yeare when he dyed."

Sometimes, too, he asked so many questions that his friends took pleasure in teasing him : *Dr. John Newton—he told me he was borne in Bedfordshire, but would not tell me where :* while at other times his repeated queries seem to have exasperated them : *The Earle of Carnarvon does not remember Mr. Brown, and I ask't his Lordship lately if any of his servants doe ; he assures me NO.* That this was no isolated instance is proved by Aubrey's own sharpness with Anthony Wood : *On Sunday last I dined with Mr. Ashmole, who bids me answer you POSITIVELY that Sir Richard Nepier never did write anything and sayes that he haz acquainted you thus much before by letter.*

But though he could extend his reach back to the Elizabethan age by this method : *Old Sergeant Hoskins the Poet (grandfather to this Sir John Hoskins, Baronet, my honoured friend) was well acquainted with Mr. Nicholas Hill, by which meanes I have this tradicion which otherwise had been lost ; as also his very name :* it had its disappointments too. *Mr. Baron Brampton hath invited me to his chamber to give me a farther account of Generall Monk. I let slip the Opportunity, and my honoured friend is dead,* Aubrey said sadly on one occasion, and on another : *I thought to have taken Memoires of him ; but deferring it Death took away Sir Jonas.* And ever after a loss like this, Aubrey nursed a secret regret, as he showed in his life of Edmund Waller : *Mr. Thomas Big of Wickham haz been dead these 20 yeares, who could have told me the cause of his madness,* he said then. *I beleeve that I am right. You see how things become antiquated.*

Anything that could be checked was checked, however, with scrupulous care. *Thomas Hobbes, Malmesburiensis, Philosophus, was borne at his father's house in Westport,* Aubrey recorded, *being that extreme howse that pointes into, or faces, the Horse-fayre ; the farthest howse on the left hand as you goe to Tedbury, leaving the Church on your right. To prevent mistakes, and that hereafter may rise no doubt what house was famous for this Famous man's Birth ; I doe here testifie that in April, 1659, his brother Edmond went with me into this house, and into the Chamber where he was borne. Now things begin to be antiquated, and I have heard some guesse it might be at the howse where his brother Edmund lived and dyed. But this is so, as I here deliver it. This house was given by Thomas, the Vicar, to his daughter, whose daughter or granddaughter possessed it, when I was there. It is a firme house, stone-built and tiled, of one roome (besides a buttery, or the like, within) below, and two chambers above. 'Twas in the innermost where He first drew breath.*

Despite all this research for Anthony Wood, Aubrey still found time to carry on several projects of his own, for the distractions of the past had vanished when, at the age of forty-six his financial ruin was complete. From 1670 onwards he enjoyed *a sweet otium,* because when he had his horoscope calculated, in 1671, he discovered a scapegoat for all his misfortunes. " The nativity," said Henry Coley, the astrologer, " is a most Remarkeable opposition, and 'tis much pitty the starres were not more favourable to the Native." For, it seems, they " threaten ruin to land and estate ; give Superlative Vexations in Matters Relating to Marriag, besides wondrous Contests in Law-suits : all of which vexations, I suppose the native hath had a Greater portion than ever was desired." And even though another horoscope, cast this time by John Gadbury, an astrologer who was, unlike Coley, as yet unacquainted with Aubrey himself " looks no more like Esq: Aubrey than an apple is like an Oyster," Aubrey seems to have found it a real relief to be able to blame his own incompetence upon the stars.

He was, in fact, so enthralled with the predictions that, not only did he make selections from the forty volumes of Nativities which William Lilly had assembled : *Mr. Ashmole turnes and reads,* he said, *and I doe write :* but he also set about collecting, on his own account, the precise hours of the birth of most of his friends, which he entered in a little book entitled *A Collection of Genitures Well Attested. Walter Charleton M.D. borne at Shepton-Malet in com. Somerset, Feb. 2ᵈ, 1619, about 6 h. P.M. his mother being then at supper,* he notes, but not all con-finements were as uneventful as this. *Sir William Dugdale was born September 12, 1605. That afternoon a Swarme of Bees pitch't under his Mother's chamber window, as it were an omen of his laborious Collections,* and worst of all perhaps was the case of Mris. Jane Smyth, for *when she was born it thundered and lightened and the house was on fire.* Anthony Ettrick, the friend with whom he had been in danger of drowning on his return from Ireland, was more fortunate : he came quietly into the world on a Sunday. *His mother would say he was a Sundaye's Bird.* But once again, Aubrey found himself baulked for lack of information : Christopher Wren had told him that *the bell rang VIII as his mother fell in Labour with him,* but Aubrey complained to Wood that *he hath putt a trick on us, as it seems ; for he hath made him selfe a yeare younger then indeed he is, though he needs not be ashamed of his age, he hath made such admirable use of his time : 'tis a poore spirited thing, if he will not resolve me.* Anthony Wood's reply to this must have been interesting reading, for he had just tried to reduce his forty years to twenty-five, by writing to Aubrey : " My Nativity I cannot yet retrive ; but by talking with an ancient servant of my father's, I find I was born on the 17 of Decem, but the year when I am not certain : 'twas possibly about 1647 : " and this from a man who had written an eye-witness account of King Charles I's entry into Christ Church in 1636.

But it was not birth alone that counted in astrology ; every date was significant. If you fell ill, the time you took to your bed was of the utmost importance : *Sir Robert Henley, of Bramswell, Hants, Baronet, decubuit, Thursday, about 3 P.M., Feb. 14, Valentine's Day. He was taken ill a hunting about noon, I think the Tuesday before :* and Aubrey was always careful to transfer the leases of his fast vanishing estates at the most propitious moment. *Eston-Pierse possession,* one horoscope is marked, and underneath is written : *25 March 1671. 1 P.M. possession given by Jonathan Rogers to Mr. Sherwin.* The exact time at which an honour was granted was also most important and Aubrey several times repeated that *Sir Christopher Wren was Knighted at Whitehall on Friday, 14th November 1673, at 5 h A.M. (From Mr. Robert Hooke, the next day).* Even a man's figure depended on the heavens, for Aubrey noted of Sir William Petty : *Jupiter in Cancer makes him fatt at heart. John Gadbury also sayes that Vomits would be excellent good for him :* and the stars had an even worse effect on poor William Marshall, the sculptor : *Conjunction of Mercury and Leo made him stutter.* It was no wonder, therefore, that Edward Davenant said *he thankt God his father did not know the houre of his birth ; for that it would have tempted him to have studyed Astrologie, for which he had no esteeme at all.*

Throughout the nineteenth century, the pious clergymen who bowdlerised Aubrey's work fell particularly hard on him for this superstition. But in this they merely revealed their lack of historical knowledge, for though astrology had become gross superstition by their days, it was not always so. Until the publication of Newton's theory showed the fallacy of the beliefs on which the celestial scheme or horoscopes was founded, astrology had been one of the most serious attempts to explain the world scientifically. And it was in this scientific spirit that Aubrey approached the problem. *We have not that Science yet perfect,* he said, *'tis one of the Desiderata. The way to make it perfect is to gett a Supellex of true Genitures ; in order wherunto I have with much care collected these ensuing, which the Astrologers may rely on, for I have sett doune none on randome, or doubtfull, information, but from their own Mouthes : quod N.B.* And when in 1673, *Sir Leoline Jenkins was sent with Sir Joseph Williamson, Plenipotentiaries to Nemeghen,* Aubrey gave striking proof of his empirical attitude. *I remember that very time they went away was opposition of Saturn and Mars. I sayd then to the Earl of Thanet that if that Ambassade came to any good I would never trust to Astrologie again.* It cannot be held against Aubrey that he at last decided, on the evidence before him, that astrology was the key to truth, for as Jeremy Bentham has said, " He who thinks, and thinks for himself, will always have a claim to thanks ; it is no matter whether it be right or wrong, so as it be explicit. If it is right, it will serve as a guide to direct : if wrong, as a beacon to warn."

In those days a warning beacon was badly needed, for one of the first results of the Reformation had been a tremendous outburst of superstition, and the Puritans, encouraged by their literal acceptance of the truth of the Bible, soon spread their delusions throughout Europe. Aubrey realised this as well as anyone. *Though it was then the fashion to fall upon the church of Rome,* he said, *yet these men were as superstitious, but did not know it.* In Germany, Luther himself accused the Devil of having created flies purposely to distract him while writing good books, and in Calvin's Geneva several people went to the stake for the detestable crime of spreading the plague. It was not until the middle of Elizabeth's reign that the symptoms of this wild credulity began to appear in England, where as the Puritan influence became dominant, it brought with it a renewed belief in Witchcraft. Little action was taken by the State against those unfortunates during the Queen's reign, however, for Elizabeth disapproved most strongly of this particular superstition, very probably because her mother had not only been universally accounted to be a witch, but had also been sentenced "to be beheaded or burned at the Kings pleasure." No such family scruples held back the Stuarts, though, and on the accession of James I, the prosecutions started, which were to result in the execution of seventy thousand witches in England alone before 1680. Indeed King James himself, in his book on "Daemonologie," gave a terrific fillip to the witch-trials, although he soon came up against so many frauds that he recanted his views. Aubrey tells two stories that must have contributed to the King's change of heart. First he says, *One Mris. Katharine Waldron (a Gentlewoman of good Family) pretended to be bewitched by a certain woman. She had acquired such a strange habit, that She would endure exquisite torments, as to have pinnes thrust into her flesh, nay under her Nailes. His Majesty being in these parts went to see her in one of her Fitts : she lay on a bed : and the King saw her endure the torments aforesayd. The Roome (as it is easily to be believed) was full of Company. His Majesty gave a sodain pluck to her Coates, and topt them over her head, and discovered ALL to the standers by : which surprise (it seemes she had some innate modesty in her) not imagining of such a thing made her immediately start, and detected the Cheate.* And then there was the case of *Richard Heydock, M.D. quondam Fellow of New College in Oxford, an Ingenious, and a learned Person : but much against the Hierachie of the Church of England. He had this Device to gaine Proselytes by preaching in his Dream : which was much noised abroad, and talk't of as a Miracle. But King James 1st. being at Salisbury went to heare him : He observed that this Harangue was very methodicall &c. that he did but counterfeit a Sleep. He surprized the Doctor by drawing his sword, and swearing Gods waunes I will cutt-off his head : at which the Dr. startled, and pretended to awake. So the Cheat was detected.*

But not all his subjects proved so astute as their sovereign, and although King James threw the whole weight of his influence and that of his Council, the Star Chamber and the Episcopate, into the struggle against the growing mania, it was too late. Wherever the Puritans, and later the Parliament, held sway, the persecution broke out afresh, and books, pamphlets and sermons poured from the press. It was, surprisingly, the educated class which was most obsessed by the belief in witchcraft, and it must be admitted that all the evidence available supported its existence ; though perhaps Chief Justice Hale went somewhat too far in laying it down as a law that there must be such things as witches, since there were laws against witches, and it was not conceivable that laws had been made against something which did not exist. The witches themselves were never convicted without their voluntary confessions, usually under torture it is true, but even without this persuasion, many of the unfortunate creatures, like those present-day women who complain of non-existent sexual attacks, vociferously protested that they were in truth in league with the Devil. And the catalogue, which Aubrey has left, of the evils for which witches were held to be accountable, explains the astounding number of persons who suffered death for this crime. *Twisting of trees, tearing and turning up Oakes by the roots,* he listed. *Raysing tempests ; wracking ships ; throwing down steeples ; blasting plantes ; dwindle away young children. To overlooke 'and binde the spirits and phantasy ; bewhattling and making men impotent, woemen miscarry (Countesse of Carlisle). Whirlewinds ; haracanes ; Spirits in 'em.* He went on to explain the organisation of the witch's sabbath, which seems to have moved with the times, for they now held *the session, à la mode de Royal Society, with Balloting-box. Memorandum,* he concludes, *Sir Henry Billingsley said wise men alwaies saw that as some malicious woemen increased in years, increased also in malice : set howses on fire, mischiefe to children, etc. Thought it better to have them underground then above ground and raise storms : the familiars could not handsomely knock 'em in the head.* It was no wonder, therefore, that *when there was a Cabal of Witches detected at Malmesbury, they were examined by Sir James Long of Dracot-Cerne, and committed by him to Salisbury Gaole. I think there were 7 or 8 old women hanged. There were odd things sworne against them, as the strange manner of the dyeing of H. Dennys Horse : of flying in the Air on a staffe, etc. These examinations, &c. Sr. James hath fairly written in a Book, which He promised to give to the Royall Society.* Despite this seeming support for the persecution amongst even the most scientific men, scepticism was slowly growing : *Mr. Anth. Ettrick of the Middle Temple (a very judicious Gentleman) was a curious Observer of the whole Triall, and was not satisfied,* says Aubrey on another occasion. *The crowd of spectators made such a noise that the Judge could not heare the Prisoner, nor the Prisoner the Judge ; but the words were handed from one to the other by Mr. R. Chandler, and sometimes not truly reported.*

In the infancy of science, every theory, no matter how absurd it might seem superficially, had to be checked before it could be safely discarded ; and nowadays Aubrey would not be maligned as a credulous fool, but would be praised as an anthropologist and a collector of folk-lore. *Old Customs and old wives fables are grosse things,* he admits, *but yet ought not to be buried in Oblivion ; there may be some trueth and usefulnesse be picked out of them, besides 'tis a pleasure to consider the Errours that enveloped former ages : as also the present.* And the errors of the present were not confined to Aubrey, even though he noted them down with such a will. *William Lawd (Arch-bishop of Canterbury) in a Sermon Preached before the Parliament, about the beginning of the Reign of King Charles I affirms the power of Prayer to be so great, that though there be a Conjunction or Opposition of Saturn or Mars (as there was one of them then) it will overcome the malignity of it.* As the Church believed, so did the State : *A little before the Death of Oliver Protector, a Whale came into the River Thames and was taken at Greenwich. 'Tis said, Oliver was troubled at it.* Nor was Science itself free from the taint, for the astronomer Kepler was convinced that the planets, by their revolutions, produced " a music of the spheres," which was audible only to the sun, which he believed to be the body of a divine spirit ; while the great Newton himself accounted for the tangential velocities of the planets, which prevent them from falling into the sun, by supposing that, initially, they had been hurled by the hand of God.

Although he shared in some of the delusions of his time, Aubrey made many reservations in his beliefs. He says of *Phantomes : Though I myselfe never saw any such things, yet I will not conclude that there is no Truth at all in these reports. I believe that (extraordinarily) there have been such Apparitions ; but where one is true, a hundred are Figments. There is a Lecherie in lyeing : and imposeing on the Credulous : And the Imagination of fearfull People is to admiration.*

Even though he sifted the mass of evidence which he had collected in this critical spirit, he was so much more of an antiquary than a scientist that he could never bring himself to discard any of the stories which he had so laboriously discovered. *It may seem nauseous to some,* he apologised, *that I have rakt up so many Western vulgar Proverbs ; which I confess I disdeigne not to quote ; Pliny himself being not afraid to call them Oracles. For Proverbes are drawn from the Experience and Observations of many Ages : and are the ancient Natural Philosophy of the Vulgar, preserved in old English and worse Rythmes, handed down to us for our curious moderne Philosophers to examine.* And many years later, in 1688, Aubrey gathered all these anecdotes and traditions into one volume, *The Remaines of Gentilisme and Judaisme,* in which he laboriously drew a parallel between the superstitions of his own country and those of Greece and Rome, and preserved for ever those meaningless customs that are so dear to the hearts of anthropologists. *In several parts of Oxfordshire,* he reports solemnly, *particularly at Lanton, it is the custom for the Maid Servant to ask the Man for Ivy to dress the Hous, and if the Man denies or neglects to fetch in Ivy, the Maid steals away a pair of his Breeches and nails them up to the gate in the yard, or highway.*

In these collections, he tried sincerely not to rely purely upon hearsay. *Mr. Hierome Banks as he lay on his Death Bed in Bell-yard, said Three Days before he died, that Mr. Jennings of the Inner-Temple (his great Acquaintance, Dead a Year or two before) gave Three Knocks, looked in, and said, Come away. He was as far from believing things as any man,* Aubrey said, and he reinforced the story by a similar experience of his own : *Three or four Dayes before my Father died,* he writes, *as I was in my Bed about Nine a Clock in the Morning perfectly awake, I did hear three distinct Knocks on the Beds-head, as if it had been with a Ruler or Ferula.* But even though Aubrey had experienced this case of haunting himself, he was not blind to the possibilities of charlatanry in other cases. *In the time of King Charles II.,* he reports, *the Drumming at the House of Mr. Monpesson of Tydworth made a great Talke over England. They did have some times Knockings : and if they sayd : Devill, knock so many knocks : so many knocks would be answered : But Mr. Ettrick sometimes whispered the words : and it was then no returne.* But, says Aubrey with admirable common-sense, *he should have spoken in Latin, or French, for the detection of this. Another time,* he adds, *Sir Christopher Wren went thither and lay there : He could see no strange things ; but sometimes he should heare a drumming, as one may drumm with ones hand upon wainscot : But he observed that this drumming was not, but onely, when a certain Maid-servant was in the next Room : But all these remarqued, that the Devill kept no very unseasonable houres, sc. it seldom knock't after twelve at night : or before 6 in the morning.* This does not look like the writing of a grossly credulous man, especially when one considers the completely different state of mind of our ancestors.

For the habit of doubt is an extremely recent growth, almost wholly subsequent to Newton in fact, and Aubrey often showed a scepticism that was most praiseworthy in an age when any statement was accepted just because it was made. This completely uncritical state of mind is hard for us to visualise, because it has vanished almost entirely from the modern world ; except in Eire, where the people are still more likely to accept, than to reject, even the most obvious falsehood, and where, in consequence, the banshees and the fairies and the leprechauns have kept their last foothold in Europe. And in England in the seventeenth century critical thought was especially rare in connection with religion. However much the various sects might differ in their interpretation of the Bible, not one of them doubted for an instant that every word in it was absolutely and literally true ; and the Bible constantly mentioned witches and spectres and portents. So Aubrey's reservations with regard to the following story are very laudable. *Anno* 1679, he says, *After the Discovery of the Popish Plot, the Penal Laws were put in execution against the Roman Catholicks : So, that if they did not receive the Sacrament according to the Church of England in their Parish Church, they were to be severely proceeded against according to Law : Mr. Ployden, to avoid the Penalty, went to his Parish Church at Lasham near Alton in Hampshire : when Mr. Laurence (the Minister) had put the Chalice into Mr. Ployden's hand, the Cup of it (wherein the Wine was) fell off. 'Tis true, it was out of order before ; and he had a Tremor in his hand. The Communion was stopt by this accident.* Religion in those days being still very primitive, portents of his kind were expected : for although various pieces of *Priest-cheate* had been exposed at the Reformation, many of the rites of the Church were still attended by the grossest superstition. For instance, *Sinne-eaters* were still in existence in Aubrey's lifetime.

In the County of Hereford, he notes, *was an old Custome at Funeralls to hire poor people, who were to take upon them all the Sinnes of the party deceased. One of these (I remember) lived in a Cottage on Rosse-high way : He was a long, leane, ugly, lamentable poor raskal. The manner was that when the Corps was brought out of the house and layd on a Biere : a Loafe of bread was brought out, and delivered to the sinne-eater over the Corps, as also a Mazar-bowle of maple (Gossips bowle) full of beer, which he was to drinke up, and sixpence in money, in consideration whereof he tooke upon him (ipso facto) all the Sinnes of the Defunct, and freed him (or her) from Walking after they were dead. This custome alludes (me thinkes) something to the Scape goat in the old Lawe.* The cheapness of the price charge for the assumption of another man's sins is most surprising, for in the days before

Hell was abolished by the Privy Council, its terrors were very real, as is shown by Queen Elizabeth's dreadful deathbed vision of herself ringed by flames. *In North-Wales, the Sinne-eaters are frequently made use of,* Aubrey adds, *but there, instead of a Bowle of Beere, they have a bowle of Milke.*

The throne also, like the Church, was surrounded by signs and portents, many of them so plausible that it is no wonder that they were believed. *An Old Man (like an Hermit) Second-sighted, tooke his Leave of King James the First, when he came into England,* Aubrey reports. *He took little notice of Prince Henry,* James' eldest son, who was to die at the age of eighteen, *but addressing himself to the Duke of York (since Charles I.) fell a weeping to think what misfortunes he should undergo ; and that he should be one of the miserablest unhappy Princes that ever was.* No one believed more firmly in such omens than Charles I himself, and to the very end of his life he was dogged by these coincidences. *The Head of King Charles Is. Staff did fall off at his Tryal,* says Aubrey, *that is commonly known.*

It was at coronations, however, that superstition had the fullest play. *King Charles II. was Crowned at the very conjunction of the Sun and Mercury,* Aubrey reports. *As the King was at Dinner in Westminster Hall, it Thundered and Lightned extreamly : The Canons and the Thunder played together.* But the second Charles was no superstitious man, and it was not until the crowning of his brother that the portents worried a King again. Aubrey was present at this ceremony and he carefully recorded the catastrophes, which foreshadowed so clearly the disastrous end of King James' troublous reign. *When King James II. was Crowned (according to the Ancient Custom, the Peers go to the Throne, and kiss the King). The Crown was almost kiss'd off his Head. An Earl did sett it right : and as he came from the Abbey to Westminster-Hall, the Crown totter'd extreamly.*

The Canopy carried over King James IIs. Head by the Wardens of the Cinque Ports, was torn by a puff of Wind as he came to Westminster-hall : It hung down very lamentably : I saw it. 'Twas of Cloath of gold & my strength (I am confident) could not have rent it and it was not a windy day.

The top of his Scepter (Flower de Lis) did then fall, which the Earl of Peterborough took up. Nor was this all. *Upon Saint Mark's day, after the Coronation of King James II, were prepared stately Fire-works on the Thames. It happened, that they took fire all together, and it was so dreadful, that several Spectators leap'd into the River, choosing rather to be drown'd than burn'd. In a Yard by the Thames was my Lord Powys's Coach and Horses : The Horses were so frightened by the Fire works, that the Coachman was not able to stop them, but ran over one who with great difficulty recovered.*

These accidents seemed to prove that the throne was once again of interest to the supernatural powers, for the profligacy of Charles II was so gross that, according to Anthony Wood, " in the latter end of Nov. 1675, a pillion was set behind the statue of King Charles II on horseback at Stoks Market and on the horse's brest writ on paper :—Hast, post-hast for a Midwife," and serious doubts had begun to arise as to whether he could really be the instrument of God's healing. *Dr. Ralph Bathurst, Dean of Wells and one of the Chaplains to King Charles, who is no Superstitious Man, protested to me that the curing*

*of the King's Evill by the Touch of the King does puzzle his Philosophie:
for whether they were of the House of Yorke, or Lancaster, it did.* 'Tis true
*(indeed) there are Prayers read at the Touching, but neither the King minds
them nor the Chaplains.* Nevertheless the belief in the King's miraculous
power was still strong. *Arise Evans,* says Aubrey, *had a fungous Nose,
and said, it was reveal'd to him, that the King's Hand would Cure him: And
at the first coming of King Charles II into St. Jame's Park he kiss'd the King's
Hand, and rubb'd his Nose with it ; which disturb'd the King, but Cured
him.* But Aubrey was not deceived by this seeming proof. *In Somersetshire,* he added, *'tis confidently reported that some were Cured of the
King's-evil, by the Touch of the Duke of Monmouth: The Lord Chancellor
Bacon saith, That Imagination is next Kin to Miracle-working Faith.*

And so it seems that belief in the supernatural was not entirely
pointless, when it could be turned to such excellent practical uses.
Nor was it confined entirely to medical aid : advice about careers was
sometimes given in this roundabout way : *Mr. Brograve of Hamel near
Puckbridge in Hertfordshire when he was a young Man, Riding in a Lane
in that Country, had a blow given him on his Cheek (or Head): He look'd
back, and saw that no body was near, behind him ; anon, he had such another
Blow : I have forgot if a Third. He turn'd back and fell to the Study of the
Law ; and was afterwards a Judge.* And the whereabouts of lost wills
and buried treasure were so constantly being hinted at in dreams,
that it led occasionally to the most unfortunate results : *One Daniel
Healy, of Donaghmore, in Ireland, having three different times dreamed that
Money lay concealed under a large Stone in a field near where he lived, procured
some Workmen to assist him in removing it, and when they had dug as far as
the foundation, it fell suddenly and killed Healy on the spot.* However the
best use of the gullibility of the time was made by *Mris. Abbott, the
wife of a poor Cloathworker at Guildford,* who, by means of an elaborate
confidence trick, procured *so good an education for her son that the child
came, by degrees, to be Arch-Bishop of Canterbury.*

It can be seen, therefore, that a proper use of superstition could
bring a rich reward ; and it was also an admirable excuse for in-
efficiency. For instance, after a vast amount of money had been spent
on boring for coal in Surrey, only to end in failure, *Mr. William Lilly
(Astrologer) was quick to blame the Subterranean Spirits: For as fast as
the Irons were put in they would snap off.* It was this use which Aubrey
made of astrology. *Thomas Morgan was unfortunate and idle,* he says
of one of his friends, *seemed to have Saturne much his Enemie.* And
having convinced himself that in like manner the loss of his own estates
was due entirely to the stars being against him, Aubrey turned back
to his life without repining *when all was gone.*

Only one regret still lingered. *I wished Monastarys had not been
putt down,* he complained, *that the Reformers would have been more moderate
as to that point. Nay, the Turkes have Monasteries. The Reformers in the
Lutheran Countrys were more prudent then to destroy them : only altered the
religion. Why should our Reformers be so severe?* For now that he was
run out of his estates, Aubrey could have made good use of *the Convenience of Religious houses,* for he thought it *fitt there should be receptacles
and provision for Contemplative men. What a pleasure 'twould have been
to have travelled from Monastery to Monastery,* he sighed, and wished

himself back in the old Catholic England, *before the Pope, with all his Authority, was clean banished the Realm.*

Then the Crusado's to the Holy-warres were most magnificent and glorious, Aubrey says, *and the rise I beleeve of the adventures of Knights Errants, and Romances. The solemnities of Processions in and about the Churches, and the Perambulations in the Fields, besides their convenience, were fine pleasing diversions. The Priestes went before in their Formalities, singing the Latin-service, and the people came after making their good-meaning-responses. The Reverence given to Holy-men was very great : then were the Churches open all day long, men and women going in and out hourely to and from their Devotions. Then were the Consciences of the people kept in so great awe by Confession : that Just dealing and vertue was habitual.*

This Countrey, he continues, speaking of his native Wiltshire, *was very full of Religious howses : a man could not have travelled but he must have mett Monkes, Fryars, Bonne Hommes, &c. in their several habits, black, white, gray, &c: and the tingle-tangle of the Convent-bells I fancie made very pretty musique, like College bells at Oxford.*

Then were no Free-schooles : the boyes were educated at the Monasteries. The young mades (not at Hakney, Say schooles, &c. to learn pride and wanton-nesse) but at the Nunneries, where they had examples of Piety, humilitie and modestie to imitate and practise. Here they learned Needle-worke, and the art of Confectionary : Surgery (anciently no apothecaries or Surgeons—the gentlewoemen did cure their poore neighbours : their hands are now too fine) Physicke, Writing, Drawing, etc.

Old Jacquer (who lived where Charles Hadnam did) could see from his House, the Nuns of the Priory of St. Mary (juxta Kington) come into the Nymph-Hay with their Rocks and Wheels to spin, and with their Sowing Work. He would say that he hath told threescore and ten : tho' of Nuns there were not so many : but in all, with Lay-Sisters, as Widows, old Maids, and young Girles, there might be such a Number. This was a fine way of breeding-up young woemen, who are led more by Example, then Precept ; and a good Retirement for Widows and grave single Women, to a civil, vertuous, and holy Life.

Plato saies that the foundation of Government is the Education of youth : by this meanes, it is most probable that this was a Golden-age.

And now Aubrey was well away on his reminiscences. *Let us imagine then what kind of Countrie this was in the time of the ancient Britons,* he says, *by the nature of the soile, which is a soure, woodsere land, very natural for the production of oaks especially. One may conclude that this North-division was a shady dismall wood ; and the inhabitants almost as salvage as the Beasts, whose Skins were their only rayment. They were 2 or 3 degrees I suppose less salvage than the Americans.*

The Romans subdued and civilised them, however, *but after they withdrew, here was a mist of Ignorance for 600 years. They were so far from knowing Arts, that they could not build a wall with stone. They lived sluttishly in poor houses, where they eat a great deal of beef and mutton, and drank good Ale in a brown mazard ; and their very Kings were but a Sort of Farmers.*

After the Christian Religion was planted here, it gave a great Shoote, and the Kings and great men gave vast revenues to the Church, who were ignorant enough in those Days. The Normans then came and taught them civility and building ; which though it was Gothiq, as also their Policy (Feudalis Lex), yet they were magnificent.

For the Government, 'till the time of King Henry 8, it was like a nest of boxes ; for Copy-holders (who till then were Villaines) held of the Lords of the Mannor, who held of a superior Lord, who held perhaps of another superior Lord or Duke, who held of the King. Upon any occasion of Bustling, or Tournaments in those Days, one of these great Lords sounded his Trumpets (the Lords then kept Trumpeters ; even to King James) and summon'd those that held under them. Those again sounded their trumpetts, and so downward to the Copy-holders.

The Lords (then Lords in deed as well as Title) liv'd in their countries like petty Kings, had jura regalia belonging to their signories, had their Castles and Burroughes, and sent Burgesses to the Lower House ; had Gallows within their Liberties where they could try, condemn, hang and drawe ; never went up to London but in Parliament-time, or once a yeare to do their homage and duty to the King.

No younger brothers then were, by the Custom and constitution of the Realme, to betake themselves to Trades, but were Church-men, or Retainers or Servants to great Men : rid good horses (now and then took a purse) and their bloud that was bred at the good Tables of their Masters was upon every occasion freely lett out in their Quarrels. It was then too common amongst their Masters to have Feuds with one another, and their servants at Market or where they met (in that slashing age) did commonly bang one anothers Bucklers.

The poor boyes did turn the Spitts, and lick't the dripping-pan, and grew to be huge lusty knaves.

In those dayes the Gentry begott their own servants and copyhold tenants (the custom of Lying with the Bride the first night).

No Ale-houses nor yet Innes then, unless upon great roades : when they had a minde to drinke they went to the Friaries ; and when they travilled they had entertainement at the Religious howses for 3 dayes, if occasion so long required. The meeting of the Country was not then at tipling-howses, but in the Fields or Forests with their Hawkes or Howndes, with their bugle-hornes in silken baudries.

Such Joy and merriment was every Holiday ; which dayes were kept with great Solempnitie and reverence. In Herefordshire and parts of the Marches of Wales, the Tabor and pipe were exceeding common. Many beggars begd with it : and the Peasants danced to it in the Churchyard on Holy dayes and Holy-day-eves. Now it is almost lost : the Drumme and Trumpet have putt that peaceable Musique to silence.

In those times (besides the jollities already mentioned) they had their Pilgrimages to several shrines, as chiefly hereabout, to St. Joseph of Arimathea at his Chapil in Glastonbury-abby. In the roades thither were severall howses of entertaynment built purposely for them.

The disappearance of these *howses of entertaynement* was obviously a great blow to Aubrey, but he was not long in finding out their modern counterpart. Though he was by now divested of all, he was safe by means of his family connections from actual want, for as he puts it *Providence raysed me (unexpectedly) good friends*, with one or other of whom he managed to spend the remainder of his days. There was *the Right Honourable Nicholas, Earl of Thanet, with whom I was delitescent at Hethfield in Kent neer a yeare : Sir Christopher Wren : Mr. Ogilby :*

then Edmund Wyld Esq. R.S.S. tooke me into his Armes, with whom I most commonly take my Diet and sweet Otium's. This latter was a man after Aubrey's own heart, as is shown by Roger North's description of him. " One Mr. Wyld, a rich Philosopher, lived in Bloomsbury. He was single, and his house a sort of knick-knack-atory. This gentleman was of a superior order, and valued himself upon new inventions of his own. He sowed salads in the morning to be cut for dinner ; and claimed the invention of painted curtains, in varnish, upon silk ; which would bend and not crack ; and his house was furnished with them : and he delighted in nothing more than in showing his multifarious contrivances." So it can be imagined that Aubrey was in his element in this place, helping in the experiments, wondering why in the autumn beads of sweat appeared on his host's patent curtains, and drinking and talking his fill. *Mr. Wyld,* he says proudly, *will undertake to prepare an Earth ('twill be neare a halfe a yeare preparing) that shall produce Wheate without sowing : and he believes he can doe the like for Pease.* And so sure was his host of success that he was prepared to back his judgement with solid cash. *Edmund Wyld, Esq. R.R.S.,* Aubrey explained at greater length, *hath had a pott of Composition in his garden these 7 yeares, that beares nothing at all : not so much as grasse, or mosse. He makes this Challenge, if any Man will give him twenty pounds, he will give him an hundred if it doth not beare* Wheat spontaneously : *and the Party shall keep the Key : and he shall sift the Earth Composition with a fine Sieve ; so that he may be sure, there are no graines of Wheat in it. He hath also a Composition for Pease : but that he will not warrant not having tryed it.* But the wager found no takers, for Edmund Wyld was famous for his skill in gardening. *London. Bloomesbery. August 12. 1684.,* Aubrey noted on another occasion, *my honoured Friend Edmund Wyld, Esq. did just before we sate down to dinner, sow in an Earthen Porringer of prepared Earth, Seeds of Parsley, Prunella, Balme, &c. The Porringer was sett on a chafing dish of Coales : and by the time we had ended Dinner (which was about an hower $\frac{1}{2}$) seeds sprang visibly up, scilicet, nineteen, or 20 young plants. Their Leaves as big as common Pinnes heads : by and by appeared more, so that the Dish was full : Some of the Plants being drawn-out with a paire of pliers, the stalkes were about $\frac{1}{2}$ inch long. About two or three houres after the Soweing, the Dish was exposed in the garden subdio : That night it happened to raine very hard all night, yet they all lived, and flourished till about the middle of September : and then they began to wither. Some of them lived till Michaelmass : and some till 8th or 10th of October following. I was one of the Four (besides Mr. Wyld) that was an Eye-witnesse of this Experiment. The Dish remaines in the Garden to this day (Feb. 7. 16$\frac{89}{90}$),* he concludes, *but no vegetable at all did ever growe in it since.* And to make this the ideal home for Aubrey " most of the ingenious persons about town visited " his host ; it is no wonder, therefore, that he sounded so complacent when he noted : *I now indulge my genius with my friends and pray for the young angels.*

Aubrey had now begun to reap the reward of his sensible recognition that *to be good and agreeable company is a virtue.* For though he had lost his fortune, he never lost a friend, and the warmth with which he continued to be regarded everywhere is shown by the following poem, which has been accidentally preserved amongst his papers.

" To his most honourd frend John Aubrey Esquire in imitation of
Mr. Greaves verses, etc." runs the heading, but the author's name is
missing :

> " If thou, my dearest Friend, in whose safe breast
> I store my joys, and make my greifes take rest ;
> Who art alone to me instead of all
> This World doth Wit, or Mirth, or Pleasure call :
> If thou should'st ask, why I so little care
> What interest or repute with most I beare ?
> Why with so very few my selfe I mate ?
> To th' rest regardless of their love or hate ?
> In short I'll tell the, 'tis 'cause I would be
> From noise of businesse and all troubles free.
> Lies, False News, impertinence I hate,
> And all things else which contradict my Fate,
> With losse of Knowledge, truth and liberty
> By affording every fool my company.
> Yet what I love, with whom I would converse.
> And freely consort, I'le unask'd rehearse :
> One, whome by experience I truly find
> To be my friend, and suited to my mind :
> Reserv'd to others, but open unto me,
> And has a Soul from base dissembling free,
> And modest too ; who thinks the greatest wit
> Consists in the wise government of it :
> Utters no secrets, constant to his friend,
> Nor can his thoughts to wicked fallsehood bend :
> One that Flies sadnesse, hates to be severe,
> But with facetiousnesse unbends his care.
> Yet one that's studious too, whose boundlesse mind
> Scarce within Learning's limits is confin'd,
> But chiefly Nature loves ; and farre does pry
> Into her secrets with his piercing eye.
> These and like things I love ; but to say true
> I've all this while been but describing You.
> You are the Man, my friend, whome I can love,
> The love of others I do not much approve."

One disadvantage did arise, however, from Aubrey's dependence
on his friends. *Edmund Wyld lives in the great square in Bloomsbery,*
he wrote, *on the south side, next dore to the Blackmores head,* and by the
most unfortunate chance his stomach, which he said *had been till then
so tender that I could not drinke claret without sugar, nor white wine, but
would disgorge,* chose this very moment to recover. And Aubrey was
never one for half measures, with the result that his writing became
even more untidy and more inaccurate. *If I had but either one to come
to me in a morning with a good Scourge,* came the familiar lament, *or did
not sett-up till one or two with Mr. Wyld, I could doe a great deal of
businesse.*

That no blame really attaches to Edmund Wyld for his guest's incurable sociability is made only too clear by the Diaries of the period, where Aubrey constantly appears, drinking in taverns, talking in coffee-houses or helping his friends in their work. " Mr. Aubery and I observed the Resistance of air to be duplicate to the velocity or rather in a musicall proportion," Robert Hooke wrote in 1674, and four years later he added, " Observed with Aubery the Moon Eclipsed." The same source provides us with more details of Aubrey's life in London. " With Mr. Aubery at Lord Brounkers, Mr. Colwalls, Sir Jo: Moors, Cap. Sherbourns ", Hooke says on one day, and nearly every night he notes, " At Garways with Mr. Hill, Mr. Hoskins, Mr. Wild, Mr. Aubery, Godfry, Blackburn, Lodowick, &c." Then there were frequent excursions to Knightsbridge to see the Bishop of Salisbury or to visit his other friends. " I dind with Boyle, it agreed well," says Hooke, " then with Aubery visited Harrington and Gadberry. Both mad but of Divers humours." And every Thursday there was the Royal Society to attend, with the promise of some drinking afterwards. " Agreed upon new clubb to meet at Joes," wrote Robert Hooke on December the tenth, 1675. " Mr. Hill, Mr. Lodowick, Mr. Aubery and I and to joyn to us Sir Jo: More, Mr. Wild, Mr. Hoskins. We now began our New Philosophicall Clubb ", he added on New Year's Day, " and Resolvd upon Ingaging ourselves not to speak of any thing that was then reveald *sub sigillo* to any one nor to declare that we had such a meeting at all. We began our first Discourse about light upon the occasion of Mr. Newton's Late Papers," and it was Aubrey who led off the discussion. All this activity cost money though, and poor bankrupt Aubrey was soon reduced to borrowing from his friends. " Lent Aubery 10sh. and before 20sh. and since 5 : he promised to repay it," run the entries, but when the time of reckoning came, no cash was forthcoming. " Bought of Mr. Aubery, Euclides Works Greek and Latin 10sh., Plunia *Purpur* 1s., Censorinus *de mensura Anni* 8d., Duret *Histoire des Langues,* and Scaliger *Contra Caldanum* 6s. 4d., Baytins *de re Navali* 2sh.," wrote Robert Hooke, "acquitted the former 20sh. lent." But five days later another entry occurs in the Diary, " Lent Aubery 20sh. more."

Aubrey had hoped that the completion of his ruin would allow him to increase the work which he had been carrying on all through the crisis of his fortunes. *Notwithstanding all these embarassments,* he had said, *I did pian piano (as they occur'd) take notes of Antiquity ; and having a quick draught, have drawne landskips on horse-back symbolically.* For Aubrey was still only forty-five when he lost his fortune and, being in the prime of life, he thought that he would be able to concentrate on his work at last, now that he was free from the continual distraction of trying to control his obstreperous accounts and to wriggle out of the lawsuits by which he had always been entangled in the past. *Anno* 1671, he says happily, *having sold all and disappointed as aforesaid of moneys I received, I had so strong an Impulse to (in good part) finish my Description of Wilts, two volumes in folio, that I could not be quiet till I had donne it, and that with danger enough, tanquam canis e Nilo* [like a dog at the Nile] *take a lap and away for feare of the Crocodiles, i.e. Catch-polls—And indeed all that I have donne and that little that I have studied have been just after that fashion, so that had I not lived long my want of Leisure would have afforded but a slender Harvest. My head was alwaies working ; never idle, and even travelling (which from 1649 till 1670 was never off horse-back) did gleane some observations, of which I have a collection in folio of 2 quiers of paper plus a dust basket, some whereof are to be valued.*

As if to disprove still further his theory that *a man's Spirit rises and falls with his fortunes : makes me lethargique,* Aubrey had branched off in yet another direction. In a letter to Anthony Wood at this time, he says : *I am writing a Comedy for Thomas Shadwell, which I have now almost finished since I came here. And I shall fit him with another, The Country Revell, both humours untoucht, but of this, Mum ! for 'tis very satyricall against some of my mischievous enemies which I in my tumbling up and down have collected.* About the worth of his plays, Aubrey had no illusions, for he saw that the Civil War had utterly destroyed the English stage. By forbidding the performance of any play, the Puritans successfully broke the link with the great days of Shakespeare and Jonson, while the bigotry of their rule during the Commonwealth was largely responsible for the licentiousness of the early Restoration drama. As Professor Trevelyan has pointed out in his 'English Social History' : " These unhappy conditions were peculiar to England : the age of Wycherley over here was the age of Molière, Corneille and Racine in France. There the drama, comic as well as tragic, was decent and was serious, and the French have ever since taken their drama seriously, as the Elizabethan English took theirs, regarding it as a civilising influence and a criticism of life." But although Aubrey sadly noted : *Now our present writers reflect so much upon particular persons and coxcombeities, that twenty yeares hence they will not be understood,* he followed the popular model, and sketched (between the lines of some old legal documents) the design for a grossly obscene farce. For *the Countrey Revell* was written to expose both the coarse-ness of the simple country people (amongst whom was *Squeaker, a shee-Balladsinger*) and the vices of the gentry, and amongst the latter Aubrey included many thinly disguised portraits of his acquaintances, *Courtoise, a Knight of the Bath and Protector of distressed Ladies,* was really old Thomas Tyndale, Aubrey's Wiltshire neighbour, *Justice Wag-staffe* was Sir John Dunstable, and Aubrey's great enemy, Gwyn, the Earl of Oxford's secretary, appeared as *Sir Fastidious Overween. Sir Surly Chagrin, Captain Exceptious Quarrelsome, Squire Fitz-Ale* and *Sir Libidinous Gourmand* are also recognisable portraits of his con-temporaries, and in the notes for these characters, Aubrey has left a scathing comment on the efficiency of his times. *Plato saies perpetuall drunkenness is the Reward of virtue,* says Squire Fitz-Ale at one point, and Sir Hugh the Vicar confesses to be *one of the old red-nosed Clergy, orthodox and canonicall. All the Parsons hereabout in Wiltshire,* Aubrey noted after this, *are Alehouse-hunters. James Long, Esq., hunted Sir Hugh driefoote to the Alehouse with his pack of hounds to the griefe of the revered Divine.* And of Sir John Dunstable, he says : *The Cellar he calls his Library,* and he continues, *Parliament men prepare themselves for the businesse of the Nation with Ale in the morning. Some Justices doe sleepe on the Bench every assizes.* One final note about this character shows that the Army was no less corrupt than the Church and the

[lxvii]

Law. *At Chippenham, the Deputye Lieutenants mett to see the Order of the Militia. After a taedious setting (at dinner, and drinking after dinner) the Drummes beate and the Soldiers began to march before the windowe to be seen by the Deputy Lieutenants. Justice Wagstaffe (Colonell) had not marcht before 'em many yardes but downe a falls all along in the dirt. His Myrmidons, multâ vi, heav'd him up, and then a cryed out, Some drinks, ho! and so there was an end of the Businesse.*

The plot deals with the fortunes of an adultress, who, pursued by her husband, is following her lover disguised in page's attire, and the play ends with most of the characters dead on the stage. *Raynes,* wrote Aubrey, who in his excitement seems to have inserted the real name of the injured husband, *comes and invades Sir Fastidious Overween, and is slayne by him ; and then Sir Fastidious neglects her ; she comes and stabbes him, and then herselfe.*

Naturally enough the play was never finished, for in 1672 Henry Coley wrote " to his much honoured Freind Mr. John Aubrey at the Right Honourable the Earle of Thanet's house at Hethfield in Kent," saying " you are much wanted at London, and dayly expected and therefore I hope you will not be long absent. Interest calls for your appearance." For at last a job was in prospect. *Dr. Christopher Wren, my deare friend, without my knowledge contrived an employment for me, which he referred to me to consider of it,* Aubrey reported to Anthony Wood. *'Tis this—Mr. Ogilby is writing the History of all England : the map is mending already. Now the Doctor told him that if that were all, it would be no very great matter. He was pleased to tell him that he could not meet with a fitter man for that turne than J. A. Now it's true it suites well enough with my Genius ; but he is a cunning Scott, and I must deale warily with him, with the advice of my friends. It will be February next before I begin, and then between that and November followeing I must scurry all over England and Wales. The King will give me protection and letters to make enquiries.*

In the end Aubrey's task was limited to a single county only, and he *enter'd upon the Perambulation of the County of Surrey July 1 1673, and left off about the middle of September following.* In those two and a half months, he wandered about the county, noting with equal interest, *here a Ruinated Castle,* there a peculiarly ingenious automatic water closet. *Oatelands,* he says *was formerly one of the Palaces belonging to the Crown of England. Here was a Fair Park, well stor'd with Deer, but dispark'd by the late Usurpers. In the Park was once a Paddock, with a Standing, where Queen Elizabeth was us'd to shoot with a Cross-Bow.* And in the parish of Godalming, he stumbled upon *a Mannour called Catteshulle, held from the King, as Master of his Concubines.*

His main task was the gathering of inscriptions from the parish churches. *This searching after Antiquities is a wearisome Taske. I wishe I had gonne through all the Church monuments,* he complained. *Though of all studies I take the least delight in this, yet methinkes I am carried on with a kind of divine aestrum : for nobody els hereabout hardly cares for it, but rather makes a scorne of it : But, me thinkes, it shewes a kind of gratitude and good nature, to revive the Memories and memorialls of the pious and charitable benefactors long since dead and gonne.* And a formidable array of inscriptions he has assembled ; for, in his day, tombstones were not so stereotyped as they are now. Poems, jokes, advertisements even, found their place on the walls of the churches, but the design was most often to shock :

> Thus Youth and Age and all Things pass away,
> Thy Turn is now as His was Yesterday ;
> To morrow shall another take thy room,
> The next day He a prey for Worms become,
> And ore your dusty Bones shall others tread,
> As you now walk and trample on the Dead ;
> 'Till neither Stone nor Memory appear,
> That ever you had Birth or Being here.

And life itself, which was so fleeting, was often held up to scorn :

> This World to her was but a traged Play,
> She came and saw't, dislikt, and pass'd away,

cries the epitaph on a ten-year-old child, Susanna Barford, and another answers :

> Wealth, Honour, Bubbles are,
> long life a Blast.
> That Good this Virgin chose
> shall everlast.

But the walls of the churches did not reflect only the melancholy side of seventeenth-century life : its prosperity and pride appeared too. For when they had made their fortunes, the newly enriched London merchants had begun to retire into the country, and the flamboyant tombstones, commemorating *Citizen and Fishmonger* or *Citizen and Haberdasher,* unselfconsciously reflect the prosperity they had attained. But the habits of a lifetime die hard, and some of the epitaphs were used to continue to drum up business even from the grave :

> Here Lockyer lyes interred, enough his Name
> Speakes one hath few Competitors in Fame ;
> A Name so great, so gen'ral, it may scorn
> Inscriptions, which do vulgar Tombs adorn ;
> His Vertues and his Pills are so well known,
> That Envy can't confine them under Stone ;
> This Verse is lost, his PILL embalmes him safe
> To future Times without an Epitaph.

Another feature of Stuart life which stands out from the tombs is the incredible frequency with which both men and women married. At *Stretham,* Aubrey noted down this epitaph : *Here beneath Sleepe in the Lord Jesus, his gracefull Servantes (Wives of Thomas Hobbes, Esq;)* and to have been just once wed was considered sufficiently startling to be recorded on one's tomb : *Dame Martha, 3ª Daughter to Robert Wilson, Esqr. onely Wife to Sir Edward Grophy of Brendon in the County of Durham, Bart.* Nor was the humour of this situation missed by the citizens of that time :

> *That you have layd my Body here,*
> *By that first Side I lov'd so deare,*
> *I thank you Husband,* runs one epitaph.
> *But yet I have another Boone,*
> *When Fates shall come (as come full soon*
> *It will and will not be deny'd)*
> *That you would close my other Side.*
> *Y'have thought it worthy to be Read,*
> *You once were Second to my Bed ;*
> *Why may you not like Title have,*
> *To this my Second Bed the Grave.*
> *This Stone will cover us all Three,*
> *And under it we shall be free,*
> *From Love or Hate, or least Distrust*
> *Of Jealousy to vex our Dust ;*
> *For here our Bodyes do but wayte*
> *The Summons for their glorious State.*

This sentiment would have been most unpopular with the occupant of a tomb at Barnes : *The best of Husbands, John Squier, late Faithful, and (oh ! that for so short a Time) Painful Rector of this Parish.* And the following epitaph would have pleased him even less :

> *Here lies a Traveller old madam Besse,*
> *Honest Charles Hales his wife I guesse.*
> *She was his dear one, wee'le not belie her ;*
> *And so's mine too ; wou'd she lay by her.*

Aubrey's time, however, was not taken up wholly by *this wearisome Taske.* Wandering from church to church, he found time to visit the Spas like Epsom, which were just then achieving popularity and were replacing the mediæval pilgrimages as an excuse for holidays, and also to stay at the country houses on his way : *I must not forget my noble Friend, Mr. Charles Howard's Cottage of Retirement (which he call'd his Castle) which lay in the Middle of a vast Heathy Country, where in the troublesome Times, he withdrew from the wicked World, and enjoy'd himself here, where he had only one Floor, his little Dining Room, a Kitchen, a Chapel and a Laboratory.* And in these places Aubrey heard many anecdotes which he was unable to resist introducing quite irrelevantly into his narrative. At Godalming, for instance, he met *Mr. Samuel Speed (the famous and valiant Sea Chaplain and Sailor). In a Poem made by Sir John Birkenhead, on the Sea-fight with the Dutch, he takes Notice of our Vicar in this Manner.*

> *His Chaplain, he plyed his wonted Work,*
> *He prayed like a Christian, and fought like a Turke,*
> *Crying now for the King, and the Duke of York*
> *With a thump, a thump, thump ;*

while at Dulwich College he noted that *the Tradition concerning the Occasion of the Foundation runs thus ; That Mr. Alleyne, being a Tragedian, and one of the Original Actors in the celebrated Shakespeare's Plays, in one of which he play'd a Daemon, with six others, and was in the midst of the Play surpris'd by an Apparition of the Devil, which so work'd on his Fancy, that he made a Vow, which he performed at this Place.* But it was at Croydon that Aubrey stumbled on a piece of information after his own heart. *There was one Oak,* he reports, *in the great Wood call'd Norwood, that had Miselto, a Timber Tree, which was felled about* 1657. *Some Persons cut this Misselto, for some Apothecaries in London, and sold them a Quantity for Ten Shillings, each time, and left only one Branch remaining for more to sprout out. One fell lame shortly after : Soon after, each of the others lost an Eye, and he that fell'd the Tree, about* 1678 *(tho' warned of these Misfortunes of the other Men) would not withstanding, adventure to do it, and shortly after broke his Leg ; as if the Hamadryades had resolved to take an ample Revenge for the Injury done to that sacred and venerable Oak.* Aubrey mentions elsewhere that *When an Oake is felling (before it falles) it gives a kind of shriekes, or groanes, that may be heard a mile off, as if it were the Genius of the Oake lamenting. I cannot omit here taking Notice,* he continues excitedly, *of the great Misfortunes in the Family of the Earl of Winchelsea, who at Eastwell in Kent, felled down a most curious Grove of Oaks, near his noble Seat, and gave the First Blow with his own Hands. Shortly after, his Countess died in her Bed suddenly, and his eldest Son, the Lord Maidstone, was killed at Sea by a Cannon Bullet. It has been not unusually observed, that to cut Oak-Wood is unfortunate,* Aubrey concludes, and this family should have been particularly wary of flouting any superstition, for had not *My Lady Seymer dreamt, that she found a Nest, with Nine Finches in it. And so many Children she had by the Earl of Winchelsey, whose name is Finch.*

Coming to the end of his Perambulation, Aubrey returned to London, where he noted an interesting sidelight on the Reformation. *Robert de Wharton,* he says, *the last Prior of the Monastery dedicated to St. Saviour at Bermondsey, surrendered this Convent into the King's Hands,* 1 *January* 1538. *He obtained a pension of £333. 6. 8d. per Annum.* That this generosity could have its disadvantages for the throne, however, is shown by the subtle revenge wreaked by another dispossessed pensioner. *The Last Lady Abbesse of Amesbury was a Kirton : who after the Dissolution married to one Appleton of Hampshire,* Aubrey reports. *She had during her life a Pension from King Henry IIX : she was one hundred and fourty yeares old when she dyed.*

Aubrey finished his tour with a description of the Surrey side of the Thames, directly opposite the City of London. *On the Bank Side were two Bear Gardens,* he says, *the Old and the New, wherein Bears, Bulls, Otters, &c. were kept to be baited by Dogs bred to that Sport, for the Diversion of the Spectators, the Destruction of the innocent Creatures, and the Gratification of a barbarous and savage Temper, which never more displays itself then in shewing a Complacency and Delight in these cruel Spectacles.*

Near this Garden was a Theatre, known by the name of the GLOBE Play-House, to which Beaumont, Fletcher, and Philip Massinger belonged and wrote for ; and though the most eminent Place for Tragedies, Comedies, and Interludes, was, because of its Situation, only used in the hot Summer Months.

Not far from this Place were the Asparagus-Gardens, and Pimblico-Path, where were fine walks, cool Arbours, &c. much used by the Citizens of London and their Families, and both mentioned by the Comedians at the Beginning of 1600. ' To walk in Pimblico' became Proverbial for a Man handsomely drest ; as these walks were frequented by none else.

Next the Bear-Garden on this Bank was formerly the Bordello, or Stewes, so called from the severall licensed Houses for the Entertainment of lewd Persons, in which were Women prepared for all Comers. The Knights Templars were notable wenchers ; for whose convenience and use these Stewes on the Bankside (over against the Temple) were erected and constituted. They were subject to several Laws and Regulations (viz. No single Woman to take Money to lye with any Man, except she lye with him all Night, till the Morrow) and their Manner of Life and priviledged Places received several Confirmations from the Crown, as one in 1345 from King Edward III. In 1506, King Henry VII, for some Time shut up these Houses, which were in Number Eighteen ; and not long after renewed their Licence, and reduced them to Twelve ; at which Number they continued till their final Suppression by Sound of Trumpet in 1546, by King Henry VIII, whose tender Conscience startled at such scandalous and open Lewdness. The single women that were Retainers to, or Inmates in, these Houses, were Excommunicate, not suffered to enter the Church while alive, or if not reconciled before their Death, prohibited Christian Burial, and were interred in a Peice of Ground called the Single-Women's Church-Yard, set apart for their use only. These Houses were distinguished by several Signs painted on their Fronts, as, a Boar's Head, The Crane, the Cardinal's Hat, the Swan, the Bell, the Crosse-Keys, the Popes Head, and the Gun.

John Evelyn assured the author that " with incredible satisfaction have I perus'd your Natural History of Surrey, &c ; and greatly admire both your Industry in undertaking so profitable a Work, and your Judgement in the several Observations which you have made. It is so useful a Piece, and so obliging that I cannot sufficiently applaud it. Something I would contribute to it, if it were possible ; but your Spicilegium is so accurate, that you have left nothing almost for those who come after you." But now that the tour was over and the rough draft made, the inevitable happened, and eighteen years later Aubrey was to write, *In the Year 1673, it was my Intention to have describ'd the pleasant County of Surrey, which I am sorry I did not compleat.* The notes themselves would probably have disappeared completely, had not Anthony Wood seen them and desired Aubrey to *transcribe them fair, and to preserve them, there being many good Remarks that deserve not to be bury'd in Oblivion. I wish I had done it soon after my Perambulation, whilst the Idea of them was fresh and lively,* Aubrey lamented, *I should then have given it more Spirit. The Papers are like Sybillina Folia. I shall not take the Paines to digest them in better Order (which would require the Drudgery of another Transcribing) and I now set things down tumultuarily, as if tumbled out of a Sack, as they come to my Hand, Mixing Antiquities and Natural Things together, as I have here done them. They will be of some use to such as love Antiquities or Natural History ; and on that Account I expose them to the View of the Candid Reader wishing him as much Pleasure in the Perusal of them, as I had in the Seeing of them. Vale.* Despite this hopeful ending, the book was not printed until Aubrey had been dead for twenty-two years, and even then the learned Dr. Rawlinson had to put the work into some semblance of order ; for it fell to him to collate it, as he said with justifiable exasperation, from two manuscripts " both wrote with the Author's own Hand, and both huddled together in a very confused and immethodical Order."

As soon as he had finished his Perambulation, Aubrey found himself surrounded by a multitude of jobs. First, a new edition of Camden's " Britannia " was foreshadowed and a set of queries relating to it was printed and *considered at several meetings by Christ. Wren, John Hoskyns, R. Hooke, J. Ogilby, John Aubrey, Gregory King.* On top of this, Aubrey was assisting in the production of two more books, Dugdale's " Monasticon " and the English version of Wood's " Historia at Antiquitates Universitatis Oxoniensis." His help with the latter work was so considerable that Anthony Wood, besides acknowledging it handsomely in the book itself, wrote Aubrey a special letter of thanks on its publication. " I am verie glad that you have satisfied me in so many things and cease not to send into divers parts for further information of other men : I speake in my conscience (for I have told other men of it already) that I have had, and shall have more from you as to these things than all people besides whatsoever. What I have had hitherto besides has been for the most part by mine owne industry and purse." And all this time Aubrey was busy collecting the anecdotes for Wood's other book " Athenae Oxoniensis " and the two antiquaries were at the peak of their friendship. " I am as carefull of your health and wellfare as any friend you have," Wood assured Aubrey, and the latter so delighted in his company that he wished to share him with all his acquaintances. *I sent you 2 lettres by my friend Mr. George Ent, together with a bundle of bookes,* Aubrey wrote to Wood in August 1674. *He is a very honest gentleman and his Rhodomantades you will easily pardon.* And George Ent must have been prompt in his delivery of the letter of introduction which Aubrey had given him, for in November Aubrey wrote *I am very glad you two good folke are acquainted ; according to my desire.* By March next year, however, matters were very different. *I am exceeding sorry for Mr. Ent's strangenesse to you,* Aubrey wrote apologetically to Anthony Wood, *but 'tis confesst his friends must beare with him ; and he being cholerique, &c : I read only that paragraph, where He introduced into your company two Boy-bachelors, and upbraided you of dotage.*

In the midst of all this work, moreover, disaster threatened. 1673, *die Jovis, St. Martin 9h.15+P.M.,* Aubrey noted with excusable exactness, *J.A. arrested by Gardiner, Sergeant, a lusty faire-haired solar Fellow, prowd, insolent, et omnia id genus.* For his financial difficulties were upon him again, and in his plight he enlisted the aid of his friends in the Royal Society to obtain a post for him, for he had been not unhelpful to them. " They made him their drudge," said one of his contemporaries, " for when any curious experiment was to be donne, they would lay the task on him." He therefore expected great things from *Mr. Secretary Wren's indefinite Kindnesse,* and from Lord Brouncker, the President, and by now he was ready to accept any kind of job. *There are peaceable places among Souldiers,* he mused, *and now the navy offices thrive, and a man can nowhere so well hide himself in an office as there.*

[lxxiii]

'cause 'tis out of the way. This last idea was doubly attractive because another member of the Royal Society, Samuel Pepys, was already firmly entrenched there.

Nothing came of these projects, however, and by 1675, even Aubrey had begun to despair of ever recovering his fortunes in England and so he turned his gaze towards the New World. But he was quite unable to make up his mind where to settle, for no sooner had Edmund Wyld offered to buy him an estate in New York, than the Earl of Thanet put him off it. "I perceive that Mr. Wild," the Earl had written, "has a mind to buy some land in New-York, which place you suppose to be a Fine Country. You are the first that ever I heard terme that part a delicious Country. Corne, indeed I heare will grow there, and in the summer they may have fatt Beefe, and Mutton : But in the Winter, which is very long and tedious, They are like the Norvegians, that live upon Salt meates, and Fish, and have such vast Snowes, that they are forced to digge their wayes out of their houses else they will be stiffled." Having by now thoroughly discouraged poor Aubrey, Lord Thanet continued : "If he will by land in America, lett it be in the Bermudas, where health abounds, and safety is had, two chiefe things which a wise Man, as he, should looke after, and soe much with my humble service pray let him knowe." The truth of the matter was that Lord Thanet owned land in Bermuda and had tried before to persuade Aubrey to go out there, and he was not alone in his desire to have so pleasant a companion on his estates. Only the previous year, Aubrey had appalled Anthony Wood by saying, *I am like to be spirited away to Jamaica by my Lord Vaughan, who is newly made Governor there, and mighty earnest to have me goe with him, and will look out some employment worth a Gentleman for me :* an offer which Sir William Petty strongly advised Aubrey to accept. *In Jamaica,* he told him, *500 pounds gives 100 per annum : take a Chymist with me,* Aubrey noted, *for brandy, suger, etc. and goe halfe with him.*

Cecil Calvert, Lord Baltemore, Absolute Lord and Proprietary of Maryland and Avalon, who had been at Aubrey's college, made yet another offer and that the most tempting. *Now if I would be rich,* Aubrey day-dreamed, *I could be a prince. I could goe into Maryland, which is one of the finest countrys of the world ; same climate with France ; between Virginia and New England. I can have all the favour of my Lord Baltemore I could wish. His brother is his Lieutenant there ; and a very good natured gentleman. Plenty of all things : ground there is 2000 miles westwards. I could be able I believe to carry a colony of rogues ; another of ingenious Artificers ; and I doubt not one might make a shift to have 5 or 6 ingeniose companions, which is enough.*

But somehow all these plans languished, probably from the very number of offers, and Aubrey made no move. For emigration was still a dangerous business and, as Professor Trevelyan has pointed out, "more than three quarters of the first colonists died prematurely, succumbing to the miseries of the voyage, or to disease, famine, exposure and Indian War." *Sir John Dugdale saith that John Davenport was a Non-Conformist,* Aubrey told Anthony Wood, *and he hath enquired of his Relations, who know nothing of him, if dead or alive, but they believe he is dead. He went over sea ; he thinkes to the Barbadoes, or some of these plantations, or to Holland :* whereas actually he was Pastor at New Haven in New England. And the sociable Aubrey was the last person to submit himself to an artificial death like this : if he had to be separated from his friends it would be by the grave, not by the sea. *For why,* he sensibly asked himself, *should I at this time of day, and being of a Monastic humour, make my selfe a slave and roast my self for Wealth ?*

The expansion of the English race oversea was a comparatively recent development. Until Elizabeth's reign every English sovereign had tried to make England a great Continental power, and the titles which Mary Tudor accumulated on her marriage to Philip II show how near that ideal came to realisation. A book that Aubrey mentions is dedicated *to the most mightie and most puissant Princess Marie, by the grace of God, Queen of England, Spaine, both Sicilies, France, Jerusalem, and Ireland : Defender of the Faith : Archduchesse of Austria ; Duchess of Milaine, Burgundie and Brabant : Countesse of Haspurge, Flanders, Tyroll, etc.* But Mary died childless and left England free to pursue her true destiny. In the next reign, England changed her national weapon, substituting the broadside for the long-bow, and this revolution in naval tactics, and the consequent advantage in sea fighting which it gave her, caused England to turn towards the Western Ocean and the lands beyond it as her rightful domain. The other powers remained peculiarly blind to the possibilities of these floating batteries, and " as late as 1511," Professor Trevelyan says, " the Spaniards fought the Turks at Lepanto, by sea tactics the same as those by which the Greeks had defeated the Persians at Salamis." The English, however, were fully conscious of the potentialities of the new weapons, and with them they laid the foundations of their sea power and their Empire.

Aubrey's continual hesitations had by now begun to irritate his friends. " Weare not I a married man," the Earl of Thanet told him crossly, " and so consequently tyed by the Legg in England, or at the best my Chain being to reach noe further, then a voyage to Bourbon, or Provence ; I would infallibly waite upon that noble kinsman of mine, my Cousin Charles Howard, in that Voyage for the Bermudas." But Aubrey, though unmarried, was no less firmly " tyed by the Legg " to London and Oxford, to the Royal Society and to his friends. For he had come now to dread even the suggestion of a job : *if I should have it,* he said on one occasion, *I should be like the weaned child, to leave Mr. Wyld : who are inseparable, and dote together till* 12 *or* 1, *at night.*

Even when he had himself become a landowner in the colonies, Aubrey could not be tempted out of England. *Captain Poyntz (for service that I did him to the Earle of Pembroke and the Earl of Abingdon) did very kindly make me a Grant of a Thousand acres of Land in the Island of Tobago, anno Domini* 1686. *Febr. 2d. He advised me to send over people to plant and to gett Subscribers to come in for a share of these* 1000 *Acres, for* 200 *Acres would be enough for me.* But still he made no move, even though he knew that *in this delicate Island is Lac lunae (the mother of Silver).*

In the selfsame year, another windfall came his way. *William Penn, Lord Proprietor of Pennsylvania, did ex mero motu et ex gratia speciali* [from a genuine impulse and as a mark of his special favour] *give me a Graunt under his seale, of Six hundred acres in Pennsylvania, without my seeking or dreaming of it. He adviseth me to plant it with French Protestants for seaven yeares gratis and afterwards make them to pay such a Rent. Also he tells me, for 200 Acres ten pounds per annum Rent for ever, after three yeares.* This generous gift was Penn's last attempt to persuade Aubrey to join him in his experiment in the New World. But before making this grant, he had tried both persuasion and direct invitations, and among Aubrey's papers is a letter, the intention of which is obvious, in which William Penn paints as alluring a picture as possible of his territory.

Dated " Philadelphia, 13th of the 4th Month, called June, 1683," it runs as follows : " Esteemed Friend, We are the wonder of our neighbours as in our coming and numbers, so to our selves in our health, Subsistence and Success : all goes well, blessed by God, and provision we shall have to spare, considerably, in a year or Two, unless very great quantitys of People croud upon us. The Aier, heat and Cold Resemble the heart of France : the Soyls good, the Springs many and delightfull, the fruits, roots, corns and Flesh, as good as I have commonly eaten in Europe, I may say most of them better. Strawberry's ripe in the woods in Aprill, and in the Last Month, Peas, beans, Cherrys and mulberrys. Much black walnutt, Chesnutt, Cyprus, or white Cedar and mulberry are here. The Sorts of fish in these parts are excellent and numerous. Sturgeon leap day and night that we can hear them a bow Shot from the Rivers in our beds. We have Roasted and pickeled them, and they eat like veal one way, and Sturgeon the other way. Mineral here is great Store, I shall send some suddainly for Tryall. Vines are here in Abundance everywhere, some may be as bigg in the body as a man's thigh. I have begun a Vineyard by a French man of Languedock, and another of Poictou, near Santong. Severall people from other Colonys are retireing hither, as Virginia, Mary Land, New England, Road Island, New York &c : I make it my businesse to Establish vertuous Economy and therefore Sett twice in Councell every week, with good Success, I thank god. My Reception was with all the show of Kindness the rude State of the Country could yield ; and after holding the Genrll Assemblys, I am not uneasy to the People. They to express their Love and gratitude gave me an Impost that might be worth 500 pounds per annum, and I returned it to them with as much Creditt. This is our present posture. I am Debtor to thy kindness for two Letters : wether this be pay or no, pray miss not to Continue to yield that Content And Liberality to Thy very True Freind William Penn."

But to return to 1675. Aubrey, it seems, was once more hopeful of getting a place in England, for in that year Lord Thanet wrote to him : " I am glad you have soe good an opportunity to make your addresses to that excellent Lady, the Younger Countess Dowager of Pembroke, who if yore Starrs be favourable, may, through the interest of the Dutches of Portsmouth, procure you some good imployment, if not neglected by a wonted trapishness incident in You. The freedom I take in menconing that you will, I hope, easily forgive, since I doe it not by way of check, but by a friendly advertisement to beware of it." Aubrey's efficiency is well attested by the offers of emigration which he had received, for life was still so hard in the Plantations that no one but a fool, and the first colonists were far from that, would have suggested taking with them anyone who could not more than pull his own weight ; and so it must have been his " wonted trapishness " that caused this job, like all the others, to fall through.

The result was that Aubrey was immediately overwhelmed, yet again, by his financial difficulties (*upon a threatning of my brother to threw me in Gaole*) and in this predicament a strange letter arrived from the Earl of Thanet. " J. Aubrey," it began curtly, " With this you will receive a Protection according to your desire, which when useless returne. I send it you under this provisoe, that yow are my Sollicitor to looke after my business in London ; and for your Sallary that is agreed on. My mother hath lent me Thanet house garden, where I intend to fit up two or three chambers for my use when I come to London privately, and intend to stay not long there, one of which as my meniall Servant you may make use of when fitted up, and when it is you shall have notice. I would have you in future to take more time in writing your letters, for your last was soe ill writ that I had a great deale of trouble to read some part of it. Thanet." Poor Aubrey must have been appalled to receive such a letter from a man whom he had always looked upon as one of his greatest friends, but the next post set his mind at rest. " Sir," wrote Lord Thanet then, " I am not soe ignorant as not to knowe the Stile of myne of the third Instant is much unbefitting to writ unto a Gentleman of youre Birth. The reason why I make my selfe such a proud ill bread Fellowe in it, is the better to disguise the business You lately enjoyned me to doe for You. And on the same Score my Letters in the future shall be, by your permission, as little civill, then in case any thing should be questioned in the account you knowe of, in producing such, writ in soe imperious a manner, will induce all to believe that the business, although very unbefitting, of your belonging to me is noe otherwise then reall. Although this small service can hardly be inrolled under the notion of a Courtesy, yet I assure You 'tis the first Protection I ever gave : although I have been in this nature solicited by many. Weare there anything of moment that I could serve you in," he concludes, " you might freely command him who is in great reallity Your most affectionate and humble Servant : Thanet."

Even armed with this powerful protection, however, Aubrey still felt unsafe (*if my brother should know of it,* he wrote, *he would fall upon me like a Tygre*) and to avoid any possibility of imprisonment for debt, he constantly changed his dwelling. " Yor lodging," Lord Thanet said, " like an inchanted Castle, being never to be found out, I shall in the future direct my Letters to Mr. Hookes chamber in Gressam Colledge as you desire."

Matters had, in fact, become so serious that Aubrey was even toying with the idea of entering the Church. *Fough ! The Cassock stinkes ; it would be ridiculous,* he had said when the idea first came up two years before, but a letter to Anthony Wood shows that his objections were now taking a more practical turn. *I am stormed by my chiefest freinds afresh, viz. Baron Bertie, Sir William Petty, Sir John Hoskyns, Bishop of Sarum, etc. to turne Ecclesiastique ; but the King of France growes stronger and stronger, and what if the Roman Religion should come-in againe ? Why then, say they, cannot you turne too ? You, I say, know well that I am no puritan, nor an enimy to the old Gentleman on the other side of the Alpes. Truly, if I had a good Parsonage of 2 or 300 pounds per annum (as you told me) it would be a shrewd temptation.* That Aubrey was unlearned in theology and had a stutter caused not the slightest difficulty, for the standard was not high and Aubrey himself said of one of the most learned divines, Robert Sanderson, Lord Bishop of Lincoln : *He had no great memorie : I am certain not a sure one : when I was a Fresh-man and heard him read his first Lecture, he was out in the Lord's Prayer.*

The question of his taking any services did not really arise. " If the heasitation in your speech doth hinder," one of his friends suggested, " gett a Parsonage of 4 or 500 pounds per annum, and give a Curat 100 pounds per annum to officiate for you."

This allotment of one-fifth of the revenue to the incumbent was very generous, for during his perambulation of Surrey, Aubrey had been so greatly shocked to find curates who received only sixteen or twenty pounds a year for doing the whole work of a parish that he was for once moved to anger. *I cannot here pass by without animadvertising on this poor mean Pittance, set aside for the Vicar, while the Lay Impropriator sacrilegiously fattens on the Revenue of the Church, and enjoys what neither in right Reason or Conscience was never design'd for, or belongs to the Laity,* he said. *Could Impropriators be once persuaded to set aside for the Service of the Altar a just Proportion (for the Age is too degenerate to expect a Surrender of the whole to the pious Uses first designed by the Donors) it might, in some measure, atone for the Rapine of their Ancestors.* But so frail is the human conscience that when Aubrey himself had the chance *to fatten on the Revenues of the Church,* he proposed to keep a mere four-fifths of the income for his own use.

This corruption was all the more serious when one considers the overwhelming importance of the Church in those days. " Though it was an age of reading and writing in the conduct of the ordinary affairs of life," says Professor Trevelyan, " very little printed matter came in the way of the less educated. This gave all the greater importance to the sermon, which dealt as freely with political as with religious doctrines." And though Charles II capped his aphorism about Presbyterianism being no religion for a gentleman, by saying that Anglicanism was no religion for a Christian, there was no doubt about its entertainment value. For science had had as yet had so little effect on the character of religious belief that the Church felt sure enough of itself to tolerate the kind of jesting that now seems irreverent. " My Lord, my Lord," cried one preacher to the dozing Landerdale, " you snore so loud, you will wake the King." And it was with obvious satisfaction that Anthony Wood noted in his Journal : " August 26, Sunday : a baudy Sermon at S. Marie's in the afternoon." Though baudiness was a rare delight, jokes were common in church and preachers vied with each other in attracting the largest audiences for their performances. Some preached in their sleep, like that poor man who was so sadly discomfited by James I, and Meredith Lloyd told Aubrey that *when Dr. Powell preacht, that a Smoake would issue out of his head ; so great agitation of spirit he had,* which led Aubrey to ask in true scientific fashion : *Why might not such accidents heretofore be a Hint to the glories, which the Painters putt about the heads of canonized Saints.* As a final proof of the importance of the sermon in everyday life, Aubrey remarks that *Sir William Croftes, eldest brother to the now Bishop of Hereford, built a house in Leominster, to live there, to heare John Tombes preach.* Nor were the pleasures of religion confined to the actual service. *At Danby Wisk, in the North Riding of Yorkshire,* Aubrey says, *it is the custom for the parishioners, after receiving the Sacrament, to goe from church directly to the ale-house, and there drink together, as a testimony of charity and friendship.*

Aubrey still hesitated, though, very probably because he thought a parsonage was beneath him, for the clergy had not yet reached the pitch of gentility which they were to achieve in the next two centuries ; and Clarendon, though he was a tireless supporter of the Anglican Church, noted with disgust that after the Civil War, " the daughters of noble and illustrious Families bestowed themselves upon divines or other low and unequal matches."

Aubrey's misgivings about the consequences of a change in religion were already growing out of date, as is shown by the tone in which he himself mentions the queasy consciences of the recent past. *John Barclay was in England tempore regis Jacobi,* he writes solemnly. *He was then an old man, white beard ; and wore a hatt and a feather, which gave some severe people offence.* And there can be no doubt at all about the spirit in which he recorded that *in Sir Charles Scarborough's time (he was of Caius College) Dr. Batchcroft, the Head of that House, would visit the boyes' Chambers, and see what they were studying ; and Charles Scarborough's Genius let him to the Mathematics, and he was wont to be reading of Clavius upon Euclid. The old Dr. had found in the title 'e Societate Jesu', and was much scandalized at it. Sayd he, By all meanes leave-off this author, and read Protestant Mathematicall bookes.* And when Aubrey mentioned the death, in 1671, of his friend, *Edward Bagshawe, a Prisoner to Newgate 22 weekes for refusing to take the Oath of Allegiance (he boggled at the word ' willingly ' in the oath*) he hastened to add that *he was buried in the fanatique burying-place by the Artillery-ground in Moor-fields.*

The truth of the matter, as Aubrey realised perfectly well, was that the Wars of Religion had proved so disastrous that they had caused a definite reaction in favour of tolerance, and in the very next year after Aubrey had expressed his misgivings, the death penalty for heresy was finally abolished. " Since their belief of their contrary truths is confessedly a work of divine revelation, why a man should be hanged because it has not yet pleased God to give him his spirit, I confess I am yet to understand," Robert Boyle had written when Parliament was trying to stamp out " the spreading impostures of the sectaries " during the Commonwealth, and he was driven to the conclusion that " it is strange that men should rather be quarrelling for a few trifling opinions, wherein they dissent, than to embrace one another for those many fundamental truths wherein they agree."

In this attitude Boyle was soon joined by most educated men, though not all of them would have agreed with Sir William Davenant, who confessed to Aubrey that *his private opinion was that Religion, at last, e.g. a hundred yeares hence, would come to Settlement, and that in a·kind of ingeniose Quakerisme.* Aubrey himself was completely in sympathy with this civilised attitude : *George Webb, Bishop of Limrick,* he says, *dyed and was buried in Limerick about two or three daies before the Towne was taken by the Irish, who digged up the body again ; it was about* 1642. *I confess I doe not like that super-zeale in the Canon Lawe, not to let alone there the bodys of Heretiques. It is too inhuman.*

Even Roman Catholicism was coming to be tolerated as a religion, although it was still hated as a political weapon, and Aubrey numbered among his personal friends *Capt. Pugh, a Rubroliterate gent, my acquaintance, a writer and a Poet. Bred up in Societate Jesu ; but turn'd out because he was a Captaine in the late Warres. When his studie was searcht, his Orders were there found, and also a letter from the Queen-Mother (Whose Confessor he had sometimes been) to the King, that, if he should fall into any danger of the Lawe, upon sight of that lettre he should obtaine his Majesties pardon.* And very necessary this letter was to prove, for Aubrey continues : *All his bookes were seized on ; amongst others his almanac, wherein he entred omnia Caroli II deliramenta et vitia* [all Charles II's follies and vices] *which was carried to the Council board.*

Despite outbursts of popular hysteria, like the one caused by Titus Oates, Catholicism had been looked on with sympathy by the upper classes ever since the Reformation. *When he lay dyeing,* Aubrey writes of his great grandfather, *he desired them to send for a good man ; they thought he meant Dr. Goodman, Deane of St. Paules, but he meant a Priest, as I have heard my cosen John Madock say. Capt. Pugh was wont to say that civilians (as most learned and Gent.) naturally incline to the Church of Rome ; and the Common lawyers, as more ignorant and Clownish, to the church of Geneva.* And Aubrey had heard even John Tombes, the Baptist, *who seemed to be a very pious and zealous Christian, say (though he was much opposite to the Romish Religion) that truly, for his part, should he see a poor zealous Friar goeing to preach, he should pay him respect.*

This attitude is the more surprising, when one realises that Catholicism then appeared to the mass of Englishmen in very much the same light as Communism nowadays strikes the Americans. For by its immediate success, Luther's revolution was even more startling than Marx's ; and it was no less violent. " Whoso can strike, smite, strangle, or stab secretly or publicly," enjoined Luther, " such wonderful times are these that a prince can better merit Heaven with bloodshed than another with prayer," and in his political thought he showed himself a true German, the first in the lamentable procession of that nation's modern colossi. " No one need think that the world can be ruled without blood," he thundered, " the civil sword shall and must be red and bloody." Faced with this threat, it was no wonder that the Papacy reacted so violently : and with Christendon in danger, the Church adopted in self-defence a policy which had been outlined a century before by the Bishop of Verden. " When the Church is threatened," he had said, " she is released from the commandments of morality ; with unity as the end, the use of every means is sanctified, even cunning, treachery, violence, prison, death. For all order is for the sake of the community, and the individual must be sacrificed to the common good." In pursuance of this totalitarian policy, the Papacy sided with every enemy of England for the next two hundred years, besides ceaselessly plotting revolution inside the country. Rebellion against a Protestant monarch was held to be the duty of every true Christian, and a procession of Jesuits passed between the Continent and the tightly organised and obedient Catholic families of England, to foster this end. It was largely for these political reasons that Catholicism was excluded from all measures of toleration, long after they had been extended to every other sect. And it was because of this political danger that Aubrey was so alarmed when his own sympathies became too widely known. *When I was comeing one time out of All-souls,* he wrote to Anthony Wood in 1688, *the Gape-abouts, at the gate pointed at me, one sayd Romano-Catholicus : I pray God bless you and deliver you from effronts.*

But still Aubrey made no decision, even though he was reduced to such straits by 1677 that he had to sell the last of his possessions, his precious books. That he was still hopeful, however, is shown by a note : *I expect preferment through Sir Leoline Jenkins,* who was not only some *remote kin to him,* but also owed his rise entirely to the efforts of the Aubrey family. When this worthy was made *Principall Secretary of Estate,* therefore, Aubrey was quick to *wayte on him to congratulate for the Honour his Majestie had been pleased to bestowe on him,* but though he reported that *he recieved me with his usual courtesie, and sayd that it had pleased God to rayse-up a poore worme to doe his Majestie humble service,* he showed no sign of wishing to repeat the process and poor Aubrey went unsatisfied. And in 1683 the final blow fell : *It pleased God at Whitsuntide last,* he wrote, *to bereave me of a deare, usefull, and faithfull friend (Mr. Johnson) who had the reversion of the place of Master of the Rolles ; who generously, for friendship and neighbourhood sake (we were borne the same weeke and within 4 miles and educated together) gave me the Graunt to be one of his Secretaries. He was a strong lustie man and died of a malignant fever, infected by the Earl of Abingdons brother, making of his Will. It was such an Opportunity that I shall never have the like again,* Aubrey bewailed. *His death is an extraordinary losse to me, for that had he lived to have been Master of the Rolles I had been one of his Secretarys, worth 600 pounds or more.*

This disappointment seems to have brought Aubrey's age home to him, for he was now in his fifty-eighth year, and we hear no more of prospective jobs. But the habit of a lifetime dies hard and in his *Faber Fortunae* he continued to jot down, as they occurred to him, ideas for recouping his fortunes. *Put somebody upon marrying the Thames and Avon, and gett a share in it,* he said hopefully, or *Gett a Patent to digge for the Coale that I have discovered in Slyfield-common in Surrey, near Gilford.* In all, sixty-two projects were noted down by him, but it is the last entry that is of the greatest interest, for Aubrey was far in advance of his time when he suggested *a Register Generall of People, Plantations, and Trade of England.* His idea was *to gett an*

Office for such a Registrie for the collecting the Accounts for the severall particulars following, viz :

(1) *Of all the Births, Marriages, Burialls throughout all England : and to see them duly kept : that his Majestie may have a yearly account of the increase and decrease of his subjects.*

(2) *An account of the Harths, and Houses in England : as also of the People, by their Age, Sex, Trade, Titles, and Office.*

(3) *An account of the Trade is to be deduced from the Customs-house Bills, and Prices currant (upon the Exchange).*

(4) *A particular account of the Excise, according to the last collections of subfarmes.*

(5) *An account of the severall Payments that have been made by Land-taxes, Polls, Subsidies, Benevolence, and particular Imposts.*

(6) *An account of all the Church Revenues.*

(7) *A Villare Anglicanum, sc. an account of all the Cities, Townes, Villages, great Houses, Rodes, carriages, principal Innes and Families of England, with the Post-stages of the same.*

(8) *An account of all the Scholars in the Universities : and public schooles.*

(9) *An account of all the Prisoners from time to time, and of all Executions.*

(10) *A particular account of the Shipping of England, and all Foreign parts : and the Sea-men resident in each Port.*

(11) *The Prices currant of the principall Commodities in each Market of England.*

(12) *The true number of Irish Cattle imported.*

(13) *The number of Attorneys in each Countie : now : and what heretofore.*

The design, he summed up, *is to have Abstracts of all the above particulars in order to compare them one with another, so as to give the King a true State of the Nation at all times.* And for his own advice Aubrey noted : *Be at Sir Leoline Jenkins to gett a Patent to authorize me to use all lawfull waies and means to procure accounts of the premisses, and that all the King's Officers be assistant to me therein gratis. Sir Wm. Petty hath promised me, to assist me in it.*

The consideration of these ingenious projects was never allowed to interfere with his writing, however, and when Thomas Hobbes died in 1679, Aubrey, as his oldest friend, immediately set about preparing an informal biography to supplement the more impersonal Latin life which Hobbes had written at his request. *'Tis Religion to performe the Will of the Dead,* Aubrey says in the preface to his book, *which I here dischardge, with my Promise (1667) to my old friend, in setting forth his Life and performing the last Office to my honoured Friend Mr. Thomas Hobbes, whom I have had the honour to know from my child-hood, being his Countryman and borne in Malmesbury Hundred and having both the same Schoolmaster.*

Since no body knew so many particulars of his Life as my selfe, Aubrey explained, *he desired that if I survived him, it should be handed to Posterity by my hands, which I declare and avow to do ingenuously and impartially, to prevent misreports and undeceive those who are scandalized.*

One sayes that when a learned man dyes, a great deal of Learning dyes with him. He was a flumen ingenii [a river of talent] *never dry. The recrementa* (Remaines) *of so learned a Person are valueable. Amongst innumerable Observables of Him which had deserved to be sett downe, thus few (that have not scap't my Memory) I humbly offer to the Present Age and Posterity, tanquam tabulam naufragii* [like fragments of a shipwreck] *and as plankes and lighter thinges swimme, and are preserved, where the more weighty sinke and are lost. And as with the light after Sun-sett—at which time clear ; by and by, comes the crepusculum* [dusk] *; then, totall darknes—in like manner is it with matters of Antiquitie. Men thinke, because every body remembers a memorable accident shortly after 'tis donne, 'twill never be forgotten, which for want of registring, at last is drowned in Oblivion ; which reflection haz been a hint that by my meanes many Antiquities have been reskued and preserved (I myselfe now inclining to be Ancient)—or else utterly lost and forgotten.*

For that I am so minute, I declare I never intended it, but setting downe in my first draught every particular with purpose, upon review, to cutt off what was superfluous and trivall) I shewed it to some Friends of mine (who also were of Mr. Hobbes's acquaintance) whose judgements I much value, who gave their opinion : and 'twas clearly their judgement, to let all stand ; for though to soome at present it might appeare too triviall ; yet hereafter 'twould not be scorned but passe for Antiquity.

And besides I have Precedents of Reverend writers to plead, who have in some Lives recited things as triviall, nay, the sayings and actions of good woemen. (Dean Fell hath recorded his Mother's jejune sayings and actions, and triviall remarques of Dr. Hammond in his life, written by him.)

I am also to beg pardon of the Reader, he concludes, *for two long Digressions, viz. Malmesbury and Gorambery ; but this also was advised as the only way to preserve them, and which I have donne for the sake of the Lovers of Antiquity. I hope its novelty and pleasantness will make compensation for its length.*

Anthony Wood, hearing that Aubrey was engaged on this task, was quick to warn him " to have a care what he does, if he have a hand in it—that he write faire things or else sombody will be upon his back." For it was on this very subject that Wood himself had come to grief just six years back. *Anno Domini* 1674, Aubrey noted, *Mr. Anthony à Wood sett forth an elaborate Worke of eleven yeares study, intituled The History and Antiquities of the University of Oxford, wherin, in every respective Colledge and Hall, he mentions the Writers there educated and what Bookes they wrote. The Dean of Christ-church (Dr. John Fell) having Plenipotentiary power of the Presse there, perused every sheet before 'twas to be sent to the presse ; and maugre the Author and to his sore displeasure did expunge and inserted what he pleased in Mr. Hobbes's life.*

Hereupon, the Author acquaints John Aubrey, Mr. Hobbes's correspondent, with all that had passed ; J.A. acquaints Mr. Hobbes. Mr. Hobbes takeing it ill, was resolved to vindicate himselfe in an Epistle to the Author. Accordingly an epistle dated Apr. 20, 1674, was sent to the Author in Manuscript, with an Intention to publish it when the History of Oxford was to be published. Upon the reciept of Mr. Hobbes's Epistle by Anthony à Wood, he forthwith repaired, very honestly and without any guile, to the Deane of Christ Church to communicate it to him. The Deane read it over carelessly, and not without scorne, and when he had donne, bid Mr. Wood tell Mr. Hobbes, that he was an old man, had one foote in the grave, that he should mind his latter end, and not trouble the world any more with his papers, etc., or to that effect.

In the meane time Mr. Hobbes meetes with the King in the Pall-mall, in St. James's parke ; tells him how he had been served by the Deane of Christ Church, and withall desires his Majestie to be pleased to give him leave to vindicate himself. The King seeming to be troubled at the dealing of the Deane, gave Mr. Hobbes leave, conditionally that he touch no-body but him who had abused him, neither that he should reflect upon the Universitie.

Mr. Hobbes understanding that this Historie would be published at the common Act at Oxon, about 11 *July, the said yeare* 1674, *prints his Epistle at London, and sends downe divers Copies to Oxon, which being dispersed at Coffee-houses and Stationers shops, a Copie forthwith came to the Deane's hands, who upon the reading of it fretted and fumed at it as a most famous Libell, sent for the Author of the History and chid him, telling withall that he had corresponded with his Enemie (Hobbes). The Author replied that surely he had not forgot what he had donne, for he had communicated to him before what Mr. Hobbes had sayd and written ; whereupon the deane, recollecting himselfe, told him that Hobbes should suddenly heare more of him ; so that the last sheete of paper being then in the presse and one leafe thereof being left vacant, the Deane supplied it with his answer.*

To this scurrilous Answer the old Gentleman never made any Reply, but slighted the Dr.'s passion and forgave it, Aubrey adds. *But 'tis supposed it might be the cause why Mr. Hobbes was not afterwards so indulgent, or spared the lesse to speake his Opinion, concerning the Universities and how much their Doctrine and Method had contributed to the late Troubles.*

As Aubrey had been in the very centre of this controversy, he hardly needed reminding of the prejudice that a life of Hobbes was likely to arouse ; even the King had to move warily when dealing with him, as Aubrey has recorded. For Hobbes had presented Charles II with his *History of England from* 1640 *to* 1660, *which the King has read and likes extreamely, but tells him there is so much Truth in it he dares not license for feare of displeasing the Bishops.* And Aubrey was naturally careful in these matters, as he had in his own family an excellent example of the perils of authorship. *In Queen Elizabeth's time,* he states, *one Penry of Wales wrote a booke called Martin-Mar-prelate. He was hanged for it. He was kin to my great-grandfather.* In Aubrey's own lifetime there had been the case of *George Withers, an easie rymer, and no good Poet whose witt was Satyricall. I thinke the first thing he wrote,* says Aubrey, *was 'Abuses Whipt and stript',* for which *he was committed to Newgate.* With examples like these before them, authors were very wary about printing their works. *This Earle of Clarendon told me,* says Aubrey, *he has his father's Life written by himselfe, but 'tis not fitt so soon to publish it,* and John Rushworth, the historian, wrote to him, " I being neere of kin to Sir Thomas Fairfax, the Parliament's Generall, he made choice of me to be his secretary in the Wars, by which means I am beter inabled to give account of military affairs, both in the first Wars and in the second which hapened in the year 1648—all of which I am now Perfeting the same, but the times favors not the Comeing of it forth." Aubrey himself had been driven to a similar concealment, for in the year before his death he wrote to Thomas Tanner : *I gave my Holyoake's Dictionary to the Museum. Pray looke on the blanke leaves at the end of it, and you will find a thundering Copie of Verses that Henry Birkhead gave me in the praise of this King of France. Now he is dead, it may be look't-upon.*

Whatever the reason was, Aubrey, without reading it over, sent the manuscript of his *Life of Hobbes* to Anthony Wood who, after he had extracted what he wanted, lent it to Richard Blackburne, *a generall scholar, prodigious memorie, sound judgement ; but 30 yeares old now*, who promptly produced a Latin biography of the philosopher, founded largely on Aubrey's material ; help which he acknowledged merely by including among a list of Hobbes' friends, " John Aubrey of the Royal Society, Esq., a man born rather for the public good than his own, who chiefly encouraged me to the undertaking this work, and kindly supplied me with materials."

Unlike Silas Taylor, who, in similar circumstances, ejaculated, *Soe I should have the fflitted milke for my entertainment and he goe away with the cream and all under his own name too*, Aubrey seemed to bear little resentment against the people who so ruthlessly stole the fruit of his labours. *In the meane time I suffer the grasse to be cutt under my feet, for Dr. Blackbourne will have all the Glory*, Aubrey grumbled, but he busied himself, nonetheless, with collecting laudatory verses with which to preface Blackburne's edition. *I never yet knew a witt (unless he were a piece of an Antiquary) write a proper Epitaph, but have the reader ignorant, what countreyman, &c : only tickles his ears with Elogies*, Aubrey wrote to Anthony Wood in 1680. *I have engaged the Earle of Dorset, my Lord John Vaughan, to write verses, and they will engage my Lord Mowgrave, and the Earl of Rochester. I first engaged Mr. Dreyden ; and Mr. Waller, who is willing he tells me (for they were old acquaintances) but he is something afrayd of the Ecclesiastiques.*

Towards Anthony Wood, Aubrey felt nothing but gratitude. *'Twill be a pretty thing and I am glad you putt me on it*, he wrote benevolently about the Brief Lives, *I doe it playingly* : and later he said, *my Memoires of Lives is now a booke of 2 quires, close written : and after I had begun it I had such an impulse in my spirit that I could not be at quiet till I had donne it. I beleeve never any in England were delivered so faithfully and with so good authority.* For Aubrey had become even more enthralled with this work since Anthony Wood had cunningly suggested to him that he might win fame by publishing his own version of the Lives at a later date : and it must have been encouraging, with this idea in mind, to see into what a lamentably pompous style Wood was translating his notes. Aubrey had written of Thomas Chaloner, *He was as far from a Puritan as the East from the West. He was of the Naturall Religion, and of Henry Martyn's Gang, and one who loved to enjoy the pleasures of this life :* whereas Wood's heavy-handed and self-righteous version ran, " This Thomas Chaloner, who was as far from being a puritan or a presbyterian as the east is from the west, for he was a boon companion, was of Henry Martin's gang, was of the natural religion, and loved to enjoy the comfortable importances of this life, without any regard of laying up for a wet day, which at last he wanted." Where Wood pointed a moral, Aubrey adorned a tale.

On Ascension Day, 1680, therefore, Aubrey sent the Minutes of his Lives to Anthony Wood at Oxford and for the next twelve years the volumes shuttled to and fro between them, growing ever more involved and more untidy. And now Aubrey felt free to work out a notion which he had first conceived in 1669 : *An Idea of Education of Young Gentlemen, viz. From the Age of 9 or ten yeares ; till 17, or 18 ;* and his views on this subject were so far in advance of his age, that it was not until this century that they were even given a trial.

The basic idea of his school he outlined as follows : *Plato saies, that the Education of Children is the Foundation of Government : it will follow, that the Education of the Nobless must be the Pillars and Ornaments of it : they are the Atlasses that beare-up the weight of it. 'Tis true, there is an ample provision made in both our Universities for the Education of Clerkes : but not care hath yet been taken for the right breeding-up of Gentlemen of Qualitie.*

The methods by which Aubrey wished to train the gentlemen of England for their task of government were astonishingly liberal. *The common way of teaching is so long, tedious, and praeposterous,* he said, *that it breakes the spirit of the fine tender ingeniose youths and causes 'em perfectly to hate learning,* and he attacked particularly *the ordinary school-masters' tyrannicall beating and dispiriting of children which many tender ingeniose children doe never recover again. Dr. Busby,* he admits, *hath made a number of good Scholars, but I have heard several of his Scholars affirme, that he hath marred by his severity more than he hath made :* an awful accusation when one considers that, during his reign at Westminster, Busby not only produced the greatest architect of the age Sir Christopher Wren, the greatest poet John Dryden and the greatest philosopher John Locke, but that his pupils so monopolised the highest positions in the Church that the Bishop of Rochester thanked God " that he was a Bishop although not a Westminster." Aubrey nevertheless held to his doctrine that *Youth should be indulged as to all lawfull Pleasures,* and two hundred years before its time he produced the theory that *'Tis a very ill thing to cross children ; it makes them ill-natured ; wherefore let them not be cross'd in things indifferent.*

Aubrey had adopted the revolutionary idea that *a Schoole should be indeed the house of play and pleasure ; and not of feare and bondage,* and his aim was to get his pupils to take *so great a delight in their Studies, that they would learn as fast as one could teach them.* He therefore decided *never to overcloude their tender memories : but let them, when they begin to be weary, turn the Globes and play with them.* Nor were more strenuous forms of exercise ignored. *Young men doe much want Ayring,* he thought, *especially those of a sulphurous complexion, they are apt to kindle a Feaver without it ;* and so riding tours round the countryside were encouraged, and these expeditions had the added advantage of serving discipline as well as health. For the withdrawal of permission to share in these jaunts would serve as an adequate punishment for any breach of the lax discipline. For more serious misdemeanours, *Not to eat Tarts, and Fruit, or drinke Wine would be a penance,* Aubrey thought, but he had some doubts about the safety of this latter method : *It is observed, that those children who are too severely prohibited to drink wine, doe generally prove Drunkards,* besides which it was acknowledged to be *a good medicine against the Wormes.* Scrupulous in observing his rule *the scholars not to be beaten about the head,* he decided at last that thumb-screws would have to be employed to discourage the most serious naughtiness. From the health point of view, Aubrey also set special store in letting *the children sleep-out their full Sleep. No scholar to rise too early (especially in Winter)*, runs one rule, *because it checks their Perspiration and so, dulls them; and it stints their growth. Some friends of mine*, he added, *impute their unluckiness to their too early rising at Westminster.* And in the garden, Aubrey intended to provide his pupils with *a noble Bassin to learn the Art of Swimming, and wash themselves in warme weather.*

His friend, Dr. Ezreel Tonge (ever famous as *the inventor of the Way of teaching Children to write a good hand in twenty dayes' time, by writing over with black Inke, Copies printed from Copper-plates in red Inke, by which meanes Boyes learn to admiration)* had, according to Aubrey *an excellent schoole, and followed precisely the Jesuites method of teaching; and boyes did profit wonderfully, as needes they must, by that method.* In imitation of his friend, therefore, Aubrey decided to limit his instruction to modern subjects, such as *Cookery, Chemistry, Cards (They may have a Banke for wine, of the money that is wonne at play every night), Merchants Accompts, the Mathematicks*, and *Dancing*, trusting that his pupils would be unconsciously forced into learning Latin by *the Ten or 12 Swisse, or Dutch, or Scotish Boyes of about fifteen years old (French boies will be naught*, he added curtly, *like the shearing of Hogges they make a great crie and little wool: thir mindes do chiefly run on the propagation of their race)* whom he intended to educate free, in return for a promise to restrict their conversation to Latin. And the cook, the scullions, and the porter, *a lusty young Swiss with a long sword*, were likewise pledged to speak Latin only.

By these means, he hoped, the boys would pick up the classical tongues despite themselves, and another of his devices to this end was borrowed direct from Dr. Tonge's school, *where was a long gallery, and he had severall printed heads of Caesar's, &c; verbes under such a head, governed by a Dative case; under another an Ablative. The boyes had it as readie as could be.* Aubrey was convinced of the value of this pictorial method of education, even in later life: *Sir Ralph Hopton (since L^a) was wont to say that he learn't more Philosophy once from a painted cloath in an Alehouse then in all the bookes he had read: sc.*

> *Never lament or make any mone*
> *For either ther's Remedy, or there is none.*

Another rule laid it down that *the Scholars were Not to be dressed à la mode till Dinner-time*, for Aubrey had been acutely aware that he was working against time ever since his friend, Mr. J. Ward, had told him that he had found *by experience, that the only time of Learning is from nine to sixteen, afterwards Cupid beginns to Tyrannize.* And in case any one should misunderstand exactly what Mr. Ward meant by that, Aubrey mentioned that *Mr. Hobbes told me, that G. Duke of Buckingham had at Paris when he was about twenty yeares old, desired Him to reade Geometrie to him: his Grace had great naturall parts, and quicknesse of witt; Mr. Hobbes read, and his Grace did not apprehend, which Mr. Hobbes wondered at: at last, Mr. Hobbes observed that his Grace was at mastrupation (his hand in his Codpiece). This is a very improper age ; for that reason for learning.*

Aubrey was under no illusion about the opposition which his plan would meet, nor from what direction that opposition would come, for the book concludes : *But now (me thinkes) I see a black Squadron marching from Oxford led up by a Crosier Staffe (Jo: Fell, Bᵖ. Oxon) to discomfit this pretty Flock : and so my pleasing Dream*

is at an
END.

Although Aubrey headed this work, *A Private Essay only,* he took more trouble over it after its completion, than over any of his other books. Not only did he choose the sites where he wished his schools to be, for he considered that half a dozen establishments would cover the needs of the whole country, but he continued for several years to make strenuous efforts to find a patron, or rather six patrons, who would put his schemes into practice. *Sir,* he wrote to Anthony Henley in 1694, *I hope this Child of mine will be presented to you in a lucky houre. I am much joy'd to heare that excellent character you give of the Earl of Leicester : He may be a meanes to promote this Designe : the Earl of Pembroke hath read it all over, and excerped some things : he approves of it : but is not active. I have some hopes that the Marquess of Worcester (to whom my brother is well known) may propagate this Design in Wales : I am not over confident of my Lord Weymouth.* Unfortunately, however, he had over-estimated the public spirit of all the other peers in whom he had placed such high hopes : for although they all admired the design, none took any practical steps to carry it out. *God's will be done,* was Aubrey's reaction. *If the Nobless have a mind to have their Children be put into the Clergie's pockets, much good may it do 'em.* And at last even he despaired of seeing his *Idea* take practical shape : *But I forsee that it will lie coffined up, and nobody have that Generosity to set affoote this noble Designe.*

Deare Friend, Aubrey wrote to Anthony Wood on May 11, 1686. *In January last, after a very great conflict of affliction, I rowsed up my spirits and writt a lettre to you, and immediately fell to worke with my Naturall History of Wilts, which I had just donne April 21, rough hewn, and finished the last chapter, when at the evening I heard of the sad news of the Decease of my deare and ever honoured mother : who died at Chalke, but my brother has buried her with my father in North Wilts (Kingston S. Michael). My head has been a fountain of teares, and this is the first lettre (except of businesse) that I have writt since my Griefe. I am now involved in a great deale of trouble, and Chalke must be sold ; but I hope to make some reservations for my selfe, and I hope before I dye to be able to make an honourable present to you : for I am for the Spaniards way ; sc. not to make my soule my Executor. I shall shortly goe to Chalke to see how matters goe there : and as soon as I can pick up a little money intend to see you at Oxon, and thinke the time very long till I am with you. God blesse you and comfort me, that I may but live to finish and publish my papers.*

Tuissimus, J.A.

Let me desire you to write to me by the next post, to let me know how you doe : yor letter will be a Cordial to me : therefore pray fail not. Fabian Philips is yours. I am sorry for the losse of our facetious friend Parson Hodges. I must make hast with my papers, for I am now 60.

[lxxxviii]

Deborah Aubrey was 15 *yeares old and as much as from January to June when she was married,* John Aubrey says, and as he was her first child, there was less difference in years between them than there was between Aubrey and his brother, William. It was no wonder, therefore, that his mother's death brought home to him so forcibly his own age and the perilous condition of his works. *His Writings had the usual fate of those not printed in the Author's life-time,* Aubrey had written many years before about Nicholas Hill, and his *Minutes of Lives* are full of similar references. *George Herbert writt a folio in Latin,* he noted, *which because the Parson of Hineham could not read, his widowe condemned to the uses of good houswifry,* and he mentioned many other manuscripts besides which had *wrapt Herings by this time* or had *been putt under Pyes.* The examples were so unending : *George Sandys, Poet, had something in Divinity ready for the presse, which his niece my Lady Wyat lost in the Warres—the title of it shee does not remember :* and the Fire of London had caused such widespread destruction, that even plagiarism was excusable in that age. *'Tis certaine,* Aubrey says, *that John Wallis is a person of reall worth, and may stand very gloriously upon his owne basis, and need not be beholding to any man for Fame, yet he is so extremely greedy of glorie, that he steales feathers from others to adorne his own cap ; e.g. he lies at watch, at Sir Christopher Wren's discourse, Mr. Robert Hooke's, Dr. William Holder, &c ; putts downe their notions in his Note booke, and then prints it, without owneing the Authors. This frequently, of which they complain. But though he does an injury to the Inventors, he does good to Learning, in publishing such curious notions, which the author (especially Sir Christopher Wren) might never have the leisure to write of himselfe.*

There was one example, however, which appalled Aubrey by its similarity in every detail to his own case. *One Mr. Gerard of Castle Carey in Somerset, collected the Antiquities of that county, Dorset, and that of Devon,* he said, *which I cannot for my life retrive. His Executor had them, whose Estate was seized for debt ; and they utterly lost.* And so, before setting out for Wiltshire to settle his mother's affairs, Aubrey made an elaborate will, although he had nothing to leave except instructions as to the fate of his manuscripts, and in it he charged Robert Hooke with the task of preparing his Wiltshire papers for the press. For to the men of the seventeenth century, their reputation after death was a matter of the utmost concern, and though few of them went so far as Machiavelli in believing that fame was the only immortality of which the individual was capable, the desire for a good and a lasting reputation was so general, that Aubrey recorded with astonishment the reply Charles I made, when Mr. Ross endeavoured to persuade him to pay for the engraving of a manuscript by saying that *it would appeare glorious in historie after his Majestie's death. Pish, sayd He, I care not what they say of me in History when I am dead.*

Aubrey, however, cared most particularly and he eagerly accepted Elias Ashmole's suggestion that he should entrust his manuscripts to the newly founded Ashmolean Museum at Oxford ; an idea with which his friends were not all in favour as the following letter shows. *Mr. Wood,* Aubrey began coldly, *Last Teusday I went to see Mr. Ashmole, whom I found ill. He lately received a letter from Dr. Plot, about the things that I sent to Oxford ; and says that he desired you to send to the Museum,*

but you denyed it, and would not let him see the Catalogue, that I sent. Mr.
Ashmole desired to speake with me about it, and is most outragiously angry ;
and charg'd me to write to you as soon as I could and to order you to putt the
Box in the Museum : for he looks upon you as a Papist, and sayeth so does the
whole Universitie, and there was present at this angry fitt of his, an Oxford
scholar (I thinke his Kinsman) who owned, what Mr. Ashmole sayd. Mr.
Ashmole saies that now there is such care and good method taken, that the
Books in the Museum are more safe than those in the Librarie, or Archives ;
and he says he expects to heare of your being plunder'd, and papers burnt,
as at the Spanish Ambassador's, at Wild house, where were burnt MSS and
Antiquities invaluable, such as are not left in the world : and he further bids
me tell you, that if you shall refuse to deliver the things sent downe by me, to
Oxford, that he will never looke on you as Friend, and will never give a farthing
more to the University of Oxford. Since therefore it is so ordered, I do desire
and appoint you to send my Box forthwith (you may keep the Key) for feare
that all my MSS. &c. should be rifled by the Mobile (which God forbid,
but Mr. E. Ashmole and I doe much feare) besides my Guift will make a
better shew, in the Museum ; than when dispersed in 2 places. I have severall
other MSS. of my own and Mr. Mercator's. That of mine that I most value
is my Idea of Education of Young Gentlemen, which is in a Box as big as that
sent to you ; with choice Grammaticall bookes, ancient and modern, for the
Informator to peruse and study. If I should die here, they will be lost or seized
upon by Mr. Kent's son : if I send them to the Museum, the Tutors would
burn it, for it crosses their Interest exceedingly : if in your hands when you
die your Nephew will stop gunnes with them. I intended the Earl of Abingdon,
but he has now other Fish to fry. I think the Earl of Pembroke would do
best, but had I money to pay an Amanuensis, I would leave a Copie in the
hands of each of those 2 peeres. Tuissimus, J. Aubrey.

All his works, therefore, were deposited in the Ashmolean, except
for *The Minutes of Lives,* which Anthony Wood still kept, and *The
Remaines of Gentilisme and Judaisme,* which Aubrey had finished that
very year, and had dedicated *To His ever honoured Friend Edmund Wylde,
Esqr. as a small token of ancient Friendship.* As if to repay Aubrey for
his sharpness to Anthony Wood, his bequest was no sooner settled
than the museum was robbed, and there vanished among other things
his *Picture in miniature, by Mr. S. Cowper (which at an auction yields* 20
*Guineas) and Archbishop Bancroft's, by Hillyard, the famous Illuminer in
Q. Elizabeth's time.* But his papers were untouched.

It was only fair that Aubrey should see his life-work settled safely
before his death, for he had expended a great deal of energy in rescuing
other people's libraries from dispersal. In 1683, he had attempted
to get the Royal Society or the University of Oxford to purchase the
mathematical collections of his old friend Sir Jonas Moore. Getting
no response from either of these bodies, he had approached Isaac
Newton, but with no more success, for Newton pointed out that
Trinity College had incurred such heavy charges over its new buildings
that the purchase was out of the question for them, and the University
of Cambridge was likely to prove no better prospect, " their chest
being at present very low."

Nor was it books alone that roused the easy-going Aubrey to such
endeavours. When the havoc of the Civil War was succeeded by the

disastrous Fire of London, he redoubled his efforts to preserve the dwindling number of antiquities that still remained. *'Tis pitty that in noblemen's galleries, the names are not writt on or behind the pictures,* he thought, and therefore in his life of Milton he made this note : *Write his name in red letters on his Pictures, with his widowe, to preserve.* In another case, he tried to kill two birds with one stone and failed in both attempts : *Mr. Inigo Jones (Architect to King James I, and to King Charles I) was wont to wayte upon their Majesties when they went their Progress,* he said. *He design'd admirably well : and in these Progresses he drew a great many Prospects of the old Gothick, or ancient Castles, in sheetes of paper. He bought the Mannour of Burley neer Glastonbury (once belonging to it ; but very unfortunate to the late Possessors) where in a large Parlour, I saw these Draughts of Castles : they did furnish the Roome round ; one of them was falln downe, and in a childs hands, which I rescued : and hung it up my selfe. I have often intimated this to our Gravers to make them publick : but I cannot perswade them to it. But had the ingeniose Mr. Wenceslaus Hollar lived, he would have donne it, upon my request. Of these once stately Castles, there is not now a stone left upon a stone.* In many other cases, too, Aubrey came too late to do anything but record the damage already done. *In the Abbey-church of Dowre are two remaynders of mayled and cross-legged monuments,* he reported, *one sayd to be of a Lord Chandois, th'other, the Lord of Eywas-lacy. A little before I sawe them a Mower had taken one of the armes to whett his syth.* This ignorant destruction was bad enough, but the thoughtlessness of the educated classes was even harder to bear : *Franciscus Linus made the Jesuits College at Liège the finest Dialls in the World. The like dialls he made (which resemble something of Candlesticks) in the garden at Whitehall, which were one night, Anno Domini 1674, broken all to pieces (for they were of glasse spheres) by the Earl of Rochester, Lord Buckhurst, Fleetwood Shephard, etc. comeing in from their Revells. What, said the Earl of Rochester, doest thou stand heer to marke time ? Dash they fell to worke. Ther was a watchman alwayes stood there to secure it.*

Aubrey was no blind admirer of old things, however, for he said, *the old windowes of the Church of Clerken-well are of great antiquitie, as appears by their shape, and their uglinesse,* and he recorded with equal care vanishing legends : *The tradition is that the Bell of Lincoln's-Inne was brought from Cales* [Cadiz], *tempore Reginae Elizabethae, plundered in the expedition under the Earl of Essex :* and passing curiosities : *Mr. Emanuel Decretz (Serjeant Painter to King Charles 1st) told me in 1649, that the Catafalco of King James at his funerall (which is a kind of Bed of State, erected in Westminster Abbey, as Robert Earl of Essex had, Oliver Cromwell, and General Monke) was very ingeniosely designed by Mr. Inigo Jones, and that he made the 4 heades of the Cariatides (which bore up the Canopie) of playster of Paris, and made the drapery of them of white Callico, which was very handsome and very cheap, and shewed as well as if they had been cutt out of white marble.* Even the changes in the language were recorded by him, for his book *Villare Anglicanum* is subtitled : *Derivation of English Place names—A Collection of so many British words, as come to my memorie, that are endemized, and now current English : and have escaped the fury of the Saxon Conquest. How these curiosities would be quite forgott,* he added, *did not such idle fellowes as I am putt them downe!*

Now that his works were at last in safe custody, Aubrey set about revising them *so as to speed them to the Presse ;* but as his revision consisted entirely of adding more haphazard notes, they came no nearer to publication until, in 1692, Thomas Tanner, afterwards Bishop of St. Asaph, promised to arrange *The Naturall Historie of Wiltshire* for the printer. " I shall go towards Lavington on Saturday next," the nineteen-year-old Tanner wrote to him. " My principal business is to drive on our Common design, viz. the *Antiquities of Wilt.hire,* which I hope will find encouragement. If it does not I will never undertake anything more for the publick. I am heartily sorry your *Monumenta* meets with no better incouragement in this age, but I like it never the worse for that. It hath been the ill fortune of the best books that they have not borne the Charges of their own impression. It is well known that no Bookseller would give Sir Henry Spelman five pounds in books for his incomparable Glossary, and you know that Sir Walter Raleigh burnt the latter part of his admirable History of the World, because the former had undone the printer. The Christian Scriptures and the Monasticon, volumes now worth old Gold, had never been printed had not the former been carried on by a publick fund, the other by the sole charges of the Editor. I hope to live to see the *Monumenta Britannica* in as good vogue as the best of them." But though Tanner was to live for another forty years, he was not even to see Aubrey's book in print, let alone in vogue. For without a patron to pay for the publishing, few works came out in those days ; and to have a patron often meant interference, as Anthony Wood had found to his cost in his dealings with John Fell. Nor was this the only disadvantage to be encountered, for Aubrey mentions the case of *Thomas Goodwyn, who was a generall Scholar, and had a delicate Witt ; was a great Historian, and an excellent Poet. The Journey into France, crept in Bishop Corbet's poems, was made by him ; by the same token it made him misse of preferment at Court, Mary the Queen-mother remembring how he had abused her brother, the King of France ; which made him to accept of the place at Ludlowe, out of view of the World.* Aubrey, however, was to enjoy neither the advantages nor the disadvantages of the system, and his works remained unpublished for all the world as if he had lived in the days *when the Price of Writing of Manuscripts, before the use of Printing, was xxx shillings per quire.*

The *Monumenta Britannica,* which Tanner mentioned, had had its origin in the command given by Charles II to print an account of Avebury, but Aubrey had proceeded so slowly with the work and had added so many facts about other antiquities that five separate dedications of the book were made, as death took away one hoped-for patron after another, before it even got near the press. Now, however, " Proposals for Printing Monumenta Britannica Written by Mr. John Aubrey, Fellow of the Royal Society " were issued at long last. " The whole Work will consist of about 160 Sheets, and will be Printed in Folio with abundance of Cuts " ran the advertisement, which gave the price as eighteen shillings, nine down and nine on delivery, and assured the public " that the Booke will be printed by Candlemas next." *In the Declension of the Roman Empire,* runs a sample page on the back of the prospectus, *the Britains being drawn away to defend other*

Provinces, their own Country lay open to the Incursion of the Invaders : In that miserable state of things, the Learned Men fled for Refuge into Ireland ; upon which occasion Learning did flourish there a long time ; but the memory of things here *became obliterated. Books perish'd, and Tradition was forgot. The Saxon Conquerors ascribed Works great and strange to the Devil, or some Giants, and handed down to us only Fables. 'Twas in that Deluge of History, the Account of these British Monuments utterly perished ; the Discovery whereof I do here endeavour (for want of written Record) to work out and restore after a kind of Algebraical Method, by compering them that I have seen, one with another and reducing them to a kind of Aequation : to (being but an ill Orator my self) to make the Stones give Evidence for them-selves.* Although this extract sounds enticing, the plan seems to have languished, for the book never appeared. Edmund Gibson, who had seen the manuscript, probably gave the true reason, when he wrote to Thomas Tanner some years later. " There is not in Mr. Aubrey's books what I had expected," he said then. " The accounts of things are so broken and short, the parts so much disordered, and the whole such a mere Rhapsody, that I cannot but wonder how that poor man could entertain any thoughts of a present Impression. They will be serviceable enough, however," he admits, " especially in Counties where Intelligence falls short ; but in the rest, we shall not make much use of them."

In the same year, 1692, another letter passed between John Aubrey and Anthony Wood. *Accidentally I spoke with Mr. Gadbury, who is extremely incens't against you,* it ran. *He sayes that you have printed lyes concerning him.* For the first volume of " Athenae Oxoniensis " had now appeared in London and in it Wood had raked up an old scandal about the astrologer's father, who, according to Aubrey, *when he was a taylor, takes the measure of a young Lady for a gowne, and clappes up a match. He tells me what you have wrote,* Aubrey's letter continues, *and I am sorry for it, for he was civil to you, and was an ingeniose loyall Person.* In October of the same year, he wrote to Wood again : *I shewed your letter to Mr. Gadbury, wherin you tell him that what he desires should be amended as to Himselfe shall be donne in the Appendix to be printed : but he huff't and pish't, saying that your Copies are flown abroad and the Scandalls are irrevocable and that he will have a fling at you in Print to vindicate himselfe.* But Wood remained blind to the indiscretion he had committed. " I wonder at nothing more," he said, " then that Mr. Gadbury should take it amiss of those things that I say of him : for whereas the generalitie of scholars did formerly take him to have been bred an Academician because he was borne at Oxon, and so, consequently, not to be much admired, now their eyes being opened and knowing that his education hath been mechanical they esteeme him a Prodigie of Parts and therefore are much desirous that his picture may hang in the public gallery at the Schooles." This storm was but a foretaste of what was to follow, for with the appearance of Wood's second volume, disaster finally overwhelmed the long collaboration between the two antiquaries.

Now that Anthony Wood's work was published, Aubrey received back from him *The Minutes of Lives,* only to find that the manuscript had been mutilated. *INGRATITUDE,* wrote poor Aubrey on the first of the remaining pages. *This part the second, Mr. Wood haz gelded from page 1 to page 44 and other pages too are wanting wherein are contained Truths, but such as I entrusted no body with the sight of, but himselfe : whom I thought I might have entrusted with my Life. There are severall papers that may cutt my throate. I find too late Memento diffidere* [Take care to distrust] *was a Saying worthy one of the Sages. He hath also embezilled the Index of it—quod N. B. It was stitch't up when I sent it to him. Novemb. 29, 1692.* Aubrey's anxiety was well founded : for Anthony Wood had cut out the lives of James I and the Duke of Monmouth amongst others, and his behaviour to his devoted assistant had been so bitter of late that Aubrey did well to have doubts about the safety of his throat.

The reason for Wood's unforgivable conduct soon became apparent, however, for the second volume of "Athenae Oxoniensis" had no sooner appeared than he found himself surrounded by threats. " Mr. Henry Cruttenden told me," he confided to his Journal, " that in New Coll. common-chamber severall of their fellowes said that I had abused their relations and that when dark nights come they would beat me." Nor was this the worst, for a rumour floated down from London " that the Presbyterians will raise a tax (two hundred thousand pounds) to give to the King that he will hang me." For in his book Wood had not scrupled to tell the truth, particularly if it was unpleasant, and as ill luck would have it, it was a remark that he had copied from Aubrey that precipitated the storm. In his life of Judge Jenkins, Wood had foolishly repeated Aubrey's story about Lord Chancellor Hyde's corruption, and though Hyde had been banished for these very practices twenty-eight years before and had been dead for twenty years, his son, Lord Clarendon, issued a writ against Anthony Wood for libel.

It was this affair that finally changed Wood's attitude towards John Aubrey. Hearne has reported the humorous relationship of their early friendship : " Anthony used to say of him, when he was at the same time in company : Look, yonder goes such a one, who can tell you such and such stories, and I'le warrant Mr. Aubrey will break his neck downstairs rather than miss him." This amiable attitude was now to disappear forever and Aubrey became in Wood's view " roving and magotie-headed, and sometimes little better than crased."

One thing has always been said, though, in Anthony Wood's favour ; that he confined his accusations of Aubrey to his Journal and never mentioned in court the source of the libellous statement, even though his whole defence rested on the fact that " those things that are excepted against are not of the author's invention but what he found in letters sent to him from persons of knowne reputation, of which he is ready at any time to take his oath in any court of judicature. Which letters being at larg written, he for his own security did curtaile and contract them to what they now are without mentioning the name of the person. Yet notwithstanding this they are excepted against." And notwithstanding this, Anthony Wood was fined forty pounds, was expelled from the University and, on the last day of July, 1693, saw his book publicly burnt at Oxford by the common hangman.

But hidden amongst Tanner's papers there lies a letter that passed between Aubrey and Anthony Wood in December, 1692. *All the last week I was ill,* it ran, *but on sunday I went to my Lord Abingdon, who saluted me with a sad aspect, and a sadder Intimation : sc. that he was exceedingly grieved for the Trouble that was comeing upon me : I was mightily surprized : sayd he, the Earl of Clarendon hath told me, that Mr. Wood hath confessed to him, that he had the Libell from me : as also the other informations. I do admire that you should deale so unkindly with me; that have been so faithfull a friend to serve you ever since 1665, as to doe so by me. The Libell was printed, and not uncommon : Could not you have sayd, that you bought it : or had it of George Ent : or some body that is dead—To be short, my Lord is resolved to ruine me : pray let me know by the next post, what 'tis that you have donne against me, that I may be the better enabled to make my Defences. My heart is ready to breake : thus hoping to hear from you I rest, Yours J. Aubrey.* But no reply came : no reply for over eighteen months : and this biographer is confirmed in his opinion of Anthony Wood's treachery.

Early next year, Aubrey deposited his precious *Lives* in the Ashmolean, with special instructions that Anthony Wood was never to know about the bequest, for he still feared the vindictiveness of his late friend. But even so, his kindness of heart did not allow him to upbraid Wood for his shabby treatment of the *Lives,* until over a year after the debacle which he had unwittingly caused ; and then he took the edge off his complaint by suggesting the resumption of their friendship. *Mr. Wood,* he wrote from Boarstall on September 2nd, 1694, *I thought I should have heard from you ere this time. I have been ill ever since I came from Oxford, till within these 5 days, of a Surfeit of Peaches, etc ; so that I was faine to send to Kit White for a good Lusty Vomit. I could not eat a bitt of flesh for six days, but abstinence hath pretty well settled me again. Your unkindnes and choleric humour was a great addition to my ilnes. You know I have allwayes loved you, and never thought I tooke paines enough to serve you : and I was told by severall at Oxford, and so the last yeare, that you can never afford me a good word. You have cutt out a matter of 40 pages out of one of my volumnes, as also the Index : (Was ever any body so unkind ?) and I remember you told me comeing from Hedington, that there were some things in it that would cutt my throat. I thought you so deare a friend that I might have entrusted my life in your hands, and now your unkindnes doth almost break my heart.* Having made this complaint, Aubrey was unable to carry his resentment any farther. *I would have you come the next week,* he continued, *for a fortnight hence Sir John Aubrey goes into Glamorganshire, and will have me with him. You cannot imagine how much your unkindnes vext and discomposed me. So God bless you. Tuissimus, J. A. I would have you come hither as early as you can,* Aubrey added in postscript, *because of perusing the MS. and seeing the gardens, for the afternoon will be taken up with good fellowship.*

This letter at last stirred Anthony Wood into answering Aubrey's previous accusation. " I must tell you," he wrote, " that in your letter dated 3 Dec. 1692 you go forward to plague and disturb my thoughts without examination. At length when you came to towne an yeare after you told me it was a Banter. Now I appeal to all the world whither this was not an unworthy thing that you did never let me know it by letter to comfort my thoughts, only by word of mouth a yeare after and that by accident." After which Anthony Wood upbraids Aubrey on many counts, referring again and again to " your most wicked and silly letter," and proving himself to have been so kindly and faithful friend that this biographer feels bound to reject Wood's version of the affair. Having Aubrey at a disadvantage, however, Wood seized the opportunity to bring up every grievance that had ever occurred to him. Aubrey had deserted him in his trouble, Aubrey had left a book to Trinity College Library that really belonged to him, and, worst of all, in " that rascally letter that had been soaked in a pucket of ale," he had been unjustly accused of cutting up Aubrey's *Lives*. Not content with this written reprimand, Anthony Wood welcomed their suggested meeting as an opportunity to continue the quarrel. " If you bring any body with you," he said ominously, " let him be only a servant, because I have several things to say to you."

And on this note, this strange friendship ended, for no further letters passed between the two, and on November 28th, 1695, Anthony Wood died a solitary and painful death in his attic room at Oxford. *I am extreemely sorrowfull for the death of my dear Friend, and old Correspondent Mr. Anthony Wood,* Aubrey wrote to Tanner when the news reached Llantrithid, *who (though his spleen used to make him chagrin, and to chide me) yet we could not be asunder, and he would alwayes seek me at my Lodgeings with his darke-Lanthorne, which should be a Relick. I hoped that he would have lived, to have given me a cast of his office, in naming the place of my obyt and grave ; which I hope will be here : here is fine red earth, but not deep. I am glad you have all his papers, who will be faithfull to him, and finish what he left undone.*

Aubrey was now in his seventieth year, and having transferred his papers to Thomas Tanner, he at last had the leisure to complete a book for publication. " John Aubrey talkes desperately of putting his *Monumenta Britannica* in the Press," wrote Edmund Gibson at this time, but it was a very different work that was eventually to appear. *My Lord,* runs the dedication to the Earl of Abingdon, *When I enjoyed the Contentment of Solitude in Your pleasant Walks and Gardens at Lavington the last Summer, I reviewed several scattered Papers which had lain by me for several Years ; And then presumed to think, that if they were put together they might be somewhat entertaining : I therefore digested them there in this Order, in which I now present them to Your Lordship. It was my intention to have finished my Description of Wilts (half finished already) and to have Dedicated it to Your Lordship : but My Age is now too far spent for such Undertakings : I have therefore devolved that Task on my Countrey-man, Mr. T. Tanner, who hath Youth to go through with it, and a Genius proper for such an Undertaking. Wherefore, I humbly beseech Your Lordship to accept of this small Offering, as a grateful Memorial of the profound Respect which I have for You, who have for many Years taken me into your Favour and Protection. My Lord, May the Blessed Angels be Your careful Guardians : such are the Prayers of Your Lordship's Most Obliged and Humble Servant, J. Aubrey.*

Aubrey's enduring reputation as a superstitious fool came from this book, the only publication of his long life. For although he said elsewhere, *I know that some will nauseate these old Fables : but I doe profess to regard them as the most considerable pieces of Antiquity, I collect : and that they are to be registred for Posterity, to let them understand the Encroachment of Ignorance on Mankind : and to see what strange Absurdity Man can by Custome and education be brought to believe :* he made no such reservation in regard to this work, which is a hotch-potch of myths and gullibility entitled :—

MISCELLANIES
VIZ.

i. Day-Fatality.	*xii.* Marvels.
ii. Local-Fatality.	*xiii.* Magick.
iii. Ostenta.	*xiv.* Transportation in the Air.
iv. Omens.	*xv.* Visions in a Beril, or Glass.
v. Dreams.	*xvi.* Converse with Angels+Spirits.
vi. Apparitions.	*xvii.* Corps-Candles in Wales.
vii. Voices.	*xviii.* Oracles.
viii. Impulses.	*xix.* Extasie.
ix. Knockings.	
x. Blows Invisible.	*xx.* Glances of { Love. / Envy.
xi. Prophesies.	*xxi.* Second-Sighted-Persons.

Collected by J. Aubrey, Esq ;

Although Aubrey included too large a number of dreary coincidences under these enticing headings, he managed also to bring in many fascinating stories. Some are connected directly with the superstitions of the time : *At Paris, when it begins to Thunder and Lighten,* he says, *they do presently Ring out the great Bell at the Abbey of St. German, which they do believe makes it cease. The like was wont to be done heretofore in Wiltshire ; when it Thundred and Lightned, they did Ring St. Adelm's at Malmesbury Abbey. The curious do say, that the Ringing of Bells exceedingly disturbs Spirits :* and again : *It is a thing very common to nail Horse-shoes on the Thresholds of Doors : Which is to hinder the power of Witches that enter into the House. Most Houses of the West-end of London have the Horse shoe on the Threshold. It should be a Horse-shoe that one finds.* Other passages are purely descriptive. *At Leghorn, and other Ports in Italie, when Shippes arrive, the Courtizans runne to the Mariners with their Lutes and Ghitarres, playing and singing, with their Haire dissheveld, and Breasts naked, to allure them. In like manner at Gosprit, neer Portsmouth, where the Seamen lye, the Towne is full of wanton wenches, and there is never a house but hath a Virginall in it : and (they say) scarce 3 honest women in the Town.*

Near Letterkenny in the County of Donegall, Aubrey says, reverting to superstition, *a party of the Protestants had been surpriz'd sleeping by the Popish-Irish, were it not for several Wrens that just wakned them by dancing and pecking on the Drums as the Enemy were approaching. For this reason the wild Irish mortally hate these Birds to this day, calling them Devils Servants, and killing them wher ever they catch them ; They teach their Children to thrust them full of Thorns : You'll see sometimes on Holidays a whole Parish running like mad-men from Hedg to Hedg a Wren-hunting.* In the chapter on *Impulses,* Aubrey says, *Oliver Cromwell had certainly this Afflatus.*

One that I knew, that was at the Battle of Dunbar, told me that Oliver was carried on with a Divine Impulse ; he did Laugh so excessively as if he had been drunk ; his Eyes sparkled with Spirits. He obtained a great *Victory ; but the Action was said to be contrary to Human Prudence. The same fit of Laughter seiz'd Oliver Cromwell, just before the Battle of Naseby ; as a Kinsman of mine, and a great Favourite of his, Colonel J. P. then present, testifi'd. Cardinal Mezarine said, that he was a lucky Fool.*

In the *Miscellanies* Aubrey was not above showing how some superstitious beliefs could misfire : *I have seen some Rings made for sweet-hearts,* he said, *with a Heart enamelled held between two right hands. See an Epigramme of G. Buchanan on two Rings that were made by Q. Elizabeths appointment, which being layd one upon the other shewed the like figure. The Heart was 2 Diamonds, which joined made the Heart. Q. Eliz. kept one moeitie and sent the other as a Token of her constant Friendship to Mary Queen of Scotts ; but she cutt off her Head for all that.* Nor is Aubrey's irrepressible sense of humour absent, as the following tales show. *This is an old piece of Priest-cheate,* he says. *The Image of the B. Virgin nodded at St. Bernard, and said (id est, the Priests boy with a tube behind the statue) Good morrow Father Bernard. I thanke your Ladyship, qd he, but St. Paul saieth that it is not lawfull for women to speake in the church.* And of his own time, Aubrey reported that *the second Lady of Sr. Walter Long (whither voluntarily, or upon Sr. Walter's desire I have forgott) did make a Solemn Promise to him, on his Death-bed, that she would not marry after his Decease. But not long after, one Sir Somerset Fox, a very Beautiful young Gentleman, did win her Love : so that notwithstanding her Promise aforesaid, she married him at South-wrax-hall. As he lead her by the hand from the Church into the Parlour, the Picture of Sr. Walter, that then hung over the Parlour-dore (the String being eaten off with the rust of the naile) fell down upon her Ladyship, and crack'd in the fall : (it was painted on wood as the fashion was in those days). This made her Ladyship reflect on her Promise, and drew some Tears from her Eyes.*

It is reported concerning the Lord Duffus (in the Shire of Murray) his Predecessors, says Aubrey, *that upon a time, when he was walking abroad in the Fields near to his own House, he was suddenly carried away, and found the next Day at Paris in the French King's Cellar with a Silver Cup in his Hand ; that being brought into the King's Prescence and question'd by him, Who he was ? And how he came thither ? He told his name, his Country, and the place of his Residence, and that on such a Day of the Month (which proved to be the Day immediately preceeding) being in the Fields, he heard the noise of a Whirl-wind, and of Voices crying Horse and Hattock (this is the Word which the Fairies are said to use when they remove from any place) whereupon he cried (Horse and Hattock) also, and was immediately caught up, and transported through the Air, by the Fairies to that place, where after he had drunk heartily he fell a sleep, and before he awoke, the rest of the Company were gone, and had left him in the posture wherein he was found. It's said, the King gave him the Cup which was found in his Hand, and dis-miss'd him.* But not all *Transportation in the Air* was as uneventful as this, and Aubrey has left a record of one of the earliest air disasters, albeit an indirect one : *A Gentleman of my Acquaintance was in Portugal, Anno 1655,* he says, *when one was Burnt by the Inquisition for being brought thither from Goa in East India, in the Air, in an incredible short time.* This subject always fascinated Aubrey, and he mentioned many other cases of flying in the course of his works. Indeed he went further still, for amongst his inventions is the following note : *Fill or force in smoake into a Bladder and try if the Bladder will not be carryed up in the Ayre. If it is so, several bladders may drawe a man up into the ayre a certain hight, as the Holly-berrys arise to the middle of water in a glass. Memorandum try to what hight they will ascend in a deep vessell, and also try other Berryes if any will doe so.* He even proposed building a flying machine, but wise man that he was, he was going to take no risk without a parachute : *Memorandum to propose that Mr. Packer sends to Norfolk or Suffolke to the gentleman that hath with much curiosity measured the feathers in the wings of severall Birds and taken the proportions of them and the weight of their bodies, and to send to Mr. Francis Potter for his notions of Flying and of being safely delivered upon the ground from great Heights with a sheet, etc.*

This book being finished, or as nearly finished as anything Aubrey ever did (for even the printed book is full of gaps and references and hints for further research) he set out once more upon his travels. But in his seventy-second year he was growing very infirm : *January 5th* 169¾, he had written three years before, *an apoplectick fitt, circiter* 4ʰ. *P.M. :* and as he passed through his beloved Oxford on his way to Lady Long's in Wiltshire, death at last struck him down.

Aubrey had no dread of death : *If Solomon counts the day of ones death better than the day of ones birth,* he had said in his *Miscellanies, there can be no Objection why that also may not be reckoned amongst ones Remarkable and Happy days :* and his own sudden release from life would no doubt have pleased him, for he was ever concerned at the miseries of old age. Speaking of *Gideon de Laune, Apothecary to Mary the Queen mother, a very wise man, and as a signe of it left an estate of 80,000 pounds,* he said, *Sir William Davenant was his great acquaintance and told me of him, and that after his returne into England he went to visit him, being then octogenary, and very decrepit with the Gowt, but had his sight and under-standing. He had a place made for him in the Kitchen chimney ; and, non obstante he was master of such an estate, Sir William sawe him slighted not only by his daughter-in-lawe, but by the cooke-mayd, which much affected him— misery of old age.* And if the rich were treated thus, how much worse would be the case of a penniless gentleman, for Aubrey was haunted by the thought of John Rushworth, who like himself was an historian and something of a drunkard. *Yesterday I saw Mr. Rushworth,* he had written to Anthony Wood in 1689, *which was a great mortification. He hath quite lost his memory with drinking Brandy : remembred nothing of you, etc. His Landlady wiped his nose like a child. He was about 83, onwards to 84. He had forgot his children before he died.*

But however grateful Aubrey would have been to die while he was still vigorous, he would have grieved to know that his passing would go unnoticed. For though he was buried by his young friend Thomas Tanner, now Fellow of All Souls, no tomb was erected, despite the design and the instructions that he had prepared so care-fully. *I would desire that this Inscription should be a stone about the bigness of a royal sheet of paper scilicet, about 2 foot square. Mr. Reynolds of Lambeth, Stonecutter (Foxhall) who married Mr. Elias Ashmole's Widow will help me to a Marble as square as an imperial sheet of paper for 8 shillings.*

Many years before, Aubrey had discovered a tomb called Gawen's Barrow on his farm at Broad Chalk. *I never was so sacralegious as to disturbe, or rob his urne,* he said. *Let his Ashes rest in peace : but I have oftentimes wish't, that my Corps might be interred by it : but the Lawes Ecclesiastick denie it. Our Bones in consecrated ground never lie quiet : and in London once in ten yeares (or thereabout) the Earth is carried to the Dung-wharf.* But though Aubrey was not buried in Wiltshire, at least his desire to lie undisturbed in his grave was granted. For the very time and place of his burial was forgotten, and not for one hundred and fifty years was an entry uncovered in the Register of the Church of St. Mary Magdalene—" 1697, JOHN AUBERY A Stranger was Buryed June 7th."

And even now there is no memorial to this famous man at Oxford, save his life's work safely lodged in Sir Thomas Bodley's Library across the way.

These remains of his, which were then in the Ashmolean Museum, disprove once for all the accusation that John Aubrey frittered his life away. For even though several volumes of his manuscripts have vanished since his death, there still remain nine major works to his credit, besides innumerable others less substantial.

Many scholars, taking their cue from Anthony Wood, have nonetheless dismissed Aubrey as of little importance : but the fault lies much more in their misunderstanding of his talents, than in his lack of them. For they have persisted in looking on Aubrey as an historian, and then running him down for his shortcomings in that field : whereas if one accepts James Bryce's dictum that " the secret of historical composition is to know what to neglect," it is obvious that Aubrey cannot be considered as an historian, for his genius was for collection, rather than selection. But a poor historian may be nonetheless a fine historical scholar, and the vividness of his stories and the pith of his quotations shows the very real skill and scholarship that Aubrey applied to his task. For though he has often been condemned for his unreliability, the charge is once again based on muddled thinking : he was sometimes inaccurate, it is true but he was never untruthful, and the distinction is a most important one. For Aubrey's belief in astrology in no wise affected his trustworthiness on other subjects, as Malone pointed out so clearly in the next century. " If the representation attempted to be given of this ingenious and unfortunate gentleman were just and well founded," he said, " if it were true that every one who is weak in one place must necessarily be weak in all ; that all those persons who in the last century were idle enough to put their faith in judicial astrology; and to give credit to preternatural appearances of the dead, were fools ; and their judgement or testimony of no value on any subject whatever, however unconnected with these weaknesses ; then, in this large list of ninnies,

[c]

must we class, with Mr. Aubrey, the accomplished and literate Charles the First ; the grave and judicious Clarendon ; the witty Duke of Buckingham ; the fertile and ingenious Dryden ; and many other names of equal celebrity :—they must all ' bench by his side,' and must be set down as persons not capable of forming a true judgement on any matter whatsoever presented to them, and wholly unworthy of credit." Aubrey summed up his own position perfectly when he wrote in his life of Hobbes : *But one may say of him, as one sayes of Jos. Scaliger, that where he erres, he erres so ingeniosely, that one had rather erre with him then hitt the mark with Clavius.*

No one, however, has tried to deny Aubrey's skill as a writer : and when he himself asked, *Is my English style well enough ?* even Anthony Wood felt bound to answer " 'Tis well," instead of falling hard upon him as he usually did for his queries. " You should never ask these questions, but do them out of hand. You have time enough," was a more typical response.

Time, which is as kind to books as it is to wine, has even added to the quality of Aubrey's style ; for the two and a half centuries that have passed since his death have caused Aubrey's work to mature in two separate ways. " There is no beauty that hath not some strangeness in the proportion," Bacon has said and it is in this direction that the years have had their first effect. Words, no less than men, have a history of their own, and in reading Aubrey after so great a lapse of time, the sharpness of every phrase and sentence is particularly striking. Unblunted by use, bare of acquired meanings and monotonous echoes, the words affect us with the freshness of a foreign tongue, and like a foreign language, they make everything seem doubly significant. The second effect of time is quite different. *It is said of Antiquaries, they wipe off the mouldinesse they digge, and remove the rubbish,* Aubrey remarked disapprovingly, and the trivialities that he therefore insisted, against the advice of all his friends, on including in his works, have now become their greatest strength. As he moves slowly through the darkness of his vanished century, bringing one person after another into a ring of light, the contemporary details, which he had jotted down so casually, bring the very noise of the seventeenth century into our ears. Through him one gets the most vivid sense of the presence of the past, of that feeling which Rossetti summed up when he wrote :

> " As much as in a hundred years she's dead
> Yet is today the day on which she died."

For Aubrey's writing was addressed not to the mind alone, but to the imagination, and the unerring skill with which he chose just that episode in a man's life when his personality was most extravagantly in bloom, gives even the shortest of his biographies a vividness which has never been excelled. *Thomas Fuller,* he says, *was of a middle stature ; strong sett ; curled haire ; a very working head, in so much that, walking and meditating before dinner, he would eate-up a penny loafe, not knowing that he did it. His naturall memorie was very great, to which he added the Art of Memorie : he would repeat to you forwards and backwards all the signes from Ludgate to Charing-crosse.* And his technique was so perfect that he was able to render precisely the effect that he wished to produce, even in a single sentence. *William Cartwright's son having many children lives not handsomely and haz lost his Learning,* he says, and similar examples of his skill are unending :—*Mr. Philips, author of Montelion and Don Juan Lamberto, is very happy at Jiggish Poetry and Gypsies and Ballads—Mariana Morgan. She is a swidging lustie woman—Nicholas Mercator is of a soft temper, of great temperance (amat Veneram aliquantum) : of a prodigious invention, and will be acquainted (familiarly) with no body—Mr. Gore. He is a fidling peevish fellow—Thomas Willis, M.D. was middle stature : darke brindle haire (like a red pig) stammered much—the Duke of Monmouth's mother : Mrs. Lucy Walters, who could deny no body—Robert Greville, Lord Brookes, was killed at the Siege of Lichfield, March the 2d (St. Chad's day, to whom the Church is dedicated) 1643 by a Minister's sonne, born deafe and dumbe, out of the church. He was armed cap à pied ; only his Bever was open—William Sanderson dyed at Whitehall (I was then there) : went out like a spent candle : died before Dr. Holder could come to him with the Sacrament—William Outram was a tall spare leane pale consumptive man ; wasted himself much, I presume, by frequent preaching—Sir Francis Stuart was a Sea-captaine and (I thinke) he was one Summer, a Vice or Rere-Admirall. He was a learned Gentleman, and one of the Club at the Mermayd, in Fryday street, with Sir Walter Ralegh, etc, of that Sodalitie : Heroes and Witts of that time—Richard Martin, Recorder of London, was a very handsome man, a gracefull speaker, facetious, and well-beloved. I thinke he dyed of a merry Symposiaque with his fellow-Witts. He was Recorder but a moneth before his death—George Sandys, Poet, lies buried in the Chancel neer the dore on the south side, but without any remembrance or stone : which is pitty so sweet a Swan should lye so ingloriously.*

Aubrey's skill was so great, in fact, that he could conjure a living being out of a mere list of facts. *Mrs. Abigail Sloper borne at Broad Chalke, near Salisbury, A.D. 1648. Pride ; lechery ; ungratefull to her father ; maried ; runne distracted ; recovered.* And again : *Richard Stokes, M.D. His father was Fellow of Eaton College. He was bred there and at King's College. Scholar to Mr. W. Oughtred for Mathematiques (Algebra). He made himselfe mad with it, but became sober again, but I feare like a crackt-glasse. Became a Roman-catholique : maried unhappily at Liege, dog and catt, etc. Became a Sott. Dyed in Newgate, Prisoner for debt April 1681.*

As the stories lengthen, the impression becomes ever clearer. *John Partridge, the son of an honest waterman at Putney in Surrey. He was taught to read, and a little to write. He was bound Apprentice to a Shoemaker ; where he was kept hard to his Trade. At 18 he gott him a Lillie's Grammar, and Goldman's Dictionary, and a Latin Bible, and Ovid's Metamorphoses. He is of indefatigable industrie and in a few yeares he made himself a competent master of the Latin tongue, well enough to reade any Astrologicall book, and quickly became a master of that Science. He then studyed the Greek tongue, and also the Hebrew, to neither of which he is a stranger. He then studyed good Authors in Physique, and intends to make that his Profession and Practyse : but is yet (1680) a shoemaker in Convent Garden—Mr. Attorney Generall Noy was a great Lawyer and a great Humorist. There is a world of merry stories of him. A Countrey clowne asked for a good Inne, and he bids him ride into Lincoln's Inne, and asked if his Horse went to hay or to grasse. He caused the Breeches of a Bencher of Lincolne's Inne to be taken-in by a Tayler and made him believe that he had the Dropsie. Another time Noy and Pine of Lincolne's Inne went afoot to Barnet with clubbes in their hands, like countrey-fellowes. They went to the Red Lyon Inne; the people of the house were afrayd to trust them, fearing they might not pay—Richard Meriton: his true name was Head. He had been amongst the Gipsies. He looked like a knave with his gogling eies. He could transforme himselfe into any shape. Brake 2 or 3 times. Was at last a Bookeseller in Little Britaine, or towards his later end. He maintained himselfe by Scribbling: 20s. per sheet. He was drowned goeing to Plymouth by long Sea about 1676, being about 50 yeares of age—Saint Dunstan. He was a Somersetshire Gentleman. He was a great Chymist. The storie of his pulling the Devill by the nose with his tongues in his Laboratorie, was famous in church-windowes. Meredith Lloyd had, about the beginning of the Civill Warres, a MS. of this Saint's concerning Chymistrey, and sayes that there are severall MSS. of His up and downe in England. He could make a fire out of Gold, with which he could sett any combustible matter on fire at a great distance. Meredith Lloyd tells me that, three or 400 yeares ago, Chymistry was in a greater perfection, much, then now; their proces was then more Seraphique and Universall: now they looke only after medicines.* The mediæval hunt for the Philosopher's Stone had only recently been abandoned, however. Even in the previous century, Aubrey reported, *Thomas Charnock attained the secret from his master at Salisbury close, who dying left his worke with him. He lost it by fireing his Tabernacle on a New yeare's day. About this time being 28 yeares of Age, he learned the secret againe of the Prior of Bathe. He continued it nine monthes; was within a month of his reckoning; the crowe's head began to appeare black.* But once again the elusive secret escaped his grasp, for a friend told Aubrey " that he kept a fire in, divers yeares; that his daughter lived with him; that once he was gone forth, and by her neglect (whome he trusted it with in his abscence) the fire went out and so all his worke was lost: the Brazen head was very neare comeing to speake, but so was he disappointed."

Sometimes Aubrey helped out one of his purely factual lives with a single story, and together they provide the complete portrait of a man. *Sir Mathew Hale, Judge,* he wrote, 1609, *natus November 1ˢᵗ in the evening, his father then being at his prayers.* 1640, *maried the first time.* (*He was a great Cuckold.*) 1656, *His second mariage to his servant Mayd, Mary.* 1660, *made Lord Chief Baron.* 1671, *Lord Chiefe Justice of England,* 18 *May.* 1676, *Christmas day, he dyed.* I remember, Aubrey told Anthony Wood some years later, *about 1646 (or 1647) that Mr. John Maynard (now Sir John, and serjeant) came into Middle Temple hall, from Westminster-hall, weary with business, and hungry, when we had newly dined. He sate-downe by Mr. Bennet Hoskyns (the only son of Serjeant Hoskyns, the Poet) since Baronet, and some others; who having made an end of their Commons, fell unto various Discourse, and what was the meaning of the Text (Rom. v. 7.) 'For a just man one would dare to die; but for a good man one would willingly die.' They askt Mr. Maynard what was the difference between a just man and a good man. He was beginning to eate, and cryed:—Hoh! you have eaten your dinners, and now have leasure to discourse; I have not. He had eate but a Bitt or two when he reply'd:—I'le tell you the difference presently : serjeant Rolle is a just man, and Mathew Hale is a good man ; and so fell to make an end of his dinner. And there could not be a better interpretation of this Text. For serjeant Rolle was just, but by nature penurious ; and his wife made him worse : Mathew Hale was not only just, but wonderfully Charitable and open handed, and did not sound a trumpet neither, as the Hypocrites doe.*

The same Serjeant figures in one of Aubrey's other stories. *The Lady Hele gave by her Will 800 pounds per annum to be layd out for Charitable Uses and by the advice and prudence of Serjeant Maynard. He did order it according to the best of his understanding, and yet he sayd that he haz lived to see every one of these Benefactions abused.* Mankind, even then, was apt to treat a favour as a right, as the following unhappy tale shows only too clearly. *Madam Curtin, a good Fortune of 3000 pounds, daughter to Sir William Curtin, the great Merchant, lately married her footman, who, not long after marriage, beates her, getts her money, and ran away :* a double disaster for the poor lady, for even in those days servants were almost as hard to come by as another fortune. *The dayly concurse of Servants out of the Country to London, makes Servants Wages deare in the Countrey, and makes scarcity of Labourers,* Aubrey complained angrily. *Mr. Fabian Philips affirmes to me that when he came first to London sc. 1619, an ordinary servant-mayds wages was but sixteen shillings per annum and now tis 3, or 4 pounds per annum.*

So unchanging are the troubles of the human race when looked at by a contemporary, a fact which Aubrey recognised only too well. *Mr. William Prynne's advice to me for the reading of our English Historie,* he had recorded carefully, *was to read the Authors, that wrote of their owne Time.* Unless we look at the past through its own eyes, we can be hopelessly misled by the differences in emphasis. For the law of perspective seems to work contrariwise down the centuries : the figures grow larger as they walk away. But as Aubrey leads us amongst his friends and we find bawdy verses written on Philip Sidney's famous death, or see Sir Walter Raleigh discomfited at dinner by his son and catch the poet Suckling cheating at cards, the heroic figures lose their formal pose, and we see them once again as living men.

Aubrey's were the first biographies that did not point a moral ; in fact, they were really a record of his unselfconscious gossip with his friends. For he would have agreed with Hazlitt, who liked " a friend the better for having faults that one can talk about," and he had, like W. H. Mallock, " the very highest opinion of scandal. It is founded on the most sacred of things—that is, Truth, and it is built up by the most beautiful of things—that is, Imagination." But Aubrey was so kind a man that his gossip rarely turned to scandal, and his wit, in Disraeli's phrase, was excessively good-natured, and, like champagne, not only sparkled, but was sweet. *Will this not give offence?* Aubrey asked on more than one occasion, to be answered by Anthony Wood : " Perhaps no." John Ray, however, offered more detailed advice : " Whatever you may conceive may give Offence, may by the wording of it be so softned and sweetned as to take off the Edge of it, as Pills are gilded to make them less ungrateful."

In the letter which Aubrey attached to *the Minutes of Lives,* when he first sent them to Anthony Wood in 1680, he fully explained his aims and intentions. *Sir !* he said then, *I have, according to your desire, putt in writing these Minutes of Lives tumultuarily, as they occurr'd to my thoughts or as occasionally I had information of them. They may easily be reduced into order at your leisure by numbring them with red figures, according to time and place, &c.* 'Tis a Taske that I never thought to have undertaken till you imposed it upon me, sayeing that I was fitt for it by reason of my generall acquaintance, having now not only lived above a halfe a Centurie of yeares in the world, but have also been much tumbled up and downe in it which hath made me much knowne ; besides the moderne advantage of Coffee-howses in this great Citie, before which men knew not how to be acquainted, but with their owne Relations, or societies. I might add that I come of a longaevous race, by which meanes I have imped some feathers of the wings of Time, for severall Generations ; which does reach high. When I first began, I did not thinke I could have drawne it out to so long a Thread.*

I here lay-downe to you (out of the conjunct friendship between us) the Trueth, and, as neer as I can and that religiously as a Poenitent to his Confessor, nothing but the trueth : the naked and plaine trueth, which is here exposed so bare that the very pudenda are not covered, and affords many passages that would raise a Blush in a young Virgin's cheeke. So that after your perusall, I must desire you to make a Castration (as Raderus to Martial) and to sowe-on some Figge-leaves—i.e. to be my Index expurgatorius.

What uncertainty doe we find in printed Histories ? they either treading too neer on the heeles of trueth that they dare not speake plaine, or els for want of intelligence (things being antiquated) become too obscure and darke ! I doe not here repeat any thing already published (to the best of my remembrance) and I fancy my selfe all along discourseing with you ; alledgeing those of my Relations and acquaintance (as either you knew or have heerd of) ad faciendam Fidem : so that you make me to renew my acquaintance with my old and deceased Friends, and to rejuvenescere (as it were) which is the pleasure of old men. 'Tis pitty that such minutes had not been taken 100 yeares since or more : for want wherof many worthy men's Names and Notions are swallowd-up in oblivion ; as much as these also would have been, had it not been through your Instigation : and perhaps this is one of the usefullest pieces that I have scribbeld.

I remember one sayeing of Generall Lambert's, that ' the best of men are but men at the best ' ; of this, you will meet with divers examples in this rude and hastie collection. Now these Arcana are not fitt to lett flie abroad, till about 30 yeares hence, he concludes, *for the author and the Persons (like Medlars) ought to be rotten first.*

The measure of his success is in the following pages, and is complete. For Aubrey had the rare gift of creating, and not just recording, life, and he has himself summed up his achievement in words that cannot be bettered : *These Remaines are tanquam Tabulata Naufragy* [like fragments of a shipwreck] *that after the Revolution of so many Years and Govenments have escaped the Teeth of Time and (which is more dangerous) the Hands of mistaken Zeale. So that the retriving of these forgotten Things from Oblivion in some sort resembles the Art of a Conjuror, who makes those walke and appeare that have layen in their graves many hundreds of yeares : and to represent as it were to the eie, the places, Customes and Fashions, that were of old Times.*

AUBREY'S BRIEF LIVES

GEORGE ABBOT

[Born 1562. Archbishop of Canterbury. Educated at Guildford Grammar School and Balliol College, Oxford. In 1592 he was appointed private chaplain to Lord Buckhurst, the Chancellor of the University, and in 1597 he became Master of University College, where he wrote for his pupils *A Briefe Description of the whole World,* which included an account of America. He was an extreme Puritan and, besides accusing Laud of Papacy and heresy, he burnt religious pictures in the market-place. His pamphleteering made him unpopular at Oxford when he was Vice-Chancellor, and in 1605 he committed one hundred and forty undergraduates to prison for sitting *with their hats on* in his presence at St. Mary's Church. He revised the New Testament for the *Authorised Version.* Having won James I's approval by his efforts to re-establish episcopacy in Scotland, he was made Bishop of Coventry and Lichfield in 1609, and was translated to London in 1610. The next year, Secretary Calvert remarked : *By a strong north wind coming out of Scotland, Abbot was blown over the Thames to Lambeth.* As Archbishop of Canterbury, Abbot continued his struggle against Arminianism, burning two members of that faith and torturing another. He lost favour by his opposition to the Countess of Essex's divorce, but, having re-established his position in 1615 by the introduction of George Villiers (later Duke of Buckingham) at Court, he seized the opportunity to make his elder brother Bishop of Salisbury. In 1621, he accidentally shot a gamekeeper with a cross-bow while hunting, and though he settled £20 a year on the keeper's widow, *which soon procured her another husband,* and was also formally pardoned by the King, the Bishops Elect, of whom Laud was one, refused to be consecrated by him. In 1627 he was stripped of all authority by Charles I, and although, when he was restored to favour in 1628, the other prelates, who were *gaping after his Benefice,* were warned that *his Grace perhaps may eat the Goose which shall graze upon his grave,* he never again took any part in affairs of State, but lived in retirement until his death in 1633.]

WHEN Arch-Bishop Abbot's Mother (a poor Cloath-worker's Wife in Gilford) was with Child of him, she did long for a Jack or Pike, and she dreamt that if she should Eat a Jack, her Son in her Belly should be a *great Man.* Upon this she was indefatigable to satisfy her Longing, as well as her Dream. She first enquir'd out for this Fish : but the next Morning, goeing with her Payle to the River-side (which runneth by the Howse, now an Ale-house, the Signe of the 3 Mariners) to take up some Water, a good Jack accidentally came into her Payle. She took up the much desir'd Banquet, dress'd it, and devour'd it almost all her selfe, or very neare. This odd Affair made no small Noise in the Neighbourhood, and the Curiosity of it made severall People of Quality offer themselves to be Sponsors at the Baptismal Fount when she was deliver'd. This their Poverty accepted joyfully, and three were chosen, who maintained him at School, and University afterwards, his father not being able. This is generally recieved for a trueth.

It was Bred up a Scholar in the Town, and by degrees, came to be Arch-Bishop of Canterbury. Old Nightingale was his servant, and weepes when he talkes of him. Every one that knew, loved him. He was sometimes Cholerique.

THOMAS ALLEN

[Born 1542. Mathematician. Educated at Trinity College, Oxford. Bachelor of Arts 1563. Fellow 1565. Master of Arts 1567. He obtained the patronage of the Earl of Northumberland, but refused the offer of a bishopric from the Earl of Leicester, as he preferred a life of retirement. He was described by Fuller as having succeeded to the skill and scandal of Friar Bacon. Died 1632.]

MR. ALLEN was a very cheerfull, facetious man, and every body loved his company, and every Howse on their *Gaudie-dayes* were wont to invite him.

The great Dudley, Earle of Leicester, made use of him for casting of Nativities, for he was the best Astrologer of his time. Queen Elizabeth sent for him to have his advice about the new Star that appeared in the Swan or Cassiopeia (but I think the Swan) to which he gave his Judgement very learnedly.

In those darke times, Astrologer, Mathematician, and Conjurer were accounted the same things ; and the vulgar did verily beleeve him to be a Conjurer. He had a great many Mathematicall Instruments and Glasses in his Chamber, which did also confirme the ignorant in their opinion, and his servitor (to impose on Freshmen and simple people) would tell them that sometimes he should meet the Spirits comeing up his staires like Bees. Now there is to some men a great Lechery in Lying, and imposing on the understandings of beleeving people, and he thought it for his credit to serve such a Master.

He was generally acquainted, and every long Vacation he rode into the Countrey to visitt his old Acquaintance and Patrones, to whom his great learning, mixt with much sweetnes of humour, rendred him very welcome. One time being at Hom Lacy in Herefordshire, at Mr. John Scudamore's (grand-father to the Lord Scudamor) he happened to leave his Watch in the Chamber windowe. (Watches were then rarities.) The maydes came in to make the Bed, and hearing a thing in a case cry *Tick, Tick, Tick,* presently concluded that that was his Devill, and tooke it by the String with the tongues, and threw it out of the windowe into the Mote (to drowne the Devill). It so happened that the string hung on a sprig of an elder that grew out of the Mote, and this confirmed them that 'twas the Devill. So the good old Gentleman gott his Watch again.

LANCELOT ANDREWES

[Born 1555. Divine. Sometime Dean of Westminster and Chaplain-in-ordinary to Queen Elizabeth. Under James I, he rose into great favour and was made successively Bishop of Chichester, of Ely and, in 1618, of Winchester. He attended the Hampton Court Conference and was general editor of the Authorised Version of the Bible. Bishop Andrewes was a man of the very greatest learning and it is said that the awe of his presence was wont to restrain King James from that unseemly levity in which he was rather too prone to indulge. Died 1626.]

LANCELOT ANDREWES, Lord Bishop of Winton, was borne in London; went to Schoole at Merchant Taylors schoole. Mr. Mulcaster was his schoolemaster, whose picture he hung in his Studie.

Old Mr. Sutton, a very learned man in those dayes, of Blandford St. Maries, Dorset, was his school fellow, and sayd that Lancelot Andrewes was a great long boy of 18 yeares old at least before he went to the University.

The Puritan faction did begin to increase in those dayes, and especially at Enamuel College. This party had a great mind to drawe in this learned young man, whom (if they could make theirs) they knew would be a great honour to them. They carried themselves outwardly with great sanctity and strictnesse. They preached up very strict keeping and observing the Lord's day: made, upon the matter, damnation to breake it, and that 'twas less Sin to kill a man. Yet these Hypocrites did bowle in a private green at their colledge every Sunday after Sermon; and one of the Colledge (a loving friend to Mr. L. Andrewes) to satisfie him, one time lent him the Key of a Private back dore to the bowling green, on a Sunday evening, which he opening, discovered these zealous Preachers with their Gownes off, earnest at play. But they were strangely surprised to see the entry of one that was not of the Brotherhood.

There was then at Cambridge a good fatt Alderman that was wont to sleep at Church, which the Alderman endeavoured to prevent but could not. Well! this was preached against as a signe of Reprobation. The good man was exceedingly troubled at it, and went to Andrewes his Chamber to be satisfied in point of Conscience. Mr. Andrewes told him, that it was an ill habit of Body, not of Mind, and that it was against his Will; advised him on Sundays to make a more sparing meale, and to mend it at Supper. The Alderman did so, but Sleepe comes on again for all that, and was preached at; comes againe to be resolved with Teares in his eies. Andrewes then told him he would have him make a good heartie meal as he was wont to doe, and presently take out his full sleep. He did so, came to St. Maries, where the Preacher was prepared with a Sermon to damne all who slept at Sermon, a certain signe of Reprobation. The good Alderman, having taken his full nap before, lookes on the Preacher all Sermon time, and spoyled the design. But I should have sayd that Andrewes was most extremely spoken against and preached against for offering to assoile or excuse a sleeper in sermon time. But he had learning and witt enough to defend himselfe.

His good learning quickly made him known in the University, and also to King James, who much valued him for it, and advanced him, and at last made him Bishop of Winchester: which Bishoprick he ordered with great Prudence as to government of the Parsons, preferring of ingeniose persons that were staked to poore livings and did *delitescere*. He made it his Enquiry to find out such men. Amongst severall others (whose names have escaped my memorie) Nicholas Fuller (he wrote *Critica Sacra*), Minister of Allington, neer Amesbury in Wilts, was one. The Bishop sent for him, and the poor man was afrayd and knew not what hurt he had donne. Makes him sitt downe to Dinner and, after the Desert, was brought in, in a dish, his Institution and Induction, or the donation of a Prebend; which was his way.

He dyed at Winchester house in Southwark, and lies buried in a Chapell at St. Mary Overies, where his Executors have erected (but I beleeve according to his Lordship's will, els they would not have layed out 1000 pounds) a sumptuose Monument for Him. ·

He had not that smooth way of Oratory, as now. It was a shrewd and severe animadversion of a Scotish Lord, who, when King James asked him how he liked Bp. A.'s sermon, said that he was learned, but he did play with his Text, as a Jack-an-apes does, who takes up a thing and tosses and playes with it, and then he takes up another, and playes a little with it. Here's a pretty thing, and there's a pretty thing!

[7]

FRANCIS BACON: VISCOUNT ST. ALBANS

[Born 1561. Philosopher and statesman. He went through the various steps of the legal profession, entered Parliament in 1584, and then wrote papers on public affairs, including *A Letter of Advice to Queen Elizabeth* urging strong measures against the Catholics. He made the acquaintance of the Earl of Essex, who treated him with generosity and endeavoured to advance him in his career; nevertheless, having been appointed to investigate the causes of Essex's revolt in 1601, he was largely responsible for the Earl's conviction. The accession of James I gave a favourable turn to Bacon's fortunes and he was knighted in 1603; becoming Solicitor-General in 1607, Attorney-General in 1613, Lord Keeper in 1617, Lord Chancellor and Baron Verulam in 1618, and Viscount St. Albans in 1621. In the same year, a Parliamentary Committee on the Administration of the Law charged him with corruption under twenty-three counts; and so clear was the evidence that he made no attempt at defence. He was sentenced to a fine of £40,000; to be committed to the Tower during the King's pleasure (which was that he should be released in a few days); to be perpetually banished from Court; and to be incapable of holding office or sitting in Parliament ever again. The remaining years of his life were spent in literary and philosophical work. It was Bacon's ambition to create a new system of philosophy, based on a right interpretation of nature, to replace that of Aristotle; and his development of inductive philosophy did in fact revolutionise future thought, for he did more than anyone else to free the intellect from preconceived notions and to direct it to the unbiased study of facts. He wrote *The Advancement of Learning, The History of Henry the Seventh, The New Atlantis, Maxims of the Law* and his *Essays*. Bacon died in 1626, leaving debts of £22,000. Pope described him as *the wisest, brightest, meanest of mankind*.]

IN his Lordship's prosperity, Sir Fulke Grevil, Lord Brooke, was his great Friend and acquaintance; but when he was in disgrace and want, he was so unworthy as to forbid his Butler to let him have any more small Beer, which he had often sent for, his stomach being nice, and the small beere of Gray's Inne not liking his pallet. This has donne his memorie more dishonour then Sir Philip Sidney's friendship engraven on his monument hath donne him Honour.

Richard, Earle of Dorset, was a great admirer and friend

of the Lord Chancellor Bacon, and was wont to have Sir Thomas Billingsley along with him, to remember and to putt downe in writing my Lord's sayings at Table.

Mr. Ben Johnson was one of his friends and acquaintance, as doeth appeare by his excellent verses on his Lordship's birthday, and in his *Underwoods,* where he gives him a Character, and concludes that about his time and within his view were borne all the Witts that could honour a Nation or helpe studie.

The learned and great Cardinal Richelieu was a great admirer of the Lord Bacon.

He came often to Sir John Danvers at Chelsey. Sir John told me that when his Lordship had wrote *The History of Henry* 7, he sent the Manuscript copie to him to desire his opinion of it before 'twas printed. Qd. Sir John, Your Lordship knowes that I am no Scholar. 'Tis no matter, said my Lord : I knowe what a Schollar can say ; I would know what you can say. Sir John read it, and gave his opinion what he misliked (which I am sorry I have forgott) which my Lord acknowledged to be true, and mended it ; Why, said he, a Scholar would never have told me this.

Mr. Thomas Hobbes was beloved by his Lordship, who was wont to have him walke with him in his delicate groves where he did meditate : and when a notion darted into his mind, Mr. Hobbs was presently to write it downe, and his Lordship was wont to say that he did it better then any one els about him ; for that many times, when he read their notes he scarce understood what they writt, because they understood it not clearly themselves.

In short, all that were great and good loved and honoured him. (Sir Edward Coke, Lord Chiefe Justice, alwayes envyed him, and would be undervalueing his Lawe, as you may find in my Lord's lettres, and I knew old Lawyers that remembred it.)

He was Lord Protector during King James's Progresse into Scotland, and gave Audiences in great State to Ambassadors in the Banquetting-house at Whitehall.

The Aviary at Yorke House was built by his Lordship ; it did cost 300 pounds.

At every meale, according to the season of the yeare, he had his Table strewed with Sweet Herbes and Flowers, which he sayd did refresh his spirits and memorie.

When his Lordship was at his Country-house at Gorhambery, St. Albans seemed as if the Court were there, so Nobly did He live. His servants had Liveries with his Crest (a Boare) ; his Watermen were more imployed by Gentlemen then any other. even the King's.

King James sent a Buck to him, and he gave the keeper fifty pounds.

He was wont to say to his servant Hunt (who was a notable thrifty man and loved this World, and the only servant he had that he could never gett to become bound for him) *The World was made for man, Hunt, and not man for the World.* Hunt left an estate of 1000 pound per annum in Somerset.

None of his servants durst appeare before him without Spanish leather bootes; for he would smelle the neates leather, which offended him.

The East India Merchants presented his Lordship with a Cabinet of Jewells, which his Page, Mr. Cockaine, received, and deceived his Lord.

Three of his Lordship's servants kept their Coaches, and some kept Race-horses.

His Lordship would many times have Musique in the next roome where he meditated. I have now forgott what Mr. Bushel sayd, whether his Lordship enjoyed his Muse best at night or in the Morning.

His Lordship was a good Poet, but conceal'd, as appeares by his Letters :

> *The world's a Bubble, and the life of man*
> *Less than a span ;*
> *In his conception wretched, from the wombe*
> *So to the tombe ;*
> *Curst from his cradle, and brought up to yeares*
> *With cares and feares.*
> *Who then to frail mortality shall trust*
> *But limmes in water or but writes in dust.*
>
> *Yet since with sorrow here we live opprest,*
> *What life is best ?*
> *Courts are but onely superficiall scholes*
> *To dandle fooles :*
> *The rurall parts are turn'd into a den*
> *Of savage men ;*
> *And wher's a city from all vice so free,*
> *But may be term'd the worst of all the three ?*
>
> *Domestick cares afflict the husband's bed*
> *Or paines his hed ;*
> *Those that live single take it for a curse,*
> *Or doe things worse ;*

Some would have children ; those that have them mone,
  Or wish them gone.
What is it then to have, or have no wife,
But single thraldome or a double strife ?

Our owne affections still at home to please
  Is a disease ;
To crosse the sea to any foreine soyle,
  Perills and toyle ;
Warres with their noise affright us ; when they cease
  W' are worse in peace.
What then remaines ? but that we still should cry
Not to be borne, or, being borne, to dye.

He was a παιδεραστής His Ganimeds and Favourites
tooke Bribes ; but his Lordship alwayes gave Judgement
secundum aequum et bonum [according as was just and good].
His Decrees in Chancery stand firme, i.e. there are fewer of his
Decrees reverst then of any other Chancellor.

His Dowager married her Gentleman-usher Sir Thomas
(I thinke) Underhill, whom she made deafe and blinde with too
much of Venus. She was living since the beheading of the
late King.

He had a uterine brother, Anthony Bacon, who was a very
great states-man, and much beyond his brother Francis for the
Politiques, a lame man ; he was a Pensioner to, and lived with
the Earle of Essex. And to him he dedicates the first Edition
of his *Essayes*, a little booke no bigger then a Primer, which
I have seen in the Bodlyan Library.

His sisters were ingeniose and well-bred ; they well understood the Use of the Globes, as you may find in the preface
of Mr. Blundevill *Of the Sphaere : I began this Arithmetique more
than 7 yeares since for that vertuous Gentlewoman Mris. Elizabeth
Bacon : and though at her request I had made this Arithmetique so
plaine and easie as was possible (as to my seeming) yet her continuall
sicknesse would not suffer her to exercise herself therin.*

He had a delicate, lively, hazel Eie ; Dr. Harvey tolde me
it was like the Eie of a viper.

His Lordship being in Yorke-house garden, lookeing on
Fishers as they were throwing their Nett, asked them what
they would take for their Draught ; they answered *so much* ;
his Lordship would only offer *so much*. They drew up their
Nett and there were only 2 or 3 little fishes : his Lordship
then told them it had been better for them to have taken his
Offer. They replied, they hoped to have had a better Draught.

But, sayd his Lordship, Hope is a good Breakfast but an ill Supper.

When his Lordship was in disfavour, his neighbours, hearing how much he was indebted, came to him with a Motion to buy Oake-wood of him. His Lordship told them, He would not sell his Feathers.

The Earle of Manchester being removed from his Place of Lord chiefe Justice of the Common-Pleas to be Lord President of the Councell, told my Lord (upon his Fall) that he was sorry to see Him made such an Example. Lord Bacon replied *it did not trouble him, since he was made a President.*

The Bishop of London did cutte-downe a noble Clowd of Trees at Fulham. The Lord Chancellor told him that he was a good Expounder of darke places.

Upon his being in Dis-favour his Servants suddenly went away ; he compared them to the flying of the Vermin when the Howse was falling.

One told his Lordship it was now time to looke about him. He replyed : I do not looke about me, I looke above me.

Sir Julius Caesar (Master of the Rolles) sent to his Lordship in his necessity a hundred pounds for a Present.

His Lordship would often drinke a good draught of strong Beer (March-beer) to-bedwards, to lay his working Fancy asleep, which otherwise would keepe him from sleeping great part of the night.

I remember Sir John Danvers told me, that his Lordship much delighted in his curious pretty garden at Chelsey, and as he was walking there one time he fell downe in a dead-sowne. My Lady Danvers rubbed his face, temples, etc., and gave him cordiall water ; as soon as he came to himselfe, sayde he, *Madam, I am no good footman.*

I will write something of Verulam, and his House at Gorhambery. At Verulam is to be seen, in some few places, some remaines of the Wall of this Citie. This magnanimous Lord Chancellor had a great mind to have made it a Citie again : and he had designed it, to be built with great uniformity : but Fortune denyed it Him, though she proved kinder to the great Cardinal Richelieu, who lived both to designe and finish that specious Towne of Richelieu, where he was borne ; before, an obscure and small Vilage.

Within the bounds of the Walls of this old Citie of Verulam (his Lordship's Baronry) was Verulam-howse ; which his Lordship built, the most ingeniosely contrived little pile, that ever I sawe. No question but his Lordship was the chiefest

Architect ; but he had for his assistant a favourite of his, a St. Albans man, Mr. Dobson, who was his Lordship's right hand, a very ingeniose person (Master of the Alienation Office) ; but he spending his estate upon woemen, necessity forced his son Will Dobson to be the most excellent Painter that England hath yet bred.

This howse did cost nine or ten thousand the building, and was sold about 1665 or 1666 by Sir Harbottle Grimston, Baronet, to two Carpenters for fower hundred poundes ; of which they made eight hundred poundes. I am sorry I measured not the front and breadth ; but I little suspected it would be pulled downe for the sale of the Materials. There were good Chimney pieces ; the roomes very loftie, and all were very well wainscotted. There were two Bathing-roomes or Stuffes, whither his Lordship retired afternoons as he sawe cause. All the tunnells of the Chimneys were carried into the middle of the howse ; and round about them were seates. The top of the howse was very well Leaded : from the Leads was a lovely Prospect to the Ponds, which were opposite to the East side of the howse, and were on the other side of the stately Walke of Trees that leades to Gorhambery-howse : and also over that Long Walke of Trees, whose topps afford a most pleasant variegated verdure, resembling the workes in Irish-stitch. In the middle of this howse was a delicate Staire-case of wood, which was curiously carved, and on the posts of every interstice was some prettie figure, as of a grave Divine with his booke and spectacles, a Mendicant Friar, etc., not one thing twice. On the dores of the upper storie on the outside (which were painted darke Umber) were the figures of the gods of the Gentiles, viz. on the South dore, 2d storie, was Apollo ; on another, Jupiter with his Thunderbolt, etc., bigger then the life, and donne by an excellent hand ; the heightnings were of hatch-ings of gold, which when the Sun shone on them made a most glorious shew.

The upper part of the uppermost dore on the East side had inserted into it a large Looking-glasse, with which the Stranger was very gratefully decieved, for (after he had been entertained a pretty while, with the prospects of the Ponds, Walks, and countrey, which this dore faced) when you were about to returne into the roome, one would have sworn (*primo intuitu* [at first glance], that he had beheld another Prospect through the Howse : for, as soon as the Straunger was landed on the Balconie, the Conserge that shewed the howse would shutt the dore to putt this fallacy on him with the Looking-glasse. This was his Lordship's Summer-howse : for he sayes (in his essay) one should have seates for Summer and Winter as well as Cloathes.

From hence to Gorhambery in a straite line (about a little mile, the way easily ascending, hardly so acclive as a Deske) leade three parallel walkes : in the middlemost three coaches may passe abreast : in the wing-walkes two.

About the mid-way from Verolam-house to Gorambery, on the right hand, on the side of a Hill which faces the Passer-by, are sett in artificiall manner severall stately Trees of the like groweth and heighth, whose diversity of greens on the side of the hill are exceeding pleasant. These delicate walkes and prospects entertaine the Eie to Gorambery-howse, which is a large, well-built Gothique howse, built (I thinke) by Sr Nicholas Bacon, Lord Keeper, father to this Lord Chancellor, to whom it descended by the death of Anthony Bacon his middle brother, who died sans issue. The Lord Chancellor made an addition of a noble Portico, which fronts the Garden to the South ; opposite to every arch of this Portico, and as big as the arch, are drawn by an excellent hand (but the mischief of it is, in water-colours) curious pictures, all Emblematicall, with Motto's under each. For example, one I remember is a ship tossed in a storm, the Motto, *Alter erit tum Tiphys* [There will come another Tiphys].

Over this Portico is a stately Gallerie, whose Glasse-windowes are all painted : and every pane with severall figures of beest, bird, or flower : perhaps his Lordship might use them as Topiques for Locall memorie. The windowes looke into the Garden : the side opposite to them no window ; but is hung all with pictures at length, as of King James, his Lordship, and severall Illustrious persons of his time. At the end you enter is no windowe, but there is a very large picture, thus : In the middle on a Rock in the sea stands King James in armour with his regall Ornaments ; on his right hand stands (but whether or no on a Rock I have forgott) King Hen. 4 of France, in armour ; and on his left hand the King of Spaine in like manner. These figures are (at least) as big as the life : they are donne only with umbre and shell-gold ; all the heightning and illuminated part being burnisht gold and the shadowed umbre, as in the pictures of the Gods on the dores of Verulam-howse. The roofe of this Gallerie is semi-cylindrique, and painted by the same hand and same manner, with heads and busts of Greek and Roman Emperours and Heroes.

In the Hall (which is of the auncient building) is a large storie very well painted of the Feastes of the Gods, where Mars

[14]

is caught in a nett by Vulcan. On the wall, over the Chimney, is painted an Oake with Akornes falling from it, the Word, *Nisi quid potius* [Failing some better chance] and on the wall over the Table is painted Ceres teaching the Soweing of Corne, the Word, *Moniti meliora* [We now have better counsel].

The garden is large, which was (no doubt) rarely planted and kept in his Lordship's time. Here is a handsome Dore, which opens into Oake-wood ; over this dore in golden letters on blew are six verses.

The Oakes of this wood are very great and shadie. His Lordship much delighted himselfe here : under every tree, he planted some fine flower, or flowers, some wherof are there still (1656) viz. Paeonies, Tulips.

From this Wood a dore opens into a place as big as an ordinary Parke, the west part wherof is Coppice-wood, where are Walkes cut-out as straight as a line, and broad enoug for a coach, a quarter of a mile long or better. Here his Lordship much meditated, his servant Mr. Bushell attending him with his pen and inke horne to sett downe his present Notions.

The east of this Parquet was heretofore, in his Lordship's prosperitie, a Paradise ; now is a large ploughed field. The walkes, both in the Coppices and other Boscages, were most ingeniosely designed : at severall good Viewes, were erected elegant Sommer-howses well built of Roman-architecture, well wainscotted and cieled ; yet standing, but defaced, so that one would have thought the Barbarians had made a Conquest here.

The figures of the Ponds were thus : they were pitched at the bottomes with pebbles of severall colours, which were work't in to severall figures, as of Fishes, etc., which in his Lordship's time were plainly to be seen through the cleare water, now over-grown with flagges and rushes. If a poore bodie had brought his Lordship half a dozen pebbles of a curious colour, he would give them a shilling, so curious was he in perfecting his Fish-ponds, which I guesse doe containe four acres. In the middle of the middlemost pond, in the Island, is a curious banquetting-house of Roman architecture, paved with black and white marble ; covered with Cornish slatt, and neatly wainscotted.

His Lordship was wont to say, *I will lay my mannor of Goram-bery on't,* to which one Judge made a spightfull reply, saying he would not hold a wager against that, but against any other Mannour of his Lordship's, he would. Now this Illustrious Lord Chancellor had only this Mannor of Gorambery.

In April, and the Springtime, his Lordship would, when

it rayned, take his Coach (open) to recieve the benefit of Irrigation, which he was wont to say was very wholsome because of the Nitre in the Aire and the *Universall Spirit of the World*.

Mr. Hobbs told me that the cause of his Lordship's death was trying an Experiment; viz. as he was taking the aire in a Coach with Dr. Witherborne (a Scotchman, Physitian to the King) towards High-gate, snow lay on the ground, and it came into my Lord's thoughts, why flesh might not be preserved in snow, as in Salt. They were resolved they would try the Experiment presently. They alighted out of the Coach and went into a poore woman's house at the bottom of Highgate hill, and bought a Hen, and made the woman exenterate it, and then stuffed the body with Snow, and my Lord did help to doe it himselfe. The Snow so chilled him that he immediately fell so extremely ill, that he could not returne to his Lodging (I suppose then at Graye's Inne) but went to the Earle of Arundel's house at High-gate, where they putt him into a good bed warmed with a Panne, but it was a damp bed that had not been layn-in in about a yeare before, which gave him such a colde that in 2 or 3 dayes as I remember Mr. Hobbes told me, he dyed of Suffocation.

This October, 1681, it rang over all St. Albans that Sir Harbottle Grimston, Master of the Rolles, had removed the Coffin of this most renowned Lord Chancellour to make roome for his owne to lye-in in the vault there at St. Michael's church.

ISAAC BARROW

[Born 1630. Mathematician. At the age of thirty he obtained the Greek Chair at Cambridge and, in 1662, the Gresham Professorship of Geometry, which he resigned on being appointed first Lucasian Professor of Mathematics in the same University. In 1669 he resigned in favour of his pupil, Isaac Newton. He was made a Doctor of Divinity by mandate in 1670, and having preached a celebrated sermon that lasted for three and a half hours, said he felt tired from *standing* so long. In 1672 he became Master of Trinity College, Cambridge, where he founded the library. Died 1677.]

HIS Father, Thomas Barrow, was the second son of Isaac Barrow of Spinney abbey in the Countie of Cambridge, Esq., who was a Justice of the Peace there above fourtie yeares. The father of Thomas never designed him for a Tradesman, but he was so severe to him he could not endure to live with him, so he came to London and was apprentice to a Linnen-draper. He kept shoppe at the Signe of the White-Horse in Forster-Lane, near St. Forster's Church, in St. Leonard's parish; and his son was christened at St. John Zacharie's in Forster Lane, for at that time St. Leonard's Church was pulled downe to be re-edified.

He went to schoole, first to Mr. Brookes at Charter-house, two yeares. His father gave to Mr. Brookes 4 pounds per annum, whereas his pay was but 2 pound, to be carefull of him; but Mr. Brookes was negligent of him, which the Captain of the school acquainted his father (his Kinsman) and sayd that he would not have him stay there any longer than *he* did, for that he instructed him.

Afterwards to one Mr. Holbitch, about fower years, at Felton in Essex, from whence he was admitted of Peterhouse College in Cambridge first, and went to schoole a yeare after. Then he was admitted to Trinity College in Cambridge at 13 yeares old.

His father dealt in his Trade to Ireland, where he had a great losse, neer 1000 pounds; upon which he wrote to Mr. Holbitch, a Puritan, to be pleased to take a little paines more than ordinary with him, because the times growing so bad, and such a losse then received, that he did not know how he might be able to provide for him; and so Mr. Holbitch tooke him away from the Howse where he was boarded to his owne Howse, and made him Tutor to my Lord Viscount Fairfax, ward to the Lord Viscount Say and Seale, where he continued so long as my Lord continued.

This Viscount Fairfax, being a schooleboy, married a Gentleman's daughter in the towne there, who had but a thousand pounds. So leaving the schoole, would needs have Mr. Isaac Barrow with him, and tolde him he would maintain him. But my Lord Say was so cruel to him that he would not allow anything; 'tis thought he dyed for want. The 1000 pounds could not serve him long.

During this time, olde Mr. Thomas Barrow was shutt-up at Oxford, which was then a Garrison for the King, and could not heare of his Sonne. But young Isaac's Master, Holbitch, found him out in London, and courted him to come to his Schoole, and that he would make him his Heire : But he did not care to goe to schoole again.

When my Lord Fairfax faild, and that he saw he grewe heavy upon him, he went to see one of his Schoolefellowes, one Mr. Walpole, a Norfolk Gent., who asked him what would he doe ? He replyed he knew not what to doe ; he could not goe to his father at Oxford. Mr. Walpole then tolde him : I am goeing to Cambridge to Trinity College and I will maintaine you there ; and so he did for halfe a yeare till the Surrender of Oxford ; and then his Father enquired after him and found him at Cambridge. And the very next day after old Mr. Barrow came to Cambridge, Mr. Walpole was leaving the University and (hearing nothing of Isaac's father) resolved to take Isaac along with him to his Howse. His father then asked him what profession he would be of, a merchant or etc. ? He begged of his father to lett him continue in the University. His father then asked what would maintain him. He told him 20 pounds per annum. I warrant you, sayd he, I will maintaine myselfe with it. His father replyed, I'le make a shift to allow you that. So his father then went to his Tutor and acquainted him. His Tutor, Dr. Duport, told him he would take nothing for his Reading to him, for that he was likely to make a brave Scholar, and he would helpe him to halfe a chamber for nothing. And the next news his father heard of him was that he was chosen in to the Howse. Dr. Hill was then Master of the College. He mett Isaac one day, and layd his hand upon his head, and sayd, Thou art a good boy, 'tis pitty thou art a Cavalier.

His Humour when a Boy, and after :—merry and cheerfull, and beloved wherever he came. His grandfather kept him till he was seven yeares old ; his father was faine to force him away, for he would have been good for nothing there.

A good Poet, English and Latin. He spake 8 severall Languages.

He was a strong and stowt man and feared not any man. He would fight with the Butchers boyes in St. Nicholas shambles, and be hard enough for any of them.

He went to Travell three or four yeares after the King was beheaded, upon the Colledge account. He was a Candidate for the Greeke Professor's place and had the consent of the University, but Oliver Cromwell put in Dr. Widrington, and then he travelled.

He was abroade about 5 yeares, viz. in Italie, France, Germany, Constantinople. As he went to Constantinople, two men of warre, Turkish Shippes, attacqued the Vessell wherin he was. In which engagement he shewed much valour in defending the vessell; which the men that were in that engagement often testifye, for he never told his father of it himself.

Upon his return, he came in Ship to Venice, which was stowed with Cotton-wooll, and as soon as ever they came on Shore the ship fell on fire and was utterly consumed, and not a man lost, but not any goods saved—a wonderfull preservation.

At Constantinople, being in company with the English Merchants, there was a Rhadamontade that would fight with any man and bragged of his Valour, and dared any man there to try him. So no man accepting, said Isaac (not then a Divine) Why, if none els will try you I will; and fell upon him and chastised him handsomly that he vaunted no more amongst them.

After he had been three years beyond sea, his Correspondent dyed, so that he had no more supply; yet he was so well beloved that he never wanted.

At Constantinople, he wayted on the Consul, Sir Thomas Bendish, who made him staye with him, and kept him there a yeare and a halfe, whether he would or no.

At Constantinople, Mr. Dawes, a Turkey merchant, desired Mr. Barrow to stay but such a time and he would returne with him, but when that time came he could not goe, some Businesse stayed him. Mr. Barrow could stay no longer; so Mr. Dawes would have had Mr. Barrow have 100 pistolles. No, said Mr. Barrow, I know not whether I shall be able to pay you. 'Tis no matter, said Mr. Dawes. To be short, forced him to take fifty pistolls, which at his return he payd him again.

I have heard Mr. Wilson say that when he was at study, was so intent at it when the bed was made, or so, he heeded it not nor perceived it, was so *totus in hoc* [absorbed]; and would sometimes be goeing out without his hatt on.

He was by no means a spruce man, not a Dr. Smirke, but most negligent in his dresse. As he was walking one day in St. James's parke, his hatt up, his cloake halfe on and halfe off, a gent. came behind him and clapt him on the Shoulder and sayd, Well goe thy wayes for the veriest scholar that ever I mett with.

He was a strong man, but pale as the Candle he studyed by.

His pill (an opiate, possibly Matthews his pil) which he was wont to take in Turkey, which was wont to doe him good, but he took it preposterously at Mr. Wilson's, the Saddlers, neer Suffolk House, where he was wont to lye and where he dyed, and 'twas the cause of his death.

As he laye unravelling in the agonie of death, the Standers-by could hear him say softly, *I have seen the Glories of the world.*

FRANCIS BEAUMONT AND
JOHN FLETCHER

[Playwrights. Francis Beaumont was born in 1584 and collaborated with John Fletcher in the writing of plays from 1606 until his death in 1616. Dryden states that Beaumont was so accurate a judge of plays that Ben Jonson submitted all his writings to his censure. His superior faculty for the construction of plots is discernible in some of the plays that he wrote with Fletcher. Beaumont was educated at Oxford, and John Fletcher, who was born in 1579, was at Cambridge. Fletcher wrote fifty-two plays in all, fifteen of them with Beaumont, sixteen by himself, and the rest in collaboration with Rowley, Middleton, Massinger, Ben Jonson and Shakespeare. He died in 1625.]

MR. FRANCIS BEAUMONT was the son of Judge Beaumont. There was a wonderfull consimility of phansey between him and Mr. John Fletcher, which caused that dearnesse of frendship between them.

I thinke they were both of Queen's College in Cambridge.

I have heard Dr. John Earles, since Bishop of Sarum, who knew them, say, that Mr. Beaumont's maine Businesse was to lop the overflowings of Mr. Fletcher's luxuriant Fancy and flowing Witt.

They lived together on the Banke side, not far from the Play-house, both batchelors; lay together; had one Wench in the house between them, which they did so admire; the same cloathes and cloake, &c.; betweene them.

He writt (amongst many other) an admirable Elegie on the Countesse of Rutland. John Earles in his Verses on him, speaking of them,

> *A monument that will then lasting bee,*
> *When all her Marble is more dust than shee.*

Mr. Edm. Waller on him:

> *I never yet the Tragick Scene assaid*
> *Deterr'd by thy inimitable* Mayd *:*
> *And when I striv'd to reach the Comick Stile*
> Thy Scornfull Lady *seem'd to mock my toile.*

John Fletcher, invited to goe with a Knight into Norfolke or Suffolke in the Plague-time 1625, stayd but to make himselfe a suite of Cloathes, and while it was makeing, fell sick of the Plague and dyed. This I had (1668) from his Tayler, who is now a very old man, and Clarke of St. Mary Overy's in South-wark. Mr. Fletcher had an Issue in his arm (I thought it had not used so long ago). The Clarke (who was wont to bring him Ivy-leaves to dresse it) when he came, found the Spotts upon him. Death stopped his Journey and laid him low here.

SIR JOHN BIRKENHEAD

[Born 1616. Poet and journalist. Probationer Fellow of All Souls, Oxford 1640. Devised and mostly wrote *Mercurius Aulicus,* the weekly journal of the Royalists at Oxford, 1642–45. He was imprisoned, after the surrender of Oxford, and subsequently, according to Anthony Wood, *he lived by his wits in helping young gentleman out at dead lifts in making poems, songs, and epistles to their respective mistresses, as also in translating and writing several little things and other petite employments.* In exile with the Prince of Wales 1648. Knighted at St. Germains 1649. M.P. for Wilton 1661. Fellow of the Royal Society. His poems were mainly satirical. Died 1679.]

SIR JOHN BIRKENHEAD, Knight, was borne at Nantwych, in Cheshire. His father was a Sadler there, and he had a brother a sadler, a Trooper in Sir Thomas Ashton's regiment, who was quartered at my father's, who tolde me so.

He went to Oxford University, and was first a Servitor of Oriall Colledge: he wrote an excellent hand, and, when William Laud, ABC, was last there, he had occasion to have some things well transcribed, and this Birkenhead was recommended to him, who performed his businesse so well, that the archbishop recommended him to All Soules College to be a Fellow, and he was accordingly elected. He was Scholar enough, and a Poet.

After Edgehill fight, when King Charles I first had his Court at Oxford, he was pitched upon as one fitt to write the Newes, which Oxford Newes was called *Mercurius Aulicus,* which he writt wittily enough, till the surrender of the Towne.

After the surrender of Oxford, he was putt out of his Fellowship by the Visitors, and was faine to shift for himselfe as well as he could. Most part of his time he spent at London, where he mett with severall persons of quality that loved his company, and made much of him.

He went over into France, where he stayed some time, I thinke not long. He received grace there from the Dutches of Newcastle, I remember he told me. He gott many a fourty shillings (I beleeve) by Pamphlets, such as that of *Col. Pride,* and *The Last Will and Testament of Philip Earle of Pembroke,* &c.

He was exceedingly bold, confident, witty, not very grateful to his benefactors ; would Lye damnably. He was of midling stature, great goggli eies, not of sweet aspect.

He was chosen a Burghes of Parliament at Wilton in Wiltshire, anno Domini 1661, i.e. of the King's long parliament. Anno 1679 upon the choosing of *this* Parliament, he went downe to be elected, and at Salisbury heard how he was scorned and mocked at Wilton (whither he was goeing) and called *Pensioner,* etc. : he went not to the Borough where he intended to stand ; but returned to London, and tooke it so to heart that he insensibly decayed and pined away ; and so dyed at his Lodgeings in Whitehall, and was buried Saturday, December 6, in St. Martyn's churchyard in-the-fields, neer the church, according to his Will and Testament ; his reason was because he sayd they removed the bodies out of the Church.

I remember at Bristow (when I was a boy) it was a common fashion for the woemen to get a Tooth out of a Sckull in the Church yard ; which they wore as a preservative against the Tooth-ach. Under the Cathedral-church at Hereford is the greatest Charnel-house for bones, that ever I saw in England. In A° 1650 there lived amongst those bones a poor old woman that, to help out her fire, did use to mix the deadmen's bones : this was thrift and poverty : but cunning alewives putt the Ashes of these bones in their Ale to make it intoxicateing.

SIR HENRY BLOUNT

[Born 1602. Traveller. On 7th May, 1634, he left Venice in
a Venetian galley on his well-known voyage to the Levant. Sailing
down the Adriatic, he landed at Spalatro in Dalmatia : thence he
crossed the Dinaric Alps and descended into the plains of Bosnia,
arriving at Sarajevo, the capital, after a journey of nine days. Departing thence with the Turkish troops proceeding to the war in Poland,
he arrived at Valiero in Servia. Three days later he reached Belgrade
and then proceeded by way of Nissa, Sophia in Bulgaria and Philippoli
to Adrianople, finally reaching Constantinople after a land journey of
fifteen hundred miles in fifty-two days. He then sailed for Alexandria
with the Turkish Fleet, visiting Rhodes on the way. Thence he reached
Cairo by water in five days, from which he made an excursion to the
interior of the great pyramid at Gizeh. Leaving Cairo in November,
he took passage on board a French vessel at Alexandria, bound for
Palermo. Re-embarking at Trepassi for Naples, he returned via
Rome, Florence and Bologna, to Venice, where he arrived after
eleven months, having journeyed about six thousand miles. Published
Voyage to the Levant, 1636. Knighted 1640. Sided with the Royalists
in the Civil War. Died 1682.]

SIR HENRY BLOUNT, Knight, was borne (I presume) at
Tittinghanger in the Countie of Hertford. It was heretofore
the summer seate of the Lord Abbot of St. Alban's.

He was pretty wild when young, especially addicted to
common wenches. He was a second brother.

He was a Gentleman Pensioner to King Charles I, on whom
he wayted (as it was his turne) to Yorke (when the King
deserted the Parliament) : was with him at Edgehill fight ;
came with him to Oxford ; and so returned to London ; walkt
into Westminster Hall with his Sword by his side ; the
Parliamentarians all stared upon him as a Cavaleer, knowing
that he had been with the King ; was called before the House
of Commons, where he remonstrated to them he did but his
duty, and so they acquitted him.

In those dayes he dined most commonly at the Heycock's-
ordinary, near the Pallzgrave head taverne, in the Strand, which
was much frequented by Parliament men and gallants. One
time Colonel Betridge being there (one of the handsomest
men about the Towne) and bragged how much the woemen
loved him. Sir H. Blount did lay a wager, that let them two

goe together to a Bordello, he only without money, with his handsome person, and Sir Henry with a twenty-shilling piece on his bald croone, that the wenches should choose Sir Henry before Betridge; and Sir H. won the wager. Edmund Wyld, Esq., was one of the witnesses.

There was a Pamphlet (writt by Henry Nevill, Esq.) called the *Parliament of Ladies,* wherin Sir Henry Blount was the first to be called to the Barre, for spreading abroad that abominable and dangerous Doctrine that it was far cheaper and safer to lye with Common Wenches then with Ladies of Quality.

His estate left him by his father was 500 pounds per annum, which he sold for an annuitie of 1000 pounds per annum; and since, his elder brother dyed.

He was made one of the Comittee for Regulating the Lawes. He was severe against Tythes, and for the abolishing them, and that every Minister should have 100 pounds per annum and no more.

Since he was —— year olde he dranke nothing but water or Coffee. 1647, or therabout, he maryed to Mris. Hester Wase, daughter of Christopher Wase, who dyed 1679, by whom he haz two sonnes, ingeniose young Gentlemen. Charles Blount (his second sonne) hath writt *Anima Mundi* (burnt by order of the Bishop of London) and of *Sacrifices.*

I remember twenty yeares since he inveighed much against sending youths to the Universities—*quaere* if his sons were there—because they learnt there to be debaucht, and that the learning that they learned there they were to unlearne againe, as a man that is buttond or laced too hard, must unbutton before he can be at his ease. Drunkeness he much exclaimed against, but wenching he allowed. When Coffee first came in he was a great upholder of it, and hath ever since been a constant frequenter of Coffee houses, especially Mr. Farre at the Rainbowe, by Inner Temple Gate, and lately John's coffee house, at Fuller's rents.

The first Coffe howse in London was in St. Michael's Alley in Cornehill, opposite to the church, which was sett up by one Bowman (Coachman to Mr. Hodges, a Turkey merchant, who putt him upon it) in or about the yeare 1652. 'Twas about four yeares before any other was sett up, and that was by Mr. Far. Jonathan Paynter, opposite to St. Michael's Church, was the first apprentice to the Trade, viz. to Bowman. The Bagneo, in Newgate Street, was built and first opened in December 1679, built by Turkish Merchants.

He is a Gentleman of very cleare Judgement, great experience, much Contemplation, not of very much Reading, of great

[26]

Foresight into Government. His conversation is admirable. When he was young, he was a great collector of Bookes, as his sonne is now.

He was heretofore a great Shammer, i.e. one that tells falsities not to doe any body any injury, but to impose on their understanding ; e.g. at Mr. Farre's, that at an Inne (nameing the signe) in St. Albans, the Innekeeper had made a Hogs-trough of a free-stone coffin, but the pigges after that grew leane, dancing and skipping, and would run upon the topps of the houses like goates. Two young Gents., that heard Sir H. tell this *sham* so gravely, rode the next day to St. Albans to enquire ; comeing there, nobody had heard of any such thing, 'twas altogether false. The next night as soon as they allighted, they came to the Rainbowe and found Sir H., looked louringly on him, and told him they wondered he was not ashamed as to tell such stories, etc. Why, Gentlemen, sayd Sir H., have you been there to make enquiry? Yea, sayd they. Why truly, gentlemen, sayd Sir H. I heard you tell strange things that I knew to be false. I would not have gonne over the threshold of the dore to have found you out in a Lye, at which all the Company laught at the two young Gents.

He was wont to say that he did not care to have his servants goe to Church, for there servants infected one another to goe to the Alehouse and learne debauchery ; but he did bid them goe to see the Executions at Tyeburne, which worke more upon them than all the oratory in the Sermons.

He is now (1680) neer or altogether 80 yeares, his Intellectuals good still ; and body pretty strong.

This last weeke of Sept. 1682, he was taken very ill at London, and his Feet swelled ; and removed to Tittinghanger.

EDMUND BONNER

[Born 1495. Divine. Chaplain to Cardinal Wolsey 1529. He appealed in person to Pope Clement VII against Henry VIII's excommunication after his marriage to Anne Boleyn in 1533. Bishop of Hereford and Ambassador to the French Court 1538. Bishop of London 1539. Ambassador to the Emperor 1542. Bonner was three times imprisoned for his opposition to Edward VI's religious policy and was deprived of his bishopric. Restored to his see on Mary's accession in 1553, he joined with such great severity in the Marian persecution that he became one of the chief villains in Foxe's Book of Martyrs, where he is referred to as the Bloody Bishop : he was said to have *delightedly followed the accusation and found means to indite Richard Mekins, a child not past his fifteenth year, who had heard folkes talke, and in his innocence had chanced to speake against the Sacrament of the Altar. The poore boy for the safeguard of his life would gladly have said that the twelve apostles taught it hym, for he had not cared whom he had named, such was his childish innocence and feare,* and had him burned to death at Smithfield. He refused the Oath of Supremacy to Elizabeth and was again deprived of his bishopric. He died in prison in 1569 and, although Foxe noted angrily that Bonner *had long feasted and banqueted in durance at the Marshalsea,* he held that his *stinking death* was a certain sign of God's wrath against *the children of the murdering mother church of Rome.*]

BISHOP BONNER was of Broadgate hall ; he came thither a poor boy, and was at first a skullion boy in the kitchin, afterwards became a Servitor, and so by his industry raysed to what he was.

When he came to his greatnes, in acknowledgement from whence he had his Rise, he gave to the Kitchin there a great brasse-pott, called Bonners-pott, which was taken away in the Parliament time. Mr. Steevens has shewed the Pott to me, I remember. It was the biggest, perhaps, in Oxford.

CAISHO BOROUGH

MR. CAISHO BURROUGHS was one of the most beautiful Men in England, and very Valiant, but very proud and blood-thirsty : There was then in London a very Beautiful Italian Lady, who fell so extreamly in Love with him, that she did let him enjoy her, which she had never let any Man do before : Wherefore, said she, I shall request this favour of you, never to tell anyone of it. The Gentlewoman died : and afterwards in a Tavern in London he spake of it : and there going to make water, the Ghost of the Gentlewoman did appear to him. He was afterwards troubled with the Apparition of her, even sometimes in company when he was drinking ; but he only perceived it : Before she did appear he did find a kind of Chilness upon his Spirits.

Sir John Burroughes being sent Envoy to the Emperor by King Charles I, did take his Eldest Son Caisho Boroughes along with him, and taking his Journey through Italy, left his son at Florence to learn the Language ; where he having an Intrigue with a beautiful Courtisan (Mistress of the Grand Duke) their Familiarity became so public, that it came to the Duke's Ear, who took a Resolution to have him Murdered, but Caisho having had timely notice of the Duke's design by some of the English there, immediately left the City without acquainting his Mistress with it, and came to England ; whereupon the Duke being disappointed of his Revenge fell upon his Mistress in most reproachful Language, she on the other side resenting the sudden Departure of her Gallant of whom she was most passionately enamour'd, killed her self. At the same moment that she expired, she did appear to Caisho at his Lodgings in London. Collonel Remes was then in Bed with him, who saw her as well as he ; giving him an account of her Resentments of his Ingratitude to her, in leaving her so suddenly, and exposing her to the Fury of the Duke, not omitting her own Tragical EXIT, adding withall, that he should be slain in a Duell, which accordingly happened ; and thus she appeared to him frequently, even when his younger Brother (who afterwards was Sir John) was a Bed with him. As often as she did appear, he would cry out with great shrieking, and trembling of his Body, as anguish of Mind, saying, *O God ! here she comes, she comes*, and at this rate she appeared 'till he was killed; she appeared to him the morning before he was killed.

This Story was so common, that King Charles I sent for Caisho Burroughes's Father whom he examined as to the Truth of the Matter; who did (together with Collonel Remes, averr, the Matter of Fact to be true, so that the King thought it worth his while to send to Florence, to enquire at what time this unhappy Lady killed herself. It was found to be the same Minute that she first appeared to Caisho being a Bed with Colonel Remes. This Relation I had from my worthy Friend Mr. Monson, who had it from Sir John's own Mouth, Brother of Caisho; he had also the same Account from his own Father, who was intimately acquainted with old Sir John Burroughes and both his Sons, and says, as often as Caisho related this, he wept bitterly.

JAMES BOVEY

JAMES BOVEY, Esq. was the youngest son of Andrew
Bovey, Merchant, Cash-keeper to Sir Peter Vanore, in
London. He was borne in the middle of Mincing-lane, in
the parish of St. Dunstan's in the East, London, anno 1622,
May 7th, at six a clock in the morning. Went to schoole at
Mercers Chapell, under Mr. Augur. At 9 sent into the Lowe
Countreys ; then returned, and perfected himselfe in the Latin
and Greeke. At 14, travelled into France and Italie, Switzerland, Germany, and the Lowe Countreys. Returned into
England at 19 ; then lived with one Hoste, a Banquier, 8
yeares : was his cashier 8 or 9 yeares. Then traded for himselfe
(27) till he was 31 ; then maried the only daughter of William
de Vischer, a Merchant ; lived 18 yeares with her, then continued single. Left off trade at 32, and retired to a Countrey
life, by reason of his indisposition, the ayre of the Citie not
agreing with him. Then in these Retirements he wrote *Active
Philosophy* (a thing not donne before) wherin are enumerated
all the Arts and Tricks practised in Negotiation, and how thev
were to be ballanced by counter-prudentiall Rules.

Whilest he lived with Mr. Hoste, he kept the Cash of the
Ambassadors of Spaine that were here ; and of the Farmers,
called by them *Assentistes,* that did furnish the Spanish and
Imperiall armies of the Low-Countreys and Germany ; and
also many other great Cashes, as of Sir Theodore Mayern, etc.
(his dealing being altogether in money-matters) by which meanes
he became acquainted with the Ministers of State both here and
abroad.

When he was abroad, his chiefe employment was to observe
the affaires of State and their Judicatures, and to take the
Politique Surveys in the Countreys he travelled thorough,
more especially in relation to Trade. He speakes the Low-
Dutch, High-Dutch, French, Italian, Spanish, and Lingua
Franco, and Latin, besides his owne.

When he retired from Businesse he studied the Lawe-
Merchant, and admitted himselfe of the Inner Temple, London,
about 1660. His Judgment haz been taken in most of the great
Causes of his time in points concerning the Lawe Merchant.

For his health he never had it very well, but indifferently, alwaies a weake stomach, which proceeded from the agitation of the Braine. His Dyet was alwayes fine diet : much Chicken.

From 14 he began to take notice of all Prudentiall Rules as came in his way, and wrote them downe, and so continued till this day, Sept. 28, 1680, being now in his 59th yeare. He made it his businesse to advance the Trade of England, and many men have printed his Conceptions. He wrote a Table of all the Exchanges in Europe.

He hath writt (which is in his custodie, and which I have seen, and many of them read) these treatises, *viz.*

1. *The Characters, or Index Rerum :* in 4 tomes.
2. *The Introduction to Active Philosophy.*
3. *The Art of Building a Man : or Education.*
4. *The Art of Conversation.*
5. *The Art of Complyance.*
6. *The Art of Governing the Tongue.*
7. *The Art of Governing the Penn.*
8. *The Government of Action.*
9. *The Government of Resolution.*
10. *The Government of Reputation.*
11. *The Government of Power :* in 2 tomes.
12. *The Government of Servients.*
13. *The Government of Subserviency.*
14. *The Government of Friendshipp.*
15. *The Government of Enmities.*
16. *The Government of Law-suites.*
17. *The Art of Gaining Wealth.*
18. *The Art of Preserving Wealth.*
19. *The Art of Buying and Selling.*
20. *The Art of Expending Wealth.*
21. *The Government of Secresy.*
22. *The Government of Amor Conjugalis :* in 2 tomes.
23. *Of Amor Concupiscentiae.*
24. *The Government of Felicity.*
25. *The Lives of Atticus, Sejanus, Augustus.*
26. *The Causes of the Diseases of the Mind.*
27. *The Cures of the Mind, viz. Passions, Diseases, Vices, Errours, Defects.*
28. *The Art of Discerning Men.*
29. *The Art of Discerning a Man's selfe.*
30. *Religion from Reason :* in 3 tomes.
31. *The Life of Cum-fu-zu, soe farr wrote by J. B.*
32. *The Life of Mahomett, wrot by Sir Walter Raleigh's papers, with some small addition for methodizing the same.*

I have desired him to give these MSS. to the library of the **Royal Society**.

As to his person, he is about 5 foot high, spare slender body, strait, haire exceeding black and curling at the end, a dark hazell eie, of a midling size, but the most sprightly that I have beheld, browes and beard of the colour as his haire. A person of great Temperance, and deepe Thoughts, and a working head, never Idle. From 14 he had a Candle burning by him all night, with pen, inke, and paper, to write downe thoughts as they came into his head; that he might not loose a Thought. Was ever a great Lover of Naturall Philosophie. His whole life has been perplex't in Lawe-suites (which haz made him expert in Humane affaires) in which he alwaies overcame. He had many Lawe-suites with powerfull Adversaries; one lasted 18 yeares. Red-haired men never had any kindnesse for him.

In all his Travills he was never robbed.

RICHARD BOYLE: EARL OF CORK

[Born 1566. Statesman. Went to Ireland 1588. Escheator to James Crofton, the Escheator General 1590. Imprisoned on a charge of embezzling the records 1592. Later he was again accused of fraud, but this time was acquitted. Conveyed to Queen Elizabeth the news of the victory near Kinsale 1601. Purchased for £1000 Sir Walter Raleigh's Irish estates, out of which he rapidly acquired a huge fortune. Knighted 1603. Privy Councillor for Munster 1606, and for Ireland 1612. Created Lord Boyle, Baron of Youghal 1616, and Viscount Dungarvan and Earl of Cork 1620. Lord Justice of Ireland 1629. Lord High Treasurer 1631. Died 1643.]

RICHARD, the first Earle of Cork, being born a private Gentleman, and younger Brother of a younger Brother, to no other Heritage than is expressed in the Device and Motto, which his humble Gratitude inscribed on all the Palaces he built,

God's Providence, mine Inheritance ;

by that Providence, and his diligent and wise Industry, raised such an Honour and Estate, and left such a Familie, as never any Subject of these three Kingdomes did, and that with so unspotted a Reputation of Integrity that the most invidious scrutiny could find no blott, though it winnowed all the methods of his Rising most severely.

Thomas, Earl of Strafford made him disgorge 1500 pounds per annum, which he restored to the Church.

Earl of Corke bought of Captaine Horsey fourtie Ploughlands in Ireland for *fourtie pounds*. (A. Ettrick assures me, I say againe fourtie ploughlands.)

Master Boyl, after Earle of Cork (who was then a Widdower) came one morning to waite on Sir Jeofry Fenton, at that time a great Officer of State in that Kingdome of Ireland, who being ingaged in business, and not knowing who it was who desired to speake with him, a while delayed him access ; which time he spent pleasantly with his young Daughter in her Nurse's Arms. But when Sir Jeoffry came, and saw whom he had made stay somewhat too long, he civilly excused it. But Master

Boyl replied, he had been very well entertayned ; and spent his time much to his satisfaction, in courting his Daughter, if he might obtaine the Honour to be accepted for his Son-in-lawe. At which Sir Jeoffry, smiling (to hear one who had been formerly married, move for a Wife carried in Arms, and under two years old) asked him if would stay for her ? To which he frankly answered him he would, and Sir Jeoffry as generously promised him he should then have his consent. And they both kept their words honourably. And by this virtuous Lady he had thirteen Children, ten of which he lived to see honourably married, and died a grandfather by the youngest of them.

My Lady Petty sayes he had a wife or two before, and that he maried Mris. Fenton without her father's consent.

This Noble Lord, by his prudent and pious Consort, no lesse an Ornament and Honour to their Descendants than himself, was blessed with five sonnes (of which he lived to see four Lords and Peeres of the Kingdome of Ireland, and a fifth, more than these Titles speak, a Soveraigne and Peerlesse in a larger Province, that of universall nature, subdued and made obsequious to his inquisitive mind) and eight Daughters.

THE HONOURABLE ROBERT BOYLE

[Born 1627. Natural philosopher and chemist. He was the fourteenth child of the great Earl of Cork. His voluminous writings exhibit vividly the fruitfulness of the experimental method, and his observations added greatly to existing knowledge, especially in regard to pneumatics : his experimental proof of the proportional relation between the elasticity and pressure of gases is still known as *Boyle's Law*. It was Robert Boyle, in his *Skepticall Chymist* (1661), who destroyed the *Elements* of the Ancients and gave to the word its modern meaning. One of the founders of the Royal Society, he declined the presidency from a scruple about oaths. His interest in religion was so intense that he taught himself *as much Greek and Hebrew as sufficed to read the Old and New Testaments*, so as not to have to rely on translations. *A Chaldee grammar I likewise took the pains of learning,* he continued, *to be able to understand that part of Daniel, and those few other portions of Scripture that were written in that tongue ; and I have added a Syriac grammar purely to be able one day to read the divine discourses of our Saviour in His own language.* He was Governor of the Corporation for the Spread of the Gospel in New England from 1661 to 1689, and a Director of the East India Company. He died in 1691.]

THE Honourable Robert Boyle, Esq., that profound Philosopher, accomplished Humanist, and excellent Divine, I had almost sayd Lay-Bishop, as one hath stiled Sir Henry Savil, was borne at Lismor in the County of Corke. He was nursed by an Irish Nurse, after the Irish manner, wher they putt the child into a pendulous Satchell (insted of a Cradle) with a slitt for the Child's head to peepe out.

When a boy at Eaton was verie sickly and pale. Went to the University of Leyden. Travelled France, Italy, Switzerland. I have oftentimes heard him say that after he had seen the Antiquities and architecture of Rome, he esteemed none any where els.

He speakes Latin very well, and very readily, as most men I have mett with. I have heard him say that when he was young, he read over Cowper's *Dictionary* : wherin I thinke he did very well, and I beleeve he is much beholding to him for his Mastership of that Language.

His father in his Will, when he comes to the Settlement

and Provision for his son Robert, thus :—*Item, to my son Robert, whom I beseech God to blesse with a particular Blessing, I bequeath, &c.* Mr. Robert Hooke, who has seen the Rentall, sayes it was 3000 pounds per annum : the greatest part is in Ireland.

He is very tall (about six foot high) and streight, very temperate, and vertuouse, and frugall : a Batcheler ; keepes a Coach ; sojournes with his sister, the Lady Ranulagh. His greatest delight is Chymistrey. He haz at his sister's a noble Laboratory, and severall servants (Prentices to him) to looke to it. He is charitable to ingeniose men that are in want, and foreigne Chymists have had large proofe of his bountie, for he will not spare for cost to gett any rare Secret : *vide* Oliver Hill's book, where he is accused of grosse Plagiarisme.

At his owne costs and chardges he gott translated and printed the New Testament in Arabique, to send into the Mahometan countreys. He has not only a high renowne in England, but abroad ; and when foreigners come to hither, 'tis one of their curiosities to make him a Visit.

His Works alone may make a Librarie.

HENRY BRIGGS

[Born 1561. Mathematician. M.A. St. John's College, Cambridge 1585 ; fellow 1588 ; first Professor of Geometry at Gresham College, London 1596–1620. He succeeded Sir Henry Savile in the Professorship of Astronomy, which he had founded at Oxford. He visited Lord Napier in Scotland and the idea of tables of logarithms having 10 for their base, as well as the actual calculation of the first table of this kind, was due to Briggs. When the two great mathematicians met, says William Lilly, the astrologer, *almost one quarter of an hour was spent, each beholding the other almost with admiration, before one word was spoke.* Lilly goes on to say that Napier *was a great lover of astrology, but Briggs the most satirical man against it that hath been known.* He called it *a system of groundless conceits.* He published and left in manuscript many works on mathematics and navigation, including *A Table to find the Height of the Pole* and *A tract on the North-west Passage to the South Sea through the Continent of Virginia.* He was a member of the company trading to Virginia. He died at Merton College, Oxford, on the 26th January, 1630, and a Greek epitaph that was written on him by Henry Jacob, one of the Fellows of Merton, ends by saying that *his soul still astronomises and his body geometrises.*]

LOOKING one time on the mappe of England he observed that the two Rivers, the Thames and that Avon (which runnes to Bathe and so to Bristowe) were not far distant, *scilicet,* about 3 miles. He sees 'twas but about 25 miles from Oxford ; getts a horse and viewes it and found it to be a levell ground and easie to be digged. Then he considered the chardge of cutting between them and the convenience of making a mariage between those Rivers which would be of great consequence for cheape and safe carrying of Goods between London and Bristow, and though the boates goe slowly and with meanders, yet considering they goe day and night they would be at their journey's end almost as soon as the Waggons, which often are overthrowne and liquours spilt and other goods broken. Not long after this he dyed and the Civill Warres brake-out.

It happened by good Luck that one Mr. Matthewes of Dorset had some acquaintance with this Mr. Briggs and had heard him discourse of it. He was an honest simple man, and had runne out of his Estate and this project did much run in his head. He would revive it (or els it had been lost and forgott) and went into the Country to make an ill survey of it (which he printed) but with no great encouragement of the Countrey or others.

Upon the restauration of King Charles II he renewed his designe and applyed himselfe to the King and Counsell. His Majestie espoused it more (he told me) then any one els. In short, for want of management and his non-ability, it came to nothing, and he is now dead of old age. But Sir Jonas Moore (an expert Mathematician and a practicall man) being sent to survey the mannor of Dantesey in Wilts (which was forfeited to the Crowne by Sir John Danvers his foolery) went to see these Streames and distances. He told me the streames were too small, unlesse in winter; but if some prince or the Parliament would rayse money to cutt through the hill by Wotton-Basset which is not very high, then there would be water enough and streames big enough. He computed the chardge, which I have forgott, but I thinke it was about 200,000 pounds.

Mr. William Oughtred calls him the English Archimedes.

ELIZABETH BROUGHTON

MRIS. ELIZABETH BROUGHTON was daughter of Edward Broughton of Herefordshire, an ancient Family. Her father lived at the Mannour-house at Cannon-Peon. Whether she was borne there or no, I know not ; but there she lost her Mayden-head to a poor young fellow, then I beleeve handsome, but, in 1660, a pittifull poor old weaver, Clarke of the Parish. He had fine curled haire, but gray. Her father at length discovered her inclinations and locked her up in the Turret of the house, but she getts down by a rope ; and away she gott to London, and did sett up for her selfe.

She was a most exquisite beautie, as finely shaped as Nature could frame ; had a delicate Witt. She was soon taken notice of at London, and her price was very deare—a second Thais. Richard, Earle of Dorset, kept her (whether before or after Venetia I know not, but I guess before). At last she grew common and infamous and gott the Pox, of which she died.

I remember thus much of an old Song of those dayes, which I have seen in a Collection : 'twas by way of litanie, *viz* :

> *From the Watch at Twelve a Clock,*
> *And from Bess Broughton's buttond smock,*
> *Libera nos Domine.*

In Ben Johnson's *Execrations against Vulcan,* he concludes thus :—

> *Pox take thee, Vulcan. May Pandora's pox*
> *And all the Ills that flew out of her Box*
> *Light on thee. And if those plagues won't doe,*
> *Thy Wive's Pox take thee, and Bess Broughton's too.*

I see that there have been famous Woemen before our times.

I doe remember her father in 1646, neer 80, the handsomest shaped man that ever my eies beheld, a very wise man, and of an admirable Elocution. He was a Committee man in Herefordshire and Glocestershire ; he was Commissary to Colonel Massey. He was of the Puritan Party heretofore, had a great guift in Praying, etc. His wife (I have heard my grandmother say, who was her neighbor) had as great parts as he. He was the first that used the Improvement of Land by Soape-ashes when he lived at Bristowe, where they then threw it away, and the Haven being like to be choaked up with the Soape-ashes (for which severall Complaints and Indictments) considering that grounds were improved by Compost, he made an experiment of improving by soape-ashes, having land neer the City; and mightily emproved it. This I had from himselfe.

THOMAS BUSHELL

[Born 1594. Speculator and Mining Engineer. Page and Seal Bearer to Francis Bacon, who *imparted to him many secrets in discovering and extracting minerals.* When Bacon became Lord Chancellor, Bushell accompanied him to Court, where he attracted the notice of James I by the gorgeousness of his attire. His walks and fountains at Enstone in Oxfordshire were visited by Charles I and Henrietta Maria in 1636, and though the King's visit was unexpected, his ingenious host managed to improvise for him *an entertainment of artificial thunders and lightnings, rain, hail-showers, drums beating, organs playing, birds singing, waters murmuring all sorts of tunes,* &c. Farmed the Royal Mines in Wales 1636. Master of the Mint at Aberystwyth 1637, at Shrewsbury 1642, and at Oxford 1643. Held Lundy Island for the King till 1647 and then lived in concealment. Gave Parliament security for his good behaviour and leased the Crown Mines from the Protector 1652. Died 1674.]

M R. THOMAS BUSHELL was one of the Gentlemen that wayted on the Lord Chancellour Bacon. 'Twas the fashion in those dayes for Gentlemen to have their Suites of Clothes garnished with Buttons. My Lord Bacon was then in Disgrace, and his Man Bushell having more Buttons than usuall on his Cloake, etc., they sayd that his Lord's breech made Buttons and Bushell wore them : from whence he was called Buttond Bushell.

He was only an English Scholar, but had a good witt and a working and contemplative head. His Lord much loved him.

His Genius lay most towards naturall philosophy and particularly towards the Discovery, drayning and improvement of the Silver mines in Cardiganshire, etc. He wrote a stich't Treatise of Mines and improving the adits to them and Bellowes to drive-in Wind.

Mr. Bushell was the greatest Master of the Art of running in Debt (perhaps) in the world : and lived so long that his depts were forgott, so that they were the great-grandchildren of the creditors. He died one hundred and twenty thousand pounds in dept. He had so delicate a way of making his Projects alluring and feazible, profitable, that he drewe to his Baits not only rich men of no designe, but also the craftiest Knaves in the countrey, such who had cosened and undon others; e.g. Mr. Goodyeere, who undid Mr. Nicholas Mees' father, etc.

He had the strangest bewitching way to drawe-in people (yea, discreet and wary men) into his projects that ever I heard of. His tongue was a Charme, and drewe in so many to be bound for him, and to be ingaged in his Designes, that he ruined a number.

As he had the art of running in dept, so sometimes he was attacqued and throwen into Prison; but he would extricate himselfe again straingely.

After his master the Lord Chancellor dyed, he maried, and lived at Enston, Oxon; where having some land lyeing on the hanging of a hill facing the South, at the foot wherof runnes a fine cleare stream which petrifies, and where is a pleasant Solitude, he spake to his servant, Jack Sydenham, to gett a Labourer to cleare some Boscage which grew on the side of the Hill, and also to dig a Cavity in the hill, to sitt and read, or contemplate. The Workman had not worked an hower before he discovers not only a Rock, but a rock of an unusuall figure with Pendants like Icecles as at Wokey Hole, Somerset, which was the occasion of making that delicate Grotto and those fine Walkes.

The Grotto belowe lookes just South; so that when it artificially raineth, upon the turning of a cock, you are enterteined with a Rainbowe. In a very little pond (no bigger then a Basin) opposite to the rock, and hard by, stood a Neptune, neatly cutt in wood, holding his Trident in his hand, and ayming with it at a Duck which perpetually turned round with him, and a Spanniel swimming after her—which was very pretty, but long since spoyled.

Here in fine weather he would walke all night. Jack Sydenham sang rarely: so did his other servant, Mr. Batty. They went very gent. in cloathes, and he loved them as his children.

He did not encumber him selfe with his wife, but here enjoyed himselfe thus in this Paradise till the War brake out, and then retired to Lundy isle.

Anno 1647 or 8, he came over into England, and when he landed at Chester, and had but one Spanish three pence (this I had from some-one of Great Tew to whom he told it) and, sayd he, I could have been contented to have begged a penny like a poor man. At that time he sayd he owed, I forgett whether it was 50 or sixty thousand pounds: but he was like Sir Kenelm Digby, if he had not 4d., wherever he came he would find Respect and Credit.

[43]

He had donne something (I have now forgott what) that made him obnoxious to the Parliament or Oliver Cromwell, about 1650; would have been hang'd if taken; printed severall letters to the Parliament, etc., dated from beyond Sea, and all that time laye privately in his Howse in Lambeth marsh, where the pointed pyramis is. In the garret there is a long Gallery, which he hung all with black, and had some death's heads and bones painted. At the end where his Couch was, was in an old Gothique Nich (like an old Monument) painted a Skeleton recumbent on a Matt. At the other end, where was his pallet-bed, was an emaciated dead man stretched out. Here he had se erall mortyfying and divine Motto's (he imitated his Lord as much as he could) and out of his windowes a very pleasant prospect. At night he walked in the garden and orchard. Only Mr. Sydenham, and an old trusty woman, was privy to his being in England.

He was a handsome proper Gentleman when I sawe him at his house aforesayd at Lambith. He was about 70, but I should not have guessed him hardly 60. He had a perfect healthy constitution : fresh, ruddy face, hawke-nosed, and was temperate.

Mr. Edmund Wyld sayes that he tap't the mountaine of Snowdon in Wales, which was like to have drowned all the countrey ; and they were like to knock him and his men in the head.

In the time of the Civill Warres his Hermitage over the Rocks at Enston were hung with black-bayes ; his bed had black Curtaines, etc., but it had no bed posts but hung by 4 Cordes covered with blak-bayes instead of bed-postes. When the Queen-mother came to Oxon to the King, she either brought (as I thinke) or somebody gave her, an entire Mummie from Egypt, a great raritie, which her Majestie gave to Mr. Bushell, but I beleeve long ere this time the dampnesse of the place haz spoyled it with mouldinesse.

SAMUEL BUTLER

[Born 1612. Satirist. The son of a farmer. In early youth he was page to the Countess of Kent, and thereafter Clerk to various Puritan Justices. After the Restoration he became Secretary to the Lord President of Wales. At this time he married a widow of means, which however were soon dissipated. In 1663 the first part of *Hudibras* appeared and the other two in 1664 and 1678. *Hudibras*, which stands at the head of the satirical literature of England, is the most remarkable document of the reaction against Puritanism at the Restoration, and might be taken as the seamy side of *The Pilgrim's Progress*, being directed not against righteousness, but against self-righteousness. This book was immensely popular and King Charles II always carried a copy with him. Nevertheless, Butler died in extreme poverty in 1680.]

HIS father was a man but of slender fortune, and to breed him at schoole was as much education as he was able to reach to. When but a Boy he would make observations and reflections on every Thing one sayd or did, and censure it to be either well or ill. He was never at the University, for the reason alledged.

He came when a young man to be a servant to the Countesse of Kent, whom he served severall yeares : she gave her Gentlemen 20 pounds per annum a-piece. Here, besides his Study, he employed his time much in painting and drawing, and also in Musique. He was thinking once to have made painting his Profession. His love to and skill in painting made a great friendship between him and Mr. Samuel Cowper (the Prince of Limners of this Age.)

He was Secretarie to the Duke of Bucks, when he was Chancellor of Cambridge. He might have had Preferments at first ; but he would not accept any but very good ones, so at last he had none at all, and dyed in want.

He then studied the Common Lawes of England, but did not practise. He maried a good Jointuresse, the relict of one Morgan, by which meanes he lived comfortably.

John Cleveland was a fellow of St. John's Colledge in Cambridge, where he was more taken notice of for his being an eminent Disputant, then a good Poet. Being turned out of his Fellowship for a malignant he came to Oxford, where the

King's Army was, and was much caressed by them. After the King was beaten out of the field, he came to London, and retired in Grayes Inne. He, and Sam Butler, &c. of Grayes Inne, had a Clubb every night.

In my fathers time, they had a Clubb (*fustis*) at the school-dore: and when they desired leave *exeundi foras* (two went together still) they carried the Clubbe. I have heard that this was used in my time in Country-schooles before the Warres. When Monkes or Fryars goe out of their Convent, they always are licensed by couples; to be witnesses of one anothers actions or behaviour. We use now the word Clubbe for a Sodality at a Taverne or Drinking-house.

He printed a witty Poeme called *Hudibras*, which tooke extremely; so that the King and Lord Chancellor Hyde (who haz his picture in his Library over the Chimney) would have him sent for, and accordingly he was sent for. They both promised him great matters, but to this day he haz got *no* Employment, only the King gave him 300 pounds.

After the restauration of his Majestie when the Court at Ludlowe was againe sett-up, he was then the King's Steward at the castle there.

He haz often sayd, that way (e.g. Mr. Edmund Waller's) of Quibling with Sence will hereafter growe as much out of fashion and be as ridicule as quibling with words.

His verses on the Jesuites, not printed:—

> No *Jesuite* ever took in hand,
> To plant a church in barren Land;
> Or ever thought it worth his while
> A Swede or Russe to reconcile;
> For where there is not store of wealth,
> Souls are not worth the charge of health.
> Spaine on America had 2 designes
> To sell their Ghospell for their mines;
> For had the Mexicans been poore,
> No Spaniard twice had landed on their shore.
> 'Twas Gold the Catholick Religion planted,
> Which, had they wanted Gold, they still had wanted.

Satyricall Witts disoblige whom they converse with; and consequently make to themselves many Enemies and few Friends; and this was his manner and case. He was of a leonine-coloured haire, sanguino-cholerique, middle sized, strong; a severe and sound judgement, high coloured; a good fellowe. He haz been much troubled with the Gowt, and particularly

1679, he stirred not out of his chamber from October till Easter.

He dyed of a Consumption, September 25 ; and buried 27, according to his Appointment, in the Church-yard of Convent Garden ; *scil.* in the north part next the church at the east end. His feet touch the wall. His grave, 2 yards distant from the Pillaster of the Dore, (by his desire) 6 foot deepe.

About 25 of his old acquaintance at his Funerall. I myself being one of the eldest, helped to carry the Pall. His coffin covered with black Bayes.

WILLIAM BUTLER

[Born 1535. Physician. Licensed to practise medicine. He attended Henry, Prince of Wales, who died in 1612 in his eighteenth year. Died 1618.]

WILL BUTLER, physitian; he was of Clare-hall in Cambridge, never tooke the Degree of Doctor, though he was the greatest Physitian of his time.

The occasion of his first being taken notice of was thus: About the comeing in of King James, there was a Minister a few miles from Cambridge, that was to preach before his Majestie at Newmarket. The parson heard that the King was a great Scholar, and studyed so excessively that he could not sleepe, so somebody gave him some opium, which had made him sleep his last, had not Doctor Butler used this following remedy. He was sent for by the Parson's wife. When he came and sawe the Parson, and asked what they had donne, he told her that she was in danger to be hanged for killing her husband, and so in great choler left her. It was at that time when the Cowes came into the Backside to be milkt. He turnes back and asked whose Cowes those were. She sayd, her husband's. Sayd he, Will you give one of those Cowes to fetch your husband to life again? That she would, with all her heart. He then causes one presently to be killed and opened, and the parson to be taken out of his Bed and putt into the Cowes warme belly, which after some time brought him to life, or els he had infallibly dyed.

He was a man of great Moodes, a humorist. One time King James sent for him to Newmarket, and when he was gonne halfe-way left the Messenger and turned back; so then the messenger made him ride before him.

I think he was never maried. He lived in an Apothecary-shop in Cambridge, Crane's, to whom he left his estate, and he in gratitude erected the Monument for him at his own chardge, in the fashion he used. He was not greedy of money, except choice Pieces of Golde, or Rarities.

Once, on the rode from Cambridge to London, he took a fancy to a chamberlayne or tapster in his Inne, and took him with him and made him his favourite, by whom only accession was to be had to him, and thus enriched him.

[48]

He would many times (I have heard say) sitt among the Boyes at St. Maries' Church in Cambridge (and just so would the famous attorney general Noy in Lincoln's Inne, who had many such froliques and humours).

He kept an old mayd whose name was Nell. Dr. Butler would many times go to the Taverne, but drinke by himself. About 9 or 10 at night old Nell comes for him with a candle and lanthorne, and sayes, Come you home, you drunken Beast. By and by Nell would stumble; then her Master calls *her* drunken beast; and so they did drunken beast one another all the way till they came home.

A Serving man brought his Master's water to Doctor Butler, being then in his Studie (with turn'd Barres) but would not bee spoken with. After much fruitlesse importunity the man tolde the doctor he was resolved he should see his Master's water; he would not be turned away, threw it on the Dr.'s head. This humour pleased the Dr., and he went to the Gent. and cured him.

A gent. lying a-dyeing, sent his Servant with a horse for the doctor. The horse, being exceeding dry, ducks downe his head strongly into the water, and plucks downe the Dr. over his head, who was plunged in the water over head and ears. The Dr. was madded, and would return home. The man swore he should not; drewe his sword, and gave him ever and anon (when he would returne) a little prick, and so drove him before him.

The Dr. lyeing at the Savoy in London next the water side, where there was a Balcony look't into the Thames, a Patient came to him that was grievously tormented with an Ague. The Dr. orders a boate to be in readinesse under his windowe, and discoursed with the patient (a Gent.) in the Balcony, when, on a signall given, two or three lusty Fellowes came behind the Gentleman and threwe him a matter of 20 feete into the Thames. This surprize absolutely cured him.

A Gent. with a red ugly, pumpled face came to him for a cure. Said the Dr., I must hang you. So presently he had a device made ready to hang him from a Beame in the roome, and when he was e'en almost dead, he cutt the veines that fed these pumples and lett out the black ugley Bloud, and cured him.

That he was chymical I know by this token, that his mayd came running in to him one time like a slutt and a Furie; with her haire about her eares, and cries, Butler! come and looke to your Devilles your selfe, and you will; the stills are all blowne up! She tended them, and it seems gave them too

[49]

greate a heate. Old Dr. Ridgely knew him, and I thinke was at that time with him.

He was much addicted to his humours, and would suffer persons of quality to wayte sometimes some hours at his dore, with Coaches, before he would receive them. Dr. Gale, of Paule's School, assures me that a French man came one time from London to Cambridge, purposely to see him, whom he made staye two howres for him in his Gallery and then he came out to him in an old blew gowne. The French gentleman makes him 2 or 3 very lowe Bowes to the ground. Dr. Butler whippes his Legge over his head, and away goes into his chamber, and did not speake with him.

WILLIAM CAMDEN

[Born 1551. Antiquary and historian. He was appointed Head-master of Westminster School in 1593. He made tours of antiquarian investigation up and downe England, and published his *Britannia* in 1586. In 1597 he was made Clarencieux King-at-Arms, which freed him from his academic duties and enabled him to devote more time to his historical work. His other principal books are *Annals of the Reign of Elizabeth, Monuments and Inscriptions in Westminster Abbey* and a collection of *Ancient English Historians.* He wrote principally in Latin, but his *Britannia* was translated into English by Philemon Holland in 1610. Died 1623.]

D R. NICHOLAS MERCATOR has Stadius's *Ephemerides,* which had been one of Mr. Camden's; his name is there (I knowe his hand) and there are some notes by which I find he was Astrologically given.

In his *Britannia* he haz a remarkable Astrologicall observation, that when Saturn is in Capricornus a great Plague is certainly in London. He had observed it all his time, and setts downe the like made by others before his time. Saturn was so posited in the great plague 1625, and also in the last great plague 1665. He likewise delivers that when an Eclipse happens in Scorpio that 'tis fatall to the Towne of Shrewsbury.

Mr. Camden told Sir Robert Filmore that he was not suffered to print many things in his *Elizabetha,* which he sent over to his acquaintance and correspondent Thuanus, who printed it all faithfully in his *Annalls* without altering a word.

He was basted by a Courtier of the Queene's in the Cloysters at Westminster for denigrating Queen Elizabeth in his History.

When my grandfather went to schoole at Yatton-Keynell (neer Easton-Piers) Mr. Camden came to see the church, and particularly tooke notice of a little painted-glasse-windowe in the chancell, which (ever since my remembrance) haz been walled-up, to save the parson the chardge of glazing it.

'Tis reported, that he had bad Eies (I guesse Lippitude) which was a great inconvenience to an Antiquary.

Mr. Camden much studied the Welch language, and kept a Welsh servant to improve him in that language, for the better understanding of our Antiquities.

Sir William Dugdale tells me that he haz Minutes of King

James's life to a moneth and a day, written by Mr. William Camden (those memoires were continued within a fortnight of his death) as also his owne life, according to yeares and daye, which is very briefe, but 2 sheetes, Mr. Camden's owne hand writing. Sir William Dugdale had it from John Hacket, Bishop of Coventry and Lichfield, who did filch it from Mr. Camden as he lay a dyeing.

He lies buried in the South Cross-aisle of Westminster Abbey, his effigies $\frac{1}{2}$ on an Altar; in his hand a Booke, on the leaves wherof is writt BRITANNIA.

I have heard Sir Wm. Dugdale say, that though Mr. Camden had the Name, yet Mr. Glover was the best Herald that did ever belong to the Office. He tooke a great deale of paines in searching the Antiquities of severall Counties. He wrote a most delicate hand, and pourtrayed finely.

There is (or late was) at a Coffee house at the upper end of Bell-yard (or Shier-lane) under his owne hand, a Vistation of Cheshire, a most curious piece, which Sir Wm. Dugdale wish't me to see; and he told me that at York, at some ordinary house (I thinke a house of entertainment) he sawe such an elaborate piece of Yorkshire. But severall Counties he surveyd, and that with great exactnes, but after his death they were all scattered abroad, and fell into ignorant hands.

WILLIAM CARTWRIGHT

[Born 1611. Dramatist and divine. He was educated at the Free School at Cirencester and afterwards, as a King's Scholar, at Westminster, whence he was chosen in 1628 Student of Christ Church, Oxford. Having taken the degree of M.A. in 1635, he entered into holy orders and became, according to Anthony Wood, *the most florid and seraphical preacher in the University.* On the 1st of September, 1642, he was nominated one of the Council of War and on the 16th of September he was imprisoned by the Lord Say, but was released on bail and next April was chosen Junior Proctor of the University. He died at Oxford on the 29th of November, 1643, of a malignant fever (called the camp-disease) and was buried on the 1st of December at the upper end of the north aisle of Christ Church Cathedral. His reputation amongst his contemporaries was enormous, and Fell said of him: *Cartwright was the utmost man could come to.* Lloyd is still more enthusiastic in his praise: *To have the same person cast his net and catch souls as well in the pulpit as on the stage! A miracle of industry and witt, sitting sixteen hours a day at all manner of knowledge, an excellent preacher in whom hallowed fancies and reason grew visions and holy passions, raptures and extasies, and all this at thirty years of age!* When *The Royal Slave*, a *Tragi-Comedy*, was performed before the King and Queen by the students of Christ Church in 1636, the Court *unanimously acknowledg'd that it did exceed all things of that nature which they had ever seen,* and his early death was felt to deal a mortal blow to the stage. The King, who was then at Oxford, being asked why he wore black on the day of Cartwright's funeral, replied that *since the Muses had so much mourned for the loss of such a son, it would be a shame for him not to appear in mourning for the loss of such a subject.*]

GLOCESTERSHIRE is famous for the birth of William Cartwright at a place called Northway neer Tewksbury. Were he alive now he would be sixty-one. (This I have from his brother, who lives not far from me, and from his sisters whom I called upon in Glocestershire at Leckhampton. His sister Howes was 57 yeares old the 10 March last: her brother William was 4 yeares older.)

His father was a gentleman of 300 pounds per annum. He kept his Inne at Cirencester, but a year or therabout, where he declined and lost by it too. He had by his wife 100 pounds per annum, in Wiltshire, an impropriation, which his son has now (but having many children, lives not handsomely and haz lost his Learning: he was by the second wife, whose estate this was).

He writt a Treatise of Metaphysique, as also Sermons, particularly the Sermon that by the King's command he preached at His return from Edge-hill fight.

William Cartwright was buried in the south aisle in Christ Church, Oxon. Pitty 'tis so famous a Bard should lye without an Inscription.

'Tis not to be forgott that King Charles 1st dropt a teare at the newes of his death.

LUCIUS CARY: VISCOUNT FALKLAND

[Born 1610. Poet, statesman, courtier. Imprisoned in the Fleet to prevent him fighting a duel 1630. Vainly sought service in Holland before serving as a volunteer against the Scots 1639. Member of the Short and Long Parliaments. Spoke against Laud's ecclesiastical tyranny and for Strafford's attainder, but opposed the abolition of Episcopacy 1641. Secretary of State 1642. Accompanied Charles I to York and was sent to negotiate with Parliament 1642. Present at the siege of Gloucester. Despairing of peace, he threw away his life at Newbury fight in September 1643. His verses and philosophical tractates were published posthumously.]

HE maried Letice, the daughter of Sir Richard Morison, by whom he had two sonnes; the eldest lived to be a man, died *sine prole* [without issue], the second was father to this Lord Falkland now living.

This Lady Letice was a good and pious Lady, as you may see by her Life writt about 1649 or 50, by John Duncomb D.D. But I will tell you a pretty story from William Hawes, of Trin. Coll., who was well acquainted with the Governor aforesaid, who told him that my Lady was (after the manner of woemen) much governed by, and indulgent to, the Nursery: when she had a mind to beg any thing of my Lord for one of her mayds, nurses, etc., she would not doe it by herselfe (if she could helpe it) but putt this Gentleman upon it, to move it to my Lord. My Lord had but a small estate for his Title; and the old gentleman would say, Madam, this is so unreasonable a motion to propose to my Lord that I am certaine he will never grant it; e.g. one time to lett a Farme twenty pound per annum: under value. At length, when she could not prevaile on him, she would say that, I warrant you, for all this, I will obtaine it of my Lord: *it will cost me but the expence of a few Teares*. Now she would make her words good: and this great Witt, the greatest master of Reason and Judgement of his time, at the long runne, being stormed by her *Teares* (I presume there were kisses and secret embraces that were also ingredients) would this pious Lady obtain her unreasonable desires of her poor Lord.

[55]

My Lord in his Youth was very wild, and also mischievous, as being apt to stabbe and doe bloudy mischiefs; but 'twas not long before he tooke up to be serious, and then grew to be an extraordinary hard student. I have heard Dr. Ralph Bathurst say that, when he was a boy, my Lord lived at Coventrey (where he had then a House) and that he would sett up very late at nights at his study, and many times came to the Library at the Schoole there.

The Studies in fashion in those dayes (in England) were Poetrey; and Controversie with the Church of Rome. My Lord's Mother was a Zealous Papist, who being very earnest to have her son of her Religion, and her son upon that occasion, labouring hard to find the Trueth, was so far at last from setling on the Romish church, that he setled and rested in the Polish (I meane Socinianisme.) He was the first Socinian in England; and Dr. Hugh Crescy, of Merton Coll. (Dean of Leighlin in Ireland, afterwards a Bendictin Monke) told me that he himselfe was the first that brought Socinus's bookes; shortly after, my Lord comeing to him, and casting his eie on them, would needs presently borrow them, to peruse; and was so extremely taken and satisfied with them, that from that time was his Conversion.

My Lord much lived at Tue, which is a pleasant seat, and about 12 miles from Oxford; his Lordship was acquainted with the best Witts of that University, and his House was like a Colledge, full of Learned men. Mr. William Chillingworth, of Trinity College in Oxford (afterwards D.D.) was his most intimate and beloved favourite, and was most commonly with my Lord. His chaplaine Charles Gataker was an ingeniose young Gentleman, but no Writer. For learned Gentlemen of the Country, his acquaintance was Mr. Sandys, the Traveller and Translator; Ben. Johnson; Edmund Waller, Esq.; Mr. Thomas Hobbes, and all the excellent of that peacable time.

In the Civill-warres he adhered to King Charles I, who after Edge-hill fight made him Principall Secretary of Estate (with Sir Edward Nicholas) which he dischardged with a great deal of Witt and Prudence, only his advice was very unlucky to his Majestie, in perswading him (after the victory at Rownd-way-downe, and the taking of Bristowe) to sitt-downe before Glocester, which was so bravely defended by that incomparably vigilant Governor, Col. Massey, and the diligent and careful soldiers and citizens (men and woemen) that it so broke and weakened the King's Army, that 'twas the procatractique cause of his ruine. After this, all the King's matters went worse and worse. At the fight at Newbery, my Lord Falkland being there, and having nothing to doe to chardge ; as the two armies were engageing, rode in like a mad-man (as he was) between them, and was (as he needs must be) shott. Some that were your superfine discoursing politicians and fine Gentlemen, would needs have the reason of this mad action of throwing away his Life so, to be his discontent for the unfortunate advice given to his master as aforesaid ; but, I have been well enformed, by those who best knew him, and knew intrigues behind the curtaine (as they say) that it was the griefe of the death of Mris. Moray, a handsome Lady at Court, who was his Mistresse, and whom he loved above all creatures, was the true cause of his being so madly guilty of his own Death, as afore mentioned.

The next day, when they went to bury the dead, they could not find his Lordship's body ; it was stript and trod-upon and mangled, so there was one that wayted on him in his chamber would undertake to know it from all other bodyes, by a certaine Mole his Lordship had in his Neck, and by that marke did finde it. He lies interred at Great Tue, but, I thinke, yet without any monument.

In the dining roome, there is a picture of his at length, and like him ('twas done by Jacob de Valke, who taught me to paint.) He was a little man and of no great strength of body ; he had blackish haire, something flaggy, and I thinke his eies black. Dr. Earles would not allow him to be a good poet, though a great Witt ; he writt not a smoth verse, but a great deal of Sense.

SIR CHARLES CAVENDISH

[Born 1591. Mathematician. Brother of the first Duke of Newcastle. Accompanied Sir Henry Wotton to France 1612. Knighted 1619. M.P. for Nottingham 1624, 1628 and 1640. On the outbreak of the Civil War he served for the King, under his brother, as lieutenant-general of horse 1642. Despairing of the Royal cause, he went to Hamburg in 1644 and remained on the Continent until 1651. He then returned to London, where he lived in extreme poverty as his estates had been confiscated. He was at last admitted to compound, on making submission to Parliament, and bought back Welbeck and Bolsover, which had been confiscated from his brother. Died 1654.]

SIR CHARLES CAVENDISH was the younger Brother to William, Duke of Newcastle. He was a little, weake, crooked man, and nature having not adapted him for the Court nor Campe, he betooke himself to the Study of the Mathematiques, wherin he became a great Master. His father left him a good Estate, the revenue wherof he expended on bookes and on learned men.

He had collected in Italie, France, &c., with no small chardge, as many Manuscript Mathematicall bookes as filled a Hogges-head, which he intended to have printed; which if he had lived to have donne, the growth of Mathematicall Learning had been 30 yeares or more forwarder then 'tis. But he died of the Scurvey, contracted by hard study, about 1652, and left an Attorney of Clifford's Inne, his Executor, who shortly after died, and left his Wife Executrix, who sold this incomparable Collection aforesaid, by weight to the past-board makers for Wast-paper. A good Caution for those that have good MSS. to take care to see them printed in their life-times.

He writt severall things in Mathematiques for his owne pleasure.

CHARLES CAVENDISH

[Born 1620. Royalist General. Travelled in the East 1638–1640. Served under the Prince of Orange 1641: At the beginning of the Civil War he became a volunteer in the Guards. He was given a troop after Edgehill. He raised a regiment of horse and was given command in Nottinghamshire and Lincoln. He was victorious at Grantham, Ancaster and Burton-on-Trent, but was defeated and slain at Gainsborough in 1643, at the age of twenty-three.]

CHARLES CAVENDISH, Colonel, was second son to the Right Honourable Earle of Devonshire, brother to this present Earle, William.

He was well educated, and then travelled into France, Italie, &c.; but was so extremely delighted in travelling, that he went into Greece, all over; and that would not serve his turne but he would goe to Babylon, and then his Governour would not adventure to goe any further with him; but to see Babylon he was to march in the Turks armie.

Upon his returne into England the Civill Warres brakeout, and he tooke a Commission of a Colonel in his Majestie's Cause, wherin he did his Majestie great service, and gave signall proofs of his Valour.

He was the Souldiers' Mignion, and his Majestie's Darling, designed by him Generall of the Northern Horse (and his Commission was given him) a great marke of Honour for one of about five and twenty : *Thus shall it be donne to the man whom the King delights to Honour.*

Col. Cavendish was a Princely person, and all his actions were agreable to that character : he had in an eminent degree the semblance and appearance of a man made to governe. Methinkes he gave cleare this indication, the King's Cause lived with him, the King's Cause died with him; when Cromwell heard that he was Slaine, he cried upon it *We have donne our Businesse.*

And yet two things (I must confess) this Commander knew not, pardon his ignorance, he knew not to Flie away—he knew not how to aske quarter—though an older did, I meane Henderson ; for when this bold person entred Grantham on the one side, that wary Gentleman, who should have attaqued it, fled away on the other. If Cato thought it Usurpation in Caesar to give him his Life, Cavendish thought it a greater for Traytors and Rebells of a common Size to give him his. This brave Hero might be opprest (as he was at last by numbers) but he could not be conquered.

What wonders might have been expected from a Commander so Vigilant, so Loyall, so Constant, had he not dropt downe in his blooming age? But though he fell in his green yeares, he fell a prince, and a great one too; one whose Loyaltie to his great Master nothing could shake.

An high Extraction to some persons is like the Dropsie, the greatnesse of the man is his disease, and renders him unwieldlie: but here is a Person of great Extract free from the swelling of Greatness, as brisk and active as the lightest Horseman that fought under him. In some parts of India, they tell us, that a Nobleman accounts himselfe polluted if a Plebeian touch him; but here is a person of that rank who used the same familiaritie and frankness amongst the meanest of his Souldiers, the poorest miner, and amongst his equalls; and by stooping so low, he rose the higher in the common account, and was valued accordingly as a Prince, and a Great one.

Sir Robert Harley, an ingeniose Gent. and expert Soldier, haz often sayd, that (generally) the Commanders of the King's Army would never be acquainted with their Soldiers, which was an extraordinary Prejudice to the King's Cause. A Captaine's good look, or good word (some times) does infinitely winne them and oblige them; and he would say 'twas to admiration how Souldiers will venture their Lives for an obligeing Officer.

Consider Abner in the Manner of his Fall, that was by a treacherous hand, and so fell Cavendish. *And when Abner was returned to Hebron, Joab tooke him aside in the Gate to speake with him quietly, and smote him there under the fifth Rib, that he died, for the bloud of Asahel his brother.* Thus fell Abner; and thus Cavendish,—the Colonell's horse being mired in a bog at the Fight before Gainsborough, 1643, the Rebels surround him, and take him Prisoner; and after he was so, a base raskall comes behind him, and runs him through. Thus fell two great men by treacherous handes.

And lastly, the place of his Fall, that was in Israel. Here Abner fell in his, and Cavendish fell in our Israel—the Church of England. In this Church brave Cavendish fell, and what is more then that, in this Churches quarrel.

Thus I have compared Colonel Cavendish with Abner, a fighting and a famous man in Israel; you see how he does equal, how he does exceed him.

THOMAS CHALONER

[Born 1595. Regicide. M.P. for Richmond in Yorkshire 1645–
1653. Commissioner in Munster 1647. He was one of Charles I's
judges, and although he was absent on the last day, when sentence
was given, he signed the death warrant. Councillor of State 1651.
In 1653, at the violent dissolution of the Long Parliament, Cromwell
called him a drunkard. M.P. for Scarborough 1659. Excluded from
pardon 1660. Died 1661.]

THOMAS CHALONER, Esq., was a well bred Gentleman,
and of very good naturall parts, and of an agreable Humor.
He had the accomplishments of Studies at home, and
Travells in France, Italie and Germanie.

Riding a-hunting in Yorkshire (where the Allum Workes
now are) on a Common, he tooke notice of the soyle and
herbage, and tasted the water, and found it to be like that where
he had seen the Allum workes in Germanie. Wherupon he gott
a Patent of the King (Charles I) for an Allum-worke (which
was the first that ever was in England) which was worth to
him two thousand pounds per annum, or better ; but some
Courtiers did thinke the Profitt too much for him, and prevailed
so with the King, that, notwithstanding the Patent aforesayd,
he graunted a Moietie, or more, to another (a courtier) which
was the reason that made Mr. Chaloner so interest himselfe
for the Parliament-cause, and, in revenge, to be one of the King's
Judges.

He was as far from a Puritan as the East from the West.
He was of the Naturall Religion, and of Henry Martyn's Gang,
and one who loved to enjoy the pleasures of this life. He was
(they say) a good Scholar, but he wrote nothing that I heare
of, onely an anonymous pamphlett *An Account of the Discovery
of Moyses's Tombe* ; which was written very wittily. It was about
1652. It did sett the Witts of all the Rabbis of the Assembly
then to worke, and 'twas a pretty while before the Shamme was
detected.

He had a trick sometimes to goe into Westminster-hall
in a morning in Terme-time, and tell some strange story (Sham)
and would come thither again about 11 or 12 to have the
pleasure to heare how it spred ; and sometimes it would be

[61]

altered, with additions, he could scarce know it to be his owne. He was neither proud nor covetous, nor a hypocrite : not apt to doe injustice, but apt to revenge.

After the restauration of King Charles the Second, he kept the Castle at the Isle of Man, where he had a pretty Wench that was his Concubine ; where when Newes was brought him that there were some come to the Castle to demaund it for his Majestie, he spake to his Girle to make him a Possett, into which he putt, out of a paper he had, some Poyson, which did, in a very short time, make him fall a-vomiting exceedingly ; and after some time vomited nothing but Bloud. His Retchings were so violent that the Standers by were much grieved to behold it. Within three howres he dyed. The Demandants of the Castle came and sawe him dead : he was swoln so extremely that they could not see any eie he had, and no more of his nose than the tip of it, which shewed like a Wart, and his Coddes were swoln as big as one's head.

WILLIAM CHILLINGWORTH

[Born 1602. Divine. Educated at Oxford. Falling into theological doubts, he became a convert to Roman Catholicism and studied
at the Jesuit College at Douay in 1630. In the following year he
returned to Oxford and, after further consideration of the points
at issue, he rejoined the Church of England. This exposed him to
violent attacks by the Romanists, in reply to which he published in
1637 *The Religion of the Protestants a Safe Way to Salvation*. He was
regarded as one of the ablest controversialists of the Anglican Church.
Died 1644.]

WILLIAM CHILLINGWORTH, D.D., was borne in
Oxford. His father was a Brewer.

About anno 1630, he was acquainted with one
who drew him and some other scholars over to Doway, where
he was not so well entertained as he thought he merited for his
great Disputative Witt. They made him the porter (which
was to trye his temper, and exercise his obedience) so he stole
over and came to Trinity College again, where he was fellowe.

William Laud, A.B.C., was his Godfather and great friend.
He sent his Grace weekly intelligence of what passed in the
University. Sir William Davenant (poet laureat) told me that
notwithstanding this Doctor's great Reason, he was guilty of
the detestable Crime of Treacherie. Dr. Gill, Filius Dris. Gill
(Schoolmaster of Paules-schoole) and Chillingworth held
weekely intelligence one with another for some yeares, wherein
they used to nibble at states-matters. Dr. Gill in one of his
letters calles King James and his sonne, *the old foole and the
young one,* which letter Chillingworth communicates to W. Laud,
A. B. Cant. The poore young Dr. Gill was seised, and a terrible
storme pointed towards him, which, by the eloquent intercession and advocation of Edward, Earle of Dorset, together
with the Teares of the poore old Doctor, his father, and supplica-
tions on his knees to his Majestie, were blowne-over. I am
sorry so great a witt should have such a *naeve*.

He was a little man, blackish haire, of a Saturnine complexion. He never swore to all the points of the Church of
England.

The Lord Falkland and he had such extraordinary clear
reasons, that they were wont to say at Oxon that if the great

[63]

Turke were to be converted by naturall reason, these two were the persons to convert him.

When Doctor Kettle (the president of Trin. Coll. Oxon.) dyed, which was in anno 1643, Dr. Chillingworth was Competitor for the Presidentship, with Dr. Hannibal Potter and Dr. Roberts. Dr. Han. Potter had been formerly Chaplain to the Bishop of Winton, who was so much Dr. Potter's friend, that though (as Will Hawes haz told me) Dr. Potter was not lawfully elected, upon referring themselves to their visitor (Bishop of Winton), the Bishop (Curle) ordered Dr. Potter possession; and let the fellowes gett him out if they could. This was shortly after the Lord Falkland was slaine, who had he lived, Dr. Chillingworth assured Will. Hawes, no man should have carried it against him : and that he was so extremely discomposed and wept bitterly for the losse of his deare Friend, yet notwithstanding he doubted not to have an astergance for it.

My tutor, W. Browne, haz told me, that Dr. Chillingworth studied not much, but when he did, he did much in a little time. He much delighted in Sextus Empeiricus. He did walke much in the College grove, and there contemplate, and meet with some *cod's-head* or other, and dispute with him and baffle him. He thus prepared himselfe before-hand. I thinke it was an Epidemick evill of that time, which I thinke is growne out of fashion, as unmannerly and boyish. He was the readiest and nimblest Disputant of his time in the university, perhaps none haz equalled him since.

I have heard Mr. Thomas Hobbes, Malmsb. (who knew him) say, that he was like a lusty fighting fellow that did drive his enimies before him, but would often give his owne party smart back-blowes.

He lies buried in the south side of the Cloysters at Chichester, where he dyed of the *morbus castrensis* [siphylis] after the taking of Arundel castle by the Parliament : wherin he was very much blamed by the King's soldiers for his Advice in military affaires there, and they curst *that little Priest* and imputed the Losse of the Castle to his advice. In his sicknesse he was inhumanely treated by Dr. Cheynell, who, when he was to be buryed, threw his booke into the grave with him, saying, *Rott with the rotten ; let the dead bury the dead.*

GEORGE CLIFFORD: EARL OF CUMBERLAND

[Born 1558. Courtier and Adventurer. Succeeded his father as third Earl 1570. Having run through a great part of his very handsome property, he seized on the opportunity offered by the war with Spain to re-establish himself. In 1588 he commanded the *Elizabeth Bonaventure*, a Queen's ship of 600 tons, against the Spanish Armada and, after the decisive action off Gravelines, carried the news of the victory to the camp at Tilbury. The reports of his gallantry so pleased the Queen, that she lent him the *Golden Lion*, and later the *Victory*, to undertake expeditions to the South Seas. At his own expense, he fitted out ten privateering expeditions against Spain and Spanish America between 1586 and 1598, sailing personally with those of 1589, 1591, 1593 and 1598. At Court he was in high favour with the Queen, whose glove, set with diamonds, he wore as a plume in his hat. But want of fortune or management attended all his expeditions, and his loss seemed greater than his gain. Having at his majority inherited a large property, he was nearly a thousand pounds in debt when he died in 1605.]

THIS George, Earl of Cumberland, built the greatest Fleet of shipping that ever any Subject did. The Armada of the Argonautes was but a trifle to this. He was the greatest Navigator and did the most prodigious things at sea that ever any subject did at his own cost: he had a little fleet of (I thinke 20) brave ships of his own building and manning: for doing whereof he sold the Inheritance of above sixteen thousand pounds per annum; did great things against the Spaniard, etc: in the West Indies, whose atchievements would have much more compensated his chardges. But the Queen and councell when he had donne these things, seised on all his prizes and kept his ships, saying it was not to the safety of State to have any subject doe such great things.

He had a vast Estate, and could then ride in his owne lands from Yorkeshire to Westmorland.

The best account of his Expedition with his Fleet to America is to be found in Purchas's *Pilgrim*. He tooke from the Spaniards to the value of seaven or 8 hundred thousand poundes. When he returned with this rich Cargo (the richest without doubt that ever Subject brought) the Queene's Councell (where he had some that envyed him—*Virtutis comes Invidia* : [Envy is the attendant of Greatness]) layed their heads together and concluded 'twas too much for a Subject to have, and confiscated it all to the Queen, even the Shippes and all, and to make restauration to the Spaniard, that he was forced to sell fifteene thousand pounds per annum.

This was the breaking of that ancient and noble Family ; but Robert, Earl of Salisbury (who was the chiefest Enemie) afterwards maried his Daughter, as he might well be touch't in conscience, to make some recompence after he had donne so much mischiefe.

As I take it, Sir Walter Ralegh went this brave Voyage with his Lordship ; and Mr. Edmund Wright, the excellent Navigator ; and, not unlikely, Mr. Harriot too.

SIR EDWARD COKE

[Born 1552. Judge and law writer. Educated at Norwich Free School and Trinity College, Cambridge. Went to reside in Clifford's Inn in 1571, where he soon obtained a good practice. He married Bridget Paston, who brought him £30,000, besides a considerable property in land, and throughout his life he steadily added to his possessions. Advanced by Burghley's influence, he became Recorder of London and Solicitor-General in 1592, Speaker of the House of Commons in 1593 and Attorney-General in 1594. To spite Bacon, he married Burghley's granddaughter in 1598. Began publishing his *Law Reports* 1600. He showed great rancour in the trials of Essex, Raleigh and the Gunpowder Plotters. Decided against the King's authority to make law by proclamation 1610. Compelled, through Bacon's influence and against his own wish, to become Chief Justice of the King's Bench 1613. Suspended, partly through Bacon's representations to James I, and then dismissed from this office 1616. Though he returned to power later, his chief fame rests on his *Reports,* which established the supremacy of the Common Law in England. Died 1634.]

WHEN I was first of the Middle Temple, I heard an old Lawyer, who was his country-man affirme that Sir Edward Coke, Knight, Lord Chief Justice of the King's Bench, was borne but to 300 pounds a yeare land, and I have heard some of his country say again that he was borne but to 40 pounds per annum. What shall one beleeve ?

He was of Clifford's Inne before he was of the Inner Temple, as the fashion then was first to be of an Inne of Chancery.

Old John Tussell (that was my attorney) haz told me that he gott a hundred thousand pounds in one yeare, viz. 1° Jacobi, being then Attorney-Generall. His advice was that every man of Estate (right or wrong) should sue-out his Pardon, which cost 5 pounds which belonged to him.

He left an estate of eleeven thousand pounds per annum. Sir John Danvers, who knew him, told me that he had heard one say to him, reflecting on his great scraping of wealth, that his sonnes would spend his Estate faster than he gott it ; he replyed, They cannot take more delight in the spending of it then I did in the getting of it.

His second wife, Elizabeth, the relickt of Sir William Hatton, was with Child when he maried her : laying his hand on her belly (when he came to bed) and finding a Child to stirre, What, sayd he, Flesh in the Pott. Yea, quoth she, or els I would not have maried a Cooke.

He shewed himselfe too clownish and bitter in his carriage to Sir Walter Ralegh at his Triall, where he sayes *Thou Traytor,* at every word, and *thou lyest like a Traytor.*

He will play with his Case as a Cat would with a mouse and be so fulsomely Pedantique that a Schoole boy would nauseate it. But when he comes to matter of Lawe, all acknowledge him to be admirable.

When Mr. Cuff, secretary to the Earle of Essex, was arraigned, he would dispute with him in Syllogismes, till at last one of his brethern said, Prithee, brother, leave off: thou doest dispute scurvily. Cuff was a smart man and a great Scholar and baffeld him. Said Cooke, *Dominum cognoscite vestrum* [Know your own Master] Cuff replied, *My Lord, you leave out the former part of the verse, which you should have repeated, Acteon ego sum,* reflecting on his being a Cuckold.

After he was putt out of his place of Lord Chief Justice of the King's Bench, to spite him, they made him Sheriff of Buckinghamshire; at which time he caused the Sheriff's oath to be altered, which till that time was, amongst other things, to emquire after and apprehend all Lollards. He was also chosen, after he was displaced, a Burghesse to sitt in Parliament.

He was of wonderfull painstaking, as appeares by his Writings. He was short-sighted but never used spectacles to his dyeing day, being then 83 yeares of age. He was a very handsome proper man and of a curious compexion, as appeares by his Picture at the Inner Temple, which his grandson gave them about 1668, at length, in his Atturney generall's fusted gowne, which the House haz turned into Judge's robes.

The world expected from him a Commentary on Littleton's *Tenures*; and he left them his Common-place book, which is now so much made use of.

Memorandum :—when the Play called *Ignoramus* (made by one Ruggles of Clare-hall) was acted with great applause before King James, they dressed Sir Ignoramus like Chief Justice Coke and cutt his beard like him and feigned his voyce. This drollery did sett all the Lawyers against the Clergie, and shortly upon this Mr. Selden wrote of Tythes not *jure divino.*

JEAN BAPTISTE COLBERT

[Born 1619. Statesman. Louis XIV made it a rule to work in person at what he called *his business as king*. He carried on his operations regardless of the great dignitaries of the land, closeting himself with three or four confidential ministers, and himself deciding all the important business of government in accordance with the reports they made to him. Since these ministers were men of bourgeois origin, Louis XIV imagined himself to be dealing with mere clerks who were the instruments of his will. But as a matter of fact, since they possessed experience of affairs and were acquainted with the details of administration, they were able to suggest to the King whatever decisions they desired him to make. The most active of these ministers was Colbert, for whom was created the new office of Controller-General of Finance with which he combined two other Secretaryships of State so as to concentrate in his own hands all business except the army and diplomacy. Colbert had no new ideas to contribute : in his view the most important thing was to keep the greatest possible quantity of money in the kingdom ; he therefore tried to discourage imports and to hamper the maritime trade of other countries, while encouraging the manufacture of industrial products in France by creating trading companies, each of which enjoyed a monopoly in a certain field. But all these companies went bankrupt, leaving only a few traces behind them, such as the Gobelins and Beauvais tapestry works, the mirror manufactory of Saint-Gobain and the lace of Chantilly and Alencon. While he was responsible for the navy, Colbert tried in vain to revive the galleys in the Mediterranean, but his influence produced effects on the Atlantic fleet which have lasted until the present day. For he imposed registration and compulsory service on all the sailors and fishermen of France and he founded the Naval Pensions Fund, the most ancient insurance fund in France. He died in 1683.]

MONSIEUR COLBERT was a Merchant and an excellent Accomptant, i.e. for Debtor and Creditor. He is of Scotish extraction and that obscure enough, his grandfather being a Scotish bag-piper to the Scotch regiment.

Cardinal Mezarin found that his Stables were very chardgeable to him, and was imposed upon in his Accompts. He hearing of this merchant Colbert to be a great master in this Art, sends for him and desires him to make inspection into his accounts and putt him into a better method to avoyd being abused. Which he did, and that so well that he imployed him in ordering the accounts of all his Estate and found him so usefull that he also made use of him to methodize and settle the Accompts of the King. This was his Rise.

JOHN COLET

[Born 1467. Scholar and theologian. He was the son of a wealthy citizen, who was twice Lord Mayor of London. The only survivor of a family of twenty-two, he went to Oxford and Paris, and thence to Italy; where he learned Greek and probably met Savonarola. Deciding to enter the Church, several livings were conferred on him by his family in 1485, while he was still a minor and long before he was ordained : for it was not until 1497 that he became a deacon and, the year after that, a priest. He continued to follow his studies, devoting himself chiefly to St. Paul's Epistles, on which he lectured in Latin at Oxford. He was outspoken against the corruptions of the Church, and would have been called to account but for the protection of Archbishop Warham : he was, in fact, later accused of heresy and treason. He had the spirit of a scientific enquirer, holding that the first four chapters of *Genesis* should be considered as poetry rather than fact, and that we should love God rather than know Him. He became friendly with Erasmus in 1498, and Sir Thomas More called him his *spiritual director*. In 1504 he was appointed Dean of St. Paul's. He inherited a vast fortune on his father's death in 1505, and spent £40,000 of it on the foundation of St. Paul's School. It is rather for his learning and his attitude to the advancement of knowledge, than for his own writings, that he has such a high place in the history of English literature. He died in 1519.]

JOHN COLET, D.D., Deane of St. Paule's, London. After the Conflagration (his Monument being broken) somebody made a little hole towards the upper edge of his Coffin, which was closed like the coffin of a Pye and was full of a Liquour which conserved the body. Mr. Wyld and Ralph Greatorex tasted it and 'twas of a kind of insipid tast, something of an Ironish tast. The Coffin was of Lead, and layd in the Wall about 2 foot ½ above the surface of the Floore.

This was a strange rare way of conserving a Corps : perhaps it was a Pickle, as for Beefe, whose Saltness in so many years the Lead might sweeten and render insipid. The body felt, to the probe of a stick which they thrust into a chinke, like boyld Brawne.

THOMAS COOPER

[Born 1517. Divine and scholar. The son of an Oxford tailor. It had been Cooper's intention to take Orders, but having adopted Protestant views, he found himself checked by the accession of Queen Mary. He therefore changed his pursuit, took a degree in Physic and began to practise in Oxford. In 1545 Thomas Lanquet died while writing a *Chronicle of the World*: he had brought it down from the Creation to A.D. 17, and Cooper undertook to carry it on to the reign of Edward VI. *Cooper's Chronicle A.D.* 17–1547 was published in 1549. In 1548 he had published a *Latin Dictionary*. On the death of Mary he was ordained, and in 1565 he published his *Thesaurus Linguae Romanorum,* which delighted Queen Elizabeth so much that she expressed her determination to promote the author as far as lay in her power. Cooper was therefore made Dean of Christ Church and Vice-Chancellor of Oxford in 1567, Dean of Gloucester in 1569, Bishop of Lincoln in 1570 and of Winchester in 1584. His wife was utterly profligate, but he refused to be divorced, even when the heads of the University offered to arrange it for him, declaring that he would not charge his conscience with such a scandal. He was lampooned by Martin Mar-Prelate in 1588 and 1589 and published an *Admonition* in his own defence in the latter year. He died in 1594.]

D R. EDWARD DAVENANT told me that this learned man had a shrew to his wife : who was irreconcileably angrie with him for sitting-up late at night so, compileing his *Dictionarie*.

When he had halfe-donne it, she had the opportunity to gett into his studie, tooke all his paines out in her lap, and threw it into the fire, and burnt it. Well, for all that, the good man had so great a zeale for the advancement of learning, that he began it again, and went through with it to that Perfection that he hath left it to us, a most usefull Worke. He was after wards made Bishop of Winton.

RICHARD CORBET

[Born 1582. Divine. He was friendly with the powerful Duke of Buckingham, who procured the Deanery of Christ Church for him in 1620. In 1628 when the Deanery was required by the Earl of Dorset for Brian Duppa, Corbet was elected to the vacant see of Oxford, and was translated to Norwich in 1622. He was acknowledged the best poet of all the bishops of England, and though his verse was usually in a rollicking satiric vein, he wrote one extremely bitter poem *Upon Mrs. Mallet, an unhandsome gentlewoman that made love to him.* He died in 1635.]

RICHARD CORBET, D.D., was the son of Vincent Corbet, who was a Gardner at Twicknam. He was a Westminster scholar ; old Parson Bussey, of Alscott in Warwickshire, went to schoole with him. He would say that he was a very handsome man, but something apt to abuse, and a Coward.

He was a Student of Christ Church in Oxford. He was very facetious, and a good Fellowe. One time, he and some of his acquaintance being merry at Fryar Bacon's study (where was good liquor sold) they were drinking on the Leads of the house, and one of the scholars was a sleepe, and had a paire of goode silke stockings on. Dr. Corbet (then M.A. if not B.D.) gott a paire of Cizers and cutt them full of little Holes, but when the other awaked, and perceived how and by whom he was abused, he did chastise him, and made him pay for them.

After he was Doctor of Divinity, he sang Ballads at the Crosse at Abingdon on a market-day. He and some of his Camerades were at the Taverne by the Crosse (which, by the way, was then the finest of England ; I remember it when I was a Freshman ; it was admirable curious Gothique Architecture, and fine Figures in the niches ; 'twas one of those built by King Edward I for his Queen). The Ballad-singer complayned he had no custome ; he could not putt-off his Ballads. The jolly Dr. putts-off his Gowne, and putts-on the Ballad-singer's Leathern jacket, and being a handsome man, and had a rare full Voice, he presently vended a great many, and had a great Audience.

He was made Deane of Christ Church. He had good Interest with great men, as you may find in his Poems, and with the then great Favourite, the Duke of Bucks. His excellent Witt was lettres of recommendation to him. I have forgott the story, but at the same time that Dr. Fell thought to have carried it, Dr. Corbett putt a pretty trick on, to lett him take a journey on purpose to London for it, when he had already the Graunt of it. His Poems are pure naturall Witt, delightfull and easie.

He preached a Sermon before the King at Woodstock (I suppose King James) and no doubt with a very good grace; but it happened that he was out, on which occasion there were made these verses:

A reverend Deane,
With his Ruffe starch't cleane,
  Did preach before the King:
In his Band-string was spied
A Ring that was tyed,
  Was not that a pritty thing?
The Ring without doubt
Was the thing putt him out,
  So oft hee forgot what was next;
For all that were there,
On my conscience dare sweare
  That he handled it more than his Text.

His conversation was extreme pleasant. Dr. Stubbins was one of his Cronies; he was a jolly fatt Dr. and a very good house-keeper; parson in Oxfordshire. As Dr. Corbet and he were riding in Lob Lane in wett weather ('tis an extraordinary deepe, dirty lane) the coach fell; and Dr. Corbet sayd that Dr. Stubbins was up to the elbowes in mud, he was up to the elbowes in Stubbins.

He was made Bishop of Oxford, and I have heard that he had an admirable, grave and venerable aspect.

One time, as he was Confirming, the country-people pressing in to see the Ceremonie, sayd he, *Beare off there, or I'le confirm yee with my Staffe.* Another time, being to lay his hand on the head of a man very bald, he turns to his chaplaine, Lushington, and sayd, *Some Dust, Lushington,* (to keepe his hand from slipping). There was a man with a great venerable Beard: sayd the Bishop, *You, behind the Beard.*

His Chaplain, Dr. Lushington, was a very learned and ingeniose man, and they loved one another. The Bishop sometimes would take the key of the wine-cellar, and he and his Chaplaine would goe and lock themselves in and be merry. Then first he layes downe his Episcopall hat—*There lyes the*

Doctor. Then he putts off his gowne—*There lyes the Bishop.* Then 'twas, *Here's to thee, Corbet,* and *Here's to thee, Lushington.*

He married Alice Hutton, whom 'twas sayd he bigott. She was a very beautifull woman, and so was her mother. He had a son that went to schoole at Westminster, with Ned Bagshawe: a very handsome youth, but he is run out of all, and goes begging up and downe to Gentlemen.

His Antagonist, Dr. Price the Anniversarist, was made Deane of Hereford. Dr. Watts, Canon of that church, told me that this Deane was a mighty Pontificall proud man, and that one time when they went in Procession about the Cathedral church, he would not doe it the usually way in his surplice, hood, etc., on foot, but rode on a mare thus habited, with the Common prayer booke in his hand, reading. A stone horse happend to breake loose, and smelt the mare, and ran and leapt her, and held the Reverend Deane all the time so hard in his Embraces, that he could not gett off till the horse had done his bussinesse. But he would never ride in procession afterwards.

The last words he sayd were, *Good night, Lushington.*

ABRAHAM COWLEY

[Born 1618. Poet. In childhood he was greatly influenced by reading Spenser, a copy of whose poems was in the possession of his mother. This, he said, made him a poet. His first book, *Poetic Blossoms,* was written when he was only ten and published when he was fifteen. At Cambridge he was distinguished for his graceful translations. On the outbreak of the Civil War he joined the Royalists, was turned out of his College, and in 1646 followed the Queen to Paris, where he remained for twelve years, during which time he rendered unwearied service to the royal family and was employed on delicate diplomatic missions. At the Restoration he wrote some loyal odes, but was disappointed by being refused the Mastership of the Savoy, and retired to the country. Cowley's fame among his contemporaries was much greater than that which posterity has accorded to him. He is said by Pope to have died of a fever brought on by lying in the fields after a drinking-bout in 1667.]

MR. ABRAHAM COWLEY : he was borne in Fleet-street, London, neer Chancery-lane ; his father a Grocer.

He writ when a Boy at Westminster Poems and a Comedy called *Love's Riddle,* dedicated to Sir Kenelme Digby.

A. C. discoursed very ill, and with hesitation.

In December 1648, King Charles the first, being in great trouble, and prisoner at Caeresbroke, or to be brought to London to his Triall ; Charles Prince of Wales being then at Paris, and in profound sorrow for his father, Mr. Abraham Cowley went to wayte on him ; his Highnesse asked him whether he would play at Cards, to diverte his sad thoughts. Mr. Cowley replied, he did not care to play at cards ; but if his Highness pleasd, they would use *Sortes Virgilianae* (Mr. Cowley always had a Virgil in his pocket). The Prince accepted the proposal, and prick't his pinne in the fourth booke of the *Æneids.* The Prince understood not Latin well, and desired Mr. Cowley to translate the verses, which he did admirably well, and Mr. George Ent (who lived in his house at Chertsey, in the great plague 1665) shewed me Mr. Cowley's owne hand writing.

> By a bold people's stubborn arms opprest,
> Forced to forsake the land he once possess't,
> Torn from his dearest sonne, let him in vaine
> Seeke help, and see his friends unjustly slain.

[75]

Let him to base unequal termes submit,
In hope to save his crown, yet loose both it
And life at once, untimely let him dy,
And on an open stage unburied ly.

Now as to the last part, I well remember it was frequently and soberly affirmed by officers of the army, &c. Grandees, that the body of King Charles the First was privately putt into the Sand about White-hall; and the coffin that was carried to Windsor and layd in King Henry 8th's vault was filled with rubbish, or brick-batts. Mr. Fabian Philips, who adventured his life before the King's Tryall, by printing, assures me, that the Kings Coffin did cost but six shillings: a plain deale coffin.

He was Secretarie to the Earle of St. Albans (then Lord Jermyn) at Paris. When his Majestie returned, George, Duke of Bucks, hearing that at Chertsey was a good Farme belonging to the Queene-mother goes to the Earl of St. Alban's and the commissioners to take a Lease of it. Said the Earle to him, That is beneath your Grace, to take a Lease. That is all one, qd. he, I desire to have the favour to buy it for my money. He payd for it, and had it, and freely and generously gave it to his deare and ingeniose friend, Mr. Abraham Cowley, for whom purposely he bought it: which ought not to be forgotten.

He lies interred at Westminster Abbey, next to Sir Jeffrey Chaucer, where the Duke of Bucks has putte a neate Monument of white marble; above that a very faire Urne, with a kind of Ghirland of Ivy about it. His Grace the Duke of Bucks held a tassell of the Pall.

Vide his Will, *scilicet,* for his true and lasting Charity, that is, he settles his Estate in such a manner that every yeare so much is to be payd for the enlarging of poor Prisoners cast into Gaole by cruel Creditors for small Debts. I doe think this memorable Benefaction is not mentioned in his life in print before his Workes; it is certainly the best method of Charity.

SIR CHARLES DANVERS

[Born 1568. Soldier. His brothers were Henry, Earl of Danby and Sir John Danvers. Charles Danvers was elected a Member of Parliament in 1586, when he was eighteen. He served under Lord Willoughby in the Netherlands and was knighted by his commander in 1588. He and his brother Henry were outlawed for killing a neighbour, Henry Long, in a quarrel in 1593 and they took refuge in France, where Henri IV received them kindly and interceded with Queen Elizabeth in their behalf. However, it was not until 1598 that they were pardoned. In 1599 Charles Danvers was given a colonel's commission in the army that accompanied Essex to Ireland and later joined in Essex's abortive rising in 1601. He made a full confession, admitting his guilt, and was beheaded the same year.]

SOMMERFORD magna—the Assassination of Harry Long was contrived in the parlour of the Parsonage here: R. Wisdome was then Lecturer and preacht that day, and Henry Long expired in his armes. My great-grandfather, R. Danvers, was in some trouble about it, his Horses and Men being in that Action. His Servants were hanged.

Sir John Danvers, the father, was a most beautifull and good and even-tempered person. He was of a mild and peacable nature, and his sonnes' sad accident brake his heart.

George Herbert's verses pinned on the Curtaine of the picture of old Sir John:

> Passe not by : search and you may
> Find a Treasure worth your stay.
> What makes a Danvers would you find ?
> In a faire Bodie, a faire Minde.
> Sir John Danvers' earthly part
> Here is copied out by Art :
> But his heavenly and divine
> In his Progenie doth shine.
> Had he only brought them forth
> Know that much had been his Worth.
> Ther's no Monument to a Sonne :
> Reade him there, and I have donne.

His picture is yet extant : my Cosen John Danvers (his Son) haz it.

Sir Henry Danvers, Knight, Earle of Danby and Baron of Dauntesey, was second sonn of old Sir John Danvers of Dauntesey Knight. He was of a magnificent and munificent spirit: and made that noble Physick-garden at Oxford, and endowed it with I think 30 pounds per annum.

Henry, Earl of Danby, was page to Sir Philip Sydney. He perfected his Latin when a man by parson Oldham of Dodmerton; was a perfect master of the French; a Historian; Tall and spare; Temperate; sedate and solid; a very great favorite of Prince Henry. He bred up severall brave young Gentlemen, and preferred them, e.g. Colonel Leg, since Earl of Dartmouth, and severall others; lived most at Cornbury; a great Improver of his Estate, to eleaven thousand pounds per annum at the least, neer twelve. A great Oeconomist: He allowed three thousand pounds per annum only for his Kitchin. All his servants were sober and wise in their respective places.

He was made a Knight of the Garter A.D. 1633. For many years before St. Georges Feast had not been more magnificently kept, then when this Earle with the Earle of Morton were installed Knights of the Garter. One might then have beheld the abridgment of English, and Scotish in their Attendance. The Scotish Earle (like Zeuxis his Picture) adorned with all art and costlinesse: whilst our English Earle (like to the plaine sheet of Apelles) by the gravity of habit, gott the advantage of the Gallantry of his Corrival with judicious beholders.

He never maried; and by his Will made 1639, setled his Estate on his hopefull Nephew Henry D'Anvers (only sonne of Sʳ John Danvers) snatch't away (before fully of age) to the great griefe of all good men.

Full of Honour, Wounds, and Dayes, he dyed Anno Domini 1643, and lies buried in a little Chapel made for his Monument, on the north side of Dantesey-church; near to the Vault where his father and ancestors lie.

Elizabeth Danvers, his mother, an Italian, prodigious parts for a Woman. I have heard my father's mother say that she had Chaucer at her fingers' ends. A great Politician; great Witt and spirit, but revengefull: knew how to manage her estate as well as any man; understood Jewels as well as any Jeweller. Very Beautifull, but only short-sighted.

To obtain Pardons for her Sonnes she maryed Sir Edmund Carey, cosen-german to Queen Elizabeth, but kept him to hard meate.

Sir Charles Danvers advised the Earle of Essex, either to treat with the Queen (but Sir Ferdinando Gorges did let the

Hostages goe) or to make his way through the gate at Essex-house, and then to hast away to High-gate, and so to Northumberland (the Earl of Northumberland maried his mother's sister) and from thence to the King of Scots, and there they might make their Peace; if not, the Queen was old and could not live long. But the Earle followed not his advice, and so they both lost their heads on Tower-hill, February the 6th, 1600.

His familiar acquaintance were the Earl of Oxon; Sir Francis and Sir Horace Vere; Sir Walter Raleigh, etc.—the Heroes of those times.

With all their faylings, Wilts cannot shew two such Brothers.

SIR JOHN DANVERS

[Born 1588. Regicide. Brother of Sir Charles Danvers and the
first Earl of Danby. Knighted by James I, he was Member of Parliament for Oxford University in 1625, 1626, 1628 and 1639. A colonel
in the Parliamentary Army, he sat as M.P. for Malmesbury in 1645.
He signed the death-warrant of Charles I in 1649, and from that date
until 1653 he was a member of the Council of State. He died in 1655.]

THE Mannor of Dantesey in Wilts was forfeited to the
Crowne by Sir John Danvers his foolery.

At Dantesey was a robbery committed at the Mannour
howse, on the family of the Stradlings : Sir Edward, and all
his servants, except one plowboy who hid himselfe, were
murthered : by which meanes, this whole Estate came to Anne
his sister, and heire. She married after to Sir John Danvers
(the father) a handsome gentleman, who clapt up a match with
her before she heard the newes, he, by good fortune lighting
upon the Messenger first. She lived at that time in Paternoster-
Rowe at London, and had but an ordinary portion.

This Robbury was donne on a Satterday night ; the next
day the neighbors wondered none of the family came to Church ;
they went to see what was the matter, and the Parson of the
parish very gravely went along with them, who, by the boy was
proved to be one of the company, and was, I thinke, hanged
for his paines.

Sir John Danvers told me that when he was a young man,
the principall reason of sending their sons to Travell, was to
weane them from their acquaintance and *familiarity* with the
Servingmen : for then Parents were so austere and grave, that
the Sonnes must not be company for their father, and *some*
company men must have : so they contracted a familiarity
with the Serving men, who got a *hank* upon them they could
hardly after clawe off. Nay, Parents would suffer their Servants
to domineer over their Children : and some in what they found
their child to take delight, in that would be sure to crosse them.

This young Sir John's first wife was the Lady Herbert,
a widowe, mother of the Lord Edward Herbert of Cherbury
and George Herbert, Orator. By her he had no issue ; she
was old enough to have been his Mother. He maried her for

love of her Witt. The Earl of Danby was greatly displeased with him for this disagreable match.

Sir John was a great friend of the King's partie and a Patron to distressed and cashiered Cavaliers. But to revenge himselfe of his sister, the Lady Gargrave, and to ingratiate himself more with the Protector to null his brother, Earl of Danby's, Will, he, contrary to his owne naturall inclination, did sitt in the High Court of Justice at the King's Triall.

The Pleasure and Use of Gardens were unknown to our great Grandfathers : They were contented with Pot-herbs : and did mind chiefly their Stables. But in the time of King Charles II^d Gardening was much improved, and became common. 'Twas Sir John Danvers of Chelsey (Brother and Heir to Henry Danvers Earle of Danby) who first taught us the way of Italian Gardens : He had well travelled France & Italy, and made good Observations : He had in a faire Body an harmonicall Mind : In his Youth his Complexion was so exceedingly beautifull and fine that Thomas Bond Esqr. (who was his Companion in his Travells) did say, that the People would come after him in the Street to admire Him. He had a very fine Fancy, which lay (chiefly) for Gardens, and Architecture. The Garden at Chelsey in Middlesex (as likewise the House there) doe remaine Monuments of his Ingenuity. He was a great acquaintance and Favorite of the Lord Chancellour Bacon, who took much delight in that elegant Garden.

Sir John, being my Relation and faithfull Friend, was wont in fair mornings in the Summer to brush his Beaver-hatt on the Hysop and Thyme, which did perfume it with its naturall Spirit ; and would last a morning or longer.

EDWARD DAVENANT

EDWARD DAVENANT, S. Theol. Dr., was the eldest son of Edward Davenant, Merchant of London, who was the elder brother to the Right Reverend Father in God, the learned John Davenant Bishop of Sarum.

I will first speake of the father, for he was an incomparable man in his time, and deserves to be remembred. He was of a healthy complexion (except the gout) rose at 4 or 5 in the morning, so that he followed his Studies till 6 or 7, the time that other merchants goe about their Businesse; so that, stealing so much and so quiet time in the morning, he studied as much as most men. He understood Greeke and Latin perfectly, and was a better Grecian than the Bishop: he writt a rare Greeke character as ever I sawe. He was a great Mathematician, and understood as much of it as was knowen in his time. He understood Trade very well, was a sober and good menager, but the winds and seas cross'd him. He had so great losses that he broke, but his Creditors knowing it was no fault of his, and also that he was a person of great Vertue and justice, used not extremity towards him; but I thinke gave him more Credit, so that he went into Ireland, and did sett up a Fishery for Pilchards at Wythy Island, in Ireland, where in 20 yeares he gott 10,000 pounds; satisfied and payd his Creditors; and over and above left a good estate to his son. His picture bespeakes him to be a man of judgement, and parts, and gravity extraordinary. He slipt comeing down the stone stayres at the Palace at Sarum, which bruise caused his death.

His brother, the Bishop, hung the Choire of Sarum with purple velvet, which was plundered in the Sacrilegious Times.

Dr. Edward Davenant was borne at his Father's howse at Croydon in Surrey (the farthest handsome great howse on the left hand as you ride to Bansted Downes). I have heard him say, he thankt God his father did not knowe the houre of his birth; for that it would have tempted him to have studyed Astrologie, for which he had no esteeme at all.

He went to school at Merchant Taylors' school, from thence to Queen's Colledge in Cambridge, of which house his uncle John Davenant (afterwards Bishop of Sarum) was head, where he was Fellowe. 'Twas no small advantage to him to have such a learned Father to imbue arithmeticall knowledge into him when a boy, night times when he came from schoole.

I remember when I was a young Oxford Scholar, that he could not endure to heare of the *New* (Cartesian) *Philosophy* : For, sayd he, if a new Philosophy is brought-in, a new Divinity will shortly follow ; and he was right.

When his uncle was preferred to the church of Sarum, he made his nephew Treasurer of the Church, which is the best Dignity, and gave him the Vicaridge of Gillingham in com. Dorset, and then Paulsholt parsonage, neer the Devises, which last in the late troubles he resigned to his wive's brother William Grove.

He was to his dyeing day of great diligence in study, well versed in all kinds of Learning, but his Genius did most strongly encline him to the Mathematiques, wherin he has written (in a hand as legible as print) MSS. in 4to a foot high at least. I have often heard him say (jestingly) that he would have a man knockt in the head that should write anything in Mathematiques that had been written of before. I have heard Sir Christopher Wren say that he does beleeve he was the best Mathematician in the world about 30 or 35 + yeares agoe. But being a Divine he was unwilling to print, because the world should not know how he had spent the greatest part of his time.

I have writt to his Executor, that we may have the honour and favour to conserve his MSS. in the Library of the Royal Societie, and to print what is fitt. I hope I shall obtaine my desire. He had a noble Library, which was the aggregate of his Father's, the Bishop's, and his owne.

He was of middling stature, something spare ; and weake, feeble leggs ; he had sometimes the Goute ; was of great temperance, he always dranke his beer at meales with a Toast, winter and summer, and sayd it made the beer the better.

He was very ready to teach and instruct. He did me the favour to informe me first in Algebra. His daughters were Algebrists.

He had an excellent way of improving his children's memories, which was thus : he would make one of them read a chapter or &c., and then they were (*sur le champ*) to repeate what they remembred, which did exceedingly profitt them ; and so for Sermons, he did not let them write notes (which jaded their memorie) but gave an account vivâ voce. When his eldest son, John, came to Winton-schoole (where the Boyes were enjoyned to write Sermon-notes) he had not wrote ; the Master askt him for his Notes—he had none, but sayd,

If I doe not give you as good an account of it as they doe, I am much mistaken.

He was heire to his uncle, John Davenant, Bishop of Sarum. When Bishop Coldwell came to this Bishoprick, he did lett long Leases, which were but newly expired when Bishop Davenant came to this sea; so that there tumbled into his coffers vast summes. His predecessor, Dr. Tounson, maried John Davenant's sister, continued in the see but a little while, and left severall children unprovided for, so the King or rather Duke of Bucks gave Bishop Davenant the Bishoprick out of pure charity: 'twas the only Bishoprick that he disposed of without symony, all others being made merchandise of for the advancement of his kindred. Bishop Davenant being invested, maried all his nieces to Clergie-men, so he was at no expence for their preferment. He granted to his nephew (this Dr.) the lease of the great Mannour of Poterne, worth about 1000 pounds per annum; made him Threasurer of the church of Sarum, of which the corps is the parsonage of Calne, which was esteemed to be of the like value. He made severall purchases, all of which he left him; insomuch as the churchmen of Sarum say, that he gained more by this Church then ever any man did by the Church since the Reformation, and take it very unkindly that, at his death, he left nothing (or but 50 pounds) to that Church which was the source of his Estate. How it happened I know not, or how he might be workt-on in his old age, but I have heard severall yeares since, he hadd sett downe 500 pounds in will for the Cathedral Church of Sarum.

He was not only a man of vast learning, but of great goodnes and charity; the parish and all his friends will have a great losse in him. He took no use for money upon bond. He was my singular good friend, and to whom I have been more beholding then to any one beside; for I borrowed five hundred pounds of him for a yeare and a halfe, and I could not fasten any interest on him.

SIR WILLIAM DAVENANT

[Born 1606. Dramatist. One of the founders of the Classical school of English poetry. He wrote twenty-five plays. Poet Laureate 1637. Knighted 1643. A Royalist in the Civil War, he was three times imprisoned by the Parliamentarians in the Tower, from which he was once released at the intercession of Milton. He had the satisfaction of repaying in kind these good offices when Milton, in his turn, was in danger in 1660. He owned the theatre where movable scenery and female actors were first habitually used. Died 1668.]

SIR WILLIAM DAVENANT, Knight, Poet Laureate, was borne in the City of Oxford, at the Crowne Taverne. He went to schoole at Oxon to Mr. Sylvester, but I feare he was drawne from schoole before he was ripe enough.

His father was John Davenant, a Vintner there, a very grave and discreet Citizen ; his mother was a very beautifull woman and of a very good witt, and of conversation extremely agreable.

Mr. William Shakespeare was wont to goe into Warwickshire once a yeare, and did commonly in his journey lye at this house in Oxon, where he was exceedingly respected. (I have heard Parson Robert say that Mr. William Shakespeare haz given him a hundred kisses.) Now Sir William would sometimes, when he was pleasant over a glasse of wine with his most intimate friends—e.g. Sam Butler, author of *Hudibras,* etc., say, that it seemed to him that he writt with the very spirit that did Shakespeare, and seemed contented enough to be thought his Son. He would tell them the story as above, in which way his mother had a very light report, whereby she was called a Whore.

He was preferred to the first Dutches of Richmond to wayte on Her as a Page. I remember he told me, she sent him to a famous Apothecary for some Unicornes-horne, which he resolved to try with a Spider which he incircled in it, but without the expected successe ; the Spider would goe over, and thorough and thorough, unconcerned.

He was next a servant (as I remember, a Page also) to Sir Fulke Grevil, Lord Brookes, with whom he lived to his death, which was that a servant of his (that had long wayted on him, and his Lordship had often told him that he would doe something for him, but did not, but still putt him off with delayes) as he was trussing up his Lord's pointes comeing from Stoole (for then their breeches were fastned to the doubletts with points ; then came in hookes and eies ; which not to have fastened was in my boy-hood a great crime) stabbed him. This was at the same time that the Duke of Buckingham was stabbed by Felton, and the great noise and report of the Duke's, Sir William told me, quite drowned this of his Lord's, that 'twas scarce taken notice of. This Sir Fulke G. was a good witt, and had been a good Poet in his youth. He wrote a Poeme in folio which he printed not till he was old, and then (as Sir W. said) with too much judgement and refining, spoyled it, which was at first a delicate thing.

He writt a Play or Playes, and verses, which he did with so much sweetnesse and grace, that by it he got the love and friendship of his two Mecaenasses, Mr. Endymion Porter and Mr. Henry Jermyn (since Earl of St. Albans) to whom he has dedicated his Poeme called *Madegascar*. Sir John Suckling was also his great and intimate friend.

After the death of Ben Johnson he was made in his place Poet Laureat.

He gott a terrible clap of a Black handsome wench that lay in Axe-yard, Westminster, whom he thought on when he speakes of Dalga in *Gondibert*, which cost him his Nose, with which unlucky mischance many witts were too cruelly bold : e.g. Sir John Menis, Sir John Denham, etc.

In the Civill Warres in England he was in the Army of William, Marquess of Newcastle (since Duke) where he was Generall of the Ordinance. I have heard his brother Robert say, for that service there was owing to him by King Charles the First 10,000 pounds. During that warre, 'twas his Hap to have two Alderman of Yorke his Prisoners, who were some-thing stubborne, and would not give the Ransome ordered by the Councell of Warr. Sir William used them civilly and treated them in his Tent, and sate them at the upper end of his Table *à la mode de France,* and having donne so a good while to his chardge, told them (privately and friendly) that he was not able to keepe so chargeable Guests, and bad them take an opportunity to escape, which they did : but having been gon a little way they considered with themselves that in gratitude they ought to goe back and give Sir William their Thankes ; which they did, but it was like to have been to their great danger of being taken by the Soldiers, but they happened to gett safe to Yorke.

After the King was beaten out of the field, Sir William

Davenant (who received the honour of Knighthood from the Duke of Newcastle by Commission) went into France ; resided chiefly in Paris, where the Prince of Wales then was. He then began to write his Romance in Verse called *Gondibert*, and had not writt above the first booke, but being very fond of it, prints it (before a quarter finished) with an Epistle of his to Mr. Thomas Hobbes, and Mr. Hobbes excellent Epistle to him printed before it. The Courtiers with the Prince of Wales could never be at quiet about this piece, which was the occasion of a very witty but satericall little booke of Verses writt by George Duke of Bucks, Sir John Denham, etc. :

> *That thou forsak'st thy sleepe, thy Diet,*
> *And which is more then that, our quiet.*

This last word Mr. Hobs told me was the occasion of their writing.

Here he layd an ingeniose Designe to carry a considerable number of Artificers (chiefly Weavers) from hence to Virginia ; and by Mary the queen-mother's meanes, he got favour from the King of France to goe into the Prisons and pick and choose. So when the poor dammed wretches understood what the designe was, they cryed *uno ore* [with one voice] *Tout tisseran,* i.e. We are all weavers. Will picked 36, as I remember, if not more, shipped them, and as he was in his voyage towards Virginia, he and his Tisseran were all taken by the Shippes then belonging to the Parliament of England. The Slaves, I suppose, they sold, but Sir William was brought Prisoner to England. Whether he was first a Prisoner at Caresbroke Castle in the Isle of Wight or at the Tower of London, I have forgott ; he was a Prisoner at Both. His *Gondibert* was finished at Caresbroke Castle. He expected no mercy from the Parliament, and had no hopes of escaping his life. It pleased God that the two Aldermen of Yorke aforesayd, hearing that he was taken and brought to London to be tryed for his life, which they understood was in extreme danger, they were touched with so much Generosity and goodness, as, upon their owne accounts and meer motion, to try what they could to save Sir William's life, who had been so civill to them and a meanes to save theirs, to come to London : and acquainting the Parliament with it, upon their petition, etc., Sir William's life was saved.

'Twas Harry Martyn that saved Sir William Davenant's life in the Howse. When they were talking of sacrificing one, then said Henry that in Sacrifices they always offered pure and without blemish : now yee talke of making a Sacrifice of an old rotten rascall. *Vide* H. Martyn's life, where by this very jest, then forgott, the Lord Falkland saved H. Martyn's life.

Being freed from imprisonment, because Playes (*scil.* Tragedies and Comoedies) were in those Presbyterian times scandalous, he contrives to set up an Opera *stylo recitativo,* wherein Serjeant Maynard and severall Citizens were engagers. It began at Rutland howse in Charter-house-yard ; next at the Cock-pitt in Drury-Lane, where were acted very well, *stylo recitativo,* *Sir Francis Drake,* and *the Siege of Rhodes.* It did affect the Eie and eare extremely. This first brought Scenes in fashion in England ; before, at playes, was only a Hanging.

Anno Domini 1660 was the happy restauration of his Majestie Charles II. Then was Sir William made, and the Tennis-Court in Little Lincolnes-Inne-fielde was turn'd into a Play-house for the Duke of Yorke's Players, where Sir William had Lodgeings, and where he dyed.

I was at his funerall. He had a coffin of Walnutt-tree ; Sir John Denham sayd 'twas the finest coffin that ever he sawe. His body was carried in a Herse from the Play-house to Westminster-abbey, where, at the great West dore, he was received by the Singingmen and Choristers, who sang the Service of the Church (I am the Resurrection, etc.) to his Grave, which is in the South crosse aisle, on which, on a paving stone of marble, is writt, in imitation of that on Ben Johnson : *O rare Sir Will. Davenant.*

But me thought it had been proper that a Laurell should have been sett on his Coffin—which was not donne.

JOHN DEE

[Born 1527. Mathematician and astrologer. Fellow of Trinity College, Cambridge, where the clever stage effects he introduced into a performance of Aristophanes' *Peace* procured him his lifelong reputation of being a magician. Studied at Louvain 1548. Lectured on Euclid at Paris 1550. Rector of Upton-upon-Severn 1553. Acquitted by the Star Chamber of a charge of practising sorcery against Queen Mary's life, but put under the surveillance of Bishop Bonner as a possible heretic. Suggested to Queen Mary the formation of a Royal Library of Ancient Manuscripts 1556. Visited Venice 1563. Made a voyage to St. Helena. Travelled to Hungary to present his *Monas Hieroglyphica* to Maximilian II 1563. Explained the appearance of a new star 1572. At her request, he gathered descriptions of newly discovered countries for Queen Elizabeth 1580. Made calculations to facilitate the adoption in England of the Gregorian Calendar 1583. Went to Prague and had interviews with the Emperor Rodolph II and Stephen of Poland (1584) but was compelled to leave by the representations of the Bishop of Piacenza 1585. He headed a small confraternity, which dissolved in 1589, for seeking the Philosopher's Stone and invoking the angels. Warden of Manchester College 1595–1604. Fruitlessly petitioned James I to be formally cleared of the imputation of being a magician 1604. Wrote *A Treatise of the Rosie Crucean Secrets*. He invented the phrase " The British Empire." Died 1608.]

HEE had a very faire cleare rosie complexion; a long beard as white as milke; he was tall and slender; a very handsome man. His Picture in a wooden cutt is at the end of Billingsley's *Euclid*. He wore a Gowne like an Artist's gowne, with hanging sleeves, and a slitt; a mighty good man he was.

My great Grandfather, Will: Aubrey, and he were Cosins, and intimate acquaintance. Mr. Ashmole hath letters between them, under their owne hands, viz. one of Dr. W. A. to him (ingeniosely and learnedly written) touching the *Sovraignty of the Sea,* of which J. D. writt a booke which he dedicated to Queen Elizabeth and desired my great grandfather's advice upon it. Dr. A.'s countrey-house was at Kew, and J. Dee lived at Mortlack, not a mile distant. I have heard my grandmother say they were often together.

Among the MSS. in the Bodlean library of Doctor Gwyn,

are severall letters between him and John Dee, of Chymistrey and Magicall Secrets.

Meredith Lloyd sayes that John Dee's printed booke of *Spirits,* is not above the third part of what was writt, which were in Sir Robert Cotton's Library ; many whereof were much perished by being buryed, and Sir Robert Cotton bought the field to digge after it. He told me of John Dee, etc., conjuring at a poole in Brecknockshire, and that they found a wedge of Gold ; and that they were troubled and indicted as Conjurors at the Assizes ; that a mighty storme and tempest was raysed in harvest time, the countrey people had not knowen the like.

Old Goodwife Faldo (a Natif of Mortlak in Surrey) did know Dr. Dee, and told me that he did entertain the Polonian Ambassador at his howse in Mortlak, and dyed not long after; and that he shewed the Eclipse with a darke Roome to the said Ambassador. She beleeves that he was eightie years old when he dyed. She sayd, he kept a great many Stilles goeing. That he layd the storme. That the Children dreaded him because he was accounted a Conjurer. He recovered the Basket of Cloathes stollen, when she and his daughter (both Girles) were negligent: she knew this.

He used to distill Egge-shells, and 'twas from hence that Ben: Johnson had his hint of the *Alkimist,* whom he meant.

He was a great Peace-maker ; if any of the neighbours fell out, he would never lett them alone till he had made them friends. He told a woman (his neighbour) that she laboured under the evill tongue of an ill neighbour (another woman) which came to her howse, who he sayd was a Witch.

He was sent Ambassador for Queen Elizabeth (Goody Faldo thinkes) into Poland. The Emperour of Muscovia, upon report of the great learning of the Mathematician, invited him to Mosco, with offer of two thousand pound a yeare, and from Prince Boris one thousand markes ; to have his Provision from the Emperor's Table, to be honourably received, and accounted as one of the chief men in the Land. All of which Dee accepted not.

His regayning of the Plate for a friend's Butler, who comeing from London by water with a Basket of Plate, mistooke another basket that was like his. Mr. J. Dee bid them goe by water such a day, and looke about, and he should see the man that had his basket, and he did so ; but he would not gett the lost horses, though he was offered severall angells.

Arthur Dee, his sonne, a Physitian at Norwych and intimate friend of Sir Thomas Browne, M.D., told Dr. Bathurst that (being but a Boy) he used to play at Quóits with the Plates of Gold made by Projection in the Garret of Dr. Dee's Lodgings in Prague and that he had more than once seen the Philosopher's Stone.

[90]

SIR JOHN DENHAM

[Born 1615. Poet and architect. Son of the Chief Baron of the Exchequer in Ireland. He began his literary career with a tragedy, *The Sophy* (1641), which seldom rises above mediocrity. His poem, *Cooper's Hill* (1642), is the work by which he is remembered. It is the first example in English of a poem devoted to local description and was extravagantly praised by Dr. Johnson; but the place now assigned to Denham is a much more humble one. In his earlier years he suffered for his Royalism : but after the Restoration he enjoyed prosperity. Died 1669.]

SIR JOHN DENHAM was unpolished with the small-pox : otherwise a fine complexion. He was of the tallest, but a little incurvetting at his shoulders, not very robust. His haire was but thin and flaxen, with a moist curle. His gate was slow, and was rather a Stalking (he had long legges.) His Eie was a kind of light goose-gray, not big ; but it had a strange Piercingness, not as to shining and glory, but (like a Momus) when he conversed with you he look't into your very thoughts.

He was admitted of Trinity Colledge in Oxford : I have heard Mr. Josias Howe say that he was the dreamingst young fellow ; he never expected such things from him as he haz left the world. When he was there he would Game extremely ; when he had played away all his money he would play away his Father's wrought rich gold Cappes. He was as good a Student as any in the House. Was not suspected to be a Witt.

He was much rooked by Gamesters, and fell acquainted with that unsanctified Crew, to his ruine. His father had some suspition of it, and chid him severely, wherupon his son John (only child) wrot a little Essay, *Against Gameing, and to shew the Vanities and Inconveniences of it,* which he presented to his father to let him know his detestation of it. But shortly after his Father's death (who left 2000 or 1500 pounds in ready money, 2 houses well furnished, and much plate) the money was played away first, and next the plate was sold. I remember about 1646 he lost 200 pound one night at New-cutt.

He was generally temperate as to drinking ; but one time when he was a Student of Lincolne's-Inne, having been merry at the Taverne with his Camerades, late at night, a frolick came into his head, to gett a playsterer's brush and a pott of Inke, and blott out all the Signes between Temple-barre and Charing-crosse, which made a strange confusion the next day, and 'twas in Terme time. But it happened that they were discovered, and it cost him and them some moneys. This I had from R. Estcott, Esq., that carried the Inke-pott.

At last, viz. 1640, his Play of The Sophy came out, which did take extremely. Mr. Edmund Waller sayd then of him, that he *broke-out like the Irish Rebellion : three score thousand strong,* before any body was aware.

At the beginning of the Civill Warre he was made Governor of Farnham Castle for the King, but he was but a young Soldier, and did not keepe it. In 1643, after Edgehill fight, his Poeme called *Cowper's-hill* was printed at Oxford, in a sort of browne paper, for then they could gett no better.

1647 he conveyed, or stole away the two Dukes of Yorke and Glocester from St. James's (from the Tuition of the Earle of Northumberland) and conveyed them into France to the Prince of Wales and Queen-mother.

Anno 1652, he returned into England, and being in some straights was kindly entertayned by the Earle of Pembroke at Wilton, where I had the honour to contract an acquaintance with him. He was, as I remember, a yeare with my Lord of Pembroke at Wilton and London ; he had then sold all the Lands his Father had left him.

The parsonage-house at Egham (vulgarly called The Place) was built by Baron Denham ; a house very convenient, not great, but pretty, and pleasantly scituated, and in which his son, Sir John, (though he had better seates) did take most delight in. He sold it to John Thynne, Esq. In this parish is a place called Cammomill-hill, from the Cammomill that growes there naturally ; as also west of it is Prune-well-hill (formerly part of Sir John's possessions) where was a fine Tuft of Trees, a clear Spring, and a pleasant prospect to the East, over the levell of Middlesex and Surrey. Sir John tooke great delight in this place, and was wont to say (before the troubles) that he would build there a Retiring-place to entertaine his muses ; but the warres forced him to sell that as well as the rest. He sold it to Mr. Anstey. In this parish W. and by N. (above Runney-Meade) is Cowper's Hill, from whence is a noble prospect, which is incomparably well described by that Sweet Swan, Sir John Denham.

In the time of the Civill-warres, George Withers, the Poet, begged Sir John Denham's Estate at Egham of the Parliament, in whose cause he was a Captaine of Horse. It happened that G. W. was taken prisoner, and was in danger of his Life, having written severely against the King, &c. Sir John Denham went to the King, and desired his Majestie not to hang him, for that *whilest G. W. lived, he should not be the worst Poet in England.*

He was much beloved by King Charles the first, who much valued him for his ingenuity. He graunted him the reversion of the Surveyor of His Majestie's buildings, after the decease of Mr. Inigo Jones ; which place, after the restauration of King Charles II he enjoyed to his death, and gott seaven thousand pounds, as Sir Christopher Wren told me of, to his owne knowledge. Sir Christopher Wren was his Deputie.

He burlesqued Virgil, and burnt it, sayeing that 'twas not fitt that the best Poet should be so abused. In the verses against *Gondibert,* most of them are Sir John's. He was satyricall when he had a mind to it.

His first wife was the daughter and heire of Mr. Cotton of Glocestershire, by whom he had 500 pounds per annum, one son, and two daughters.

He maried his 2nd wife, Margaret Brookes, a very beautifull young lady : Sir John was ancient and limping. The Duke of Yorke fell deeply in love with her (though I have been morally assured he never had any carnall knowledge of her). This occasioned Sir John's distemper of madness, which first appeared when he went from London to see the famous Freestone quarries at Portland in Dorset, and when he came within a mile of it, turned back to London again, and did not see it. He went to Hounslowe, and demanded rents of Lands he had sold many yeares before ; went to the King, and told him he was the Holy Ghost. But it pleased God that he was cured of this distemper, and writt excellent verses (particularly on the death of Mr. Abraham Cowley) afterwards. His 2nd lady had no child : was poysoned by the hands of the Countess of Rochester, with Chocolatte.

RENÉ DESCARTES

[Born 1596. Philosopher, mathematician and scientist. Descartes was the founder of modern philosophy, for his outlook was profoundly affected by the new physics and astronomy. He was the first philosopher since Aristotle not to accept the foundations laid by his predecessors, but to attempt to construct a complete philosophic edifice *de novo*. To obtain complete quiet, he enlisted in the Dutch army 1617. On the outbreak of the Thirty Years' War he transferred to the Bavarian army 1619. In Bavaria, during the winter of 1619, the weather being cold, he got into a stove in the morning, and stayed there all day meditating; by his own account his philosophy was half finished when he came out. In 1621 he gave up fighting, but his meditation was so constantly interrupted in civilian life that, in 1628, he joined the army that was besieging La Rochelle. From 1629 until 1649, he lived in Holland to escape persecution, but even so he himself suppressed his book, *Le Monde,* which maintained two heretical doctrines : the earth's rotation and the infinity of the universe. In September 1649, Queen Christina of Sweden sent a warship to fetch Descartes as she wanted daily lessons from him, but it turned out that she could not spare the time except at five in the morning, and this unaccustomed early rising in the cold of a Scandinavian winter was too much for Descartes, who fell ill and died in 1650.]

THE Societie of Jesus glorie in that theyr order had the educating of him.

He was too wise a man to encomber himselfe with a Wife; but as he was a man, he had the desires and appetites of a man ; he therefore kept a good conditioned hansome woman that he liked, and by whom he had some Children (I thinke 2 or 3.) 'Tis pity but comeing from the Braine of such a father, they should be well cultivated.

He was so eminently learned that all learned men made visits to him, and many of them would desire him to shew them his Instruments (in those dayes mathematicall learning lay much in the knowledge of Instruments, and, as Sir Henry Savile sayd, in doeing of tricks) he would drawe out a little Drawer under his Table, and shew them a paire of Compasses with one of the Legges broken; and then, for his Ruler, he used a sheet of paper folded double.

Mr. Hobbes was wont to say that had Des Cartes kept himselfe wholly to Geometrie that he had been the best Geometer in the world but that his head did not lye for Philosophy. He did very much admire him, but sayd that he could not pardon him for writing in the Defence of Transubstantiation, which he knew to bee absolutely against his judgement, and donne meerly to putt a compliment on the Jesuites.

SIR EVERARD DIGBY

[Born 1578. Conspirator. His father died when he was fourteen and his wardship was purchased from the Crown by Roger Manners, who sold it at an advanced price to young Digby's mother. The heir to large estates and connected with many of the greatest families in England, he soon appeared at Court, where he was appointed to an office in the Household. But he spent the greater part of his time in the country, hunting and hawking. In 1596 he married a great heiress. He was converted to Catholicism at Court by John Gerard in 1599, and his wife and mother soon followed his example. When James I came to England, Digby was among the gathering which welcomed the King at Belvoir Castle and he received the honour of knighthood there, but the Catholics were disappointed by James I and Digby joined the Gunpowder Plot. His task was to prepare for a rising in the Midlands, when the catastrophe should have been brought about, and it was settled that he should invite a large number of the disaffected gentry to meet him at Dunchurch in Warwickshire to join in a hunt, when, it was rumoured, strange news might be expected. This gathering was fixed for 5th November, 1605, but was not a success and quickly dissolved when some of the plotters arrived from London with news of their failure. Fleeing to Holbeach House in Gloucestershire, the conspirators determined to sell their lives dearly, but Sir Everard deserted them, only to be captured some days later. He was tried in Westminster Hall and was executed on Thursday, 30th June, 1606.]

SIR EVERARD DIGBY was a most gallant Gentleman and one of the handsomest men of his time.

'Twas his ill fate to suffer in the Powder-plott. When his heart was pluct out by the Executioner (who, *secundum formam,* cryed, Here is the heart of a Traytor!) it is credibly reported, he replied, Thou liest!

[96]

SIR KENELM DIGBY

[Born 1603. Author, naval commander and diplomatist. After leaving Oxford he travelled a great deal. While in France, the Queen-Mother, Marie de Medicis, whom he met at a masked ball, made immodest advances to him : to avoid her importunities, he spread a report of his death and went to Italy by sea. During the ceremony of knighthood, James I turned his face away from the naked sword, owing to constitutional nervousness, and would have thrust the point into Digby's eye had not Buckingham interposed. He was engaged in sea-fighting and conquered the French and Venetian fleets in the Mediterranean in 1627. Digby was imprisoned by the Parliament in 1642 at *The Three Tobacco Pipes nigh Charing Cross,* where his charming conversation made the prison *a place of delight.* During the Civil War he was active on the side of the King, and on the failure of his cause he was banished for a time. He was the author of several religious and quasi-scientific books, including one *On the Cure of Wounds* by means of a sympathetic powder which he imagined he had discovered : this powder was to be rubbed on the weapon causing the wound, not on the wound itself. Died 1665.]

SIR KENELME DIGBY, Knight, a Gentleman absolute in all Numbers, was the eldest son of Sir Everard Digby, who was accounted the handsomest Gentleman in England. Sir Everard sufferd as a Traytor in the Gun-powder-Treason ; but King James restored his estate to his son and heire.

He was borne at Gotehurst, Bucks on the eleventh of June : see Ben Johnson, 2d volumne :—

> *Witnesse thy Actions done at Scanderoon*
> *Upon thy Birthday, the eleaventh of June.*

(Mr. Elias Ashmole assures me, from two or 3 Nativities by Dr. Nepier, that Ben: Johnson was mistaken and did it for the ryme-sake.)

Sir Kenelme Digby was held to be the most accomplished Cavalier of his time. He went to Glocester Hall in Oxon, anno 1618. The learned Mr. Thomas Allen (then of that house) was wont to say that he was the *Mirandula* of his age.

He was such a goodly handsome person, gigantique and great voice, and had so gracefull Elocution and noble addresse, etc., that had he been drop't out of the Clowdes in any part of the World, he would have made himself respected. But the

Jesuites spake spitefully, and sayd *'twas true, but then he must not stay there above six weekes*. He was Envoyé from Henrietta Maria (then Queen-mother) to the Pope, where at first he was mightily admired; but after some time he grew high, and Hectored with his Holinesse, and gave him the Lye. The pope sayd he was mad.

Tempore Caroli I^{mi} he received the Sacrament in the Chapell at Whitehall, and professed the Protestant Religion, which gave great scandal to the Roman Catholiques; but afterwards *he looked back*.

In the Times of Confusion, the Bishop of Winchester's Lodging in Southwark, being a large Pile of Building, was made a Prison for the Royalists; and here Sir Kenelm Digby wrote his Book *of Bodies,* and diverted himself in Chymistry, and used to make artificial precious Stones, as Rubies, Emeralds, &c. out of Flint, as Sir Francis Dodington, Prisoner with him at the same Time, told me.

He was well versed in all kinds of Learning. And he had also this vertue, that no man knew better how to abound and to be abased, and either was indifferent to him. No man became Grandeur better; sometimes again he would live only with a Lackey, and Horse with a foote-cloath.

He was very generous, and liberall to deserving persons. When Abraham Cowley was but 13 yeares old, he dedicated to him a Comedy, called *Love's Riddle,* and concludes in his Epistle—*The Birch that whip't him then would prove a Bay.* Sir K. was very kind to him.

He was of undaunted courage, yet not apt in the least to give offence. His conversation was both ingeniose and innocent.

Sir John Hoskyns enformes me that Sir Kenelme Digby did translate Petronius Arbiter into English.

He maried, much against his Mother's consent, that celebrated Beautie and Courtezane, Mrs. Venetia Stanley, whom Richard Earle of Dorset kept as his Concubine, and had children by her, and setled on her an Annuity of 500 pounds per annum, which after Sir K. D. maried was unpayd by the Earle; and for which Annuity Sir Kenelme sued the Earle, after marriage, and recovered it. He would say that a handsome lusty man that was discreet might make a vertuose wife out of a Brothell-house. This Lady carried herselfe blamelessly, yet (they say) he was jealous of her. Richard, Earle of Dorset, invited her and her husband once a yeare, when with much desire and passion he beheld her, and only kissed her hand, Sir Kenelme being still by. She dyed suddenly, and hard-hearted woemen would censure him severely.

After her death, to avoyd envy and scandall, he retired in to Gresham Colledge at London, where he diverted himselfe with his Chymistry, and the Professors good conversation. He wore there a long mourning cloake, a high crowned hatt, his beard unshorne, look't like a Hermite, as signes of sorrowe for his beloved wife, to whose memory he erected a sumptuouse monument, now quite destroyed by the great Conflagration.

He was borne to three thousand pounds per Annum. What by reason of the Civil-warres, and his generous mind, he contractedst great Debts, and I know not how (there being a great falling out between him and his then only son, John) he settled his Estate upon Cornwalleys, a subtile sollicitor, and also a Member of the House of Commons, who did put Mr. John Digby to much charge in Lawe.

Mr. John Digby brought me a great book, as big as the biggest Church Bible that ever I sawe, and the richliest bound, bossed with silver, engraven with scutchions and crest (an ostrich) it was a curious velame. It was the History of the Family of the Digbyes, which Sir Kenelme either did, or ordered to be donne. There was inserted all that was to be found any where relating to them, out of Records of the Tower, Rolles, &c. All ancient Church monuments were most exquisitely limmed by some rare Artist. He told me that the compileing of it did cost his father a thousand pound. Sir Jo. Fortescue sayd he did beleeve 'twas more. When Mr. John Digby did me the favour to shew me this rare MS., This booke, sayd he, is all that I have left me of all the Estate that was my Father's.

Sir Kenelm Digby, that renowned Knight, great Linguist, and Magazen of Arts, was born and died on the Eleventh of June, and also fought fortunately at Scanderoon the same day. Hear his Epitaph, composed by Mr. Farrer :

> Under this Stone the Matchless Digby lies,
> Digby the Great, the Valiant, and the Wise :
> This Age's Wonder, for his Noble Parts ;
> Skill'd in six Tongues, and learn'd in all the Arts.
> Born on the day he died, th'Eleventh of June,
> On which he bravely fought at Scanderoon.
> 'Tis rare that one and self-same day should be
> His day of Birth, of Death, of Victory.

VENETIA DIGBY

[Born 1600. She was secretly married to Sir Kenelm Digby in the Spring of 1625 and their first child was born in the October of that year : but the marriage was not acknowledged until 1627. Absurd reports were circulated that Digby had killed her by insisting on her drinking Viper-wine to preserve her beauty. At the time of her death in 1633, Ben Jonson, Thomas May, Joseph Ruther, Owen Feltham, William Habington, Lord George Digby and Aurelian Townsend commemorated her loss in verse.]

VENETIA STANLEY was the daughter of Sir Edward Stanley. She was a most beautifull desireable Creature, and being maturo viro was left by her father to live with a tenant and servants at Enston Abbey in Oxfordshire : but as private as that place was, it seemes her Beautie could not lye hid. The young Eagles had espied her, and she was sanguine and tractable, and of much Suavity (which to abuse was great pittie.)

In those dayes, Richard, Earle of Dorset (eldest son and heire to the Lord Treasurer) lived in the greatest splendor of any nobleman in England. Among other pleasures that he enjoyed, Venus was not the least. This pretty creature's fame quickly came to his Lordship's eares, who made no delay to catch at such an opportunity.

I have now forgott who first brought her to Towne, but I have heard my uncle Danvers say (who was her contemporary) that she was so commonly courted, and that by Grandees, that 'twas written over her lodging one night *in literis uncialibus* :

PRAY COME NOT NEER,
FOR DAME VENETIA STANLEY LODGETH HERE.

The Earle of Dorset aforesayd was her greatest Gallant, who was extremely enamoured of her, and had one, if not more children by her. He setled on her an Annuity of 500 pounds per annum.

Among other young Sparkes of that time, Sir Kenelme Digby grew acquainted with her, and fell so much in love with her that he maried her, much against the good will of his mother, but he would say that a wise man, and lusty, could make an honest woman out of a Brothell-house.

Sir Edmund Wyld had her picture (and you may imagine was very familiar with her) which picture is now at Droitwych, in Worcestershire, at an Inne in an entertayning-roome, where now the Towne keepe their Meetings. (She was first a Miss to Sir Edmund Wyld.) Also at Mr. Rose's, a Jeweller in Henrietta-Street in Convent Garden, is an excellent piece of hers, drawne after she was newly dead.

She had a most lovely and sweet turn'd face, delicate darke-browne haire. She had a perfect healthy constitution ; strong ; good skin ; well-proportioned ; much enclining to a *Bona Roba* (near altogether.) Her face, a short ovall ; darke-browne eie-browe about which much sweetness, as also in the opening of her eie-lidds. The colour of her cheekes was just that of the Damaske rose, which is neither too hott nor too pale. She was of a just stature, not very tall.

Sir Kenelme had severall Pictures of her by Vandyke, &c. He had her hands cast in playster, and her feet and Face. See Ben Johnson's 2d. volumne, where he hath made her live in Poetrey, in his drawing of her both Body and Mind :

> *Sitting, and ready to be drawne,*
> *What makes these Tiffany, silkes, and lawne,*
> *Embroideries, feathers, fringes, lace,*
> *When every limbe takes like a Face ! etc.*

When these Verses were made she had three children by Sir Kenelme, who are there mentioned, viz. Kenelme, George and John.

She dyed in her bed, suddenly. Some suspected that she was poysoned. When her head was opened there was found but little braine, which her husband imputed to her drinking of viper-wine ; but spitefull woemen would say 'twas a viper husband who was jealous of her that she would steale a leape. I have heard some say, e.g. my cosen Elizabeth Falkner, that after her mariage she redeemed her Honour by her strick't living. Once a yeare the Earle of Dorset invited her and Sir Kenelme to dinner, where the Earle would behold her with much passion, and only kisse her hand.

About 1676 or 5, as I was walking through Newgate-street, I sawe Dame Venetia's Bust from off her tombe standing at a Stall at the golden Crosse, a Brasier's shop. I perfectly remembred it, but the fire had gott-off the Guilding ; but taking notice of it to one that was with me, I could never see it after-wards exposed to the street. They melted it downe. How these curiosities would be quite forgott, did not such idle fellowes as I am putt them downe.

DESIDERIUS ERASMUS

[Born 1466. The leader of the Northern Renaissance, he was the illegitimate son of a priest. His guardians, having embezzled his money, cajoled him into becoming a monk, a step which he regretted all his life. In 1493 he became secretary to the Bishop of Cambrai, which enabled him to leave the monastery and travel. Though he hated scholasticism, he was for a time at the University of Paris. In 1499 he made his first visit to England, where he liked the fashion of kissing girls. Here he made friends with Colet and More, who persuaded him to undertake serious work rather than literary trifles. He therefore started to learn Greek in 1500, and brought out a Greek Testament, with a new Latin translation, in 1516. He also tried to learn Hebrew, but gave it up. He lived in England from 1509 until 1514, where he wrote his most famous book, *The Praise of Folly*, illustrated by Holbein, which contained a scathing attack on the abuses of the Church. However, he was so disgusted by the violence of the Protestant revolt, that he sided with the Catholics, and a controversy on Free Will with Luther forced him further and further into reaction. His timidity unfitted him for the intolerance which the Reformation had engendered, and he sank into obscurity and died in 1536.]

HIS name was *Gerard Gerard,* which he translated into *Desiderius Erasmus.* Of Roterdam : he loved not Fish, though borne in a Fish-towne.

He was *begot* (as they say) *behind dores.* His father tooke great care to send him to an excellent Schoole, which was at Dusseldorf, in Cleveland. He was a tender Chitt, and his mother would not entruste him at board, but tooke a house there, and made him cordialls.

He was of the order of Augustine, whose habit was the same that the Pest-house-master at Pisa in Italie wore ; and walking in that Towne, people beckoned him to goe out of the way, taking him to be the master of the Pest-house ; and he not understanding the meaning, and keeping on his way, was there by one well basted. He made his complaint when he came to Rome, and had a dispensation for his habit.

He studied sometime in Queens Colledge in Cambridge : his chamber was over the water. He mentions his being there in one of his *Epistles,* and blames the Beere there.

Sir Charles Blount, of Maple-Durham, in Com. Oxon. (neer Reding) was his Scholar (in his *Epistles* there are some to him) and desired Erasmus to doe him the favour to sitt for his Picture, and he did so, and it is an excellent piece: which picture my cosen John Danvers, of Baynton (Wilts), haz: his wive's grandmother was Sir Charles Blount's daughter or grand-daughter. 'Twas pitty such a rarity should have been aliend from the Family, but the issue male is lately extinct. I will sometime or other endeavour to gett it for Oxford Library.

He had the Parsonage of Aldington in Kent, which is about 3 degrees perhaps a healthier place then Dr. Pell's parsonage in Essex. I wonder they could not find for him better preferment; but I see that the Sun and Aries being in the second house, he was not borne to be a rich man.

John Dreyden, Esq., Poet Laureat, tells me that there was a great friendship between his great grand-father's father and Erasmus Roterodamus, and Erasmus was Godfather to one of his sonnes, and the Christian name of Erasmus hath been kept in the family ever since. The Poet's second sonne is Erasmus.

They were wont to say that Erasmus was Interpendent between Heaven and Hell, till, about the year 1655, the Con-clave at Rome damned him for a Heretique, after he had been dead 120 yeares.

His deepest divinity is where a man would least expect it: viz. in his *Colloquies* in a Dialogue between a Butcher and a Fishmonger.

Julius Scaliger contested with Erasmus, but gott nothing by it, for, as Fuller sayth, he was like a Badger, that never bitt but he made his teeth meet.

He was the Πρόδρομος of our knowledge, and the man that made the rough and untrodden wayes smooth and passable.

THOMAS FAIRFAX : LORD FAIRFAX

[Born 1612. Soldier. Knighted 1640. Became a general for the Parliament 1642. Recaptured Leeds and captured Wakefield 1643. Commander-in-Chief of the Parliamentary Army 1645. Defeated Charles I at Naseby, where he captured a standard with his own hands, and stormed Bristol 1645. Reduced Oxford and received the thanks of Parliament 1646. Seized Charles I against his will 1647. Transmitted to the Commons the Army's demand for the King's punishment 1648. He was one of the King's judges, but endeavoured to stop his execution 1649. State Councillor and Commander-in-Chief 1649. He resigned his command from unwillingness to invade Scotland 1650. He headed the Commission sent to Charles II at the Hague in 1660, to arrange his restoration. Died 1671.]

THOMAS, Lord Fairfax of Cameron, Lord Generail of the Parliament-armie. When Oxford was surrendred, the first thing General Fairfax did was to sett a good Guard of Soldiers to preserve the Bodleian Library. 'Tis said there was more hurt donne by the Cavaliers (during their Garrison) by way of Embezilling and cutting off chaines of bookes, then there was since. He was a lover of Learning, and had he not taken this speciall care, that noble Library had been utterly destroyed, for there were ignorant Senators enough who would have been contented to have had it so.

CARLO FANTOM

CAPTAIN CARLO FANTOM, a Croatian, spake 13 languages; was a Captain under the Earle of Essex. He was very quarrelsome and a great Ravisher. He left the Parliament Party, and went to the King Ch. the first at Oxford, where he was hanged for Ravishing.

Sd. he, I care not for your Cause: I come to fight for your halfe-crowne, and your handsome woemen: my father was a R. Catholiq; and so was my grandfather. I have fought for the Christians against the Turkes; and for the Turkes against the Christians.

Sir Robert Pye was his Colonel, who shot at him for not returning a horse that he tooke away before the Regiment. This was donne in a field near Bedford, where the Army then was, as they were marching to the relief of Gainsborough. Many are yet living that sawe it. Capt. Hamden was by: The bullets went through his Buff-coat, and Capt. H. sawe his shirt on fire. Capt. Carl. Fantom tooke the Bullets, and sayd he, Sir Rob. Here, take your bullets again. None of the Soldiers would dare to fight with him: they sayd, they would not fight with the Devil.

Edmund Wyld, Esq., was very well acquainted with him, and gave him many a Treat, and at last he prevailed with him so far, towards the knowledge of this secret, that Fantom told him, that the Keepers in their Forests did know a certain herb, which they gave to Children, which made them to be shott-free (they call them Hard-men.)

In a Booke of Trialls by Duell in foli (writ by Segar, I thinke) before the Combatants fight, they have an Oath administered to them by the Herald; where is inserted (among other things) that they have not about them either Charme or Herb.

Martin Luther in his Commentaries on the First (or second Commandment, I thinke the First) saies that a Hard-man was brought to the Duke of Saxonies Court: he was brought into the great Hall and was commanded to be shott with a Musquet: the bullet drop't downe and he had only a blew Spott on his Skin, where he was struck. Martin Luther was then by, and sawe the Bullet drop-downe.

[105]

They say that a silver bullet will kill any Hardman, and can be beaten to death with cudgels. The Elector Palatine, Prince Robert's Brother, did not believe at all, that any man could make himself hard.

Robert Earl of Essex, General for the Parliament had this Capt. Fantom in high esteeme : for he was an admirable Horse-officer, and taught the Cavalry of the army the way of fighting with Horse : the General saved him from hanging twice for Ravishing ; once at Winchester, 2nd at St. Albans : and he was not content only to ravish himselfe, but he would make his soldiers doe it too, and he would stand by and look on.

He met (comeing late at night out of the Horse-shoe Tavern in Drury lane) with a Liuetenant of Col. Rossiter, who had great jingling Spurres on. Qd. he, the noise of your Spurres doe offend me, you must come over the Kennel and give me satisfaction. They drew and parted at each other and the Lieuetenant was runne thorough and died within a hour or two : and 'twas not known, who killed him.

SIR WILLIAM FLEETWOOD

[Born 1535. Recorder of London. Member of the Parliaments of 1572, 1584, 1586 and 1588. By the Earl of Leicester's influence, he was elected Recorder of London in 1571, and soon became famous for vigorously and successfully enforcing the laws against vagrants, thieves, priests and papists. In 1576 he was committed to the Fleet Prison for a short time for breaking into the Portuguese Ambassador's chapel under cover of the law against Popish recusants. In 1580 he was made Serjeant-at-Law and, in 1583, a Commissioner for the Reformation of Abuses in Printing. In the same year, he drafted a scheme for housing the poor and preventing the plague in London by maintaining open spaces. In 1588 he reported on the proceedings to be taken against Jesuits and, in 1589, on the right of sanctuary for criminals attaching to Saint Paul's Cathedral. He resigned his office in 1591, on receipt of a pension of £100 per annum and died in 1594.]

HE was a very severe Hanger of Highwaymen, so that the Fraternity were resolved to make an example of him : which they executed in this manner. They lay in wayte for him not far from Tyburne, as he was to come from his House in Bucks ; had a Halter in readinesse ; brought him under the Gallowes, fastned the rope about his neck and on the Tree, his hands tied behind him (and servants bound) and then left him to the Mercy of his Horse, which he called Ball. So he cryed, Ho Ball. Ho, Ball—and it pleased God that his horse stood still till somebody came along, which was halfe a quarter of an hour or more. He ordered that this Horse should be kept as long as he would live, and it was so ; he lived till 1646.

One day goeing on foote to Guild-hall with his Clarke behind him, he was surprised in Cheapside with a sudden and violent Loosenesse, neer the Standard. He turned up his breech against the Standard and bade his man hide his face ; For they shall never see my Arse again, sayd he.

JOHN FLORIO

[Born 1545. Author. His father, who was in 1550 preacher to a congregation of Italian Protestants in London, was forced to leave the country after charges of gross immorality had been brought against him. Florio matriculated at Magdalen, Oxford, in 1581, and according to Anthony Wood, was *a teacher and instructor of certain scholars in the University*. His first patron was the Earl of Leicester, after whose death *he lived some years in the pay and patronage* of Southampton, while to the Earl of Pembroke he was soon under heavy obligations. At the close of the sixteenth century Florio was living in London on intimate terms with all the chief literary men and their patrons. It is possible that Shakespeare modelled Holofernes in *Love's Labour's Lost* on Florio, and it is certain that his translation of Montaigne's *Essays* (which was licensed to Edward Blount in 1599, but was not published until 1603) formed the basis of Gonzago's description of an ideal state in *The Tempest*. *Montaigne speaks now good English,* wrote Sir William Cornwallis in 1600. *It is done by a fellow less beholding to nature for his fortunes than wit, yet lesser for his face than his fortune. The truth is he looks more like a good fellow than a wise man, and yet he is wise beyond either his fortune or education.* Florio died in 1625.]

JOHN FLORIO was borne in London in the beginning of King Edward VI, his father and mother flying from the Valtolin ('tis about Piedmont or Savoy) to London for Religion : Waldenses.—The family is originally of Siena, where the name is to this day.

King Edward dying, upon the persecution of Queen Mary, they fled back again into their owne countrey, where he was educated.

Afterwards he came into England, and was by King James made Informator to Prince Henry for the Italian and French tongues, and clarke to the closet to Queen Anne.

Scripsit :—First and Second Fruits, being two books of the Instruction to learne the Italian tongue : Dictionary ; and translated Montagne's Essayes.

He dyed of the great plague at Fulham anno 1625.

FRANCIS FRY

(Transportation by an Invisible Power. A Letter from the Reverend Mr. Andrew Paschal, B.D., Rector of Chedzoy in Somerset, To John Aubery, Esq; at Gresham College.)

ABOUT November last, in the Parish of Spreyton, in the County of Devon, there appeared in a Field near the Dwelling-house of Phil: Furze, to his Servant Francis Fry, being of the age of 21 next August, an aged Gentleman with a Pole in his Hand, and like that he was wont to carry about with him when living, to kill Moles withall, who told the Young Man not to be afraid of him; but should tell his Master, i.e. his Son, That several legacies that he had bequeathed were unpaid, naming 10s. to one, 10s. to another, &c. Fry replied, that the party he last named was Dead. The Spectrum replied, he knew that, but said it must be paid to (and named) the next Relation. These things being performed, he promised he would trouble him no further. These small Legacies were paid accordingly. But the young Man having caried 20s. order'd by the Spectrum to his Sister Mrs. Furze of the Parish of Staverton near Totness, which Money the Gentlewoman refus'd to receive, being sent her, as she said, from the Devil. The same Night Fry lodging there, the Spectrum appear'd to him again, whereupon Fry challenged his promise not to trouble him, and said he had done all he had desir'd him; but that Mrs. Furze would not receive the Money. The Spectrum replied, that's true indeed. But bid him ride to Totness and buy a Ring of that value, and that she would take! Which was provided for her, and receiv'd by her.

Then Fry rode homewards attended by a Servant of Mrs. Furze. But having come into Spreyton Parish, or rather a little before, he seem'd to carry an old Gentlewoman behind him, that often threw him off his Horse, and hurried him with such violence, as astonished all that saw him, or heard how horridly the Ground was beaten; and being come into his Master's Yard, Fry's Horse (a mean Beast) sprung at once 25 foot.

The trouble from the Man-Spectre ceased from this time. But the old Gentlewoman, Mrs. Furze, Mr. Furze's second Wife, whom the Spectre at his first appearance to Fry called,

That Wicked Woman my Wife (though I knew her, and took her for a very good Woman) presently after appears to several in the House, viz. to Fry, Mrs. Thomasin Gidley, Anne Langdon born in my Parish, and to a little Child which was forced to be remov'd from the House; sometimes in her own shape, sometimes in shapes more horrid, as of a Dog belching Fire, and of an Horse, and seeming to ride out at the Window, carrying only one pane of Glass away, and a little piece of Iron.

After this Fry's Head was thrust into a narrow space, where a Man's Fist could not enter, between a Bed and a Wall; and forced to be taken thence by the strength of Men, all bruised and bloody; upon this it was thought fit to Bleed him, and after that was done, the Binder was remov'd from his Arm, and convey'd about his Middle, and presently was drawn so very straight, it had almost killed him, and was cut asunder, making an ugly uncouth noise. Several other times with Handkerchiefs, Cravats and other things he was near strangled, they were drawn so close upon his Throat.

He lay one Night in his Periwig (in his Master's Chamber, for the more safety) which was torn all to pieces. His best Periwig he inclosed in a little Box on the inside with a Joindstool, and other weight upon it; the Box was snapp'd asunder, and the Wig torn all to flitters. His Master saw his Buckles fall all to pieces on his Feet: But, first I should have told you the Fate of his Shoe-strings, one of which a Gentlewoman greater than all exception, assured me that she saw it come out of his Shoe, without any visible Hand, and fling itself to the farther end of the Room; the other was coming out too, but that a Maid prevented and help'd it out, which crisp'd and curl'd about her Hand like a living Eel. The Cloathes worn by Anne Langdon and Fry (if their own) were torn to pieces on their backs. The same Gentlewoman, being the Daughter of the Minister of the Parish, Mr. Roger Specott, showed me one of Fry's Gloves, which was torn in his Pocket while she was by. I did view it near and narrowly, and do seriously confess that it is torn so very accurately in all the Seams and in other places, and laid abroad so artificially, and it is so dexterously tattered (and all done in the Pocket in a Minute's time) as nothing Human could have done it; no Cutler could have made an Engine to do it so.

Other fantastical Freeks have been very frequent, as, the marching of a great Barrel full of Salt out of one Room to another; an Andiron laying itself over a Pan of Milk that was scalding on the Fire, and two Flitches of Bacon descending from the Chimney where they hung, and laid themselves over that Andiron. The appearing of the Spectrum (when in her own shape) in the same Cloathes to seeming, which Mrs. Furze her daughter-in-law has on. The intangling of Fry's Face and Legs, about his Neck, and about the Frames of the Chairs, so as they have been with great difficulty disengaged.

But the most Remarkable of all happened in that Day that I passed by the Door in my return hither, which was Easter-eve, when Fry, returning from Work (that little he can do) he was caught by the Woman Spectre by the Skirts of his Doublet, and carried into the Air; he was quickly mist by his Master and the Workmen, and great enquiry was made for Fran. Fry, but no hearing of him; but after half an Hour after, Fry was heard Whistling and Singing in a kind of Quagmire. He was now affected as he was wont to be in his Fits, so that none regarded what he said; but coming to himself an Hour after, he solemnly protested, That the Daemon carried him so high that he saw his Master's House underneath him no bigger than a Hay-cock, that he was in perfect sense and prayed God not to suffer the Devil to destroy him; that he was suddenly set down in that Quagmire. The Workmen found one Shoe on one side of the House, and the other Shoe on the other side; his Periwig was espied next Morning hanging on the Top of a tall Tree.

It was soon observ'd, that Fry's part of his Body that had laid in the Mud, was much benum'd, and therefore the next Saturday, which was the eve of Low-Sunday, they carried him to Crediton to be let Blood; which being done, and the Company having left him for a little while, returning they found him in a Fit, with his Fore-head all bruised and swoln to a great Bigness, none being able to guess how it came, till he recover'd himself, and then he told them, That a Bird flew in at the Window with a great force, and with a Stone in it's Mouth flew directly against his Fore-head. The People looked for it, and found on the Ground just under where he sat, not a Stone, but a weight of Brass, or Copper, which the People were break-ing, and parting it among themselves. He was so very ill that he could not ride but one Mile or little more that Night, since which time I have not heard of him, save that he was ill handled the next Day, being Sunday.

Indeed Sir you may wonder that I have not Visited that House, and the poor afflicted People; especially, since I was so near, and passed by the very Door: But, besides that they have called to their assistance none but Nonconforming Ministers, I was not qualified to be welcome there, having given Mr. Furze a great deal of trouble the last Year about a

Conventicle in his House, where one of this Parish was the Preacher. But I am very well assured of the truth of what I have written, and (as more appears) you shall hear from me again.

I had forgot to tell you that Fry's Mother came to me, grievously bewailing the miserable condition of her Son. She told me that the Day before he had five Pins thrust into his Side. She ask'd, and I gave her the best Advice I could. Particularly, that her Son should declare all that the Spectre, especially the Woman gave him in Charge, for I suspect, there is *aliquid latens* [something concealed]; and that she should remove him thence by all means. But I fear that she will not do it. For I hear that Anne Langdon is come into my Parish to her Mother, and that she is grievously troubled there. I might have written as much of her, as of Fry, for she had been as ill treated, saving the Aerial Journey. Her Fits and Obsessions seem to be greater, for she Scrieches in a most Hellish tone. Thomasin Gidley (though removed) is in trouble, as I hear.

THOMAS GOFFE

[Born 1591. Divine and poet. Three of his tragedies were acted at Christ Church, Oxford, and his play *The Careless Shepherdess* was performed before the King and Queen at Salisbury. He was a woman-hater and a bachelor, until he was inveigled into marrying a parishioner at East Clandon, of which he was the incumbent from 1620 until his death. This lady was the widow of his predecessor, and she and her children by her first husband so persecuted poor Goffe that he died shortly after his marriage in 1629.]

THOMAS GOFFE the Poet was Rector here; he was buried in the Middle of the Chancel, but there is nothing in Remembrance of him; his Wife, it seems, was not so kind. I find by the Register-Book, that he was buried, July 27, 1629. His Wife pretended to fall in Love with him, by hearing him preach: Upon which, said one Thomas Thimble (one of the Squire Bedell's in Oxford, and his Confident) to him: Do not marry her: if thou dost, she will break thy Heart. He was not obsequious to his Friend's sober Advice, but for her Sake altered his Condition, and cast Anchor here.

One time some of his Oxford Friends made a Visit to him. She look'd upon them with an ill Eye, as if they had come to eat her out of her House and Home (as they say). She provided a Dish of Milk, and some Eggs for Supper, and no more: They perceived her Niggardliness, and that her Husband was inwardly troubled at it (she wearing the Breeches) so they resolv'd to be merry at Supper, and talk all in Latin, and laugh'd exceedingly. She was so vex'd at their speaking Latin, that she could not hold, but fell out a Weeping, and rose from the Table. The next Day, Mr. Goffe order'd a better Dinner for them, and sent for some Wine: They were merry, and his Friends took their final Leave of him.

'Twas no long Time before this Xantippe made Mr. Thimble's Prediction good; and when he died, the last Words he spake were: *Oracle, Oracle, Tom Thimble,* and so he gave up the Ghost.

JOHN GRAUNT

[Born 1620. Statistician. He gained such esteem by his integrity as a merchant that he was able, when he was only thirty years old, to procure the Professorship of Music in Gresham College for his friend, Dr. William Petty. In 1662 appeared the first *Natural and Political Observations made upon the Bills of Mortality by John Graunt, Citizen of London. With reference to the Government, Religion, Trade, Growth, Ayre, Diseases, and the several Changes of the said City.* This work laid the foundation of the science subsequently styled Political Arithmetic by Sir William Petty. Charles II specially recommended Graunt to be chosen an original member of the Royal Society, advising the Society that *if they found any more such tradesmen, they should be sure to admit them all without any more adoe.* After his retirement, Graunt was admitted into the management of the New River Company and was rumoured, because of his Catholicism, to have cut off the supply of water to the city the night before the Fire of London. He died in 1674.]

CAPTAINE JOHN GRAUNT (afterwards, major) was borne *240 die Aprilis,* at the 7 Starres in Burchin Lane, London, in the parish of St. Michael's Cornhill, ½ an houre before eight a clock on a munday morning, the signe being in the 9 degree of Gemini that day at 12 a clock, Anno Domini 1620.

He was bred-up (as the fashion then was) in the Puritan way ; wrote Short-hand dextrously ; and after many yeares constant hearing and writing sermon-notes, he fell to buying and reading of the best Socinian bookes, and for severall yeares continued of that Opinion. At last, he turned a Roman Catholique, of which Religion he dyed a great Zealot.

To give him his due prayse, he was a very ingeniose and studious person, and generally beloved, and rose early in the morning to his Study before shop-time. He understood Latin and French. He was a pleasant facetious Companion, and very hospitable.

He was by Trade, Haberdasher of small-wares, but was free of the Drapers-Company. A man generally beloved ; a faythfull friend. Often chosen for his prudence and justnes to be an Arbitrator ; and he was a great Peace-maker. He had an excellent working head, and was very facetious and fluent in his conversation.

He had gonne thorough all the Offices of the City as far as Common-councill-man. He was Common-councill-man two yeares. Captaine of the Trayned Band, severall yeares : Major of it, two or three yeares, and then layd downe trade and all other publique Employment for his Religion, being a Roman Catholique.

He wrote *Observations on the bills of Mortality* very ingeniosely, but I beleeve, and partly know, that he had his Hint from his intimate and familiar friend Sir William Petty, to which he made some *Additions,* since printed. And he intended (had he lived) to have writt more on the subject.

He wrott some *Observations on the Advance of the Excise,* not printed ; and also intended to have written something of Religion.

Major John Graunt dyed on Easter-eve 1674, and was buryed the Wednesday following in St. Dunstan's church in Fleetstreet in the body of the said church under the piewes towards the gallery on the north side, i.e. under the piewes (alias hoggsties) of the north side of the middle aisle (what pitty 'tis so great an Ornament of the Citty should be buryed so obscurely !) *aetatis anno* 540.

His death is lamented by all Good men that had the happinesse to knowe him ; and a great number of ingeniose persons attended him to his grave. Among others (with Teares) was that ingeniose great Virtuoso, Sir William Petty, his old and intimate Acquaintance, who was sometime a student at Brasenose College.

He had one son, a man, who dyed in Persia ; one daughter, a Nunne at (I thinke) Gaunt. His widowe yet alive.

He was my honoured and worthy Friend—*cujus animae propitietur Deus, Amen.*

EDMUND GUNTER

[Born 1581. Mathematician. Educated at Westminster and Christ Church. He took Holy Orders in 1615 and became Professor of Astronomy in Gresham College and vicar of St. George's, Southwark, in 1619. He published in 1620 a *Table of Artificial Sines and Tangents, to a radius of* 100,000,000 *parts to each minute of the Quadrant,* and assisted in the invention of Logarithms. He discovered by experiments at Deptford the variation of the magnetic needle, but this discovery seemed so strange that he suspected an error and dropped his investigations in 1622. He originated Gunter's Chain, which is still constantly used in land surveying, and first used the words cosine and cotangent, as well as inventing the decimal separator. He died in 1626.]

CAPTAIN RALPH GRETOREX, Mathematical-Instrument Maker in London, sayd that he was the first that brought Mathematicall Instruments to perfection. His *Booke of the Quadrant, Sector and Crosse-staffe* did open men's understandings and made young men in love with that Studie. Before, the Mathematicall Sciences were lock't-up in the Greeke and Latin tongues; and so lay untoucht, kept safe in some Libraries. After Mr. Gunter published his Booke, these Sciences sprang up amain, more and more to that height it is at now (1690).

When he was a Student at Christchurch, it fell to his lott to preach the Passion Sermon, which some old divines that I knew did heare, but 'twas sayd of him then in the University that our Saviour never suffered so much since his Passion as in that sermon, it was such a lamentable one—*Non omnia possumus omnes* [all things are not possible to all men.] The world is much beholding to him for what he hath donne well.

JOHN HALES

[Born 1584. Theologian. He was one of the best Greek scholars of his day and lectured on that language at Oxford. In 1616 he became chaplain to Sir Dudley Carleton, the English Ambassador at the Hague, and attended the Synod of Dort, where he was converted from Calvinism to Arminianism. A lover of quiet and learned leisure, he declined all high and responsible ecclesiastical preferment, and chose and obtained scholarly retirement in a Fellowship of Eton, of which his friends, Sir Henry Savile and Sir Henry Wotton, were successively Provost. His treatise on *Schism and Schismatics* gave offence to Laud, but Hales defended himself so well that Laud made him a Prebendary of Windsor. Refusing to acknowledge the Commonwealth, he was deprived of his fellowship and fell into poverty. Died 1656.]

WENT to School, at Bath (as I take it). Fellow of Merton Colledge: afterwards fellow of Eaton College.

He was a generall Scolar, and I beleeve a good poet: for Sir John Suckling brings him into the *Session of the Poets*:

> *Little Hales all the time did nothing but smile,*
> *To see them, about nothing, keepe such a coile.*

When the Court was at Windsor, the learned Courtiers much delighted in his company, and were wont to grace him with their company.

Mr. Hales was the common Godfather there, and 'twas pretty to see, as he walked to Windsor, how his Godchildren fell on their Knees. When he was Bursar, he still gave away all his Groates for the Acquittances to his Godchildren; and by that time he came to Windsor bridge, he would have never a Groate left.

He had a noble Librarie of bookes, and those judicially chosen, which cost him not lesse then 2500 pounds; and which he sold to Cornelius Bee, Bookeseller, in Little Britaine (as I take it, for 1000 pounds) which was his maintenance after he was ejected out of his Fellowship at Eaton-College. Mris. Powney told me that she was much against the sale of 'em, because she knew it was his Life and joy. He had then only reserved some few for his private use, to wind-up his last dayes withall.

I have heard his nephew, Mr. Sloper, say, that he much loved to read Stephanus, who was a Familist, I thinke that first wrote of that Sect of the Familie of Love : he was mightily taken with it, and was wont to say that sometime or other those fine Notions would take in the world. He was one of the first Socinians in England, I thinke the first.

The Ladie Salter (neer Eaton) was very kind to him after his Sequestration ; he was very welcome to her Ladyship and spent much of his time there : (from her Nephew.)

He lodged (after his Sequestration) at Mris. Powney's house, a widowe-woman, in Eaton, opposite to the churchyard, adjoyning to the Christopher Inne southwards. She is a very good woman and of a gratefull spirit. She told me that when she was maried, Mr. Hales was very bountifull to them in setting them up to live in the world. She was very gratefull to him and respectfull to him : a woman primitively good, and deserves to be remembred. She has been handsome : a good under-standing, and cleanlie. I wish I had her Christian name.

She has a handsome darke old-fashioned howse. The hall, after the old fashion, above the wainscot, painted cloath, with godly sentences out of the Psalmes, etc., according to the pious custome of old times ; a convenient garden and orchard.

'Tis the howse where I sawe him, a prettie little man, sanguine, of a cheerfull countenance, very gentile, and courteous ; I was recieved by him with much humanity : he was in a kind of violet-colourd cloath Gowne, with buttons and loopes (he wore not a black gowne) and was reading Thomas à Kempis ; it was within a yeare before he deceased. He loved Canarie ; but moderately, to refresh his spirits.

He had a bountifull mind. I remember in 1647, a little after the Visitation, when Thomas Mariett, Esq., Mr. William Radford, and Mr. Edward Wood (a   of Trinity College) had a frolique from Oxon to London, on foot, having never been there before ; they happened to take Windsore in their way, made their addresse to this good Gentleman, being then Fellow. Mr. Edward Wood was the Spookes-man, remonstrated that they were Oxon Scholars : he treated them well, and putt into Mr. Wood's hands Ten shillings.

This Mris Powney assures me that the poor were more relievable (that is to say) that he recieved more kindnesse from them than from the Rich. That that I putt downe of my Lady Salter is false. She had him to her house indeed, but 'twas to teach her sonne, who was such a blockhead he could not read well.

He might have been restored to his Fellowship again, but he would not accept the offer. He was not at all Covetous, and desired only to leave X pounds to bury him.

He lies buried in the Church yard at Eaton, under an altar monument of Black marble, erected at the sole chardge of Mr. Curwyn, with a too long Epitaph. He was no Kiff, or Kin to him.

EDMUND HALLEY

[Born 1656. Astronomer. Elected a Fellow of the Royal Society
at the age of twenty-two. But for Halley, Newton's *Principia* would
not have existed : his suggestions originated it and, although his
father's death had left him in poor circumstances, he printed Newton's
work at his own expense and averted the threatened suppression of
the third book. In 1691 Halley was refused the Savilian Professorship
of Astronomy at Oxford, owing to a suspicion of his being a materialist.
Assistant Secretary to the Royal Society 1685–1693. Deputy Controller
of the Mint at Ipswich 1696. William III gave him command of a
war-sloop, the *Paramour Pink,* in 1698, with orders to study the variation of the compass and to attempt to discover what land lay to the
south of the Western Ocean. Halley penetrated to the Antarctic,
and explored the Atlantic from shore to shore until 1700. The following year he published a general chart of the variation of the compass
shown by Halleyan lines. He then made a thorough survey of the
tides and coasts of the English Channel, of which he published a map
in 1702. In 1703 he was made Savilian Professor of Geometry at
Oxford. He was also elected Secretary of the Royal Society in 1713
and became Astronomer Royal in 1721. At the age of sixty-four,
he began the process of observing the moon through its complete
cycle of eighteen years and, in 1729, was elected a foreign member of
the Paris Academy of Sciences. Peter. the Great admitted him
familiarly to his table and, at Vienna, he was presented with a diamond
ring from the Emperor's own finger. Halley worked out the Law of
Inverse Squares, the first detailed description of a circulatory theory
of the Trade Winds and Monsoons, and a new method of finding the
roots of equations. He discovered the law connecting elevation in the
atmosphere with its density and first measured height by barometric
readings. He improved diving apparatus, experimented on the
dilatation of liquids by heat and, by his scientific voyages, laid the
foundations of physical geography. But his most enduring fame was
caused by his accurate prediction of the return in 1758 of the comet
(named after him) of 1531, 1607 and 1682. He died in 1742 after drinking a glass of wine against his doctor's orders.]

M R. EDMUND HALLEY, Artium Magister, the eldest
son of Edmund Halley, a Soape-boyler, a wealthy
Citizen of the City of London, of the Halleys, of
Derbyshire, a good family. He was born in Shoreditch parish,
at a place called Haggerston, the backside of Hogsdon.

At 9 yeares old, his father's apprentice taught him to write,
and arithmetique. He went to Paule's schoole to Dr. Gale :

while he was there he was very perfect in the caelestiall Globes in so much that I heard Mr. Moxton (the Globe-maker) say that if a star were misplaced in the Globe, he would presently find it. He studyed Geometry, and at 16 could make a dyall, and then, he said, thought himselfe a brave fellow.

At 16 went to Queen's Colledge in Oxon, well versed in Latin, Greeke, and Hebrew : where, at the age of nineteen, he solved this useful Probleme in Astronomie, never donne before, viz. *from 3 distances given from the Sun, and Angles between, to find the Orbe,* for which his name will be ever famous.

He went to Dantzick to visit Hevelius. December 1st, 1680, went to Paris : Cardinal d'Estrée caressed him and sent him to his brother the Admirall with a lettre of Recommendation. He hath contracted an acquaintance and friendship with all the eminentst Mathematicians of France and Italie, and holds a correspondence with them.

He gott leave and a *viaticum* of his father to goe to the Island of *Sancta Hellena,* purely upon account of advancement of Astronomy, to make the globe of the Southerne Hemisphere right, which before was very erroneous, as being donne only after the observations of ignorant seamen. There he stayed some moneths. There went over with him (amongst others) a woman, and her husband, who had no child in several yeares ; before he came from the Island, she was brought to bed of a Child. At his returne, he presented his Planisphere, with a short description, to his Majesty who was very well pleased with it ; but received nothing but Prayse.

WILLIAM HARCOURT

[Born 1610. Jesuit. His real name was Aylworth and he was born in Monmouthshire. He entered the Society of Jesus at Watten in 1641. He taught first philosophy and then theology at Liège for eleven years and then spent nine years as a missioner in Holland and England. During the excitement following Titus Oates' plot, he had some narrow escapes and a large reward was offered for his capture, but he managed to get safely to Holland. He died in 1679.]

PETRIFICATION of a Kidney.—When Father Harcourt suffered at Tyburne, and his bowells, etc. throwne into the fire, a butcher's boy standing by was resolved to have a piece of his Kidney which was broyling in the fire. He burn't his fingers much, but he got it; and one Roydon, a Brewer in Southwark, bought it, a kind of Presbyterian. The wonder is, 'tis now absolutely petrified. But 'twas not so hard when he first had it. It being alwayes carried in the pocket hardened by degrees, better then by the fire—like an Agate polished. I have seen it. He much values it.

THOMAS HARIOT

[Born 1560. Mathematician. He was mathematical tutor to Sir Walter Raleigh, who sent him to survey Virginia in 1585 : his *Brief and True Report* appears in Hakluyt's *Voyages*. He made inventions which gave algebra its modern form and used telescopes simultaneously with Galileo. Through them he observed sun-spots and the comets of 1607 and 1618. Died 1621.]

MR. HARIOT went with Sir Walter Ralegh into Virginia, and haz writt the *Description of Virginia,* which is printed. Dr. Pell tells me that he finds amongst his papers, an Alphabet that he had contrived for the American Language, like Devills.

When the Earle of Northumberland and Sir Walter Ralegh were both Prisoners in the Tower, they grew acquainted, and Sir Walter Raleigh recommended Mr. Hariot to him, and the Earle setled an Annuity of two hundred pounds a yeare on him for his life, which he enjoyed. But to Hues (who wrote *de Usu Globorum*) and to Mr. Warner he gave an Annuity but of sixty pounds per annum. These 3 were usually called the Earle of Northumberland's three Magi. They had a Table at the Earle's chardge, and the Earle himselfe had them to converse with him, singly or together.

Sir Francis Stuart had heard Mr. Hariot say that he had seen nine Cometes, and had predicted Seaven of them, but did not tell them how. 'Tis very strange : *excogitent Astronomi.*

He did not like (or valued not) the old storie of the Creation of the World. He could not beleeve the old position ; he would say *ex nihilo nihil fit* [nothing comes of nothing]. But a *nihilum* killed him at last : for in the top of his Nose came a little red speck (exceeding small) which grew bigger and bigger, and at last killed him. I suppose it was that which the Chirurgians call a *noli me tangere.*

He made a Philosophical Theologie, wherin he cast-off the Old Testament, and then the New-one would (consequently) have no Foundation. He was a Deist. His Doctrine he taught to Sir Walter Raleigh, Henry Earle of Northumberland, and some others. The Divines of those times look't on his manner of death as a Judgement upon him for nullifying the Scripture.

[123]

JAMES HARRINGTON

[Born 1611. Political theorist. He left Oxford without taking a degree and travelled to Holland, where he joined the Court of the Elector Palatine. Later he travelled through France to Rome, where he refused to kiss the Pope's toe, excusing himself afterwards to Charles I by saying that he would not kiss the foot of any prince, after kissing the King's hand. He also visited Venice, where he was greatly impressed by the system of government. In 1656 he published *Oceana,* his model of a commonwealth. Harrington's main principle is that power depends upon the balance of property, and normally of landed property. The senate prepares laws, which are voted upon by the people, and the magistrates carry them out. Elaborate systems of rotation and balloting are worked out in detail, and the permanence of the system is secured by the equilibrium of all interests. His republic is a moderate aristocracy. Harrington died in 1677.]

H IS Genius lay chiefly towards the Politiques and Democraticall Government.

Anno 1647, if not 6, he was by Order of Parliament made one of his Majestie's Bedchamber. Mr. Harrington and the King often disputed about Government. The King loved his company ; only he would not endure to heare of a Commonwealth : and Mr. Harrington passionately loved his Majestie. He was on the Scaffold with the King when he was beheaded ; and I have oftentimes heard him speake of King Charles I with the greatest zeale and passion imaginable, and that his death gave him so great a griefe that he contracted a Disease by it ; that never any thing did goe so neer to him.

He made severall Essayes in Poetry, viz. love-verses, &c. ; but his Muse was rough, and Mr. Henry Nevill, an ingeniose and well-bred Gentleman, a member of the House of Commons, and an excellent (but concealed) Poet, was his great familiar and Confident friend, and disswaded him from tampering in Poetrie which he did *invita Minervâ,* and to improve his proper Talent, viz. Politicall Reflections.

Whereupon he writ his *Oceana,* printed London 1656. Mr. T. Hobbes was wont to say that Henry Nevill had a finger in that pye ; and 'tis like enough. That ingeniose Tractat, together with his and H. Nevill's smart discourses and inculcations, dayly at Coffe-houses, made many Proselytes.

In so much that, anno 1659, the beginning of Michaelmas-terme, he had ever night a meeting at the (then) Turke's head, in the New Pallace-yard, where was made purposely a large ovall-table, with a passage in the middle for Miles to deliver his Coffee. About it sate his Disciples, and the Virtuosi. The Discourses in this Kind were the most ingeniose, and smart, that ever I heard, or expect to heare, and bandied with great eagernesse: the Arguments in the Parliament howse were but flatt to it.

Here we had (very formally) a *Balloting-box,* and balloted how things should be caried, by way of *tentamens* [experiment]. The room was every evening full as it could be cramm'd. One time Mr. Stafford and his Gang came in, in drink, from the Taverne, and affronted the Junto (Mr. Stafford tore their Orders and Minutes). The Soldiers offerd to kick them downe stayres, but Mr. Harrington's moderation and persuasion hindred it.

The Doctrine was very taking, and the more because, as to human foresight, there was no possibility of the King's returne. But the greatest part of the Parliament-men perfectly hated this designe of *Rotation by Ballotting;* for they were cursed Tyrants, and in love with their Power, and 'twas death to them, except 8 or 10, to admitt of this way, for H. Nevill proposed it in the Howse, and made it out to them, that except they embraced that Modell of Goverment they would be ruind.

Pride of Senators-for-Life is insufferable; and they were able to grind any one they owed ill will to to powder; they were hated by the armie and the countrey they represented, and their name and memorie stinkes—'twas worse then Tyranny. Now this Modell upon Rotation was that the third part of the Senate should rote out by ballot every yeare, so that every ninth yeare the Howse would be wholly alterd; no Magistrate to continue above 3 yeares, and all to be chosen by Ballot, then which manner of Choice, nothing can be invented more faire and impartiall.

Well: this Meeting continued Novemb., Dec., Jan., till Febr. 20 or 21; and then, upon the unexpected turne upon Generall Monke's comeing-in, all these aerie modells vanished. Then 'twas not fitt, nay Treason, to have donne such; but I well remember, he severall times (at the breaking-up) sayd, Well, the King will come in. Let him come-in, and call a Parliament of the greatest Cavaliers in England, so they be men of Estates, and let them sett but 7 yeares, and they will all turn Common-wealthe's men.

Anno Domini 1660, he was committed prisoner to the Tower; then to Portsey castle. His durance in these Prisons (he being a Gentleman of a high spirit and a hot head) was the procatractique cause of his deliration or madnesse ; which was not outragious, for he would discourse rationally enough and be very facetious company, but he grew to have a phancy that his Perspiration turned to Flies, and sometimes to Bees ; and he had a versatile timber house built in Mr. Hart's garden (opposite to St. James's parke) to try the experiment. He would turne it to the sun, and sitt towards it ; then he had his fox-tayles there to chase away and massacre all the Flies and Bees that were to be found there, and then shut his *Chassees* [window]. Now this Experiment was only to be tryed in Warme weather, and some flies would lye so close in the cranies and cloath (with which it was hung) that they would not presently shew themselves. A quarter of an hower after perhaps, a fly or two, or more, might be drawen-out of the lurking holes by the warmeth ; and then he would crye out, Doe not you see it apparently that these come from me? 'Twas the strangest sort of madnes that ever I found in any one : talke of any thing els, his discourse would be very ingeniose and pleasant.

He was wont to find fault with the constitution of our Government, that 'twas *by jumps,* and told a story of a Cavaliero he sawe at the Carnival in Italie, who rode on an excellent managed horse that with a touch of his toe would jumpe quite round. One side of his habit was Spanish, the other French ; which sudden alteration of the same person pleasantly surprized the spectators. Just so, said he, 'tis with us. When no Parliament, then absolute Monarchie ; when a Parliament, then it runnes to a Commonwealth.

He was wont to say that Right Reason in Contemplation, is Vertue in Action, et vice versa. Vivere secundum naturam is to live vertuously, the Divines will not have it so ; and that when the Divines would have us be an inch above Vertue, we fall an ell belowe it.

He married to his old sweet-heart Mris. Dayrell, a comely and discreete ladie. It happening so, from some private reasons, that he could not enjoy his deare in the flower and heate of his youth, he would never lye with her, but loved and admired her dearly : for she was *vergentibus annis* [sloping towards old age] when he maried her, and had lost her sweetenesse.

For above twenty yeares before he died (except his imprison-ment) he lived in the Little-Ambry (a faire house on the left hand) which lookes into the Deanes-yard in Westminster. In the upper story he had a pretty gallery, which looked into the yard, where he commonly dined, and meditated, and tooke his Tobacco.

[126]

Henry Nevill, Esq., never forsooke him to his dyeing day.
Though neer a whole yeare before he died, his memorie and
discourse were taken away by a disease ('twas a sad sight to see
such a sample of Mortality, in one whom I lately knew, a
brisque, lively cavaliero) this Gentleman, whom I must never
forget for his constant friendship, payd his visits as duly and
respectfully as when his friend was in the prime of his Understanding—a true friend.

WILLIAM HARVEY

[Born 1578. Anatomist and physiologist. Educated at Caius
College, Cambridge, and the University of Padua, then the most
famous school of physic. His theory of the circulation of the blood
was expounded to the College of Physicians in 1616, but his treatise
on the subject was not published until 1628. He died in 1657.]

WILLIAM HARVEY, Dr. of Physique and Chirurgery,
Inventor of the Circulation of the Bloud, was borne
at the house which is now the Post-house, a faire
stone-built-house, which he gave to Caius college in Cambridge,
with some lands there. His brother Eliab would have given
any money or exchange for it, because 'twas his father's,
and they all borne there; but the Doctor (truly) thought
his memory would better be preserved this way, for his
brother has left noble seates, and about 3000 pounds per
annum, at least.

William Harvey, was always very contemplative, and the
first that I heare of that was curious in Anatomie in
England. I remember I have heard him say he wrote a booke
De Insectis, which he had been many yeares about, and had
made dissections of Frogges, Toades, and a number of other
Animals, and had made curious Observations on them, which
papers, together with his goods, in his Lodgings at Whitehall,
were plundered at the beginning of the Rebellion, he being
for the King, and with him at Oxon; but he often sayd, That
of all the losses he sustained, no griefe was so crucifying to him
as the losse of these papers, which for love or money he could
never retrive or obtaine.

When Charles I by reason of the Tumults left London, he
attended him, and was at the fight of Edge-hill with him; and
during the fight, the Prince and Duke of Yorke were committed to his care. He told me that he withdrew with them
under a hedge, and tooke out of his pockett a booke and read;
but he had not read very long before a Bullet of a great Gun
grazed on the ground neare him, which made him remove his
station.

He told me that Sir Adrian Scrope was dangerously wounded
there, and left for dead amongst the dead men, stript; which

happened to be the saving of his Life. It was cold, cleer weather, and a frost that night ; which staunched his bleeding, and about midnight, or some houres after his hurte, he awaked, and was faine to drawe a dead body upon him for warmeth-sake.

I first sawe him at Oxford, 1642, after Edgehill fight, but was then too young to be acquainted with so great a Doctor. I remember he came severall times to Trinity College to George Bathurst, B.D., who had a Hen to hatch Egges in his chamber, which they dayly opened to discerne the progres and way of Generation. I had not the honour to be acquainted with him till 1651, being my she cosen Montague's physitian and friend. I was at that time bound for Italy (but to my great griefe disswaded by my mother's importunity). He was very communicative, and willing to instruct any that were modest and respectfull to him. And in order to my Journey, gave me, i.e. dictated to me, what to see, what company to keepe, what Bookes to read, how to manage my Studies : in short, he bid me goe to the Fountain head, and read Aristotle, Cicero, Avicenna, and did call the Neoteriques shitt-breeches.

He wrote a very bad hand, which (with use) I could pretty well read. He understood Greek and Latin pretty well, but was no Critique, and he wrote very bad Latin. The *Circuitis Sanguinis* [Circulation of the Blood] was, as I take it, donne into Latin by Sir George Ent.

At Oxford, he grew acquainted with Dr. Charles Scarborough, then a young Physitian (since by King Charles II Knighted) in whose conversation he much delighted ; and wheras before, he marched up and downe with the Army, he tooke him to him and made him ly in his Chamber, and said to him, Prithee leave off thy gunning, and stay here ; I will bring thee into practice.

His Majestie King Charles I gave him the Wardenship of Merton Colledge in Oxford, as a reward for his service, but the Times suffered him not to recieve or injoy any benefitt by it.

After Oxford was surrendred, which was 24 July 1646, he came to London, and lived with his brother Eliab a rich Merchant in London, who bought, about 1654, Cockaine-house, now (1680) the Excise-office, a noble house, where the Doctor was wont to contemplate on the Leads of the house, and had his severall stations, in regard of the sun, or wind.

He did delight to be in the darke, and told me he could then best contemplate. He had a house heretofore at Combe, in Surrey, a good aire and prospect, where he had Caves made in the Earth, in which in Summer time he delighted to meditate.

Ah ! my old Friend Dr. Harvey—I knew him right well.

He made me sitt by him 2 or 3 hours together in his meditating apartment discoursing. Why, had he been stiffe, starcht, and retired, as other formall Doctors are, he had known no more than they. From the meanest person, in some way, or other, the learnedst man may learn something. Pride has been one of the greatest stoppers of the Advancement of Learning.

He was far from Bigotry.

He was wont to say that man was but a great, mischievous Baboon.

He had been physitian to the Lord Chancellour Bacon, whom he esteemed much for his witt and style, but would not allow him to be a great Philosopher. Said he to me, *He writes Philosophy like a Lord Chancellor,* speaking in derision; *I have cured him.*

When Doctor Harvey (one of the Physitians College in London) being a Young Man, went to Travel towards Padoa: he went to Dover (with several others) and shewed his Pass, as the rest did, to the Governor there. The Governor told him, that he must not go, but he must keep him Prisoner. The Doctor desired to know for what reason? how he has transgrest. Well it was his Will to have it so. The Pacquet Boat Hoised Sail in the Evening (which was very clear) and the Doctor's Companions in it. There ensued a terrible Storme, and the Pacquet-Boat and all the Passengers were Drown'd: The next day the sad News was brought to Dover. The Doctor was unknown to the Governor, both by Name and Face; but the Night before, the Governor had a perfect Vision in a Dream of Doctor Harvey, who came to pass over to Calais; and that he had a Warning to stop him. This the Governor told to the Doctor the next day. The Doctor was a pious good Man, and has several times directed this Story to some of my Acquaintance.

Dr. Harvy told me, and any one if he examines himself will find it to be true, that a man could not fancy—truthfully —that he is imperfect in any part that he has, *verbi gratiâ,* Teeth, Eie, Tongue, Spina dorsi, etc. Natura tends to perfection, and in matters of Generation we ought to consult more with our sense and instinct, then our reason, and prudence, fashion of the country, and Interest. We see what contemptible products are of the prudent politiques; weake, fooles, and ricketty children, scandalls to nature and their country. The Heralds are fooles: *tota errant via* [they are on completely the wrong track]. A blessing goes with a marriage for love upon a strong impulse.

He that marries a widdowe makes himself Cuckold. *Exempli*

gratia, if a good Bitch is first warded with a Curre, let her ever after be warded with a dog of a good straine and yet she will bring curres as at first, her wombe being first infected with a Curre. So, the children will be like the first Husband (like raysing up children to your brother). So, the Adulterer, though a crime in Law, the children are like the husband.

He would say that we Europeans knew not how to order or governe our Woemen, and that the Turks were the only people used them wisely.

I remember he kept a pretty young wench to wayte on him, which I guesse he made use of for warmeth-sake as King David did, and tooke care of her in his Will, as also of his man servant.

He was very Cholerique; and in his young days wore a dagger (as the fashion then was) but this Dr. would be to apt to draw-out his dagger upon every slight occasion.

I have heard him say, that after his Booke of the *Circulation of the Blood* came-out, that he fell mightily in his Practize, and that 'twas beleeved by the vulgar that he was crack-brained; and all the Physitians were against his Opinion, and envyed him; many wrote against him. With much adoe at last, in about 20 or 30 yeares time, it was recieved in all the Universities in the world; and, as Mr. Hobbes sayes in his book *De Corpore, he is the only man, perhaps, that ever lived to see his owne Doctrine established in his life-time.*

He was Physitian, and a great Favorite of the Lord High Marshall of England, Thomas Howard Earle of Arundel and Surrey, with whom he travelled as his Physitian in his Ambassade to the Emperor at Vienna. In his Voyage, he would still be making of excursions into the Woods, makeing Observations of strange Trees, and plants, earths, etc., naturalls, and sometimes like to be lost, so that my Lord Ambassador would be really angry with him, for there was not only danger of Thieves, but also of wild beasts.

He was much and often troubled with the Gowte, and his way of Cure was thus; he would then sitt with his Legges bare, if it were a Frost, on the leads of Cockaine-house, putt them into a payle of water, till he was almost dead with cold, and betake himselfe to his Stove, and so 'twas gone.

He was hott-headed, and his thoughts working would many times keepe him from sleepinge; he told me that then his way was to rise out of his Bed and walke about his Chamber in his Shirt till he was pretty coole, i.e. till he began to have a horror, and then returne to bed, and sleepe very comfortably.

He was not tall; but of the lowest stature, round faced, olivaster complexion; little Eie, round, very black, full of spirit; his haire was black as a Raven, but quite white 20 yeares before he dyed.

I remember he was wont to drinke Coffee; which he and his brother Eliab did, before Coffee-houses were in fashion in London.

His practise was not very great towards his later end; he declined it, unlesse to a speciall friend, e.g. my Lady Howland, who had a cancer in her Breast, which he did cutt-off and seared, but at last she dyed of it. He rode on horseback with a Foot-cloath to visitt his Patients, his man following on foote, as the fashion then was, which was very decent, now quite discontinued. (The Judges rode also with their Foote-cloathes to Westminster-hall, which ended at the death of Sir Robert Hyde, Lord Chief Justice. Anthony Earl of Shafton, would have revived, but severall of the judges being old and ill horsemen would not agree to it.)

All his Profession would allow him to be an excellent Anatomist, but I never heard of any that admired his Therapeutique way. I knew severall practisers in London that would not have given 3d. for one of his Bills; and that a man could hardly tell by one of his Bills what he did aime at. (He did not care for Chymistrey, and was wont to speake against them with an undervalue.)

He had, towards his latter end, a preparation of Opium and I know not what, which he kept in his study to take, if occasion should serve, to putt him out of his paine, and which Sir Charles Scarborough promised to give him; this I beleeve to be true; but doe not at all beleeve that he really did give it him.

Not but that, had he laboured under great Paines, he had been readie enough to have donne it; I doe not deny that it was not according to his Principles upon certain occasions. But the manner of his dyeing was really, and *bonâ fide,* thus, viz. the morning of his death about 10 a clock, he went to speake, and found he had the dead palsey in his Tongue; then he sawe what was to become of him, he knew there was then no hopes of his recovery, so presently sends for his brother and young nephewes to come-up to him, to whom he gives one his Watch ('twas a minute watch with which he made his experiments), to another another thing, etc., as remembrances of him; made a signe to Sambroke, his Apothecary, to lett him blood in the Tongue, which did little or no good; and so ended his dayes. The Palsey did give him an easy Passe-port.

For 20 yeares before he dyed he tooke no manner of care about his worldly concernes, but his brother Eliab, who was a very wise and prudent menager, ordered all not only faithfully, but better then he could have donne himselfe.   He dyed worth 20,000 pounds, which he left to his brother Eliab.   In his Will he left his old friend Mr. Thomas Hobbes 10 pounds as a token of his Love.

He lies buried in a Vault at Hempsted in Essex, which his brother Eliab Harvey built ; he is lapt in lead, and on his brest in great letters

DR. WILLIAM HARVEY.

I was at his Funerall, and helpt to carry him into the Vault.

EDWARD HERBERT : LORD HERBERT OF CHERBURY

[Born 1583. Philosopher and historian. At the age of sixteen, he married a kinswoman four years his senior, while he was at the University. At his coronation in 1603, James I made him a Knight of the Bath and, in 1608, he went to the Continent, where for some years he was engaged in military and diplomatic affairs, not without his share of troubles. In 1624 he was created an Irish, and a few years later an English, peer, as Baron Herbert of Cherbury. It was in 1624 also that he wrote his treatise *De Veritate,* in which truth is distinguished from (i) revelation, (ii) the probable, (iii) the possible and (iv) the false. This was the first purely metaphysical work written by an Englishman and gave rise to much controversy. His other chief philosophical work was *De Religione Gentilium* (1663) which has been called the charter of the Deists, and was intended to prove that all religions recognise the same five main articles. He also wrote a *Life of Henry VIII* (1649) and his *Autobiography,* besides some poems of a metaphysical cast. On the outbreak of the Civil War he sided, though somewhat half-heartedly, with the Royalists, but in 1644 he surrendered to the Parliament, received a pension, and held various offices. Died 1648.]

I HAVE seen him severall times with Sir John Danvers ; he was a black man.

The Castle of Montgomery was a most Romancy seate : It stood upon a high Promontory, the north side 30+ feete high. From hence is a most delightsome prospect, 4 severall wayes. Southwards, without the Castle, is Prim-rose-hill : vide Donne's Poem :—

> *Upon this Prim-rose-hill,*
> *Where, if Heaven would distill*
> *A Showre of raine, each severall drop might goe*
> *To his owne Prim-rose, and grow Manna so ;*
> *And where their forme, and their infinitie*
>   *Make a terrestiall Galaxie,*
>   *As the small starres doe in the Skie :*

In this pleasant Solitude did this noble Lord enjoy his Muse.

This stately Castle was demolished since the late Warres at the Chardge of the Countrey.

Mr. Fludd tells me he had constantly prayers twice a day in his howse, and Sundayes would have his Chaplayne, Dr. Coote (a Cambridge scholar and a learned) read one of Smyth's Sermons.

James Usher, Lord Primate of Ireland, was sent for by him, when in his death-bed, and he would have received the sacrament. He sayd indifferently of it that *if there was good in any-thing 'twas in that,* or *if it did no good 'twould doe no hurt.* The Primate refused it, for which many blamed him. He then turned his head to the other side and expired very serenely.

GEORGE HERBERT

[Born 1593. Poet. He was educated at Westminster School and Trinity College, Cambridge, where he took his degree in 1616 and was public orator from 1619 until 1627. He became the friend of Sir Henry Wotton, Donne and Bacon, the last of whom is said to have held him in such high esteem as to submit his writings to him before publication. He acquired the favour of James I, who conferred upon him a sinecure worth £120 a year, and having powerful friends, he attached himself for some time to the Court in the hope of preferment. The death of two of his patrons, however, led him to change his views, and coming under the influence of Nicholas Ferrar, the quietist of Little Gidding, and of Laud, he took orders in 1626, becoming in 1630 Rector of Bemerton in Wiltshire, where he passed the remainder of his life, discharging the duties of a parish priest with conscientious assiduity. His chief works are *The Temple, or Sacred Poems and Private Ejaculations* (1634), *The Country Parson* (1652) and *Jacula Prudentium,* a collection of pithy proverbial sayings, the two last in prose. *The Temple,* which was published posthumously, had immediate acceptance, and according to Izaak Walton who wrote his life, twenty thousand copies were sold in a few years. Among its admirers were Charles I, William Cowper and Coleridge. Herbert wrote some of the most exquisite sacred poetry in the language, although his style, influenced by Donne, is at times characterised by artificiality and conceits. He was an excellent classical scholar and an accomplished musician. He died in 1633.]

IN Brecknockshire, about 3 miles from Brecknock, is a village called Penkelly, where is a little Castle. It is an ancient Seate of the Herberts. Mr. Herbert, of this place, came, by the mother's side, of Wgan. The Lord Cherbery's ancestor came by the second venter, who was a Miller's daughter. The greatest part of the estate was settled on the issue by the 2d venter, viz. Montgomery castle, and Aberystwith. Upon this Match with the Miller's daughter are to this day recited, or sung, by the Welsh, verses to this sence :—*O God ! Woe is me miserable, my father was a Miller, and my mother a Milleresse, and I am now a Ladie.*

In a Buriall-place in the Church at Montgomery (belonging to the Castle) is a great freestone monument of Richard Herbert, Esq. (father to the learned Lord Herbert of Cherbery, and Mr. George Herbert, who wrote the Sacred Poëms) where are the effigies of him and Magdalene his wife, who afterwards was maried to Sir John Danvers of Wilts, and lies interred at Chelsey church but without any monument. Dr. Donne, Dean of St. Paul's, preached her funerall sermon, to which are annexed severall verses, Latin and Greeke, by Mr. George Herbert, in Memorie of Her. She was buryed, as appeares by the sermon, July 1, 1627.

Mr. George Herbert was kinsman (remote) and Chapelaine to Philip, Earl of Pembroke and Montgomery, and Lord Chamberlayn. His Lordship gave him a Benefice at Bemmarton (between Wilton and Salisbury) a pittifull little chappell of Ease to Foughelston. The old house was very ruinous. Here he built a very handsome howse for the Minister, of Brick, and made a good garden and walkes. He lyes in the Chancell, under no large, nor yet very good, marble grave-stone, without any Inscription.

In the Chancell are many apt sentences of the Scripture. At his Wive's Seate, *My life is hid with Christ in God* (he hath verses on this Text in his Poëms). Above, in a little windowe-blinded, with a Veile (ill painted) *Thou art my hideing place.*

He maried Jane, the third daughter of Charles Danvers, of Bayntun, in com. Wilts, Esq. but had no issue by her. He was a very fine complexion and consumptive. His mariage, I suppose, hastened his death. My kinswoman was a handsome *bona roba* and ingeniose.

When he was first maried he lived a yeare or better at Dantesey house. H. Allen, of Dantesey, was well acquainted with him, who has told me that he had a very good hand on the Lute, and that he sett his own Lyricks or sacred poems.

Scripsit :—Sacred Poems, called *The Church,* printed, Cambridge, 1633; a Booke entituled *The Country Parson,* not printed till about 1650, 8vo. He also writt a folio in Latin, which because the parson of Hineham could not read, his widowe (then wife to Sir Robert Cooke) condemned to the uses of good houswifry. (This account I had from Mr. Arnold Cooke, one of Sir Robert Cooke's sonnes, whom I desired to aske his mother-in-lawe for Mr. G. Herbert's MSS.)

He was buryed (according to his owne desire) with the singing service for the buriall of dead, by the singing men of Sarum. Francis Sambroke (attorney) then assisted as a Chorister boy ; my uncle, Thomas Danvers, was at the Funerall.

'Tis an honour to the place, to have had the heavenly and ingeniose contemplation of this good man, who was pious even to prophesie ; e.g.

> *Religion now on tip-toe stands,*
> *Ready to goe to the American strands.*

MARY HERBERT : COUNTESS OF PEMBROKE

[Born 1561. She spent her childhood chiefly at Ludlow Castle, where her father, Sir Henry Sidney, resided as President of Wales, and she was carefully educated, acquiring a knowledge of Latin, Greek and Hebrew. Her brother Philip was her constant childhood companion. On Queen Elizabeth's suggestion she became a member of the Royal Household in 1575, and accompanied the Queen on her progresses round the country. In 1577 she became the third wife of Henry, Earl of Pembroke, and the Earl of Leicester advanced a part of her dowry, owing to her father's poverty. She suggested the composition of her brother's *Arcadia,* which she revised and added to. For, in 1586, she lost her mother, her father and her brother and, when she had recovered from this blow, she applied herself to the literary tasks which Sir Philip Sidney had left unfinished or had contemplated, and took under her protection the many men of letters to whom he had acted as patron: Edmund Spenser, Samuel Daniel, Nicholas Breton, Thomas Moffat, Thomas Nashe, Gabriel Harvey, John Donne and Ben Jonson. Her poetry, according to Sir John Harrington, should *outlast Wilton's walls.* Died 1621.]

MARY, Countesse of Pembroke, was sister to Sir Philip Sydney : maried to Henry, the eldest son of William Earle of Pembroke ; but this subtile old Earle did see that his faire and witty daughter-in-lawe would horne his sonne, and told him so, and advised him to keepe her in the Countrey and not to let her frequent the Court.

She was a beautifull Ladie and had an excellent witt, and had the best breeding that that age could afford. Shee had a pritty sharpe-ovall face. Her haire was of a reddish yellowe.

She was very salacious, and she had a Contrivance that in the Spring of the yeare, when the Stallions were to leape the Mares, they were to be brought before such a part of the house, where she had a *vidette* (a hole to peepe out at) to looke on them and please herselfe with their Sport ; and then she would act the like sport herselfe with *her* stallions. One of her great Gallants was Crooke-back't Cecill, Earl of Salisbury.

In her time, Wilton House was like a College, there were so many learned and ingeniose persons. She was the greatest Patronesse of witt and learning of any Lady in her time. She was a great Chymist, and spent yearly a great deale in that study. She kept for her Laborator in the house Adrian Gilbert (vulgarly called Dr. Gilbert) halfe-brother to Sir Walter Raleigh, who was a great Chymist in those dayes and a Man of excellent naturall Parts; but very Sarcastick, and the greatest Buffoon in the Nation; cared not what he said to man or woman of what quality soever. 'Twas he that made the curious wall about Rowlington-parke, which is the parke that adjoynes the howse at Wilton. Mr. Henry Sanford was the Earle's Secretary, a good scholar and poet, and who did penne part of the *Arcadia* dedicated to her (as appeares by the preface). He haz a preface before it with the two letters of his name. She also gave an honourable yearly Pension to Dr. Mouffet, who hath writt a Booke *De Insectis*. Also one Boston, a good Chymist, a Salisbury man borne, who did undoe himselfe by studying the Philosophers-stone, and she would have kept him, but he would have all the golde to himselfe, and so dyed, I thinke, in a Gaole. And I cannot imagine that Mr. Edmund Spencer could be a stranger here.

At Wilton is a good Library, which was collected in this learned Ladie's time. There is a Manuscript very elegantly written, viz. all the *Psalmes of David* translated by Sir Philip Sydney, curiously bound in crimson velvet. There is a MS. writt by Dame Marian *Of Hunting and Hawking,* in English verse, written in King Henry 8th's time. There is the Legier book of Wilton, one page Saxon and the other Latin, which Mr. Dugdale perused. There was a Latin Poeme, a Manuscript, writt in Julius Caesar's time; wherein amongst the Dogges, was mention of Tumblers, and that they were found no where, but in Britaine.

This curious seate of Wilton and the adjacent countrey is an Arcadian place and a Paradise. Sir Philip Sydney was much here, and there was so great love between him and his faire sister that I have heard old Gentlemen say that they lay together, and it was thought the first Philip Earle of Pembroke was begot by him, but he inherited not the witt of either brother or sister.

This Countesse, after her Lord's death, maried to Sir Matthew Lister, Knight, one of the colledge of Physitians, London. Jack Markham saies they were not maried. He was, they say, a learned and handsome Gentleman. She built then a curious house in Bedfordshire called Houghton Lodge, neer Ampthill. The architects were sent for from Italie. It is built according to the Description of Basilius's house in the firste booke of *Arcadia*. It is most pleasantly situated, and has fower

Visto's ; each prospect 25 or 30 miles. This was sold to the Earle of Elgin. The house did cost 10,000 pounds the building.

An epitaph on the Lady Mary, Countesse of Pembroke (in print somewhere) by William Browne, who wrote the *Pastoralls* :

> *Underneath this sable Herse*
> *Lies the Subject of all Verse :*
> *Sydney's Sister, Pembroke's Mother*
> *Death ! ere thou Kill'st such another*
> *Fair, and good, and learnd as SHEE,*
> *Time will throw his Dart at thee.*

WILLIAM HERBERT:
EARL OF PEMBROKE

[Born 1501. Esquire of the Body of Henry VIII. Married a sister of Queen Catharine Parr. Gentleman of the Privy Chamber 1546. Appointed one of Henry VIII's executors and a member of Edward VI's Council. Knight of the Garter and Master of the Horse 1548. Helped to quell Cornish Rising 1549. President of Wales 1550. Took part in Somerset's trial (1551) and obtained his Wiltshire estates. Created Earl of Pembroke 1551. Joined Northumberland in proclaiming Lady Jane Grey as Queen, but declared for Mary in time. Intimate with King Philip. Envoy to France 1555. Governor of Calais 1556. Lord Steward under Elizabeth 1568. Died 1570.]

HE was (as I take it) a younger brother, a mad fighting young Fellow. 'Tis certaine he was a servant to the house of Worcester, and wore their blew-coate and Badge. My cosen Whitney's great aunt gave him a golden angell when he went to London. One time, being at Bristowe, he was arrested, and killed one of the Sheriffes of the City. He made his escape through Back-street, through the (then great) Gate, into the Marsh, and gott into France.

Upon this action of Killing the Sheriffe, the City ordered the Gate to be walled-up, and only a little posterne gate or dore, with a Turnestile for a foot-passenger, which continued so till Bristowe was a Garrison for the King, and the great Gate was then opened. He was called *black Will Herbert*.

In France he betooke himselfe into the Army, where he shewd so much courage, and readinesse of witt in Conduct, that in short time he became Eminent, and was favoured by the King, who afterwards recommended him to Henry the VIII of England, who much valued him, and heaped favours and honours upon him.

He maried Anne Par, sister of Queen Katharine Par, by whom he had 2 sonnes, Henry Earle of Pembroke and Edward, the ancestor of the Lord Powys.

He was made Privy Councellor and conservator of King Henry the Eight's Will. He could neither write, nor read, but had a Stamp for his name. He was of good Naturall; but

[141]

very Cholerique. He was strong sett, but bony, reddish-favoured, of a sharp eie, sterne looke.

Upon the Dissolution of the Abbeys, He gave him the Abbey of Wilton, and a country of Lands and Mannours there about belonging to it. He gave him also the Abbey of Remesbury, in Wilts, with much lands belonging to it. He gave him Cardiff-Castle, in Glamorganshire, with the ancient Crowne-lands belonging to it.

In Queen Mary's time, upon the return of the Catholique Religion, the nunnes came again to Wilton Abbey, and this William, Earl of Pembroke, came to the gate (which lookes towards the court by the street, but now is walled up) with his cappe in hand, and fell upon his knee to the Lady Abesse and the Nunnes, crying *peccavi* [I have sinned]. Upon Queen Mary's death, the Earle came to Wilton (like a Tygre) and turned them out, crying, out, ye Whores, to worke, to worke, ye Whores, goe spinne.

He, being a stranger in our Country, and an upstart, was much envyed. And in those days (of sword and buckler) noblemen (and also great Knights, as the Longs) when they went to the Assizes or Sessions at Salisbury, etc., had a great number of Retainers following them; and there were (you have heard) in those dayes, Feudes, i.e. quarrels and animosities, between great neighbours. Particularly this newe Earle was much envyed by the then Lord Sturton of Sturton (which is a most parkely ground and Romancy pleasant place : heretofore all horrid, and woody) who would when he went or returned from Sarum (by Wilton was his rode) sound his Trumpets and give reproachfull challenging words; 'twas a relique of Knighthood Errantry.

These Lord Stourtons were possessed of a great Estate in the West till in Queen Maries dayes, the Lord Stourton was attainted by his murthering of Mr. Hargill his Steward, whom he killed and buryed in his Cellar, for which he was hanged in a silken halter at Salisbury.

There was a great Feud between this Lord Stourton and William Herbert the first Earle of Pembroke of that Family, who was altogether a Stranger in the West, and from a private Gentleman, and of no Estate, but only a Soldier of Fortune becoming a Favourite of King Henr. 8, at the dissolution of the Abbeys, in few years from nothing slipt into a prodigiouse Estate of the Church Lands : Which brought great Envy on him, from this Baron of an ancient Family and great Paternall Estate, besides the Difference in Religion. This Lord Stourton aforesayd was a person of great Spirit and Courage, and kept in his Retinew the stoutest fellowes he could heare of : Amongst others, he heard of one Hargill a mighty, stowt fellowe, who had lately killed a man, who was recommended to his Lordship for his valour : who when he came in to his family, the Lord Stourton gave the next Sunday ten groates to the Priest of the parish to say a Masse for him at Church, for the expiation of his (Hargill) sin in killing the man. A surley, dogged, crosse fellowe it seemes he was, whom at last when his Lordship had advanced to be Steward of his Estate, cosined his Lord of the Mannour of Kilmanton (the next parish.) I thinke it was a Trust : Which the Lord Stourton, who also had a good spirit, seeing his servant Hargill had so ensnared him in lowe tricks, as that he could not possibly be relieved : not able to beare so great and ungratefull an abuse, murthered him as aforesayd.

In Queen Elizabeth's time, some Bishop (I have forgott who) that had been his chaplain, was sent to the Earl of Pembroke from the Queen and Council, to take Interrogatories from him. So he takes out his pen and inke, examines and writes. When he had writt a good deale, sayd the Earle, Now lett me see it. Why, quoth the Bishop, Your Lordship cannot read it ? That's all one : I'le see it, quoth he, and takes it, and teares it to pieces. Zounds, you rascall, quoth he, d'ee thinke I will have my Throate cutt with a pen-knife ? It seems they had a minde to have pick't a hole in his Coate, and to have gott his Estate.

'Tis reported that he caused himselfe to be lett bloud, and bled so much that it was his death, and that he should say as he was expiring, *They would have Wilton, they would have Wilton,* and so gave up the Ghost.

This William (the founder of the Family) had a little reddish picked nosed Cur-dog : none of the Prettiest : which loved him, and the Earle loved the dog. When the Earle dyed, the dog would not goe from his Master's dead body, but pined away, and dyed under the hearse ; the picture of which Dog is under his picture in the Gallery at Wilton.

WILLIAM AND PHILIP HER-BERT : EARLS OF PEMBROKE

[William Herbert (1580–1630) succeeded his father as third earl in 1601. He was *immoderately given up to women* and was committed to the Fleet Prison and banished from Court for refusing to marry Mary Fitton, a Maid of Honour and a favourite of Queen Elizabeth, who was with child by him. On the accession of James I, Pembroke secured a high position at Court, becoming a Knight of the Garter, Keeper of the Forest of Clarendon and Lord Lieutenant of Cornwall. In 1604 he married Lady Mary Tálbot, a great heiress, and the wedding was celebrated by a tournament at Wilton, but Clarendon said *he paid much too dear for his wife's fortune by taking her person into the bargain.* He attended the death-bed of James I, who entreated him to testify publicly that he had died a Protestant. Pembroke carried the crown at Charles I's coronation and was made a member of the committee which advised the King on foreign affairs and of the Permanent Council of War. He was deeply interested in the New World, becoming a Member of the King's Council for the Virginia Company in 1609, the North West Passage Company in 1612, the Bermudas Company in 1615, the New England Company in 1620 and the Guiana Company 1627. He was also a member of the East India Company. He was a patron of many poets, including Massinger and Chapman, and every New Year's Day he sent Ben Jonson £20 to buy books. Inigo Jones visited Italy at his expense and he was the friend of Donne and Shakespeare, the First Folio of whose plays is dedicated *To the Most Noble and Incomparable Pair of Brethren,* William and Philip Herbert. Philip, who succeeded his brother as fourth Earl of Pembroke, was born in 1584 and was named after Sir Philip Sidney. He was the chief favourite of James I in the early years of his reign, who created him Earl of Montgomery and made him lavish grants of land. In 1628 he received the grant of Trinidad, Tobago and the Barbadoes. He was foul mouthed and quarrelsome and took the Parliamentary side in the Civil War. Died 1650.]

'TIS certain, the Earles of Pembroke were the most popular Peers in the West of England; but one might boldly say, in the whole Kingdome. The Revenue of this Family was till about 1652, 16,000 pounds per annum. But with his Offices, and all He had thirty thousand Pounds per annum. And, as the Revenue was great, so the greatnesse of his Retinue, and Hospitality were answerable. One hundred and twenty Family uprising and down lyeing : whereof you may take out six or seven, and all the rest Servants, and Retayners.

William 2^d & Philip 3^d Earles were gallant and handsome persons : they espoused not Learning, but were addicted to Field sports and Hospitality. Earle William entertained at Wilton, at his own Cost, King James the first, during the space of many moneths.

King Charles 1st did love Wilton above all places : and came thither every Sommer. It was HE, that did put Philip (1st) Earle of Pembroke upon makeing this magnificent Garden and Grotto, and to new-build that side of the House that fronts the Garden with two stately Pavilions at Each end, all al Italiano. Wilton-garden was the third garden of the Italian mode. But in the time of King Charles IId, Gardening was much improved and became common : I doe beleeve, I may modestly affirm, that there is now (1691) ten times as much gardning about London as there was in A° 1660 : and we have been since that time much improved in foreign plants : especially since about 1683, there have been exotick Plants brought into England, no lesse than seven thousand.

William Herbert, Earl of Pembroke was a most noble Person, and the Glory of the Court in the Reignes of King James and King Charles. He was handsome, and of an admirable presence. He was the greatest Maecenas to learned Men of any Peer of his time : or since. He was very generous and open handed : He gave a noble Collection of choice Bookes, and Manuscripts to the Bodlaean Library at Oxford, which remain ther as an honourable Monument of his Munificence. 'Twas thought, had he not been suddenly snatcht away by Death (to the grief of all learned, and good men) that He would have been a great Benefactor to Pembroke Colledge in Oxford ; whereas there remains only from him a great piece of Plate, that He gave there.

His Nativity was calculated by old Mr. Thomas Allen : his death was foretold, which happened true at the time praedicted, at his House at Baynards Castle in London. He was very well in health ; but because of the Fatal Direction which He lay under, he made a great Entertainment (a Supper) for his Friends : ate and dranke plentifully ; went well to bed, and died in his sleep.

Earl William was a most magnificent and brave Peer, and loved learned men. He was a good Scholar, and delighted in Poetrie : and did sometimes (for his Diversion) write some Sonnets and Epigrammes, which deserve Commendation : some of them are in print. He was of an Heroiq, and publick

Spirit, Bountiful to his Friends, and Servants, and a great Encourager of Learned Men.

Philip Earle of Pembroke (his Brother) did not delight in Books, or Poetry: but exceedingly loved Painting and Building, in which he had singular Judgement, and had the best Collection of any Peer in England, and was the great Patron to Sir Anthony van Dyck: and had most of his Painting. His Lordship's chiefe delight was in Hunting and Hawking, both which he had to the greatest perfection of any Peer in the Realm.

Wilton will appeare to have been an Academie, as well as Palace, and was (as it were) the Apiarie, to which Men, that were excellent in Armes, and Arts, did resort, and were carress't; and many of them received honourable Pensions.

As aforesaid, Philip the first Earle of that name, did not love Bookes, as his elder Brother William did: but when he was young, he had a wonderfull Sagacity or faculty of discerning Men: i.e. to espie the reality or deceit of Ambassadours and Ministers of Estate, which did render Him the more acceptable to King James the first.

Philip Earle of Pembroke (sonne of Philip aforesayd) had an admirable Witt, and was contemplative but did not much care for reading. His chiefest Diversion was Chymistrie, which his Lordship did understand very well and he made Medicines, that did great Cures.

It was the right hon. Philip (1st) Earle of Pembroke, that was the great Hunter. It was in his Lordship's time (*sc. tempore Jacobi I and Caroli I*) a serene calme of Peace, that Hunting was at its greatest Heighth that ever was in this Nation. The Roman Governours had not (I thinke) the leisure; the Saxons were never at quiet; and the Baron's Warres, and these of Yorke and Lancaster, took up the greatest part of the time since the Conquest: So that the Glory of the English Hunting breath'd its last with this Earle: who deceased about 1644, and shortly after the Forests and Parkes were sold, and converted into Arable.

'Twas after his Lordship's Decease, that I was a Hunter: that is to say with the right hon^ble William, Lord Herbert of Cardiff, the aforesaid Philip's Grandson.

This present Earl of Pembroke (1680) has at Wilton, 52 Mastives and 30 Grey-hounds, some Beares, and a Lyon, and a matter of 60 fellowes more bestiall then they.

THOMAS HOBBES

[Born 1588. Philosopher. For a great part of his life he was in the service of the Cavendish family and, in 1647, was appointed mathematical tutor to the Prince of Wales. When the Parliament of 1628 drew up the Petition of Right, Hobbes published a translation of Thucydides, with the expressed intention of showing the evils of democracy. It was not the actual occurrence of the Civil War that caused his opinions, but the prospect of it; naturally, however, his convictions were strengthened when his fears were realised and, in 1651, he published the *Leviathan,* which stressed the comfort of government. At the Restoration, Charles II awarded him a pension of £100 a year—which, however, His Majesty forgot to pay. Hobbes' atheism soon got him into fresh trouble and he was refused leave to print anything in England on controversial subjects. He continued to produce important works nevertheless and they were printed at Amsterdam. His last book was published when he was eighty-seven. Died 1679.]

THE day of his Birth was April the fifth, Anno Domini 1588, on a Fryday morning, which that yeare was Good Fryday. His mother fell in labour with him upon the fright of the Invasion of the Spaniards.

Mr. Hobbes' father was Minister of Westport juxta Malmesbury, to which Brokenborough and Charlton doe belong as Chapells of Ease: the Vicaridge of Malmesbury is but xx nobles per annum=£6 13s. 4d. He was one of the Clergie of Queen Elizabeth's time—a little Learning went a great way with him and many other ignorant Sir Johns in those days; could only read the prayers of the Church and the homilies; and disesteemed Learning (his son Edmund told me so) as not knowing the Sweetnes of it.

Westport is the Parish without the West-gate (which is now demolished) which Gate stood on the neck of land that joines Malmesbury to Westport. Here was, before the late Warres, a very pretty church, consisting of 3 aisles, or rather a nave and two aisles, dedicated to St. Mary; and a fair spire-steeple, with five tuneable Bells, which, when the Towne was taken by Sir W. Waller, were converted into Ordinance, and the church pulled-downe to the ground, that the Enemie might not shelter themselves against the Garrison. The Steeple was higher then that now standing in the Borough, which much adorned the Prospect. The Windowes were well painted, and in them were Inscriptions that declared much Antiquitie ; now is here rebuilt a Church like a Stable.

The old vicar Hobs was a good Fellow and had been at cards all Saturday night, and at church in his sleep he cries out *Trafells is troumps,* viz. clubs. Then quoth the Clark, *Then, Master, he that have Ace doe rub.*

He was a collirice man, and a parson (which I thinke succeeded him at Westport) provoked him (a purpose) at the church doore, soe Hobs stroke him and was forcd to fly for it and died in obscurity beyound London, about 80 yeares since.

As to his Father's ignorance and clownery, 'twas as good metal in the Oare which wants excoriating and refineing. A witt requires much cultivation, much paines, and art and good conversation to perfect a man.

Thomas, the Father, had an elder Brother whose name was Francis, a wealthy man, and had been Alderman of the Borough ; by Profession a Glover, which is a great Trade here, and in times past much greater. (Shall I expresse or conceale this *glover*? The philosopher would acknowledge it.) Having no child, he contributed much to, or rather altogether maintained, his Nephew Thomas at Magdalen-hall in Oxon ; and when he dyed gave him an *agellum* (a moweing-ground) called the Gasten-ground, lyeing neer to the Horse-faire, worth 16, or 18 poundes per annum ; the rest of his Landes he gave to his nephew Edmund. Edmund was neer two yeares elder then his brother Thomas, and something resembled him in aspect, not so tall, but fell much short of him in his Intellect : though he was a good plain understanding countrey-man. He had been bred at Schoole with his brother ; could have made Theme, and verse, and understood a little Greek to his dyeing day. He dyed about 13 yeares since, aetat. circiter 80.

At fower yeer old Mr. Thomas Hobbes (Philosopher) went to Schoole in Westport church till 8—then the church was painted. At 8 he could read well and number a matter of 4 or 5 figures. After, he went to Malmesbury to Parson Evans. After him, he had for his Schoolemaster, Mr. Robert Latimer, a young man of about nineteen or twenty, newly come from the University, who then kept a private schoole in Westport. This Mr. Latimer was a good Graecian, and the first that came into our Parts hereabout since the Reformation. He was a Batchelour and delighted in his Scholar, T. H.'s company, and used to instruct him, and two or three ingeniose youths more, in the evening till nine a clock.

When he was a Boy he was playsome enough, but withall

[148]

he had even then a contemplative Melancholinesse; he would gett him into a corner, and learn his Lesson by heart presently. His haire was black, and his schoolfellows were wont to call him *Crowe*.

At fourtenn yeares of age, he went away a good Schoolescholar to Magdalen-hall, in Oxford. It is not to be forgotten that before he went to the University, he had turned Euripidis *Medea* out of Greeke into Latin Iambiques, which he presented to his Master. Mr. H. told me that he would faine have had them, to see how he did grow. Twenty odde yeares agoe I searcht all old Mr. Latimer's papers, but could not find them; the Oven had devoured them.

At Oxford Mr. T. H. used, in the Summer time especially, to rise very early in the Morning, and would tye the leadencounters with Pacthreds, which he did besmere with birdlime, and bayte then with parings of cheese, and the Jack-dawes would spye them a vast distance up in the aire, and as far as Osney-abbey, and strike at the Bayte, and so he harled in the String, which the wayte of the counter would make cling about their Wings. (This story he happened to tell me, discoursing of the Optiques, to instance such sharpnes of sight in so little an eie.) He did not much care for Logick, yet he learnd it, and thought himself a good Disputant. He tooke great delight there to goe to the Booke-binders shops, and lye gaping on Mappes.

After he had taken his Batchelor of Arts degree, the than principall of Magdalen-hall (Sir James Hussee: a great encourager of towardly youths) recommended him to his yong Lord (the Earl of Devonshire) when he left Oxon, who had a conceit that he should profitt more in his learning if he had a Scholar of his owne age to wayte on him then if he had the information of a grave Doctor. He was his Lordship's page, and rode a hunting and hawking with him, and kept his privy-purse.

By this way of life he had almost forgott his Latin. He therefore bought him bookes of an Amsterdam print that he might carry in his pocket (particularly Caesar's *Commentarys*) which he did read in the Lobbey, or Ante-chamber, whilest his Lord was making his Visits.

He spent two yeares in reading romances and playes, which he haz often repented and sayd that these two yeares were lost of him—wherin perhaps he was mistaken too. For it might furnish him with copie of words.

The Lord Chancellour Bacon loved to converse with him. He assisted his Lordship in translating severall of his *Essayes* into Latin, one, I well remember, is that *Of the Greatnes of Cities* : the rest I have forgott. His Lordship was a very Contemplative person, and was wont to contemplate in his delicious walkes at Gorambery, and dictate to Mr. Thomas Bushell, or some other of his Gentlemen, that attended him with inke and paper ready to sett downe presently his Thoughts. His Lordship would often say that he better liked Mr. Hobbes's taking his thoughts, then any of the other, because he understood what he wrote, which the others not understanding, my Lord would many times have a harde taske to make sense of what they writt.

1634 : this summer—I remember 'twas in Venison season (July or August)—Mr. T. H. came into his Native Country to visitt his Friends, and amongst others he came then to see his old school-master, Mr. Robert Latimer, at Leigh-de-la-mer, where I was then a little youth at Schoole in the church, newly entred into my Grammar by him. Here was the first place and time that ever I had the honour to see this worthy, learned man, who was then pleased to take notice of me, and the next day visited my relations. He was then a proper man, briske, and in very good habit. His hayre was then quite black. He stayed at Malmsbury and in the neighborhood a weeke or better. His conversation about those times was much about Ben: Jonson, Mr. Ayton, etc. 'Twas the last time that ever he was in Wiltshire.

He was 40 yeares old before he looked on Geometry ; which happened accidentally. Being in a Gentleman's Library, Euclid's Elements lay open, and 'twas the 47 *El. libri* 1. He read the Proposition. *By G—*, sayd he (he would now and then sweare an emphaticall Oath by way of emphasis) *this is impossible !* So he reads the Demonstration of it, which referred him back to such a Proposition ; which proposition he read. That referred him back to another, which he also read. *Et sic deinceps* [and so on] that at last he was demonstratively convinced of that trueth. This made him in love with Geometry.

I have heard Mr. Hobbes say that he was wont to draw lines on his thigh and on the sheetes, abed, and also multiply and divide.

He would often complain that Algebra (though of great use) was too much admired, and so followed after, that it made men not contemplate and consider so much the nature and power of Lines, which was a great hinderance to the Groweth of Geometrie ; for that though algebra did rarely well and quickly, and easily in right lines, yet 'twould not *bite* in *solid* (I thinke) Geometry. Quod N.B.

'Twas pitty that Mr. Hobbs had not began the study of the Mathematics sooner, els he would not have layn so open. But one may say of him, as one sayes of Jos. Scaliger, that where he erres, he erres so ingeniosely, that one had rather erre with him then hitt the marke with Clavius.

After he began to reflect on the Interest of the King of England as touching his affaires between Him and parliament, for ten yeares together his thoughts were much, or almost altogether, unhinged from the Mathematiques; which was a great putt-back to his Mathematicall improvement; for in ten yeares (or better) discontinuance of that Study (especially) one's Mathematiques will become very rusty.

When the Parliament sate that began in April 1640 and was dissolved in May following, and in which many pointes of the Regall Power, which were necessary for the Peace of the Kingdome and Safety of his Majestye's Person, were disputed and denyed, Mr. Hobbes wrote a little Treatise in English, wherin he did sett-forth and demonstrate, that the sayd Powers and Rights were inseparably annexed to the Soveraignty, which soveraignty they did not then deny to be in the King; but it seemes understood not, or would not understand, that Inseparability. Of this Treatise, though not printed, many Gentlemen had copies, which occasioned much talke of the Author; and had not his Majestie dissolved the Parliament, it had brought him in danger of his life.

Bp. Manwaring (of St. David's) preach'd *his Doctrine*; for which, among others, he was sent prisoner to the Tower. Then thought Mr. Hobbes, 'tis time now for me to shift for my selfe, and so withdrew into France, and resided at Paris. This little MS. treatise grew to be his Booke *De Cive,* and at last grew there to be the so formidable LEVIATHAN; the manner of writing of which booke (he told me) was thus. He sayd that he sometimes would sett his thoughts upon researching and contemplating, always with this Rule that he very much and deeply considered one thing at a time (*scilicet,* a weeke or sometimes a fortnight). He walked much and contemplated, and he had in the head of his Staffe a pen and inke-horne, carried always a Note-book in his pocket, and as soon as a notion darted, he presently entred it into his Booke, or els he should perhaps have lost it. He had drawne the Designe of the Booke into Chapters, etc. so he knew whereabout it would come in. Thus that booke was made.

He wrote and published the *Leviathan* far from the intention either of disadvantage to his Majestie, or to flatter Oliver (who was not made Protector till three or four yeares after) on purpose to facilitate his returne; for there is scarce a page in it that he does not upbraid him.

His Majestie was displeased with him (at Paris) for a while, but not very long, by means of some's complayning of and misconstruing his writing. But his Majestie had a good Opinion of him, and sayd openly, That he thought Mr. Hobbes never meant Him hurt.

Anno 1650 or 1651, he returned into England, and lived most part in Fetter-lane, where he writt, or finished, his booke *de Corpore,* in Latin and then in English.

He was much in London till the restauration of his Majesty, having here convenience not only of Bookes, but of learned Conversation. I have heard him say, that at his Lord's house in the Countrey there was a good Library, and bookes enough for him, and that his Lordship stored the Library with what bookes he thought fitt to be bought; but he sayd, the want of learned Conversation was a very great inconvenience, and that though he conceived he could order his thinking as well perhaps as another man, yet he found a great defect. Methinkes in the country, for want of good conversation, one's Witt growes mouldy.

1660. The winter-time of 1659 he spent in Derbyshire. In March following was the dawning of the coming in of our gracious Soveraigne, and in April the Aurora. I then sent a letter to him in the Countrey to advertise him of the Advent of his Master the King and desired him by all meanes to be in London before his Arrivall; and knowing his Majestie was a great lover of good Painting I must needs presume he could not but suddenly see Mr. Cowper's curious pieces, of whose fame he had so much heard abroad and seene some of his worke, and likewise that he would sitt to him for his Picture, at which place and time he would have the best convenience of renewing his Majestie's graces to him. He returned me thankes for my friendly intimation and came to London in May following.

It happened, about two or three dayes after his Majestie's happy returne, that, as He was passing in his coach through the Strand, Mr. Hobbes was standing at Little Salisbury-house gate (where his Lord then lived). The King espied him, putt of his hatt very kindly to him, and asked him how he did. About a weeke after, he had orall conference with his Majesty at Mr. S. Cowper's, where, as he sate for his picture, he was diverted by Mr. Hobbes pleasant discourse. Here his Majestie's favours were redintegrated to him, and order was given that he should have free accesse to his Majesty, who was always much delighted in his witt and smart repartees.

[152]

The witts at Court were wont to bayte him. But he feared none of them, and would make his part good. The King would call him *the Beare*: Here comes the Beare to be bayted: (this is too low witt to be published).

He was marvellous happy and ready in his replies, and that without rancor (except provoked) but now I speake of his readinesse in replies as to witt and drollery. He would say that he did not care to give, neither was he adroit at, a present answer to a serious *quaere*: he had as lieve they should have expected an extemporary solution to an Arithmeticall probleme, for he turned and winded and compounded in philosophy, politiques, etc., as if he had been at Analyticall worke. He always avoided, as much as he could, to conclude hastily.

1665. This yeare he told me that he was willing to doe some good to the Towne where he was borne; that his Majestie loved him well, and if I could find out something in our Countrey that was in His Guift, he did beleeve he could beg it of his Majestie, and seeing he was bred a Scholar, he thought it most proper to endowe a Free-schoole there; which is wanting now (for, before the Reformation, all Monasteries had great Schooles appendant to them; e.g. Magdalen schoole and New College schoole). After enquiry I found out a piece of land in Bradon-forest (of about 25 pounds per annum value) that was in his Majesties guift, which he designed to have obtained of his Majestie for a salary for a Schoolmaster; but the Queen's Priests smelling-out the Designe and being his Enemies, hindred this publique and charitable Intention.

Mr. Samuel Cowper (the Prince of Limners of this last Age and my ever honoured Friend, who besides his Art was an ingeniose person and of great humanity) drew his Picture as like as art could afford, and one of the best pieces that ever he did: which his Majesty, at his returne, bought of him, and conserves as one of his rarities in his Closet at Whitehall.

His Lord who was a waster, sent him up and downe to borrow money, and to gett Gentlemen to be bound for him, being ashamed to speake him selfe.

In his youth he was unhealthy; of an ill complexion (yellowish): he tooke colds, being wett in his feet (there were no hackney coaches to stand in the streetes) and trod both his Shoes aside the same way. Notwithstanding he was well beloved: they lov'd his company for his pleasant facetiousness and good-nature.

From forty, or better, he grew healthier, and then he had a fresh, ruddy, complexion. He was *Sanguineo-melancholicus*; which the physiologers say is the most ingeniose complexion.

[153]

He would say that there might be good witts of all compexions ;
but good-natured, impossible.

In his old age he was very bald (which claymed a veneration) yet within dore, he used to study, and sitt bare-headed,
and sayd he never tooke cold in his head, but that the greatest
trouble was to keepe-off the Flies from pitching on the baldnes.

Face not very great ; ample forehead ; whiskers yellowish-
redish, which naturally turned up—which is a signe of a brisque
witt. Belowe he was shaved close, except a little tip under his
lip. Not but that nature could have afforded a venerable
Beard, but being naturally of a cheerfull and pleasant humour,
he affected not at all austerity and gravity to looke severe. He
desired not the reputation of his wisdome to be taken from the
cutt of his beard, but from his reason.

He had a good eie, and that of a hazell colour, which was
full of Life and Spirit, even to the last. When he was earnest
in discourse, there shone (as it were) a bright live-coale within
it. He had two kinds of lookys : when he laugh't, was witty,
and in a merry humour, one could scarce see his Eies ; by and
by, when he was serious and positive, he open'd his eies round
(i.e. his eie-lids.) He had midling eies, not very big, nor very
little.

There was a good Painter at the Earl of Devonshire's in
Derbyshire not long before Mr. Hobbes dyed, who drew him
with the great decayes of old age.

Though he left his native countrey at 14, and lived so long,
yet sometimes one might find a little touch of our pronuncia-
tion.—Old Sir Thomas Malette, one of the Judges of the King's
Bench, knew Sir Walter Ralegh, and sayd that, notwithstanding
his great Travells, Conversation, Learning, etc., yet he spake
broade Devonshire to his dyeing day.

He had very few Bookes. I never sawe (nor Sir William
Petty) above halfe a dozen about him in his chamber. Homer
and Virgil were commonly on his Table ; sometimes Xenophon,
or some probable historie, and Greek Testament, or so.

He had read much, if one considers his long life ; but
his contemplation was much more then his reading. He was
wont to say that if he had read as much as other men, he should
have knowne no more then other men.

He was wont to say that he had rather have the advice,
or take Physique from an experienced old Woman, that had
been at many sick people's Bed-sides, then from the learnedst
but unexperienced Physitian.

'Tis not consistent with an harmonicall soule to be a woman-
hater, neither had he an Abhorrescence to good wine but he

was, even in his youth (generally) temperate, both as to wine and women. I have heard him say that he did beleeve he had been in excesse in his life, a hundred times; which, considering his great age, did not amount to above once a yeare. When he did drinke, he would drinke to excesse to have the benefitt of Vomiting, which he did easily; by which benefit neither his witt was disturbt longer then he was spuing nor his stomach oppressed; but he never was, nor could not endure to be, habitually a good fellow, i.e. to drinke every day wine with company, which, though not to drunkennesse, spoiles the Braine.

For his last 30+ yeares, his Dyet, etc., was very moderate and regular. He rose about seaven, had his breakefast of Bread and Butter; and tooke his walke, meditating till ten; then he did putt downe the minutes of his thoughts, which he penned in the afternoon. He thought much and with excellent method and stedinesse, which made him seldom make a False step.

He had an inch thick board about 16 inches square, whereon paper was pasted. On this board he drew his lines (schemes). When a line came into his head, he would, as he was walking, take a rude Memorandum of it, to preserve it in his memory till he came to his chamber. He was never idle; his thoughts were always working.

His dinner was provided for him exactly by eleaven, for he could not now stay till his Lord's howre—*scil.* about two: that his stomach could not beare.

After dinner he tooke a pipe of tobacco, and then threw himselfe immediately on his bed, with his band off, and slept (tooke a nap of about halfe an howre).

In the afternoon he penned his morning Thoughts.

Besides his dayly Walking, he did twice or thrice a yeare play at Tennis (at about 75 he did it) then went to bed there and was well rubbed. This he did believe would make him live two or three yeares the longer.

In the countrey, for want of a tennis-court, he would walke up-hill and downe-hill in the parke, till he was in a great sweat, and then give the servant some money to rubbe him.

He had alwayes bookes of prick-song lyeing on his table: which at night, when he was abed, and the dores made fast, and was sure nobody heard him, he sang aloud (not that he had a very good voice) but for his health's Sake: he did beleeve it did his Lunges good, and conduced much to prolong his life.

He had the shaking Palsey in his handes; which began in France before the year 1650, and haz growne upon him by degrees, ever since, so that he haz not been able to write very legibly since 1665 or 1666, as I find by some letters he hath honoured me withall. Mr. Hobbs wase for severall yeares before he died so Paralyticall that he wase scarce able to write his name, and that in the abscence of his Amanuensis not being able to write anything, he made Scrawls on a piece of paper to remind him of the conceptions of his Mind he design'd to have committed to writing.

His extraordinary Timorousnes Mr. Hobs doth very ingeniosely confess and atributes it to the influence of his Mother's Dread of the Spanish Invasion in 88, she being then with child of him : it is very prodigious that neither the timorousness of his Nature from his Infancy, nor the decay of his Vital Heat in the extremity of old age, accompanied with the Palsy to that violence, shou'd not have chilled the briske Fervour and Vigour of his mind, which did wonderfully continue to him to his last.

His work was attended with Envy, which threw severall aspersions and false reports on him. For instance, one (common) was that he was afrayd to lye alone at night in his Chamber ; I have often heard him say that he was not afrayd of *Sprights,* but afrayd of being knockt on the head for five or ten pounds, which rogues might think he had in his chamber ; and severall other tales, as untrue.

When Mr. T. Hobbes was sick in France, the Divines came to him, and tormented him (both Roman Catholic, Church of England, and Geneva). Sayd he to them, Let me alone, or els I will detect all your Cheates from Aaron to yourselves.

Mr. Edmund Waller sayd to me, when I desired him to write some Verses in praise of him, that he was afrayd of the Churchmen : that, what was chiefly to be taken notice of in his Elogie was that he, being but *one,* and a private Person, pulled-downe all their Churches, dispelled the mists of Ignorance, and layd-open their Priest-craft.

There was a report (and surely true) that in Parliament, not long after the King was setled, some of the Bishops made a Motion to have the good old Gentleman burn't for a Heretique. Which, he hearing, feared that his papers might be search't by their order, and he told me he had burnt part of them ; among other things, a Poeme, in Latin Hexameter and Pentameter, of the Encroachment of the Clergie (both Roman and Reformed) on the Civil Power.

That he was a Christian 'tis cleare, for he recieved the Sacrament of Dr. Pierson, and in his confession to Dr. John Cosins, on his (as he thought) death-bed, declared that he liked the Religion of the Church of England best of all other.

He dyed worth neer 1000 pounds, which (considering his charity) was more than I expected : for he was very charitable to those that were the true objects of his Bounty. One time, I remember, goeing in the Strand, a poore and infirme old man craved his Almes. He, beholding him with eies of pitty and compassion, putt his hand in his pocket and gave him 6d. Sayd a Divine that stood by, Would you have donne this, if it had not been Christ's command ? Yea, said he. Why ? quoth the other. Because, sayd he, I was in paine to consider the miserable condition of the old man ; and now my almes, giving him some reliefe, doth also ease me.

Thomas Hobbs said that if it were not for the gallowes, some men are of so cruell a nature as to take a delight in killing men more than I should to kill a bird. I have heard him inveigh much against the Crueltie of Moyses for putting so many thousands to the Sword for Bowing to the Golden Calf.

Mr. Benjamin Johnson, Poet-Laureat, was his loving and familiar Friend and Acquaintance.

His nephew Francis pretty well resembled his uncle Thomas, especially about the eie ; and probably had he had good Education might have been ingeniose ; but he drowned his Witt in Ale.

When he was at Florence, he contracted a friendship with the famous Galileo Galileo, whom he extremely venerated and magnified ; and not only as he was a prodigious Witt, but for his sweetnes of nature and manners. They pretty well resembled one another as to their countenances, as by their Pictures doeth appear ; were both cheerfull and melancholique-sanguine ; and had both a consimilitie of Fate, to be hated and persecuted by the Ecclesiastiques.

Mr. Robert Hooke loved him, but was never but once in his company.

William Harvey, Dr. Of Physique and Chirurgery, Inventor of the Circulation of the Bloud, left him in his Will ten poundes, as a token of his love.

Mr. John Dreyden, Poet Laureat, is his great admirer, and oftentimes makes use of his Doctrine in his Playes—from Mr. Dreyden himselfe.

Sir Jonas Moore, Mathematicus, Surveyor of his Majestie's Ordinance, who had a great veneration for Mr. Hobbes, and was wont much to lament he fell to the study of the Mathematiques so late.

Lucius Carey, Lord Falkland was His great friend and admirer, and so was Sir William Petty ; both which I have here enrolled amongst those friends I have heard him speake of,

[157]

but Dr. Blackburne left 'em both out (to my admiration). I askt him why he had donne so? He answered because they were both ignote to Foreigners.

Des Cartes and he were acquainted and mutually respected one another. He would say that had he kept himself to Geometry he had been the best Geometer in the world but that his head did not lye for Philosophy.

I have heard him say that Aristotle was the worst Teacher that ever was, the worst Politician and Ethick—a Countrey-fellow that could live in the World would be as good: but his *Rhetorique* and *Discourse of Animals* was rare.

He had a high esteeme for the Royall Societie, having sayd that Naturall Philosophy was removed from the Universities to Gresham Colledge, meaning the Royall Societie that meetes there; and the Royall Societie (generally) had the like for him: and he would long since have been ascribed a Member there, but for the sake of one or two persons, whom he tooke to be his enemies: viz. Dr. Wallis (surely their Mercuries are in opposition) and Mr. Boyle. I might add Sir Paul Neile, who disobliges everybody.

1675, he left London *cum animo nunquam revertendi* [with the intention of never returning] and spent the remaynder of his dayes in Derbyshire with the Earl of Devonshire at Chatsworth and Hardwyck, in Contemplation and study.

These love verses he made not long before his death:—

> *Tho' I am now past ninety, and too old*
> *T' expect preferment in the Court of Cupid,*
> *And many Winters made mee ev'n so cold*
> *I am become almost all over stupid,*
>
> *Yet I can love and have a Mistresse too,*
> *As fair as can be and as wise as fair;*
> *And yet not proud, nor anything will doe*
> *To make me of her favour to despair.*
>
> *To tell you who she is were very bold;*
> *But if i' th' Character your Selfe you find*
> *Thinke not the man a Fool tho he be old*
> *Who loves in Body fair, a fairer mind.*

He fell sick about the middle of October 1679. His disease was the Strangury, and the Physitians judged it incurable by reason of his great age and naturall decay. About the 20th of November, my Lord being to remove from Chatsworth to

Hardwick, Mr. Hobbes would not be left behind; and therefore with a fetherbed laid into the Coach, upon which he lay warme clad, he was conveyed safely, and was in appearance as well after that little journey as before it. But seven or eight days after, his whole right side was taken with the dead palsy, and at the same time he was made speechlesse. He lived after this seven days, taking very little nourishment, slept well, and by intervals endeavoured to speake, but could not. In the whole time of his sickness he was free from fever. He seemed therefor to dye rather for want of the Fuell of Life (which was spent in him) and meer weaknesse and decay, then by the power of his disease, which was thought to be onely an effect of his age and weaknesse. He was put into a Woollen Shroud and Coffin, which was covered with a white Sheet, and upon that a black Herse cloth, and so carryed upon men's shoulders, a little mile to Church. The company, consisting of the family and neighbours that came to his Funerall, and attended him to his grave, were very handsomely entertained with Wine, burned and raw, cake, biscuit, etc.

A true copy of Mr. Hobbes's will.

Item, whereas it hath pleased my good Lord the Earle of Devonshire, to bid me oftentimes heretofore, and now at the making of this my last Will, to dispose therein of one hundred pounds, to be paid by his Lordship, for which I give him most humble thanks; I doe give and dispose of the same in this manner: There be five grand-children of my Brother Edmund Hobbes, to the eldest whereof whose name is Thomas Hobbes, I have heretofore given a peece of Land, which may and doth I think content him, and therefore to the other four that are younger, I dispose of the same 100 pounds the gift of my Lord of Devonshire, to be divided equally amongst them, as a furtherance to bind them Apprentices.

My Lord of Devonshire has paid the hundred pounds to Mr. Hobbes's kinred, which he bid Mr. Hobbes dispose of in his Will.

WILLIAM HOLDER

[Born 1616. Divine. Fellow of the Royal Society 1663. Canon of St. Paul's 1672. Sub-Dean of the Chapel Royal (1674) where he became so famous a disciplinarian that he was known as Mr. Snub-Dean. He published *Elements of Speech* in 1669 and various treatises on harmony and the Julian Calendar. Died 1698.]

HE is a handsome, gracefull person, and of a delicate constitution, and of an even and smooth temper ; so that, if one would goe about to describe a perfect good man, would drawe this Doctor's Character. He is very Musicall, both theoretically and practically, and he had a sweet voyce : gracefull Elocution ; his discourse so Gent. and obligeing ; cleer reason ; is a good Poet. He is extremely well qualified for his place of the Sub-Almoner of the King's Chapell, being a person abhorring covetousnes, and full of Pitty.

The only Son of Edward Popham, Admirall for the Parliament, being borne deafe and dumbe, was sent to him to learne to speake, which he taught him to doe : by what method, and how soon, you may see in the Appendix concerning it to his *Elements of Speech*. It is a most ingeniose and curious Discourse, and untouched by any other ; he was beholding to no Author ; did only consult with Nature. This Gentleman's son afterwards was a little while (upon Dr Holder's preferment to Ely) a scholar of Dr. Wallis, (a most ill-natured man, an egregious lyer and backbiter, a flatterer and fawner on my Lord Brouncker and his Miss, that my Lord may keepe up his reputation) under whom he forgott what he learnt before, the child not enduring his morose pedantique humour. Not long since in one of the *Philosophical Transactions* is entered a long mountebanking panegyrique of the Doctor's prayse for doeing so strange a thing and never makes any mention of Dr. Holder at all. Dr. H. questioning Oldenburgh (I happened to be then present) Mr. Oldenburgh (though a great friend of Dr. Wallis) acknowledged that the Doctor himselfe penned it every word ; which occasioned Dr. Holder to write against him in a pamphlet in 4to.

Mr. Thomas Hobbes writes to me, I wonder not if Dr. Wallis, or any other, that have studyed Mathematicks only to gaine Preferment, when his ignorance is discovered, convert

his study to jugling and to the gaining of a reputation of conjuring, decyphering, and such Arts. As for the matter it selfe, I
meane the teaching of a man borne deafe and dumbe to speake,
I thinke it impossible. But I doe not count him deafe and
indocible that can heare a word spoken as loud as is possible
at the very entrance to his Eare ; and he that could make him
heare (being a great and common good) would well deserve
both to be honoured and to be enriched. He that could make
him speake a few words onely deserved nothing. But he that
brags of this and cannot doe it, deserves to be whipt.

But to returne to this honest worthy Gentleman—Anno
about 1646, he went to Bletchington to his parsonage, where
his hospitality and learning, mixt with great courtesie, easily
conciliated the love of all his neighbours to him.

He was very helpfull in the Education of his brother-in-
law, Mr. Christopher Wren (now Knighted) a youth of a prodigious inventive Witt, and of whom he was as tender as if he
had been his owne Child, who gave him his first Instructions in
Geometrie and Arithmetique, and when he was a young Scholar
at the University of Oxford, was a very necessary and kind friend.

The parsonage-house at Bletchington was Mr. Christopher
Wren's home, and retiring-place ; here he contemplated, and
studied, and found-out a great many curious things in Mathematiques. About this house he made severall curious Dialls,
with his owne handes, which are still there to be seen. Which
see, as well worthy to be seen.

It ought not to be forgott the great and exemplary love
between this Doctor and his vertuose wife, who is not lesse
to be admired, in her sex and station, then her brother Sir
Christopher ; and (which is rare to be found in a woman)
her excellences doe not inflate her. Amongst many other
Guifts she haz a strange sagacity as to curing of wounds, which
she does not doe so much by presedents and Reciept bookes,
as by her owne excogitancy, considering the causes, effects,
and circumstances. His Majestie King Charles II had hurt his
hand, which he intrusted his Chirurgians to make well ; but
they ordered him so that they made it much worse, so that it
swoll, and pained him up to his shoulder ; and pained him so
extremely that he could not sleep, and began to be feaverish.
Then one told the King what a rare shee-surgeon he had in his
house ; she was presently sent for at eleven clock at night.
She presently made ready a Pultisse, and applyed it, and gave
his Majestie sudden ease, and he slept well ; next day she dressed
him, and in a short time perfectly cured him, to the great griefe
of all the Surgeons, who envy and hate her.

WENCESLAS HOLLAR

[Born 1607. Engraver. He lived in Frankfort, Cologne and Antwerp and had difficulty enough to subsist, until Thomas Howard, Earl of Arundel, brought him to England. Teacher of drawing to the Prince of Wales 1640. He fought in the ranks for the King, but was captured by Parliament and escaped to Antwerp. In 1652 he returned to England. He was appointed His Majesty's Designer in 1660. Before the introduction of photography, picture painting and engraving were important professions, and Hollar charged fourpence an hour for his work, of which 2733 examples are enumerated. Besides making copies of famous paintings and illustrating books, Hollar executed a fine map of London after the Fire, illustrated the coronation of Charles II and engraved a series of pictures of women's costumes, which have proved invaluable to historians. Died 1677.]

WINCESLAUS HOLLAR, Bohemus, was borne at Prague. His father was a Knight of the Empire and a Protestant, and either for keeping a conventicle, or being taken at one, forfeited his Estate, and was ruined by the Roman Catholiques.

He told me that when he was a Schoole-boy he tooke a delight in draweing of Mapps ; which draughts he kept, and they were pretty. He was designed by his father to have been a Lawyer, and was putt to that profession, when his father's troubles, together with the Warres, forced him to leave his countrey. So that what he did for his delight and recreation only when a boy, proved to be his livelyhood when a man.

I thinke he stayd sometime in Lowe Germany, then he came into England, wher he was very kindly entertained by that great Patron of Painters and draughts-men, Thomas Howard Lord High Marshall, Earl of Arundell and Surrey, where he spent his time in draweing and copying rarities, which he did etch (i.e. eate with *aqua fortis* in copper plates). When the Lord Marshall went Ambassador to the Emperor of Germany to Vienna, he travelld with much grandeur ; and among others, Mr. Hollar went with him (very well clad) to take viewes, landskapes, buildings, etc. remarqueable in their Journey, which wee see now at the Print-Shopps.

He hath donne the most in that way that ever any one did, insomuch that I have heard Mr. John Evelyn, R.S.S., say that at sixpence a print his Labour would come to . . . pounds (*quaere* J. E.) He was very short-sighted, and did worke so curiously that the curiosity of his Worke is not to be judged without a magnifying-glasse. When he tooke his Landskapes, he, then, had a glasse to helpe his Sight.

At Arundel-house he maried with my Ladie's wayting woman, Mrs. Tracy, by whom he haz a daughter, that was one of the greatest Beauties I have seen ; his son by her dyed in the Plague, an ingeniose youth, drew delicately.

When the Civil Warres brake-out, the Lord Marshall had leave to goe beyond sea. Mr. Hollar went into the Lowe-Countries where he stayed till about 1649.

I remember he told me that when he first came into England (which was a serene time of Peace) that the people, both poore and rich, did looke cheerfully, but at his returne, he found the Countenances of the people all changed, melancholy, spightfull, as if bewitched.

He was a very friendly good-natured man as could be, but Shiftlesse to the World, and dyed not rich. I have sayd before that his father was ruined upon the account of the Protestant religion. Winceslaus dyed a Catholique, of which religion, I suppose, he might be ever since he came to Arundel-howse. Had he lived till the 13th of July following, he had been just 70 yeares old.

ROBERT HOOKE

[Born 1635. Experimental philosopher. Curator of Experiments at the Royal Society 1662. Fellow (1663) and Secretary of the Royal Society 1677–1682. Gresham Professor of Geometry 1665. Designed Bethlehem Hospital, Montague House and the College of Physicians. He helped Newton by hints in Optics, and his anticipation of the Law of Inverse Squares was admitted by Newton. He pointed out the real nature of combustion 1665 ; proposed to measure the force of gravity by the swinging of a pendulum 1666 ; discovered the fifth star in Orion 1664 ; inferred the rotation of Jupiter ; first observed a star by daylight ; and made the earliest attempts at telescopic determination of the parallax of a fixed star. He also first applied the spiral spring to regulate watches ; expounded the true theory of the elasticity and the kinetic hypothesis of gases 1678 ; constructed the first Gregorian telescope 1674 ; described a system of telegraphy 1684 ; first asserted the true principle of the arch ; and invented the marine barometer and other instruments. Died 1703.]

MR. ROBERT HOOKE, curator of the Royall Societie at London, was borne at Freshwater in the Isle of Wight ; his father was Minister there, and of the family of the Hookes of Hooke in Hants, in the road from London to Saram, a very ancient Family and in that place for many (3 or more) hundred yeares. His father died by suspending him selfe.

John Hoskyns, the Painter, being at Freshwater, to drawe pictures, Mr. Hooke observed what he did, and, thought he, Why cannot I doe so too ? So he gitts him Chalke, and Ruddle, and coale, and grinds them, and putts them on a Trencher, gott a pencill, and to worke he went, and made a picture : then he copied (as they hung up in the parlour) the Pictures there, which he made like. Also, being a boy there, at Freshwater, he made a Diall on a round trencher ; never having had any instruction. His father was not Mathematicall at all.

When his father died, his Son Robert was but 13 yeares old, to whom he left one Hundred pounds, which was sent up to London with him, with an intention to have bound him Apprentice to Mr. Lilly the Paynter, with whom he was a little while upon tryall ; who liked him very well, but Mr. Hooke quickly perceived what was to be donne, so, thought he, why cannot I doe this by my selfe and keepe my hundred pounds ?

He went to Mr. Busby's the Schoolemaster of Westminster, at whose howse he was ; and he made very much of him. With him he lodged his hundred pounds. There he learnd to play 20 lessons on the organ. He there in one weeke's time made himselfe master of the first VI books of *Euclid*, to the Admiration of Mr. Busby. At Schoole here he was very mechanicall, and (amongst other things) he invented thirty severall wayes of Flying.

He was never a King's Scholar, and I have heard Sir Richard Knight (who was his school-fellow) say that he seldome saw him in the schoole.

Anno Domini 1658 he was sent to Christ Church in Oxford, where he had a Chorister's place (in those dayes when the Church Musique was putt-downe) which was a pretty good maintenance. He lay in the chamber in Christ Church that was Mr. Burton's, of whom 'tis whispered that, *non obstante* all his Astrologie and his booke of *Melancholie,* he ended his dayes in that chamber by hanging him selfe.

He was there Assistant to Dr. Thomas Willis in his Chymistry ; who afterwards recommended him to the Honble Robert Boyle, Esqre, to be usefull to him in his Chymicall operations. Anno Domini 1662 Mr. Robert Boyle recommended Mr. Robert Hooke to be Curator of the Experiments of the Royall Society, wherin he did an admirable good worke to the Commonwealth of Learning, in recommending the fittest person in the world to them.

Anno Domini 1666 the great Conflagration of London happened, and then he was chosen one of the two Surveyors of the Citie of London ; by which he hath gott a great Estate. He built Bedlam, the Physitians' College, Montague-house, the Piller on Fish-street-hill, and Theatre there ; and he is much made use of in Designing Buildings.

He is but of midling stature, something crooked, pale faced, and his face but little belowe, but his head is lardge ; his eie full and popping, and not quick ; a grey eie. He haz a delicate head of haire, browne, and of an excellent moist curle. He is and ever was very temperate, and moderate in dyet, etc.

As he is of prodigious inventive head, so is a person of great vertue and goodnes. Now when I have sayd his Inventive faculty is so great, you cannot imagine his Memory to be excellent, for they are like two Bucketts, as one goes up, the other goes downe. He is certainly the greatest Mechanick this day in the World.

'Twas Mr. Robert Hooke that invented the Pendulum-

[165]

Watches, so much more usefull than the other Watches. He hath invented an Engine for the speedie working of Division, etc., or for the speedie and immediate finding out the Divisor.

Before I leave this Towne, I will gett of him a Catalogue of what he hath wrote; and as much of his Inventions as I can. But they are many hundreds; he believes not fewer than a thousand. 'Tis such a hard matter to get people to doe themselves right.

Mr. Robert Hooke did in Anno 1670, write a Discourse, called, *An Attempt to prove the Motion of the Earth,* which he then read to the Royal Society; wherein he haz delivered the Theorie of explaining the coelestial motions mechanically: his words are these: I shall explaine a systeme of the world, differing in many particulars from any yet known, answering in all things to the common rules of mechanicall motions. This depends upon 3 suppositions; first, that all coelastiall bodys whatsoever have an attractive or gravitating power towards their own centers, whereby they attract not only their own parts, and keep them from flying from them, as we may observe the Earth to doe, but that they doe also attract all the other coelestiall bodys that are within the sphere of their activity, and consequently that not only the Sun and the Moon have an influence upon the body and motion of the Earth, and the Earth upon them, but that Mercury also, Venus, Mars, Saturne, and Jupiter, by their attractive powers have a considerable influence upon its motion, as, in the same manner, the corresponding attractive power of the Earth hath a considerable influence upon every one of their motions also. The second supposition is this, that all bodys whatsoever, that are putt into direct and simple motion will soe continue to move forwards in a straight line, till they are by some other effectuall powers deflected and bent into a motion describing a circle, ellipsis, or some other uncompounded curve line. The third supposition is, that these attractive powers are soe much the more powerfull in operating, by how much nearer the body wrought upon is to their own centers.

About 9 or 10 years ago, Mr. Hooke writt to Mr. Isaac Newton, of Trinity College, Cambridge, to make a Demonstration of this theory, not telling him, at first, the proportion of the gravity to the distance, nor what was the curv'd line that was thereby made. Mr. Newton, in his Answer to the letter, did expresse that he had not thought of it; and in his first attempt about it, he calculated the Curve by supposing the attraction to be the same at all distances: upon which, Mr. Hooke sent, in his next letter, the whole of his Hypothesis, *scil.* that the gravitation was reciprocall to the square of the distance : which is the whole coelastiall theory, concerning which Mr. Newton haz made a demonstration, not at all owning he receiv'd the first Intimation of it from Mr. Hooke. Likewise Mr. Newton haz in the same Booke printed some other Theories and experiments of Mr. Hooke's, without acknowledgeing from whom he had them.

This is the greatest Discovery in Nature that ever was since the World's Creation. It never was so much as hinted by any man before. I wish he had writt plainer, and afforded a little more paper.

JOHN HOSKYNS

[Born 1566. Lawyer. Fellow of New College, Oxford, 1586. M.P. for Hereford 1614. Serjeant-at-Law 1623. Welsh judge. He revised, according to tradition, the *History of the World* by Sir Walter Raleigh, with whom he became very intimate during his confinement in the Tower, and *polished* the verses of Ben Jonson so zealously as to be called Ben's *father*. Died 1638.]

HE had a brother, John, D.D., a learned man, Rector of Ledbury and canon of Hereford, who was designed to be a Scholar, but this John (the Serjeant) would not be quiet, but he must be a Scholar too. In those dayes boyes were seldome taught to read that were not to be of some learned profession. So, upon his instant importunity, being then ten years of age, he learned to reade, and, at the yeare's end, entred into his Greeke grammar. Charles Hoskyns was brother to the Serjeant and the Doctor ; a very ingeniose man, who would not have been inferior to either but killed himself with hard Study.

He was a yeare at Westminster ; and not speeding there, he was sent to Winton Schole, where he was the Flower of his time. He was of a strong constitution, and had a prodigious memorie. I remember I have heard that one time he had not made his exercise (verse) and spake to one of his Forme to shew him his, which he sawe. The Schoolmaster presently calles for the Exercises, and Hoskyns told him that he had writ it out but lost it, but he could repeate it, and repeated the other boye's exercise (I think 12 or 16 verses) only at once reading over. When the boy who really had made them shewed the Master the same, and could not repeate them, he was whipped for stealing Hoskyn's Exercise. There were many pretty stories of him when a schooleboy, which I have forgott.

The Latin verses in the quadrangle at Winton-colledge, at the Cocks where the Boyes wash their hands, where there is the picture of a good Servant, with asses eares and Hind's feet, a padlock on his Lippes, etc., very good hieroglyphick, with a hexastique in Latin underneath (which I doe not remember). It was done by the Serjeant when he went to school there ; but now finely painted.

When he came to New College, he was *Terrae filius*; but he was so bitterly Satyricall that he was expelled and putt to his shifts.

He went into Somersetshire and taught a Schole for about a yeare at Ilchester. He compiled there a Greeke Lexicon as far as M, which I have seen. He maried (neer there) a rich widowe, by whome he had only one sonne and one daughter.

After his mariage he admitted himselfe at the Middle Temple, London. He wore good Cloathes, and kept good company. His excellent Witt gave him letters of Commendacion to all ingeniose persons. At his first comeing to London he gott acquainted with the Under-Secretaries at Court, where he was often usefull to them in writing their Latin letters.

He was a close-prisoner in the Tower, *tempore Regis Jacobi*, for speaking too boldly in the Parliament-house of the King's profuse liberality to the Scotts. He made a Comparison of a Conduit, whereinto water came, and ran-out afarre-off. Now, said he, this pipe reaches as far as Edinborough. He was kept a *close prisoner* there, i.e. his windowes were boarded up. Through a small chinke he sawe once a crowe, and another time, a Kite; the sight whereof, he sayd, was a great pleasure to him.

He, with much adoe, obtained at length the favour to have his little son Bennet to be with him; and he then made a Latin Distich, thus englished by him :—

> *My little Ben, whil'st thou art young,*
> *And know'st not how to rule thy Tongue,*
> *Make it thy Slave whil'st thou art free,*
> *Least it as mine imprison thee.*

I have heard that when he came out of the Tower, his Crest was graunted him (I believe) for his bold Spirit, and (I suppose) contrived by himselfe, viz. a Lyon's head couped or, breathing fire. The Serjeant would say jocosely that it was the only Lyon's head in England that tooke Tobacco.

His great Witt quickly made him be taken notice of. Ben: Johnson called him *father*. Sir Benet told me that one time desiring Mr. Johnson to adopt him for his sonne, No, said he, I dare not; 'tis honour enough for me to be your Brother: I was your Father's sonne, and 'twas he that polished me. In shorte, his acquaintance were all the Witts then about the Towne; e.g. Sir Walter Raleigh (who was his Fellow-prisoner in the Tower, where he was Sir Walter's *Aristarchus* to review and polish Sir Walter's stile); John Donne, D.D.; Sir Benjamin Ruddyer, with whom it was once his fortune to have a quarrel and fought a Duell with him and hurt him in the Knee, but they were afterwards friends again; Sir Henry Wotton, Provost of Eaton College; *cum multis aliis.*

His verses on the fart in the Parliament house are printed in some of the *Drolleries*. He had a booke of Poemes, neatly written by one of his Clerkes, bigger then Dr. Donne's Poemes, which his sonn Benet lent to he knowes not who, about 1653, and could never heare of it since.

Was wont to say that all those that came to London were either Carrion or Crowes.

His conversation was exceedingly pleasant, and would make verses on the Roade, where he was the best Company in the world. He was a great master of the Latin and Greke languages; a great Divine; made the best Latin Epitaphs of his time. He understood the Lawe well, but worst at that.

He wrote his owne Life, which was to shew that wheras Plutarch had wrote the Lives of many Generalles, etc., Grandees, that he, or an active man might, from a private fortune by his witt and industrie attain to the Dignity of a Serjeant at Lawe— but he should have said that they must have parts like his too.

He was a very strong man, and valiant, and an early riser in the morning (*scil.*, at four in the morning). He was black-eyed and had black hayre.

I will now describe his Seate at Morhampton (Hereff.). At the Gate-house is the Picture of the old fellowe that made the fires, with a Block on his back, boytle and wedges and hatchet. In the Chapelle, over the Altar, are two Hebrewe words and underneath a distich. Here is an Organ that was Queen Elizabeth's. In the gallery, the picture of his Brother Doctor in the Pulpit, Serjeant in his Robes, the Howse, Parke, etc.; and underneath are verses. In the first leafe of his Fee-booke he drew the picture of a Purse.

In the Garden, the picture of the Gardiner, on the Wall of the Howse, with his Rake, Spade, and water-pott in his left hand. Under severall venerable and shady Oakes in the Parke, he had seates made; and where was a fine purling Spring, he did curbe it with stone.

Not many moneths before his death (being at the Assises or Sessions at Hereford) a massive countrey fellowe trod on his toe, which caused a Gangrene which was the cause of his death. One Mr. Dighton of Glocester, an experienced Chirurgian who had formerly been chirurgian in the Warres in Ireland, was sent for to cure him; but his Skill and care could not save him. His Toes were first cutt-off. The Minister of his Parish had a clubbe-foote or feete (I think his name was

Hugh). Said he, *Sir Hugh* (after his toes were cutt off) *I must be acquainted with your shoemaker.*

I remember, before the late Warres, the Ministers in Herefordshire, etc. (Counties that way) had the Title of S^r, as the Bachalours of Art have at Oxon, as Sir Richard, of Stretford ; Sir William, of Monkland. And so it was in Wilts, when my grandfather Lyte was a boy ; and anciently everywhere. In all old Wills before the Reformation it is upon Record.

Sir Robert Pye, Attorney of the Court of Wardes, was his neighbour, but there was no great goodwill between them— Sir Robert was haughty. He happened to dye on Christmas day : the newes being brought to the Serjeant, said he, The devill haz a Christmas-pye.

HENRY ISAACSON

[Born 1581. Theologian and chronologer. Master of Arts of Pembroke Hall, Cambridge. Friend of Bishop Andrews. Published *Tabula Historico-Chronologica* 1633; a *Life of Bishop Andrews* 1650; and other works. Died 1654.]

MR. HENRY ISAACSON was Secretary to Lancelot Andrews, Lord Bishop of Winton. Thomas Bourman, Dr. of Divinity, of Kingston upon Thames, did know Mr. Isaacson, and told me that he was a learned man, which I easily believed when I heard he was Secretary to that learned Prelate, who made use of none but for merit.

The Dr. told me that when he presented his *Chronologie* to his Majestie King Charles the first, 'twas in the matted Gallery at White-hall. The King presently discerned the purpose of the Treatise, and turned to his owne Birth; sayd the King, *And here's one Lye to begin with*. It seemes that Mr. Isaacson had taken it out of a foreigner, who used the other Account. Poor Mr. Isaacson was so ashamed at this unlucky rencounter, that he immediately sneak't away and stayd not for prayse or reward, both which perhaps he might have had, for his Majestie was well pleased with it.

'Twas presented in an ill Hower. An Astrologer would give something to know *that day and hower*.

DAVID JENKINS

[Born 1586. Welsh judge. Judge of Great Sessions for Car-marthen, Cardigan and Pembrokeshire 1643. An ardent Royalist, he was captured at Hereford in 1645 and steadfastly contested the right of Parliament to try him. Imprisoned until the Restoration. He published several Royalist treatises, as well as 8 *Centuries of Reports* 1661. He was a patron of the Welsh Bards in Glamorganshire, where he died in 1663.]

HE was of very good courage. Rode in the Lord Gerard's Army in Pembrokeshire, in the forlorne-hope, with his long rapier drawne holding it on-end. He was taken prisoner at Hereford. Long time prisoner in the Tower, Newgate, Wallingford, and Windsore. Never submitted to the Usurping power (I thinke, the only man). All his Estate was confiscated; and was always excepted by the Parliament in the first Ranke of delinquents.

In his Circuit in Wales at the beginning of the Warres, he caused to be Indicted severall men of those parts (that were Parliament, etc. engaged against the King) for highe Treason; and the grand jury indicted them. Afterwards, when he was prisoner in Newgate, some of these Grandees came to him to triumph over him, and told him that if they had been thus in his power, he would have hanged them. *God forbid els!* replied he: which undaunted returne they much admired.

The Parliament intended to have hanged him; and he expected no lesse, but resolved to be hangd with the Bible under one arme and Magna Charta under the other. And hangd he had been, had not Harry Martyn told them in the House that *Sanguis martyrum est semen ecclesiae* [the blood of martyrs is the seed of the Church] and that that way would doe them more mischiefe. So his life was saved, and they removed him out of the way to Wallingford Castle.

'Twas pitty he was not made one of the Judges of West-minster-hall for his long sufferings; and he might have been he told me, if he would have given money to the Chancellor Hyde: but he scornd it. He needed it not, for he had his estate againe (1500 pounds per annum) and being old and *carceribus confractus* [broken with imprisonment]. Mr. T. Hobbes, Malmesburiensis, told him one day at dinner that *that hereafter would not shew well for somebodie's Honour in History.*

[173]

SIR LEOLINE JENKINS

[Born 1623. Civilian and diplomatist. In May 1651 he was indicted *for a seminary of rebellion and sedition*. In 1655 he anticipated a threatened *bannition* by the Parliament by retiring to the Continent with his pupils. Fellow of Jesus College, Oxford, 1660; Principal 1661–73; Deputy-Professor of Civil Law 1662; he was also accustomed to conduct the foreign correspondence of the University and was appointed to receive foreign visitors of distinction. Judge of the Admiralty Court (1665) and of the Prerogative Court of Canterbury 1669. He was knighted in 1670, after he had obtained the setting aside in favour of Charles II of the Duchess of Orleans's claims to Henrietta Maria's personalty. M.P. for Hythe (1673–78) and for Oxford University 1679–85. He represented England at the Congress of Cologne in 1673 and on his voyage home, while still in the Meuse at Brielle, he fired on a Dutch man-of-war for neglecting to lower her flag, upon which the Dutchman obeyed under protest. He was also Plenipotentiary at Nymegen from 1676–79 and he marked his resentment at the bad faith displayed by Louis XIV during the negotiations by rejecting a present of his miniature, set in diamonds, though Colbert urged its acceptance to the point of importunity. Roger North calls him *the most faithful drudge of a Secretary that ever the Court had*. Despite his exemplary life, he was *inclined to laugh immoderately at a jest, especially if it were coarse*, which Charles II discovering, *failed not, after the tendency of his own fancy, to ply his Secretary with conceits of that complexion*. He died in 1685.]

SIR LLEUELLIN JENKINS, Knight, was borne at Llantrithid in the countie of Glamorgan. His father (whom I knew) was a good plaine Countrey-man, a Copyholder of Sir John Aubrey, Knight and Baronet (eldest son of Sir Thomas) whose Mannour it is.

He went to Schoole at Cowbridge, not far off.

David Jenkins, that was prisoner in the Tower (maried a sister of Sir John Aubrey) was some remote kin to him; and, looking on him as a boy towardly, diligent, and good, he contributed something towards his Education.

Anno Domini 1641, he was matriculated of Jesus College in Oxford, where he stayed till (I thinke) he tooke his Degree of *Bac. Artium*.

About that time Sir John Aubrey sent for him home to enforme his eldest sonne Lewis Aubrey (since deceased, 1659) in Grammar; and that he might take his learning the better, he was taught in the Church-house where severall boyes came to schoole, and there were 6 or 7 Gentlemen's sonnes (Sir Francis Maunsell, Bart.; Mr. Edmund Thomas; etc.) boarded in the Towne. The young Gentlemen were all neer of an age, and ripe for the University together, and to Oxford they all went under Mr. Jenkin's care about anno 1649 or 50, but by reason of the Disturbances of those Times, Sir John would not have his sonne of any College. But they all studyed at Mr. (now Sir) Sampson White's house, a Grocer, opposite to University College. Here he stayed with my Cosen about 3 yeares or better, and then, in *anno* 1655, he travelled with my Cosen and two or 3 of the other Gentlemen into France, where they stayd about 3 yeares and made themselves Masters of that Language.

He first began the Civill Lawe, viz. bought Vinnius on Justinian, 1653.

When he brought home Mr. Lewis Aubrey, he returned to Jesus College. After his Majestie's restauration Dr. Maunsell was restored to his Principallship of that house, but being very old and wearie of worldly cares, he kept it not long, before he resigned it to Mr. Jenkins.

Gilbert Sheldon, Archbishop of Canterbury, and Sir John Aubrey were *co-etanei*, and contracted a great friendship at Oxon in their youth, which continued to their deaths. In the Troublesome times after Dr. Sheldon was expelled, he was a yeare (I thinke) or two with Sir John at Llantrithid, where he tooke notice of the vertue and assiduity of the young man Mr. Jenkins. After the King's restauration Sir John Aubrey recommended Mr. Jenkins to him; made him. Anno 1668, he was Archbishop of Canterbury: Sir William Meyric, LL.D. and Judge of the Prerogative Court of Canterbury, dyed, and the Archbishop conferred that place on Mr. Jenkins.

When Mary the Queen-Mother dyed at Paris, the King of Fraunce caused her Jewells and Treasures to be locked up and sealed. His Majestie of Great Britaine sent Sir Llewellin (which is Leoline in Latin) to Paris concerning the Administration. Anno 1670, he had the Honour of Knighthood.

Anno 1673, he was sent with Sir Joseph Williamson, Plenipotentiaries, to Nemeghen: I remember that very time they went away was opposition of Saturn and Mars. I sayd then to the Earl of Thanet that if that Ambassade came to any good I would never trust to Astrologie again.

March 25, 1680, he was made Principall Secretary of Estate. When I came to wayte on him to congratulate for the Honour his Majestie had been pleased to bestowe on him, he recieved me with his usuall courtesie, and sayd that *it had pleased God to rayse-up a poore worme to doe his Majestie humble service.*

He haz a strong body for study, indefatigable, temperate and vertuous. God blesse him.

BEN JONSON

[Born 1573. Actor, poet and playwright. Educated at Westminster School. Began to work for the Admiral's Company of
Players both as player and playwright 1597. Killed a fellow-actor in
a brawl, but escaped death by benefit of the clergy 1598 : he became
a Roman Catholic during his imprisonment, but abjured twelve years
later. His *Every Man in his Humour*, with Shakespeare in the cast, was
performed by the Lord Chamberlain's Company at the Globe 1598.
His first tragedy *Sejanus* was given at the same theatre by Shakespeare's
Company in 1603. His masques, for which Inigo Jones designed the
scenery, became popular at Court, but Jonson was nevertheless imprisoned in 1605 for libelling the Scots. Although Drummond
described him *as a great lover and praiser of himself, a contemner and scorner
of others, given rather to lose a friend than a jest, jealous of every word and
action of those about him, especially after drink,* he was the friend of
Shakespeare, Donne, Bacon, Selden, Chapman, Beaumont, Fletcher,
Herrick, Suckling, Sir Kenelm Digby and Lord Falkland, and among
his patrons were the Sidneys, the Earl of Pembroke and the Duke and
Duchess of Newcastle. He was the first Poet Laureate and died in
1637.]

MR. BENJAMIN JOHNSON, Poet Laureat, was a
Warwyckshire man. 'Tis agreed that his father was
a Minister ; and by his Epistle dedicat. of *Every Man
. . .* to Mr. William Camden that he was a Westminster Scholar
and that Mr. W. Camden was his School-master.

His mother, after his father's death, maried a Bricklayer ;
and 'tis generally said that he wrought sometime with his
father-in-lawe (and particularly on the Garden-wall of Lincoln's
Inne next to Chancery Lane) and that a Knight, a Bencher,
walking thro', and hearing him repeate some Greeke verses
out of Homer, discoursing with him and finding him to have a
Witt extraordinary, gave him some Exhibition to maintaine
him at Trinity College in Cambridge.

Then he went into the Lowe-countreys, and spent some
time (not very long) in the armie, not to disgrace, as you may
find in his *Epigrammes.*

Then he came over into England, and acted and wrote,
but both ill, at the Green Curtaine, a kind of Nursery or obscure
Play-house, somewhere in the Suburbes (I thinke towards
Shoreditch or Clarkenwell).

He killed Mr. Marlow, the Poet, on Bunhill, comeing from the Green-curtain play-house.

Then he undertooke again to write a Playe, and did hitt it admirably well, viz. *Every Man* . . . , which was his first good one.

Serjeant John Hoskins of Herefordshire was his *Father*. I remember his sonne (Sir Bennet Hoskins, Baronet, who was something Poetical in his youth) told me, that when he desired to be adopted his *Son*: No, sayd he, 'tis honour enough for me to be your Brother; I am your father's son: 'twas he that polished me, I doe acknowledge it.

He was (or rather had been) of a clear and faire skin; his habit was very plaine. I have heard Mr. Lacy, the Player, say that he was wont to weare a coate like a coachman's coate, with slitts under the arme-pitts. He would many times exceed in drinke (Canarie was his beloved liquor) then he would tumble home to bed, and, when he had thoroughly perspired, then to studie. I have seen his studyeing chaire, which was of strawe, such as olde woemen used, and as Aulus Gellius is drawen in.

At riper yeares, after he had studied at Cambridge he came of his owne accord to Oxon and there entred himselfe in Christ Church and tooke his Master's degree in Oxon (or conferred on him) anno 1619. When I was in Oxon, Bishop Skinner of Oxford, who lay at our college, was wont to say that he understood an Author as well as any man in England.

Long since, in King James's time, I have heard my uncle Danvers say (who knew him) that he lived without temple Barre, at a Combe maker's shop, about the Elephant and Castle. In his later time he lived in Westminster, in the house under which you passe as you goe out of the Church yard into the old Palace; where he dyed.

'Twas an ingeniose remarque of my Lady Hoskins, that B. J. never writes of Love, or if he does, does it not naturally.

Ben Johnson had one eie lower than t'other, and bigger, like Clun the Player; perhaps he begott Clun. He mentions in his *Epigrammes,* a Sonne that he had, and his Epitaph.

He tooke a Catalogue from Mr. Lacy (the Player) of the Yorkshire Dialect. 'Twas his Hint for Clownery to his Comoedy called *The Tale of a Tub*. This I had from Mr. Lacy.

King James made him write against the Puritans, who began to be troublesome in his time.

A Grace by Ben Johnston, extempore, Before King James:

Our King and Queen the Lord-God blesse,
The Paltzgrave and the Lady Besse,

And God blesse every living thing
That Lives, and breath's, and loves the King.
God bless the Councell of Estate,
And Buckingham the fortunate.
God Blesse them all, and keepe them safe :
And God Blesse me, and God blesse Raph.

The King was mighty enquisitive to know who this Raph was. Ben told him 'twas the Drawer at the Swanne Tavernne by Charing-crosse, who drew him good Canarie. For this Drollery his Majestie gave him an hundred poundes.

B. Jonson had 50 pounds per annum for many yeares together to keepe off Sir W. Wiseman of Essex from being Sheriff. At last King James prick't him, and Ben came to his Majestie and told him he had prick't him to the heart, and then explayned himselfe : *innuendo* Sir W. W. being prick't Sheriffe : and gott him struck off.

Ben Johnson, riding through Surrey, found the Women weeping and wailing, lamenting the Death of a Lawyer, who lived there : He enquired why so great Grief for the Losse of a Lawyer ? Oh, said they, we have the greatest Loss imaginable ; he kept us all in Peace and Quietness, and was a most charitable good Man : Whereupon Ben made this Distich :

God works Wonders now and then,
Behold a Miracle, deny't who can,
Here lies a Lawyer *and an* honest *man.*

'Tis Pity that good Man's Name should not be remember'd.

This account I received from Mr. Isaac Walton (who wrote Dr.
John Donne's &c. Life) Decemb. 2, 1680, he being then eighty-seaven
years of age. This is his owne hand writing. I only knew Ben Johnson : but my Lord of Winton knew him very well, and says he was in the 6°, that is the upermost fforme in Westminster Schole. At which time his father dyed, and his mother marryed a brickelayer, who made him (much against his will) to help him in his trade. But in a short time, his scole maister, Mr. Camden, got him a better imployment, which was, to atend or accompany a son of Sir Walter Rauleyes in his travills. Within a short time after their returne, they parted (I think not in cole bloud) and with a love sutable to what they had in their travills (not to be comended) and then Ben began to set up for himself in the trade by which he got his subsistance and fame. Of which I nede not give any account. He got in time to have 100 pounds a year from the King, also a pention from the Cittie, and the like

from many of the nobility, and some of the gentry, which was well payd for love or fere of his raling in verse or prose, or boeth. My Lord of Winton told me, he told him he was (in his long retyrement and sickness, when he saw him, which was often) much afflickted that hee had profain'd the scripture in his playes ; and lamented it with horror ; yet, that at that time of his long retyrement, his pentions (so much as came yn) was given to a woman that govern'd him, with whom he livd and dyed nere the Abie in West mimster ; and that nether he nor she tooke much care for next weike, and wood be sure not to want wine ; of which he usually tooke too much before he went to bed, if not oftner and soner. My Lord tells me he knowes not, but thinks he was borne in Westminster. So much for brave Ben.

When B. J. was dyeing King Charles sent him but x pounds.

He lies buryed in the north aisle in the path of square stone (the rest is Lozenge) opposite to the Scutcheon of Robertus de Ros, with this Inscription only on him, in a pavement square of blew marble, about 14 inches square,

O RARE BENN JOHNSON

which was donne at the charge of Jack Young, afterwards knighted, who, walking there when the grave was covering, gave the fellow eighteen pence to cutt it.

RALPH KETTELL

[Born 1563. Don. Scholar of Trinity College, Oxford, 1579; Fellow 1583; Master of Arts 1586; Doctor of Divinity 1597; third President 1599. He was vigilant in dealing with College estates and discipline, and he rebuilt Trinity College Hall. Died 1643.]

RALPH KETTELL, D.D., was borne in Hartfordshire. The Lady Elizabeth Pope brought him in to be a Scholar of the House at eleaven yeares of age (as I have heard Dr. Ralph Bathurst say.)

I have heard Dr. Whistler say that he wrote good Latin, and Dr. Ralph Bathurst (whose grandmother he maried) that he scolded the best in Latin of any one that ever he knew. He was of an admirable healthy Constitution.

He dyed a year after I came to the Colledge, and he was then a good deal above 80, and he had then a fresh ruddy complexion. He was a very tall well-growne man. His gowne and surplice and hood being on, he had a terrible gigantique aspect with his sharp gray eies.

Mr. Edward Bathurst of Trinity College, Oxon, drew a Picture of Dr. Kettle some three Years after his Death, by sole Strength of Memory, he having so strong an Idea of him impressed on his Mind, that it well resembled him.

He was, they say, white very soon; he had a very venerable presence and was an excellent Governour. One of his maximes of Governing was to keepe-downe the *Juvenilis Impetus*. He was chosen President, the second after the foundation of the College.

He was a right Church of England man, and every tuesday in Terme-time, in the morning, the Undergraduates (I have forgott if Baccalaurs) were to come into the Chapell and heare him expound on the 36 Articles of the Church of England. I remember he was wont to talk much of the Rood-loft, and of the wafers; he remembred those times. On these dayes, if anyone had committed a fault, he should be sure to heare of it in the Chapell before his fellow Collegiates.

He'd have at any him that had a white Cap on; for he concluded him to have been drunke, and his head to ake. Sir John Denham had borrowed money of Mr. Whistler, the

Recorder, and after a great while the Recorder askt him for it again. Mr. Denham laught at it, and told him he never intended that. The Recorder acquainted the President, who, at a Lecture in the Chapell, rattled him, and told him, Thy father (Judge) haz hanged many an honester man. In my time, Mr. Anthony Ettrick and some others frighted a poor young freshman of Magd. Hall with conjuring, which when the old Dr. heard of: on the next Tuesday, sayd he, *Mr. Ettrick* (who is a very little man) *will conjure up a Jackanapes to be his Great-grandfather.*

He sawe how the Factions in Religion in those dayes drew, and he kept himselfe unconcerned. W. Laud, Archbishop of Canterbury, sent him one time a servant of his with Venison, which the old Dr. with much earnestness refused, and sayd he was an old man, and his Stomach weake, and he had not eaten of such Meate in a long time, and by no meanes would accept of it ; but the servant was as much pressing it on him on the other side, and told the President that he durst not carry it back againe. Well, seeing there was no avoyding it, the President asked the Servant seriously, if the Archbishop of Canterbury intended to putt in any Scholars or Fellowes into his College ?

One of the Fellowes (in Mr. Francis Potter's time) was wont to say that Dr. Kettel's braine was like a Hasty-pudding, where there was Memorie, Judgemente and Phancy all stirred together. He had all these Faculties in great measure, but they were all just so jumbled together. If you had to doe with him, taking him for a Foole, you would have found in him great Subtility and reach ; *è contra,* if you treated him as a Wise man you would have mistaken him for a Foole. A neighbour of mine, Mr. St. Low, told me heard him preach once in St. Marie's Church at Oxon. I know not whether this was the only time or no that he used this following way of conclusion : *But now I see it is time for me to shutt up my Booke, for I see the Doctor's men come-in wiping of their beardes from the Ale-house.* He could from the pulpit plainly see them, and 'twas their custom in Sermon to go there, and about the end of Sermon to returne to wayte on their masters.

He had two wives, if not three, but no child. His second wife was a Villiers (or rather I thinke the Widow of Edward Villers, Esq.) who had two beautifull daughters, co-heires. The eldest, whom severall of good estate would gladly have wedded, he would needs dispose of himselfe, and he thought nobody so fitt a husband for this Angelique creature as one Mr. Bathurst, of the College, a second brother, and of about 300 pounds per annum, but an indifferent Scholar, red fac'd, not at all handsome.

But the Doctor's fashion was to goe up and downe the College, and peepe in at the Keyholes to see whether the Boyes did follow their books or no. He seldome found Bathurst minding of his Booke, but mending of his old doublet or breeches. He was very thrifty and penurious, and upon this reason he carried away this curious creature. But she was very happy in her Issue; all her children were very Ingeniose and prosperous in the world, and most of them beautifull.

One Mr. Isham (elder brother to Sir Justinian Isham) a gentleman-commoner of this Howse, dyed of the small-pox. He was a very fine Gentleman and very well-beloved by all the Colledge, and severall of the Fellowes would have preacht his Funerall Sermon, but Dr. Kettel would not permitt it, but would doe it himselfe; which the Fellowes were sorry for, for they knew he would make a ridiculous piece of worke of it. But preach the Dr. did; takes a Text and preaches on it a little while; and then takes another Text for the satisfaction of the young Gentleman's Mother and anon takes another Text for the satisfaction of the young Gentleman's Grandmother. When he came to the Panegyrique, sayd he: He was the finest swet young Gentleman; it did my heart good to see him walke along the Quadrangle. We have an olde Proverbe that *Hungry Dogges will eate dirty puddings,* but I must needes say for this young Gentleman that he always loved *Sweet,* he spake it with a squeaking voice, *things,* and there was end.

He observed that the Howses that had the smallest beer had the most drunkards, for it forced them to goe into the towne to comfort their stomachs, wherefore Dr. Kettel alwayes had in his College excellent beere, not better to be had in Oxon, so that we could not goe to any other place but for the worse, and we had the fewest drunkards of any howse in Oxford.

He was irreconcileable to long haire; called them hairy Scalpes, and as for Perriwigges (which were then very rarely worne) he beleeved them to be the Scalpes of men cutte off after they were hang'd, and so tanned and dressed for use. When he observed the Scolars haire longer than ordinary (especially if they were Scholars of the Howse) he would bring a paire of Cizers in his Muffe (which he commonly wore) and woe be to them that sate on the outside of the Table. I remember he cutt Mr. Radford's haire with the knife that chipps the bread on the Buttery Hatch, and then he sang (this is in the old play of *Gammer Gurton's needle*):

And was not Grim the Collier finely trimm'd?
Tonedi, Tonedi.

Mr. Lydall, sayd he, how doe you decline tondeo? Tondeo, tondes, Tonedi?

He was constantly at Lectures and Excercises in the Hall, to observe them, and brought along with him his Hower-glasse; and one time, being offended with the Boyes, he threatened them that if they did not doe their excercise better he would bring an Hower-glasse two howers long.

One time walking by the Table where the Logick Lecture was read, where the Reader was telling the Boyes that a Syllo-gisme might be true *quoad formam,* but not *quoad materiam*; said the President (who would putt-in sometimes) There was a Fox that spyed a Crowe upon a tree, and he had a great mind to have him, and so getts under the tree in a hope, and layes out his tayle crooked like a Horne, thinking the Crowe might come and peck at it, and then he would seise him. Now come we (this was his word) I say the foxe's tayle is a horne: is this a true proposition or no? (to one of the boyes). Yes, sayd he (the Dr. expected he should have sayd No; for it putt him out of his designe); *Why then,* sayd he, *take him and toot him;* and away he went.

As they were reading of inscribing and circumscribing Figures, sayd he, I will shew you how to inscribe a Triangle in a Quadrangle. Bring a pig into the quadrangle, and I will sett the colledge dog at him, and he will take the pig by the eare, then come I and take the Dog by the tayle and the hog by the tayle, and so there you have a Triangle in a quadrangle; *quod erat faciendum.*

He dragg'd with one foot a little, by which he gave warning (like a rattlesnake) of his comeing. Will Egerton (Major General Egerton's younger brother) a good witt and mimick, would goe so like him that sometimes he would make the whole Chapell rise up imagining he had been entring in.

He preach't every Sunday at his parsonage at Garsington, about five miles off. He rode on his bay gelding, with his boy Ralph before him, with a leg of mutton (commonly) and some colledge bread. He did not care for the countrey Revells because they tended to debauchery. Sayd he, at Garsington revell, Here is, *Hey for Garsington!* and *hey for Cuddesdon!* and *hey Hockley!* but here's nobody cries, *hey for God Almighty!*

Upon Trinity Sunday (our Festival day) he would commonly preach at the Colledge, whither a number of the scholars of other howses would come, to laugh at him. In his prayer (where he was, of course, to remember Sir Thomas Pope, our founder, and the Lady Elizabeth, his wife, deceased) he would many times make a willfull mistake, and say, *Thomas Pope, our confounder,* but then presently recall himselfe.

He sang a thin shrill high Treble, but there was one J. Hoskyns who had a higher, and was wont to playe the wag with the Doctor, to make him straine his voyce up to his.

He was a person of great Charity. In his College, where he observed diligent boys that he ghessed had but a slender exhibition from their Friends, he would many times putt money in at their windowes ; that his right hand did not know what his left did. Servitors that wrote good hands he would sett on worke to transcribe for him, and reward them generosely, and give them good advise.

The Parsonage of Garsington belongs to the College and this good old Doctor, when one of his parish, that was an honest industrious man, happened by any accident to be in decay and lowe in the World, would let his Parsonage to him for a yeare, two or three, fourty pounds a yeare under value.

You must knowe that there was a great Faction between Dr. Kettle and the Fellowes ; and one time at a Scrutiny, the Doctor upbraiding them for their direspect to Him : Qd, Oh ! you are brave gallant Gentlemen, and *learned* men, you dispise, and snort and fart at your poor President : I am an old blind-sincks : but who was it proposed you to be fellows from poor raskall-Jacks, and Servitors : Was it not your President : and yet none of your Friends were ever so gratefull to present me with so much as a wrought Night-cap. I cry you mercy (Mr. Dr. Hobbs !) indeed. I remember, your Mother sent me once a Gammon of Bacon.

Mris. Howe, of Grendon, sent him a present of Hippocris, and some fine cheese-cakes, by a plain countrey fellow, her servant. The Dr. tastes the wine : *What,* sayd he, *didst thou take this drinke out of a Ditch?* and when he saw the cheese-cakes—*What have we here, Crinkum, Crankum?* The poor fellow stared on him, and wondered at such a rough reception of such a handsome present, but he shortly made him amends with a good dinner and halfe-a-crowne.

(Dr. Thomas Batchcroft did out-doe Dr. Kettle. One sent this Doctor a Pidgeon-pye from New-market or thereabout, and he askt the bearer whither 'twas hott, or cold ?)

In August 1642, the Lord Viscount Say and Seale came (by order of the Parliament) to visit the Colleges to see what of new Popery they could discover in the chapells. In our Chapell, on the backside of the Skreen, had been two Altars (of painting well enough for those times, and the Colours were admirably fresh and lively). That on the right hand as you enter the Chapell

[185]

was dedicated to St. Katharine, that on the left was of the taking our Saviour off from the crosse. My Lord Say sawe that this was done of old time, and Dr. Kettel told his Lordship : *Truly, my Lord, we regard them no more then a dirty Dish-clout ;* so they remained untoucht till Harris's time, and then were coloured over with green.

'Tis probable this venerable Doctor might have lived some yeares longer, and finisht his Century, had not those civill warres come on ; which much grieved him, that was wont to be absolute in the colledge, to be affronted and disrespected by rude soldiers. I remember being at the Rhetorique Lecture in the hall ; a foot soldier came in and brake his hower-glasse. The Dr. indeed was just stept out, but Jack Dowch pointed at it.

Our Grove was the Daphne for the Ladies and their gallants to walke in, and many times my Lady Isabella Thynne (who lay at Balliol College) would make her entry with a Theorbo or Lute played before her. I have heard her play on it in the Grove myself, which she did rarely ; for which Mr. Edmund Waller hath in his *Poems* for ever made her famous. She was most beautifull, most humble, charitable, etc., but she could not subdue one thing. I remember one time this Lady and fine Mris. Fenshawe (her great and intimate friend, who lay at our College) would have a frolick to make a visit to the President. The old Dr. quickly perceived that they came to abuse him : he addresses his discourse to Mris. Fenshawe, saying, Madam, your husband and father I bred up here, and I knew your grandfather. I know you to be a gentlewoman, I will not say you are a Whore ; but gett you gonne for a very woman.

Mris. Fenshawe was wont, and my Lady Thynne, to come to our Chapell, mornings, halfe dressd, like Angells. The dissoluteness of the times, as I have sayd, grieving the good old Doctor, his dayes were shortened, and dyed and was buried at Garsington.

Seneca's scholar Nero found fault with his style, saying 'twas *arena sine calce* [mortar without lime] now Dr. Kettel was wont to say that Seneca writes as a Boare does pisse, *scilicet* by jirkes.

I cannot forget a story that Robert Skinner, Lord Bishop of Oxford, haz told us : One Slymaker, a Fellow of this College long since, a fellow of great impudence, and little learning— the fashion was in those dayes to goe, every Satterday night (I thinke) to Joseph Barnes shop, the bookeseller opposite to the west end of St. Mary's, where the Newes was brought from London, etc. This impudent clowne would alwayes be hearkning to people's whisperings and overlooking their letters, that he was much taken notice of. Sir Isaac Wake, who was a very witty man, was resolved he would putt a Trick upon him, and understood that such a Sunday Slymaker was to preach at St. Mary's. So Sir Isaac, the Saterday before, reades a very formall lettre to some person of quality, that Cardinal Baronius was turned Protestant, and was marching with an Army of 40,000 men against the Pope. Slymaker hearkned with greedy Eares, and the next day in his prayer before his Sermon, beseeched God *of his infinite mercy and goodnesse to give a blessing to the Army of Cardinall Baronius, who was turnd Protestant, and now marching with an Army of forty thousand men,* and so runnes on : he had a Stentorian voice, and thunderd it out. The Auditors all stared and were amazed : George Abbot (afterwards Bishop of Sarum) was then Vice-cancellor, and when Slymaker came out of the Pulpit, sends for him, and asked his name : Slymaker, sayd he ; No, sayd the Vice-canc., 'tis *Lyemaker.*

Dr. Kettel, when he scolded at the idle young boies of his colledge, he used these names, viz. Turds, Tarrarags (these were the worst sort, rude Rakills) Rascal-Jacks, Blindcinques, Scobberlotchers (these did no hurt, were sober, but went idleing about the Grove with their hands in their pocketts, and telling the number of the trees There, or so).

To make you merry, I'le tell you a story that Dr. Henry Birket told us t'other day at his cosen Mariet's, *scilicet* that about 1638 or 1640, when he was of Trinity College, Dr. Kettel, preaching as he was wont to doe on Trinity Sunday, told 'em that they should keepe their Bodies chast and holy ; but, said he, you Fellows of the College here eate good Commons, and drinke good double Beer, and breede Seed, and that will gett-out. How would the good old Dr. have raunted and beate-up his Kettle-Drum, if he should have seen such Luxury in the College as there is now ! *Tempora mutantur.*

RICHARD KNOLLES

[Born 1550. Historian. Headmaster of the Grammar School at Sandwich in Kent, where he was engaged for twelve years on his *Generall Historie of the Turkes from the first beginning of that Nation,* which was published in 1603 and ran through many editions. Dr. Johnson said that the book showed *all the excellencies that narration can admit,* explaining Knolles' limited reputation by the fact that he wrote of a subject *of which none desires to be informed.* Byron said of the book : *I believe it had much influence on my future wishes to visit the Levant, and gave perhaps the oriental colouring which is observed in my poetry.* Southey and Coleridge also greatly admired the work, which is a fine example of the English of its time. Knolles died in 1610.]

THE Lord Burleigh, when he read Knolls *Turkish history* was particularly extremely pleased at the discription of the Battail of Lepanto ; sent for Knolles, who told him an ingeniose young man came to him, hearing what he was about, and desired that he might write that, having been in that Action.

My Lord hunted after him, and traced him from place to place, and at last to Newgate ; he was reduced to such necessity. He was hanged but a 14 night before. He unluckily lost a good opportunity of being preferred.

SIR HENRY LEE

[Born 1530. Courtier. He was educated by his uncle, Sir Thomas Wyatt, and entered the service of Henry VIII in 1545. Clerk of the Armoury 1549. Knighted 1553. M.P. for Buckinghamshire 1558 and 1572. Personal Champion to Queen Elizabeth from 1559 to 1590. Master of the Ordnance 1590. He was visited by Queen Elizabeth at his country house in 1592. Knight of the Garter 1597. He was a great builder and sheep farmer and died in 1610.]

OLD Sir Henry Lee, of Ditchley, in Oxon, Knight of the Garter, was a Gentleman of a good estate, and a strong and valiant person; and was supposed brother of Queen Elizabeth. He ordered that all his Family should be christned *Harry's*.

He was a raunger of Woodstocke Parke, and (I have heard my old cosen Whitney say) would many times in his younger yeares walke at nights in the Parke with his Keepers.

This Sir Henry Lee's Nephew and Heire (whom I remember very well: he often came to Sir John Danvers) was called *Whip and Away*. The occasion of it was this: The old Hero declining in his strength by age, and so not being able to be a Righter of his owne Wronges as heretofore, some person of quality had affronted him. So he spake to Sir Henry Lee, his heire, to lie in wayte for him about the Bell Inne, in the Strande, with halfe a dozen or more lustie fellowes at his back, and as the partie came along to give him a good Blow with his Cane and *Whip and away*; the tall fellowes should finish the revenge. Whether 'twere nicety of conscience, or Cowardice, but Sir Henry the younger absolutely refused it. For which he was disinherited and the whole estate settled on a keeper's sonne of Whitchwood forest of his owne name, a one-eied young man, no kinne to him, from whom the Earle of Lichfield now is descended, as also the Lady Norris and Lady Wharton.

He was never maried, but kept woemen to reade to him when he was a-bed. One of his Readers was parson Jones, his wife, of Wotton. I have heard her daughter (who had no more Witt) glory what a brave reader her mother was, and how Sir Harry's Worship much delighted to heare her. But his dearest deare was Mris. Anne Vavasour. He erected a noble altar monument of marble wheron his effigies in armour lay; at the feet was the *Effigies* of his mistresse, Mris. Anne Vavasour. Which occasioned these verses :

> *Here lies the good old Knight Sir Harry,*
> *Who loved well, but would not marry ;*
> *While he lived, and had his feeling,*
> *She did lye, and he was kneeling,*
> *Now he's dead and cannot feele*
> *He doeth lye and shee doeth kneele.*

Some Bishop did threaten to have this Monument defaced ; at least, to remove Mris. A. Vavasour's *effigies*.

WILLIAM LEE

[Inventor. Educated at Christ's and St. John's Colleges, Cambridge. He acquired an aversion to hand-knitting, because a young woman to whom he was paying his addresses seemed, when he visited her, to be always more mindful of her knitting than of his presence. He therefore invented the Stocking Frame, which Queen Elizabeth came to see in action. But she was disappointed by the coarseness of the work, having hoped it would make silk stockings, and refused to grant the monopoly he asked for. Lee altered the machine and produced a pair of silk stockings in 1598, which he presented to the Queen, but Elizabeth now feared that the invention would prejudice hand-knitters and it was consequently discouraged. As King James took up a similar attitude, Lee went to France, where he had been promised great rewards by King Henry IV, but the latter's assassination disappointed these hopes, and Lee died of grief at Paris in 1610.]

HE was the first Inventor of the Weaving of Stockings by an Engine of his contrivance. He was a Sussex man borne, or els lived there. He was a poor Curate, and, observing how much paines his Wife tooke in knitting a payre of Stockings, he bought a Stocking and a halfe, and observed the contrivance of the Stitch, which he designed in his Loome, which (though some of the appendent Instruments of the Engine be altered) keepes the same to this day. He went into France, and dyed there before his Loome was made there. So the Art was, not long since, in no part of the world but England. Oliver Protector made an Act that it should be Felonie to transport this Engine. This Information I tooke from a Weaver (by this Engine) in Pear-poole lane, 1656. Sir John Hoskyns, Mr. Stafford Tyndale, and I, went purposely to see it.

It ought never to be forgott, what our ingenious Countrey-Man Sir Christopher Wrenn proposed to the Silke-Stocking-Weavers of London, viz. a way to weave seven pair or nine paire of stockings at once (it must be an odd Number). He demanded four hundred pounds for his Invention : but the weavers refused it, because they were poor : and besides, they sayd, it would spoile their Trade ; perhaps they did not consider the Proverb, That Light Gaines, with quick returnes, make heavy Purses. Sir Christopher was so noble, seeing they would not adventure so much money, He breakes the Modell of the Engine all to pieces, before their faces.

RICHARD LOVELACE

[Born 1618. Cavalier and poet. He was the heir to great estates in Kent and was educated at Oxford, where he was described by Anthony Wood as *the most amiable and beautiful person that eye ever beheld*. Leaving Oxford, he repaired in great splendour to the Court and served in the Scottish expeditions of 1639. For presenting the Kentish Petition in favour of the King in 1642, he was thrown into the Gatehouse Prison, where he wrote the poem *Stone walls do not a prison make, nor iron bars a cage*. He rejoined Charles I in 1645 and served with the French King in 1646. It being reported that he was killed, his betrothed Lucy Sacheverell (Lucasta) married another man. Lovelace was again imprisoned in 1648, and while in prison he prepared his poems for the press. He had by now spent his whole fortune in support of the Royalist cause, whereupon he grew, says Wood, *very melancholy (which brought him at length into a consumption) became very poor in body and person, was the object of charity, went in ragged cloaths (whereas when he was in his glory he wore cloth of gold and silver) and mostly lodged in obscure and dirty places, more befitting the worst of beggars and poorest of servants*. He died in 1658.]

RICHARD LOVELACE, Esq. ; he was a most beautifull Gentleman.

    Obiit in a Cellar in Long Acre, a little before the Restauration of his Majestie. Mr. Edmund Wyld, etc., have made collections for him, and given him money. George Petty, Haberdasher, in Fleet Street, carried xxs. to him every Monday morning from Sir John Many and Charles Cotton, Esq., for many moneths, but was never repayd.

    One of the handsomest men in England. He was an extraordinary handsome Man, but prowd. He wrote a Poem called *Lucasta*.

HENRY MARTIN

[Born 1602. Regicide. Member of the Short and Long Parliaments, where he was the leader of anti-Royalist feeling, saying that *he did not think one man wise enough to govern all.* Charles I demanded that Martin should be tried for High Treason and excepted him from pardon. When the Civil War broke out, Martin subscribed £1200 to the Parliamentary cause and undertook to raise a regiment of horse. He was made Parliamentary Governor of Reading, but he was committed to the Tower in 1643 for saying that *it were better one family should be destroyed than many.* He was readmitted to Parliament in 1646, however, and became the leader of the extreme party. He was one of the King's judges and, when it came to Cromwell's turn to affix his name to the warrant of King Charles' execution, he wrote his signature hurriedly and then, in a burst of mirth, he smeared the ink of his pen across the face of Henry Martin, the secretary. On Charles II's return, Martin gave himself up, but was excepted from pardon and imprisoned until his death in 1680.]

HENRY MARTIN, esq., son and heir of Sir Henry Martin, Knight, Judge of the Arches, was of the University of Oxford, travelled France, but never Italie. His stature was but middling; his habit moderate; his face not good. Sir Edward Baynton was wont to say that his company was incomparable, but that he would be drunke too soone.

His father found out a rich Wife for him, whom he married something unwillingly. He was a great lover of pretty girles, to whom he was so liberall that he spent the greatest part of his estate. When he had found out a maried woman that he liked (and he had his Emissaries, male and female, to looke out) he would contrive such or such a good bargain, 20 or 30 pounds per annum under rent, to have her neer him. He lived from his wife a long time. If I am not mistaken, shee was sometime distempered by his unkindnesse to her.

King Charles I had a complaint against him for his Wenching. It happened that Henry was in Hyde parke one time when his Majestie was there, goeing to see a Race. The King espied him, and sayd aloud, Let that ugly Rascall be gonne out of the Parke, that whore-master, or els I will not see the sport. So Henry went away patiently, *sed manebat alta mente repostum* [but it lay stored up deep in his heart]. That Sarcasme raysed the whole Countie of Berks against him. He was as far from a

Puritane as light from darknesse. Shortly after (1641) he was chosen Knight of the Shire of that Countie, *nemine contradicente,* and proved a deadly Enemy to the King.

He was a great and faithfull lover of his Countrey, and never gott a farthing by the Parliament. He was of an incomparable Witt for Repartes ; not at all covetous ; humble, not at all Arrogant, as most of them were ; a great cultor of Justice, and did always in the House take the part of the oppressed.

His speeches in the House were not long, but wondrous poynant, pertinent, and witty. He was exceedingly happy in apt instances. He alone haz sometimes turned the whole House. Makeing an invective speech one time against old Sir Henry Vane ; when he had don with him, he said, But for young Sir Harry Vane ; and so sate him downe. Severall cryed out, What have you to say to young Sir Harry ? He rises up : Why ! if young Sir Harry lives to be old, he will be old Sir Harry ! and so sate downe, and set the House a-laughing, as he oftentimes did. Oliver Cromwell once in the House called him, jestingly or scoffingly, Sir Harry Martin. H. M. rises and bowes ; I thanke your *Majestie.* I always thought when you were a *King* I should be Knighted. A godly member made a Motion to have all profane and unsanctified persons expelled the Houses. H. M. stood up and moved that all Fooles might be putt out likewise, and then there would be a thin House. He was wont to sleepe much in the House (at least dog-sleepe) Alderman Atkins made a Motion that such scandalous members as slept, and minded not the businesse of the House, should be putt out. H. M. starts up : Mr. Speaker, a motion has been to turne out the Nodders, I desire the Noddees may also be turnd out.

His short lettre to his cosen Stonehouse of Radley by Abingdon that *if his Majestie should take advice of his Gunsmiths and powder-men, He would never have peace*—from Sir John Lenthall : as also of his draweing the Remonstrance of the Parliament when 'twas formed a Commonwealth—within five or six lines of the beginning he sayes *restored to it's auncient Goverment of a Commonwealth.* When 'twas read Sir Henry Vane stood up and repremanded and wondred at his impudence to affirme such a notorious Lye. H. M., standing up, meekely replied that *there was a Text had much troubled his spirit for severall dayes and nights of the man that was blind from his mother's womb whose sight was restored at last,* i.e. was restored to the sight which he should have had.

Henry Martin made a Motion in the House to call the Addressers to account (viz. those that addressed to Richard

Cromwell, Protector, to stand by him with their lives and fortunes) and that all the addressers that were of it (of the House) might be turned out as enemies to the Commonwealth of England and betrayers of their Trust to bring in Government by a single person. Had not Dick Cromwell sneak't away then, it is certain that the Rump would have cutt off his Head, as I am well assured from a deare friend of mine.

H. M. sayd that he had seen the Scripture fulfilled : *Thou hast exalted the humble and meeke ; thou hast filled the emptie, and the rich hast thou sent emptie away.*

Anno 1660 he was obnoxious for having been one of the late King's Judges, and he was in very great danger to have suffred as the others did (he pleaded only the King's Act of Proclamation at Breda which he shewd in his hand) but (as he was a Witte himselfe) so the Lord Falkland saved his life by Witt, saying, Gentlemen, yee talke here of makeing a Sacrifice ; it was the old Lawe, all Sacrifices were to be without spott or blemish ; and now you are going to make an old Rotten Rascall a Sacrifice. This Witt tooke in the House, and saved his life.

He was first a prisoner at the Tower ; then at Windsore (removed from thence because he was an eie-sore to his Majestie) from thence to Chepstowe, where he is now (1680). During his imprisonment, his wife relieved him out of her joincture, but she dyed.

When his study was searcht they found letters to his Concubine, which was printed 4to. But 'tis not to his disgrace ; there is Witt and good nature in them.

ANDREW MARVELL

[Born 1621. Poet and satirist. He travelled on the Continent
for four years. In 1653 he became tutor to Cromwell's ward, William
Dutton, and in 1657 was made Milton's assistant in the Latin secretary-
ship to the Council. After the Restoration he entered Parliament
and became a violent politician with strong Republican leanings and
wrote satires and pamphlets, attacking first the ministers, but afterwards Charles II himself. Despite this he remained a favourite with
the King, who offered him a place at Court and a present of £1000,
which were both declined. From 1660 to 1678 he wrote a series of
newsletters to his constituents at Hull, chronicling the debates in the
House of Commons. But his fame rests upon his poems written in
praise of gardens and country life. He died in 1678.]

HE was of middling stature, pretty strong sett, roundish
faced, cherry cheek't, hazell eie, browne haire. He was
in his conversation very modest, and of very few words :
and though he loved wine he would never drinke hard in
company, and was wont to say that, he would not play the good-
fellow in any man's company in whose hands he would not
trust his life. He had not a generall acquaintance.

In the time of Oliver the Protector he was Latin Secretarie.
He was a great master of the Latin tongue ; an excellent poet
in Latin or English : for Latin verses there was no man could
come into competition with him.

I remember I have heard him say that the Earle of Rochester
was the only man in England that had the true veine of Satyre.

His native towne of Hull loved him so well that they elected
him for their representative in Parliament, and gave him an
honourable pension to maintain him.

He kept bottles of wine at his lodgeing, and many times
he would drinke liberally by himselfe to refresh his spirits,
and exalt his Muse. (I remember I have been told that the learned
Goclenius (an High-German) was wont to keep bottells of
good Rhenish-wine in his studie, and, when his spirits wasted,
he would drinke a good Rummer of it.)

Obiit Londini, Aug. 18. 1678 ; and is buried in St. Giles
church in-the-fields about the middle of the south aisle. Some
suspect that he was poysoned by the Jesuites, but I cannot be
positive.

THOMAS MAY

[Born 1595. Poet and historian. The son of Sir Thomas May, he
went to Cambridge and thence to Gray's Inn, but soon discarded
law for literature. In 1622 he produced his first comedy, *The Heir,*
and also a translation of Virgil's *Georgics.* Six years later appeared
his translation of *Lucan,* which gained him the favour of Charles I,
at whose command he wrote two poems, each in seven books, *The
Reigne of King Henry II* and *The Victorious Reigne of King Edward III.*
But when the Civil War broke out, May took the side of the Parliament and was made Secretary to the Long Parliament, the historian
of which he became. *The History of the Parliament of England, which
began Nov. 3, 1640,* was published in 1647 : the narrative closes with
the Battle of Newbury (1643) and is prefaced with a short review of
the preceding reigns from that of Elizabeth. May was also the author
of several tragedies, which exhibit either featureless mediocrity or
pretentious extravagance. He died in 1650.]

AS to Tom May, Mr. Edmund Wyld told me that he was
acquainted with him when he was young, and then he
was as other young men of this Towne are, *scil.* he was
debaucht *ad omnia* : but doe not by any meanes take notice of
it ; for we have all been young. But Mr. Marvel in his Poems
upon Tom May's death falls very severe upon him.

A great acquaintance of Tom Chaloner. Would, when
inter pocula, speake slightingly of the Trinity.

He stood Candidate for the Laurell after B. Jonson ; but
Sir William Davenant caried it.

Amicus : Sir Richard Fanshawe. Mr. Emanuel Decretz
(Serjeant Painter to King Charles Ist) was present at the debate
at their parting before Sir Richard went to the King, where
both Camps were most rigorously banded.

His translation of Lucan's excellent Poeme made him in
love with the Republique, which Tang stuck by him.

Came of his death after drinking with his chin tyed with
his cap (being fatt) ; suffocated.

SIR HUGH MIDDLETON

[Born 1560. Merchant. He traded as a goldsmith, banker and cloth-maker. Alderman of Denbigh 1597. M.P. for Denbigh 1603, 1614, 1620, 1623, 1625 and 1628. He built the New River from Chadwell to London : this canal, which was about thirty-eight miles long, ten feet wide and four feet deep, was completed in 1613. King James paid half the cost in return for half the profits. Middleton also obtained large profits from the lead and silver mines in Cardiganshire 1617. Began reclaiming Brading Harbour 1620. Created baronet 1622. Died 1631.]

MR. INGELBERT was the first Inventer or Projector of bringing the water from Ware to London called *Middleton's water*. He was a poore-man, but Sir Hugh Middleton, Alderman of London, moneyed the businesse ; undertooke it ; and gott the profit and also the Credit of that most usefull Invention, for which there ought to have been erected a Statue for the memory of this poore-man from the City of London.

A Country Fellow seeing them digging the Channel for the new River said, that he would save them 2000 pounds, that is, he would turn up the Earth with a Plough ; and had strong Ploughs and Harness made purposely, which was drawn by 17 Horses, and sav'd a vast deal of Expence.

This Sir Hugh Middleton had his Picture in Goldsmyth's hall with a Waterpott by him, as if he had been the Sole Inventor. Mr. Fabian Philips sawe Ingolbert afterwards, in a poore Rug-gowne like an Almes-man, sitting by an apple-woman at the Parliament-stayres.

Memorandum : that now (1682) London is growne so populous and big that the New River of Middleton can serve the pipes to private houses but twice a weeke.

JOHN MILTON

[Born 1608. Poet and statesman. He first struck a distinctive note in the stately ode *On the Morning of Christ's Nativity*. Having given up the idea of entering the Church, for which his father had intended him, he lived at Horton in Bucks with his father, until 1637, reading the classics and preparing himself for his vocation as a poet. Here he wrote *L'Allegro* and *Il Penseroso* in 1632, *Comus* in 1634 and *Lycidas* in 1637. From 1637 to 1639, he travelled abroad and visited Grotius and Galileo. In June 1642 he married Mary Powell and next year published his pamphlet on *The Doctrine and Discipline of Divorce*, which made him notorious. In 1645 he published his *Tractate of Education* and the *Areopagitica* on the liberty of the press : but within five years Milton himself was working as Censor of Publications for the Commonwealth. After the execution of Charles I, he was appointed Latin Secretary to the newly formed Council of State and retained this post until the Restoration, when he was arrested and fined, losing the greater part of his fortune. He was soon released from custody, however, and returned to his poetry, completing *Paradise Lost* in 1664. In 1663, being now totally blind and somewhat helpless, he asked his friend Dr. Paget to recommend a wife to him : the lady chosen was Elizabeth Minshull, aged twenty-five, who survived him for fifty-three years. In 1671 *Samson Agonistes* and *Paradise Regained* were published. In Milton the influences of the Renaissance and of Puritanism met. To the former he owed his wide culture and his profound love of everything noble and beautiful, to the latter his lofty and austere character, and both these elements meet in his writings. Leaving Shakespeare out of account, he holds an indisputable place at the head of English poets. He died in 1674.]

M R. JOHN MILTON was of an Oxfordshire familie. His Grandfather was a Roman Catholic of Holton, in Oxfordshire, near Shotover.

His father was brought-up in the University of Oxon, at Christ Church, and his grandfather disinherited him because he kept not to the Catholique Religion (he found a Bible in English, in his Chamber). So therupon he came to London, and became a Scrivener (brought up by a friend of his ; was not an Apprentice) and gott a plentifull estate by it, and left it off many yeares before he dyed. He was an ingeniose man ; delighted in musique ; composed many Songs now in print, especially that of *Oriana*. I have been told that the Father composed a Song of fourscore parts for the Lantgrave of Hess, for which his Highnesse sent a meddall of gold, or a noble present. He dyed about 1647; buried in Cripple-gate-church, from his house in the Barbican.

His son John was borne the 9th of December, 1608, *die Veneris,* half an hour after 6 in the morning, in Bread Street, in London, at the Spread Eagle, which was his house (he had also in that street another howse, the Rose; and other houses in other places). Anno Domini 1619, he was ten yeares old; and was then a Poet. His school-master then was a Puritan, in Essex, who cutt his haire short.

He went to Schoole to old Mr. Gill, at Paule's Schoole. Went at his owne Chardge only, to Christ's College in Cambridge at fifteen, where he stayed eight yeares at least. Then he travelled into France and Italie (had Sir H. Wotton's commendatory letters). At Geneva he contracted a great friendship with the learned Dr. Deodati of Geneva. He was acquainted with Sir Henry Wotton, Ambassador at Venice, who delighted in his company. He was severall yeares beyond Sea, and returned to England just upon the breaking-out of the Civill Warres.

From his brother, Christopher Milton :—when he went to Schoole, when he was very young, he studied very hard, and sate-up very late, commonly till twelve or one a clock at night, and his father ordered the mayde to sitt-up for him, and in those yeares (10) composed many Copies of Verses which might well become a riper age. And was a very hard student in the University, and performed all his exercises there with very good Applause. His first Tutor there was Mr. Chapell; from whom receiving some unkindnesse (whipt him) he was afterwards (though it seemed contrary to the Rules of the College) transferred to the Tuition of one Mr. Tovell, who dyed Parson of Lutterworth. He went to travell about the year 1638 and was abroad about a year's space, chiefly in Italy.

Immediately after his return he took a lodging at Mr. Russell's, a Taylour, in St. Bride's Churchyard, and took into his tuition his sister's two sons, Edward and John Philips, the first 10, the other 9 years of age; and in a yeare's time made them capable of interpreting a Latin authour at sight. And within three years they went through the best of Latin and Greek Poetts—Lucretius and Manilius, of the Latins (and with him the use of the Globes, and some rudiments of Arithmetic and Geometry.) Hesiod, Aratus, Dionysius Afer, Oppian, Apollonii *Argonautica,* and Quintus Calaber. Cato, Varro and Columella *De re rustica* were the very first Authors they learn't. As he was severe on the one hand, so he was most familiar and free in his conversation to those to whome most sowre in his way of education. N.B. he mad his Nephews Songsters, and sing, from the time they were with him.

His first wife (Mrs. Powell, a Royalist) was brought up and lived where there was a great deale of company and merriment, dancing, etc. And when she came to live with her husband, at Mr. Russell's, in St. Bride's Churchyard, she found it very solitary; no company came to her; oftimes heard his Nephews beaten and cry. This life was irkesome to her, and so she went to her Parents at Fost-hill. He sent for her, after some time; and I thinke his servant was evilly entreated: but as for matter of wronging his bed, I never heard the least suspicions; nor had he, of that, any Jealousie.

Two opinions doe not well on the same Boulster; she was a Royalist, and went to her mother to the King's quarters, neer Oxford. I have perhaps so much charity to her that she might not wrong his bed: but what man, especially contemplative, would like to have a young wife environ'd and storm'd by the Sons of Mars, and those of the enemi partie? He parted from her, and wrote the Triplechord about divorce.

He had a middle wife, whose name was Katharin Woodcock. No child living by her.

He maried his third wife, Elizabeth Minshull, the year before the Sicknesse: a gent. person, a peacefull and agreable humour.

Hath two daughters living: Deborah was his amanuensis (he taught her Latin, and to reade Greeke to him when he had lost his eie-sight.)

His sight began to faile him at first upon his writing against Salmasius, and before 'twas full compleated one eie absolutely faild. Upon the writing of other bookes, after that, his other eie decayed. His eie-sight was decaying about 20 yeares before his death. His father read without spectacles at 84. His mother had very weake eies, and used spectacles presently after she was thirty yeares old.

His harmonicall and ingeniose Soul did lodge in a beautifull and well proportioned body. He was a spare man. He was scarce so tall as I am (*quaere,* quot feet I am high: *resp.,* of middle stature).

He had abroun hayre. His complexion exceeding faire— he was so faire that they called him *the Lady of Christ's College*. Ovall face. His eie a darke gray.

He was very healthy and free from all diseases: seldome tooke any physique (only sometimes he tooke manna): only towards his latter end he was visited with the Gowte, Spring and Fall.

He had a delicate tuneable Voice, and had good skill. His father instructed him. He had an Organ in his howse; he played on that most. Of a very cheerfull humour. He would be chearfull even in his Gowte-fitts, and sing.

He had a very good Memorie; but I believe that his excellent Method of thinking and disposing did much to helpe his Memorie.

His widowe haz his picture, drawne very well and like, when a Cambridge-schollar, which ought to be engraven; for the Pictures before his bookes are not at all like him.

His exercise was chiefly walking. He was an early riser (*scil.* at 4 a clock *manè*) yea, after he lost his sight. He had a man to read to him. The first thing he read was the Hebrew bible, and that was at 4 h. *manè*, ½ h. plus. Then he contemplated.

At 7 his man came to him again, and then read to him again, and wrote till dinner; the writing was as much as the reading. His daughter, Deborah, could read to him in Latin, Italian and French, and Greeke. Maried in Dublin to one Mr. Clarke (sells silke, etc.) very like her father. The other sister is Mary, more like her mother.

After dinner he used to walke 3 or four houres at a time (he always had a Garden where he lived) went to bed about 9.

Temperate man, rarely dranke between meales. Extreme pleasant in his conversation, and at dinner, supper, etc.; but Satyricall. (He pronounced the letter R (*littera canina*) very hard—a certaine signe of a Satyricall Witt—*from John Dreyden.*)

All the time of writing his *Paradise Lost,* his veine began at the Autumnall Aequinoctiall, and ceased at the Vernall or thereabouts (I believe about May) and this was 4 or 5 yeares of his doeing it. He began about 2 yeares before the King came-in, and finished about three yeares after the King's restauracion.

In the 4th booke of *Paradise Lost* there are about six verses of Satan's Exclamation to the Sun, which Mr. E. Philips remembers about 15 or 16 yeares before ever his Poem was thought of, which verses were intended for the Beginning of a Tragoedie which he had designed, but was diverted from it by other businesse.

He was visited much by the learned; more then he did desire. He was mightily importuned to goe into France and Italie. Foraigners came much to see him, and much admired him, and offer'd to him great preferments to come over to them; and the only inducement of severall foreigners that came over into England, was chiefly to see Oliver Protector, and Mr. John Milton; and would see the hous and chamber wher he was borne. He was much more admired abrode then at home.

His familiar learned Acquaintance were Mr. Andrew Marvell, Mr. Skinner, Dr. Pagett, M.D.

John Dreyden, Esq., Poet Laureate, who very much admires him, went to him to have leave to putt his *Paradise Lost* into a Drame in rythme. Mr. Milton recieved him civilly, and told him *he would give him leave to tagge his Verses*.

His widowe assures me that Mr. T. Hobbs was not one of his acquaintance, that her husband did not like him at all, but he would acknowledge him to be a man of great parts, and a learned man. Their Interests and Tenets did run counter to each other.

Whatever he wrote against Monarchie was out of no animosity to the King's person, or owt of any faction or interest, but out of a pure Zeale to the Liberty of Mankind, which he thought would be greater under a fre state than under a Monarchiall government. His being so conversant in Livy and the Roman authors, and the greatness he saw donne by the Roman commonwealth, and the vertue of their great Commanders induc't him to.

Mr. John Milton made two admirable Panegyricks, as to Sublimitie of Witt, one on Oliver Cromwel, and the other on Thomas, Lord Fairfax, both which his nephew Mr. Philip hath. But he hath hung back these two yeares, as to imparting copies to me for the Collection of mine. Were they made in commendation of the Devill, 'twere all one to me : 'tis the ὕψος that I looke after. I have been told that 'tis beyond Waller's or anything in that kind.

GEORGE MONK : DUKE OF ALBEMARLE

[Born 1608. Soldier. He served against the Irish Rebels, in command of a foot regiment, and returned with his Irish troops to help Charles I on the outbreak of the Civil War, but he was taken prisoner by Fairfax in 1644 and was imprisoned in the Tower. He was offered command in Ireland by Parliament on condition of taking the negative oath, after which he became Adjutant-General and Governor of Ulster. In 1650 he accompanied Cromwell to Scotland, becoming Commander-in-Chief the next year and completing the conquest of that country in 1652. He was then appointed Admiral and fought in the three great battles which practically ended the Dutch War, before resuming command of the Army in Scotland in 1654. In 1655 he greatly extended the powers of civil government which had been granted to him and his Council. He was implicitly trusted by Oliver Cromwell, on whose death he sent Richard Cromwell a letter of valuable advice. In 1659 he received Royalist overtures and marched slowly towards London, demanding the issue of writs for a new Parliament and ordering the guards to admit the secluded members. He was elected head of a new Council, General-in-Chief of the Land Forces and Joint Commander of the Navy in February 1660, but he refused the offer of supreme power for himself. He then received from the King a commission as Captain-General, authorising him to appoint a Secretary of State, and letters for the City, the Council and the Parliament, which voted the restoration of the monarchy in May. On the King's arrival, Monk was knighted and in July he was made a Knight of the Garter and created Baron Monck, Earl of Torrington and Duke of Albemarle. Monk had great influence with the new government in military matters (his own regiments being retained by the King as his Household Guard) but less influence in political matters and none in ecclesiastical questions. He remained in London throughout the Plague of 1665, maintaining order and superintending preventive measures. In 1666 he was beaten by the Dutch in a naval battle off the North Foreland, but was immediately recalled to restore order in the City after the great Fire of London. He became First Lord of the Treasury in 1667, but retired in 1668 and died in 1670.]

GEORGE MONK was borne in Devon, a second son of an ancient familie, and which had about Henry 8's time 10,000 pounds per annum (as he himselfe sayd).
He was a strong, lusty, well-sett young fellow; and in

his youth happened to slay a man, which was the occasion of his flying into the Low-countries, where he learned to be a Soldier.

At the beginning of the late Civill-warres, he came over to the King's side, where he had command.

He was a prisoner in the Tower, where his semstress, Nan Clarges, a Blacksmith's daughter was kind to him ; in a double capacity. It must be remembered that he then was in want, and she assisted him. (The trueth was, he was forgotten and neglected at Court, that they did not thinke of Exchanging him.) Here she was gott with child. She was not at all hand-some, nor cleanly. Her mother was one of the *five Woemen-Barbers*.

There was a maried woman in Drury Lane that had clapt (i.e. given the pox to) a woman's husband, a neighbour of hers. She complained of this to her neighbour gossips : so they concluded on this Revenge, viz. to gett her and whippe her and to shave all the haire off her pudenda ; which severities were executed and put into a Ballad. 'Twas the first Ballad I ever cared for the reading of ; the Burden of it was thus :—

> *Did yee ever heare the like*
> *Or ever heard the same*
> *Of five Woemen-Barbers*
> *That lived in Drewry-lane ?*

Her brother, Thomas Clarges, came a ship-board to G. M. and told him his sister was brought to bed. *Of what?* sayd he. *Of a Son. Why then,* sayd he, *she is my Wife.* He had only this Child.

I have forgott by what meanes he gott his Libertie, and an Employment under Oliver (I thinke) at Sea, against the Dutch, where he did good service ; he had courage enough. But I remember the Seamen would laugh, that instead of crying *Tack about,* he would say *Wheele to the right,* or *left.*

He had command in Scotland, where he was well-beloved by his Soldiers, and, I thinke, that countrie (for an Enemie.) Oliver, Protector, had a great mind to have him home, and sent him a fine complementall letter, to come into England to advise with him. He sent his Highnesse word, that if he pleased he would come and wayte on him at the head of 10,000 men. So that designe was spoyled.

Anno 1659/60 (as I remember) he came into London with his Army, about one a clock P.M., being then sent for by the Parliament to disband Lambert's Armie. Shortly after he was sent for to the Parliament House ; where, in the howse, a

Chaire was sett for him, but he would not in modestie sitt downe in it. The Parliament (the Rumpe of a Howse: 'twas the wooden invention of Generall Browne, a woodmonger) made him odious to the Citie, purposely, by pulling downe and burning their gates (which I myselfe sawe). The Rumpe invited him to a great Dinner, shortly after, from whence it was never intended that he should have returned (of this I am assured by one of that parliament). The members stayed till 1, 2, 3, 4 a clock, but at last his Excellency sent them word he could not come. I beleeve he suspected some treacherie.

You must know that long before these dayes, Colonel Massey, and Thomas Mariett, of Whitchurch in Warwickshire, Esqre, held correspondence with his Majestie, who wrote them letters with his owne hand, which I have seen. Both these were now in London privately. Tom Mariett laye with me (I was then of the Middle Temple) G. M. lay at Drapers Hall in Throckmorton Street. Col. Massey (Sir Edward afterwards) and T. Mariett every day were tampering with G. M. as also Col. Robinson (afterwards Liewtenant of the Tower) whom I remember they counted not so wise as King Salomon, and they could not find any inclination or propensity in G. M. for their purpose, *scil.* to be instrumentall to bring in the King. Every night late, I had an account of all these Transactions in bed, which like a Sott as I was, I did not, while fresh in Memorie, committ to writing, as neither has T. M., but I remember in the maine, that they were satisfied he no more intended the King's restauration, when he came into England, or first came to London, then his Horse did. But shortly after, finding himselfe at a Losse; and that he was purposely made Odious to the Citie, as aforsayd—and that he was a lost man—by the Parliament; and that the generality of the Citie and countrey were for the restoring the King, having long groaned under the Tyranny of other Governments; he had no way to save himselfe but to close with the citie, etc., again.

Thredneedle Street was all day long, and late at night, crammed with multitudes, crying out, *A free Parliament, a free Parliament,* that the aire rang with their clamours. One evening, he comeing out on horseback, they were so violent that he was almost afrayd of himselfe, and so, to satisfie them (as they used to doe to importunate children) *Pray be quiet, yee shall have a free Parliament.* This about 7, or rather 8, as I remember, at night. Immediately, a Loud Holla and shout was given, all the Bells in Citie ringing and the whole Citie looked as if it had been in a flame by the Bonfires, which were prodigiously great and frequent and ran like a Traine over the

Citie, and I saw some Balcones that began to be kindled. They made little Gibbetts and roasted Rumpes of mutton : nay, I sawe some very good Rumpes of Beefe. Healths to the King, Charles II, were drank in the streets by the Bonfires, even on their Knees, and this humor ran by the next night to Salisbury ; where there was like Joy : so to Chalke, where they made a great Bonfire on the top of the hill ; from hence to Blandford and Shaftesbury, and so to Land's End, and perhaps it was so all over England. So that the return of his most gracious Majestie was by the hand of God, but as by this person meerly accidental, whatever the pompous history in 8vo. sayes.

Well ! a free-Parliament was chosen, and mett ; Sir Harbottle Grimston, Knight and Baronet, was chosen Speaker. The first thing he putt to the Question was, Whether Charles Steward should be sent for, or no ? Yea, yea, *nemine contradicente.* Sir John Greenvill (now Earle of Bathe) was then in Towne, and posted away to Bruxells, found the King at Dinner, little dreaming of so good Newes, rises presently from Dinner, had his Coach immediately made readie, and that night gott out of the King of Spaine's Dominions, into the Prince of Orange's country, I thinke, Breda.

Now, as the Morne growes lighter and lighter, and more glorious, till it is perfect day, so it was with the Joy of the People. Maypoles, which in the Hypocriticall times 'twas sin to sett up, were now sett up in every crosse way ; and at the Strand, neer Drury Lane, was sett up the most prodigious one for height that (perhaps) was ever seen ; they were faine, I remember, to have the assistance of the Sea-men's art to elevate it ; that which remaines, being broken with a High Wind, I think about 1672, is but two parts of three of the whole height from the grownd, besides what is in the earth. The Juvenile and rustique folkes at that time had so much their fullnesse of desires in this kind that I think there must have been very few sett-up since. The Honours conferred on G. M. every one knowes.

His sence might be good enough, but he was slow, and heavie. He dyed and had a magnificent Funerall, suitable to his Greatnesse. His figure in his robes was very artificially donne, which laye in a Catafalco under a Canopie, in or neer the East End of Westminster Abby, a moneth or six weekes. Seth Ward, Lord Bishop of Sarum (his great acquaintance) preached his Funerall Sermon.

His eldest Brother dyed *sine prole,* about the time of the King's returne. His other Brother was made Bishop of Hereford.

G. M. and his Duchess dyed within a day or two of each other. The Bishop of Sarum told me that he did the last office of a Confessor to his Grace ; and closed his Eies (as his Lordship told me himselfe).

Some moneths before G. M.'s comeing into England, the King sent Sir Richard Grenvill (since Earl of Bath) to him to negotiate with him that he would doe him service, and to correspond with him. Said he, If opportunity be, I will doe him service, but I will not by any meanes have any correspondence with him ; and he did like a wise man in it, for he would certainly have been betrayed.

'Twas shrewd advice which Wyld, then Recorder of London, gave to the Citizens, i.e. to keep their purse-strings fast, els, the Parliament would have payd the Army, and kept out the King.

He was first an Ensigne, and after a Captain, in the Lowe-countreys, and for making false musters was like to have been . . ., which he afterwards did not forget.

This underneath was writt on the Dore of the House of Commons :

> *Till it be understood*
> *What is under Monke's hood,*
> *The Citizens putt in their hornes,*
> *Until the ten days are out,*
> *The Speaker haz the Gowt,*
> *And the Rump, they sitt upon Thornes.*

SIR JONAS MOORE

[Born 1617. Mathematician. Tutor to the Duke of York 1647, from which post he was ousted by what he called *the malicious and cunning subtlety* of Anthony Ascham. Surveyor of the Fen Drainage System 1649. Sent to report on the fortification of Tangier 1663. Knighted and Surveyor-General of the Ordnance 1663. Published *Arithmetick* and *A New System of Mathematicks*. Died 1679.]

SIR JONAS MOORE was borne at Whitelee in Lancashire, towards the Bishoprick of Durham. He was inclined to Mathematiques when a boy, which some kind friends of his putt him upon, and instructed him in it, and afterwards Mr. Oughtred more fully enformed him ; and then he taught Gentlemen in London, which was his livelyhood.

He was one of the most accomplisht Gentlemen of his time ; a good Mathematician, and a good Fellowe.

When the great Levell of the Fennes was to be surveyed, Mr. Wyld who was his Scholar and a Member of Parliament was very instrumentall in helping him to the employment of Surveying it, which was his Rise, which I have heard him acknowledge with much gratitude before severall persons of quality, since he was a Knight, and which evidenced an excellent good nature in him.

When he surveyed the Fennes, he observed the Line that the Sea made on the Beach, which is not a straight line, by which meanes he gott great Credit in keeping-out the sea in Norfolke ; so he made his Bankes against the sea of the same line that the sea makes on the Beach ; and no other could doe it, but that the sea would still breake-in upon it.

He made a Modell of a Citadell for Oliver Cromwell, to bridle the City of London, which Mr. Wyld has ; and this Citadell was to have been the Crosse building of St. Paule's church.

Sciatica : he cured it by boyling his Buttock.

The Duke of Yorke said that : Mathematicians and Physicians had no Religion : which being told to Sir Jonas More, he presented his duty to the D. Y. and wished, with all his heart that his Highnesse *were a Mathematician too* : this was since he was supposed to be a Roman Catholic.

He dyed at Godalmyng, and was buried at the Tower Chapell, with sixty peices of Ordinance (equall to the number of his yeares.) He alwayes intended to have left his Library of Mathematicall bookes to the Royall Societie, of which he was a Member; but he happened to dye without making a Will, wherby the Royal Societie have a great Losse.

His only Sonne, Jonas, had the honour of Knighthood conferred upon him, August 9, 1680, at Windsor; his Majestie being pleased to give him this Marke of his Favour *as well in consideration of his owne abilities, as of the faithfull service of his father deceased*—but young Sir Jonas, when he is old, will never be *old Sir Jonas,* for all the Gazette's elogie.

I remember Sir Jonas told us that a Jesuite (I think 'twas Grenbergerus, of the Roman college) found out a way of Flying, and that he made a youth performe it. Mr. Gascoigne taught an Irish boy that way, and he flew over a River in Lancashire (or therabout) but when he was up in the ayre, the people gave a shoute, wherat the boy being frighted, he fell downe on the other side of the river, and broke his legges, and when he came to himselfe, he sayd that he thought the people had seen some strange apparition, which fancy amazed him. This was anno 1635, and he spake it in the Royall Societie, upon the account of the Flyeing at Paris, two yeares since.

SIR ROBERT MORAY

[He was the son of Sir Mungo Moray. He served in the French Army, where he was highly favoured by Cardinal Richelieu. He returned to England at the outbreak of the Civil War and was knighted by Charles the First at Oxford in 1643. He then returned to France, where he became on good terms with Cardinal Mazarin. In 1645 he was captured in Bavaria, but was released in order to negotiate a treaty secretly between France and Scotland, by which it was proposed to attempt the restoration of Charles the First. He recommended Charles' surrender to the Scots and was with him at both Newark and Newcastle. A plan for the King's escape from Scottish custody was frustrated only by the royal captive's timidity. Moray resumed his career in France, in command of the Scots Regiment, after the downfall of the monarchy in England, and the Scottish Parliament sent cargoes of prisoners to him to recruit his corps. He joined Charles the Second in Paris, in 1654, after the collapse of the Highland rising. In 1663 Moray was appointed Lord of the Exchequer for Scotland and Deputy Secretary : thenceforward down to 1670, the government of that country was mainly carried on by Lauderdale, the King and himself. He was devoid of ambition and the King used to say, in illustration of Moray's independence of character, that *he was head of his own church.* He died in 1673.]

SIR ROBERT MORAY, Knight, was of the ancient family of the Morays in Scotland. He was borne (as I take it) in the Highlands. The Highlanders (like the Swedes) can make their owne Cloathes ; and I have heard Sir Robert say that he could doe it. I have heard some of Ol. Cromwels army say, that the Highlanders ate only oate-meale and water and milk : that their Rivers did abound with Trowtes but they had not the witt to take them till the English taught 'em.

He spent most of his time in France. After his juvenile education at Schoole and the University he betooke himselfe to military employment in the service of Lewis the 13th. He was at last a Lieuetenant-Colonel. He was a great master of the Latin tongue and was very well read. They say he was an excellent soldier.

He was far from the rough humour of the Camp-breeding, for he was a person the most obliging about the Court and the only man that would doe a kindnesse *gratis* upon an account of Friendship. A Lacquey could not have been more obsequious and diligent. What I doe now averre I know to be true upon my owne score as well as others. He was a most humble and good man, and as free from Covetousness as a Carthusian. He was abstemious and abhorred woemen. His Majesty was wont to teaze at him. 'Twas pitty he was a Presbyterian.

He was the chiefe appuy of his Countreymen and their good Angel. There had been formerly a great friendship between him and the Duke of Lauderdale, till, about a yeare or two before his death, he went to the Duke on his returne from Scotland and told him plainly that he had betrayed his Countrey.

He was one of the first Contrivers and Institutors of the Royall Societie and was our first President, and performed his charge in the Chaire very well.

He was my most honoured and obligeing friend, and I was more obliged to him then to all the Courtiers besides. I had a great losse in his death, for, had he lived, he would have got some employment or other for me before this time. He had the King's eare as much as any one, and was indefatigable in his undertakings. I was often with him. I was with him three houres the morning he dyed; he seemed to be well enough. I remember he dranke at least ½ pint of faire water, according to his usuall custome.

His lodgeing where he dyed was the leaded pavillion in the garden at Whitehall. He dyed suddenly July 4th about 8 hours P.M. A°.D. 1673. Had but one Shilling in his pocket, i.e. *in all*. The King buryed him. He lyes by Sir William Davenant in Westminster abbey.

He was a good Chymist and assisted his Majestie in his Chymicall operations.

SIR THOMAS MORE

[Born 1478. Statesman and author. While practising the law, he won the favour of Henry VIII. He was knighted in 1514 and employed on various embassies. The King kept inviting him to Court, but More would not come; at last the King came uninvited to dine with him at his house in Chelsea. More had no illusions as to Henry VIII; when complimented on the King's favourable disposition, he replied: If my head should win him a castle in France it should not fail to go. He published *Utopia* in 1516. When Wolsey fell, the King appointed More as Lord Chancellor in his stead. Contrary to the usual practice, he refused all gifts from litigants. He soon fell into disfavour, because the King was determined to divorce Catherine of Aragon in order to marry Anne Boleyn and More was unalterably opposed to the divorce. His incorruptibility when in office is shown by the fact that after his resignation he had only £100 a year. In spite of his opinions, the King invited him to his wedding with Anne Boleyn, but More refused the invitation. For refusing to take the Oath of Supremacy to Henry as head of the Church of England, More was beheaded on July 7, 1535. He was canonised in 1935.]

SIR THOMAS MORE, Lord Chancellour: his Countrey-howse was at Chelsey, in Middlesex, where Sir John Danvers built his howse. Where the gate is now, adorned with two noble Pyramids, there stood anciently a Gate-house, which was flatt on the top, leaded, from whence there is a most pleasant prospect of the Thames and the fields beyond. On this place the Lord Chancellour More was wont to recreate himselfe and contemplate. It happened one time that a Tom of Bedlam came up to him, and had a Mind to have throwne him from the battlements, saying Leap, Tom, leap. The Chancellour was in his gowne, and besides ancient and not able to struggle with such a strong fellowe. My Lord had a little dog. Sayd he, Let us first throwe the dog downe, and see what sporte that will be. So the dog was throwne over. This is very fine sport, sayd my Lord, Let us fetch him up, and try once more. While the mad man was goeing downe, my Lord fastned the dore, and called for help, but ever after kept the dore shutt.

(Till the breaking-out of the Civil-warre, Tom o Bedlam's did travell about the Countrey: they had been poore distracted men that had been putt into Bedlam, where recovering to some sobernesse they were truncated to goe a begging, e.g.

[213]

they had on their left arme an Armilla or Tinne printed in some workes : about 4 inches long : they could not gett it off. They wore about their necks a great Horne of an Oxe, in a string or Bawdrie, which, when they came to an house for Almes, they did sound ; and they did putt the drinke given them into this Horne, whereto they did putt a stopple. Since the Warres I doe not remember to have seen anyone of them.)

In his *Utopia* his lawe is that the young people are to see each other stark-naked before marriage. Sir William Roper, of Eltham, in Kent, came one morning, pretty early, to my Lord, with a proposall to marry one of his daughters. My Lord's daughters were then both together abed in a truckle-bed in their father's chamber asleep. He carries Sir William into the chamber and takes the Sheete by the corner and suddenly whippes it off. They lay on their Backs, and their smocks up as high as their arme-pitts. This awakened them, and immediately they turned on their bellies. Quoth Roper, I have seen both sides, and so gave a patt on the buttock, he made choice of, sayeing, Thou art mine. Here was all the trouble of the wooeing. This account I had from my honoured friend old Mris. Tyndale, whose grandfather, Sir William Stafford, was an intimate friend of this Sir W. Roper, who told him the story.

His discourse was extraordinary facetious. Riding one night, upon the suddaine he crossed himselfe *majori cruce,* crying out Jesu Maria ! doe not you see that prodigious Dragon in the skye ? They all lookt up, and one did not see it, and nor the tother did not see it. At length one had spyed it, and at last all had spied. Whereas there was no such phantome, only he imposed on their phantasies.

After he was beheaded, his trunke was interred in Chelsey church, neer the middle of the South wall, where was some slight Monument erected. His head was upon London bridge. There goes this story in the family, viz. that one day as one of his daughters was passing under the Bridge, looking on her father's head, sayd she, That head haz layn many a time in my Lapp, would to God it would fall into my Lap as I passe under. She had her wish, and it did fall into her Lappe, and is now preserved in a vault in the Cathedral Church at Canterbury.

The Descendant of Sir Thomas, is Mr. More, of Chilston, in Herefordshire, where, among a great many things of value plundered by the Soldiers, was his Chap, which they kept for a Relique. Methinks 'tis strange that all this time he is not Canonised, for he merited highly of the Church.

SIR THOMAS MORGAN

[Soldier. He served in the Low Countries and, under the command of Fairfax, in the Thirty Years War. Parliamentary Governor of Gloucester 1645. Captured Chepstow Castle and Monmouth 1645. Assisted General Monk in Scotland and rose to the rank of Major-General 1651–57. Appointed second in command in Flanders 1657.. Knighted on his return to England 1658. Morgan then rejoined Monk in Scotland and played a conspicuous part in the Restoration in Edinburgh. Governor of Jersey 1665. Died 1679. His alleged autobiography was published in 1699.]

LITTLE Sir Thomas Morgan, the great soldier, was of meane Parentage in Monmouthshire. He went over to the Lowe-Countrie warres about 16, being recommended by some friend of his to some Commander there, who, when he read the letter, sayd, What! has my cosen recommended a *Rattoon* to me? at which he tooke pett, and seek't his fortune (as a soldier) in Saxon Weymar.

He spake Welch, English, French, High Dutch, and Low Dutch, but never a one well. He seated himself at Cheuston, in Herefordshire.

Sir John Lenthall told me that at the taking of Dunkyrke, Marshall Turenne, and, I thinke, Cardinall Mezarine too, had a great mind to see this famous Warrior. They gave him a visitt, and wheras they thought to have found an Achillean or gigantique person, they saw a little man, not many degrees above a dwarfe, sitting in a hutt of Turves, with his fellowe soldiers, smoaking a Pipe about 3 inches (or neer so) long, and did cry-out to the Soldiers, when angry with them, *Sirrah, I'le cleave your skull!* as if the wordes had been prolated by an Eunuch.

ROBERT MURRAY

[Born 1635. Writer on trade. Took up his freedom in the Cloth-
workers' Company 1660. Invented ruled copy-books. Originated
the idea of the Penny Post in London 1681. Appointed Paymaster
of the 1714 Lottery. He published various proposals for the advancement and improvement of trade and the raising of revenue. Died
1725.]

MR. ROBERT MURRAY is a Citizen of London, a
Milliner, of the Company of Cloathworkers. His
father, a Scotchman; mother, English. Borne in
the Strand.

Mr. Murray was formerly clarke to the generall Company
for the Revenue of Ireland, and afterwards clark to the Committee of the grand Excise of England ; and was the first that
invented and introduced into this city the Club of Commerce
consisting of one of each Trade, whereof there were after very
many erected and are still continued in this city. And also
continued and sett-up the office or Banke of Credit at Devonshire house in Bishopsgate Street without, where men depositing
their goods and merchandize were furnished with bills of current
credit on ⅔ or ¾ of the value of the said Goods answering to
the intrinsique value of money, whereby the deficiency of coin
might be fully subplyed : and for rendring the same current,
a certain or competent number of traders (viz. 10 or 20 of each
trade, wherof there be 500 severall trades within the citty)
were to be associated or formed into such a society or Company
of traders as might amongst them compleat the whole body of
Commerce, whereby any possest of the said current credit
might be furnisht amongst themselves with any kind of goods
or merchandise as effectually as for money could do elsewhere.

The Penny-Post was sett up anno Domini 1680, Our Lady
day, being Fryday, a most ingeniose and usefull Project. Invented by Mr. Murray first, and then Mr. Dockery joined with
him.

RICHARD NAPIER

[Born 1559. Astrologer. Matriculated from Exeter College, Oxford, 1577. Rector of Great Linford 1590. Studied astrology under Simon Forman, an astrologer and quack doctor, who claimed miraculous powers and obtained a large and disreputable practice, chiefly among Court ladies, for which he was frequently imprisoned at the instance of medical and other authorities. Forman *was used to say he would be a Dunce,* but Napier ultimately developed so much skill that Forman on his death in 1611 bequeathed him all his manuscripts. Licensed to practise medicine 1604. Died 1634.]

MR. ASHMOLE told me, that a Woman made use of a Spell to cure an Ague, by the Advice of Dr. Nepier. A Minister came to her and severely repremanded her, for making use of a Diabolical help, and told her, she was in danger of Damnation for it, and commanded her to burn it. She did so, and her Distemper returned severely ; insomuch that she was importunate with the Doctor to use the same again : She used it, and had ease. But the Parson hearing of it, came to her again, and thundred Hell and Damnation, and frighted her so, that she burnt it again. Whereupon she fell extremely Ill, and would have had it a Third time, but the Doctor refused, saying, *That she had contemned and slighted the power and goodness of the Blessed Spirits (or Angels)* and so she died. The cause of the Lady Honywoods Desparation, was that she had used a Spell to Cure her.

In Dr. Bolton's *Sermons* is an Account of the Lady Honywood, who despaired of her Salvation. Dr. Bolton endeavour'd to comfort her : Said she (holding a Venice-glass in her Hand) I shall as certainly be Damned, as this Glass will be broken : And at that word, threw it hard on the Ground ; and the Glass remained sound ; which did give her great comfort. The Glass is yet preserved among the *Cimelia* of the Family. This Lady lived to see descended from her (I think) Ninety, which is mentioned by Dr. Bolton.

Dr. Napier was uncle and Godfather to Sir Richard Napier : he was no Doctor, but a Divine and practised Physick ; but gave most to the Poor that he got by it. When a Patient, or Querant came to him, he presently went to his Closet to Pray : It appears by his Papers, that he did converse with the Angel

Raphael, who gave him the Responses, and told to admiration the Recovery or Death of the Patient. His knees were horny with frequent Praying. 'Tis certain, he foretold his own Death to a Day and Hour; he dyed Praying upon his Knees; being of a very great Age, 1634 April the First.

Sir Richard Napier is buryed at Lindford, but died at Besels-leigh; but before he came thither he laye at an Inne, where, when the Chamberlain brought him up to his Chamber, and the Dr. look't on the bed and sawe a dead man lye in or on the bed—*What!* sayd he, *do you lodge me where a dead man lies?* Said the Chamberlain, *Sir, here is no dead man.* The Dr. look't at it again, and sawe it was himselfe. And from thence he went (ill) to Besil's-leigh, and died.

JOHN OGILBY

[Born 1600. Dancing master, author and publisher. He was entrusted with *the poetical part* of Charles II's coronation in 1661. He later became a publisher, printing many splendid books, mostly in folio, *adorned with sculpture* by Hollar and other eminent engravers : and the King issued a proclamation in 1665 forbidding anyone to represent or *counterfeit the sculpture* in them for fifteen years. To facilitate the sale of these luxurious volumes, Ogilby established a lottery under Royal patronage, in which all the prizes were books of his own editing and publishing, and Pepys was successful in one of the draws ; but Ogilby complained that the losing subscribers would not pay. John Ogilby was ridiculed by Dryden and Pope and his name has become almost proverbial for a bad poet. He died in 1676.]

M R. JOHN OGILBY would not tell where in Scotland he was borne. He sayd drollingly that he would have as great contests hereafter for the place of his Birth, as was of Homer's.

He was of a Gentleman's family, and bred to his Grammar. His father had spent his Estate, and fell to decay, and was a Prisoner of the King's Bench, whom, together with his Mother, his son relieved by his own Industry (Spangles, needles), being then but about the age of 12 or 13 yeares. By the advantage of his Sonne's industry, he raysed a small summe of Money, which he adventured in the Lottery for the advancement of the Plantation in Virginia ; and he gott out of prison by this meanes. His motto (of his lott) was,

> *I am a poor prisoner, God wott,*
> *God send me a good Lott,*
> *I'le come out of prison, and pay all my debt.*

It so happened that he had a very good Lott, that did pay his Debts.

John (the Son) bound himself Apprentice to one Mr. Draper, who kept a dancing-schoole in Grayes-Inne-lane, and in short time arrived to so great excellence in that art, that he found meanes to purchase his time of his Master and sett up for himselfe. Mr. John Lacy, the Player, from whom I take this Information, was his apprentice.

When the Duke of Buckingham's great Masque was represented at Court, he was chosen (among the rest) to performe some extraordinary part in it ; and high-danceing, i.e. vaulting and cutting capers being then in Fashion, he, endeavouring to doe something extraordinary, by misfortune of a false step when he came to the ground, did spraine a veine on the inside of his Leg, of which he was lame for ever after, which gave an occasion to say that *he was an excellent Dancing master, but never a good Leg*.

He taught 2 of the Lord Hopton's (then Sir Ralph) sisters to dance ; and Sir Ralph taught him to handle the pike and Musket, *scil.* all the Postures.

He went over into Ireland to Thomas, Earle of Strafford, Lord Liuetenant there. Mr. J. O. was in the Lord Lieutenant's Troope of Guards, and taught his Lady and Children to dance ; that was his Place. And here it was that first he gave proofe of his inclination to Poetry, by Paraphrasing upon some of Aesop's *fables*.

Upon this Mr. Chantrel putt him upon learning the Latin tongue (in the 40 aetat, plus) and taught him himself and tooke a great deale of paines with him. This was the first time he began his Latin. He printed Virgill, translated by himselfe into English verse, 8vo, dedicated to the Right Honourable William, Lord Marquesse of Hertford, who loved him very well. Aesop, in 4to, next. He writt a fine hand.

He had a warrant from the Lord Livetenant to be Master of the Ceremonies for that Kingdome ; and built a little theatre in St. Warburgh street, in Dublin. It was a short time before the Rebellion brake out, by which he was undon, and ran thorough many hazards, and particularly being like to have been blow'n-up at the Caste of Refarnum neer Dublin.

He stayed in Ireland a good while after the Warres broke-out : came into England about the yeare 1648. He was wreckt at Sea, and came to London very poor, and went on foot to Cambridge.

After he had translated Virgil, he learnt Greeke in 1653 of Mr. Whitfield, a Scotch Bishop's son, and grew so great a proficient in it that he fell-to to translate Homer's *Iliads,* 1660.

Next, as if by a prophetique spirit, foreseeing the restauration of King Charles II, and also the want there might be of Church Bibles, he printed the fairest Impression, and the most correct of English Bibles, in Royall and Imperiall paper, that ever was yet donne.

1662, he went into Ireland again, being then *by Patent* (before, but *by Warrant*) Master of the Revells (having disputed his

Right with Sir William Davenant, who had gott a Graunt) and built a noble theatre at Dublin, which cost 2000 pounds, the former being ruind and spoyled in the Troubles, and a cowhouse made of the stage.

His *Odysses* came out in 1665. People did then suspect, or would not beleeve that 'twas he was the Author of the paraphrase upon Æsop, and to convince them he published a 2ᵈ volume, which he calles his *Æsopiques*, which he did during the Sicknesse, in his retirement at Kingston upon Thames.

His *History of China*, in folio, before the Fire; then his *History of Japan*. The generall and dreadfull Conflagration burn't all that he had, that he was faine to begin the world again, being then at best worth 5 pounds.

Being thus utterly undon again by the Fire, he made his Proposalls for the printing of a faire English *Atlas*, of which he lived to finish the Historys of Africa, America, and part of Asia. And then, being encouraged by the King and the Nobility to make an actuall Survey of England and Wales, he proceeded in it so far as to an actuall Survey of the Roads both in England and Wales, which composed his Volume of his *Britannia*.

He had such an excellent and prudentiall Witt, and master of so good addresse, that when he was undon he could not only shift handsomely (which is a great mastery) but he would make such rationall proposalls that would be embraced by rich and great men, that in a short time he could gaine a good Estate again, and never failed in any thing he evr undertooke but allwayes went through with profits and glorie.

WILLIAM OUGHTRED

[Born 1574. Mathematician. Educated at Eton and King's College, Cambridge. Ordained 1603. Vicar of Albury in Surrey 1610. Published *Clavis Mathematicae* 1631. Wrote *Circles of Proportion* and other works. He invented trigonometrical abbreviations and introduced the multiplication and proportion signs. Died 1660.]

HIS Father taught to write at Eaton, and was a Scrivener; and understood common Arithmetique, and 'twas no small helpe and furtherance to his son to be instructed in it when a schoole-boy. His Grandfather came from the North for Killing a man. The last Knight of the Family was one Sir Jeffrey Oughtred. I thinke a Northumberland family.

Anno Domini 1610 he was instituted and inducted into the Rectory or Parsonage of Albury, in com. Surrey, worth a hundred pounds per annum: he was Pastor of this place fifty yeares.

William Oughtred, that was an Honour to the English Nation, maried Mrs. Caryl (an ancient Family in those parts) by whom he had nine sonnes (most lived to be men) and four daughters. None of his sonnes he could make scholars.

He was a little man, had black haire, and blacke eies (with a great deal of spirit). His head was always working. He would drawe lines and diagrams on the Dust.

His oldest son Benjamin, who lives with my cosen Boothby (who carresses him, and gives him his Dyet, and a little House near to lie in) and now an old man, he bound Apprentice to a Watchmaker; who did worke pretty well, but his sight now failes for that fine worke. He told me that his father did use to lye a bed till 11 or twelve a clock, with his Doublet on, ever since he can remember. Studyed late at night; went not to bed till eleaven a clock; had his tinder box by him; and on the top of his Bed-staffe, he had his Inke horne fix't. He slept but little. Sometimes he went not to bed in two or three nights, and would not come downe to meales till he had found out the *quaesitum*.

He was more famous abroad for his learning, and more esteemed, then at home. Severall great Mathematicians came over into England on purpose to converse with him. His countrey neighbours (though they understood not his worth) knew that there must be extraordinary worth in him, that he was so visited by Foreigners.

When Mr. Seth Ward, M.A., and Mr. Charles Scarborough, D.M., came as in Pilgrimage, to see him and admire him, Mr. Oughtred had against their comeing prepared a good dinner, and also he had dressed himselfe, thus; an old red russet cloath-cassock that had been black in dayes of yore, girt with a old leather girdle, an old fashion russet hatt, that had been a Bever, *tempore Reginae Elizabethae*. When learned Foraigners came and sawe how privately he lived, they did admire and blesse themselves, that a person of so much worth and learning should not be better provided for.

Seth Ward, M.A., a Fellow of Sydney Colledge in Cambridge (now Bishop of Sarum) came to him, and lived with him halfe a yeare (and he would not take a farthing for his diet) and learned all his Mathematiques of him. Sir Jonas More was with him a good while, and learn't; he was but an ordinary Logist before. Sir Charles Scarborough was his Scholar; so Dr. John Wallis was his Scholar; so was Christopher Wren his scholar; so was Mr. Smethwyck, R.S.S. But he did not so much like any as those that tugged and tooke paines to worke out Questions. He taught all free.

One Mr. Austin (a most ingeniose man) was his scholar, and studied so much that he became mad, fell a laughing, and so dyed, to the great griefe of the old Gentleman. Mr. Stokes, another scholar, fell mad, and dream't that the good old Gentleman came to him, and gave him good advice, and so he recovered, and is still well.

He could not endure to see a Scholar write an ill hand; he taught them all presently to mend their hands. Amongst others Mr. Thomas Henshawe, who when he came to him wrote a lamentable hand, he taught to write very well. He wrote a very elegant hand, and drew his Schemes most neatly, as they had been cut in copper. His father (no doubt) was an ingeniose artist at the Pen and taught him to write so well.

He was an Astrologer, and very lucky in giving his Judgements on Nativities; he confessed that he was not satisfied how it came about that one might foretell by the Starres, but so it was that it fell out true as he did often by his experience find; he did beleeve that some genius or spirit did help.

The Countrey people did beleeve that he could conjure, and 'tis like enough that he might be well enough contented to have them thinke so.

He has told Bishop Ward, and Mr. Elias Ashmole (who

[223]

was his neighbour) that on this spott of ground (or leaning against this Oake, or that ashe) the Solution of such or such a Probleme came into my head, as if infused by a Divine Genius, after I had thought on it without Successe for a yeare, two, or three.

Ben Oughtred told me that he had heard his father say to Mr. Allen (the famous Mathematicall Instrument-maker) in his shop, that he had found out the Longitude : *sed vix credo* [but I scarcely believe it].

I have heard Mr. Hobbes say, and very truely, that with all his great skill in Algebra, he did never add one Proposition to Geometrie : he could bind up a Bundle well.

He was a great lover of Chymistry, which he studied before his son Ben can remember, and continued it ; and told John Evelyn, of Detford, Esq., R.S.S., not above a yeare before he dyed, that if he were but five yeares (or three yeares) younger, he doubted not to find out the Philosopher's stone. It was made of the harshest cleare water that he could gett, which he lett stand to putrify, and evaporated by cimmering.

His wife was a penurious woman, and would not allow him to burne candle after Supper, by which meanes many a good notion is lost, and many a Probleme unsolved ; so that Mr. Henshawe, when he was there, bought candle, which was a great comfort to the old man.

The right hon^ble Thomas Howard, Earle of Arundel and Surrey, Lord High Marshall of England, was his great Patron, and loved him intirely. One time they were like to have been killed together by the fall at Albury of a grott, which fell downe but just as they were come out. My Lord had many Grotts about his house, cutt in the Sandy sides of hills, wherin he delighted to sitt and discourse.

In the time of the Civill Warres the Duke of Florence invited him over, and offered him 500 pounds per annum ; but he would not accept of it, because of his religion.

Notwithstanding all that has been sayd of this excellent man, he was in danger to have been Sequestred, and one Onslowe that was a great Stickler against the Royalists and a Member of the House of Commons and living not far from him—he translated his *Clavis* into English and dedicated it to him to clawe with him, and it did doe his businesse and saved him from Sequestration.

I have heard his neighbour Ministers say that he was a pittiful Preacher ; the reason was because he never studyed it, but bent all his thoughts on the Mathematiques ; but when he was in danger of being Sequestred for a Royalist, he fell to the study of divinity, and preacht (they sayd) admirably well, even in his old age.

He was a good Latinist and Graecian, as appears in a little Treatise of his against one Delamaine, a Joyner, who was so sawcy to write against him (I thinke about his *circles of Proportion*).

Nicolaus Mercator went to see him a few yeares before he dyed. 'Twas about Midsommer, and the weather was very hott, and the old gentleman had a good fire, and used Mr. Mercator with much humanity (being exceedingly taken with his excellent Mathematicall Witt) and one piece of his courtesie was, to be mighty importunate with him to sett on his upper hand next the fire ; he being cold (with age) thought he had been so too.

Before he dyed he burned a world of Papers, and sayd that the world was not worthy of them ; he was so superb. He burned also severall printed bookes, and would not stirre, till they were consumed. His son Ben was confident he understood Magique.

He dyed the 13ᵗʰ day of June, 1660, in the yeare of his age eighty-eight plus odde dayes. Ralph Greatrex, his great friend, the Mathematicall Instrument-maker, sayed he conceived he dyed with joy for the comeing-in of the King, which was the 29th of May before. *And are yee sure he is restored? Then give me a glasse of Sack to drinke his Sacred Majestie's health.* His spirits were then quite upon the wing to fly away.

The 15th of June he was buried in the chancell at Albury. I had much adoe to find the very place where the bones of this learned and good man lay (and 'twas but 16 yeares after his death). When I first ask't his son Ben, he told me that truly the griefe for his father's death was so great, that he did not remember the place—now I should have thought it would have made him remember it the better—but when he had putt on his considering cap (which was never like his father's) he told as aforesaid, with which others did agree.

I have desired Mr. John Evelyn, etc., to speake to our Patrone, the Duke of Norfolk, to bestowe a decent Inscription of marble on him, which will also perpetuate his Grace's fame.

JOHN OVERALL

[Born 1560. Divine. Regius Professor of Theology at Cambridge 1596–1607. Master of Catherine Hall 1598–1607. Dean of St. Pauls 1602. Took part in the Hampton Court Conference and the enlargement of the Church Catechism 1604. One of the Revisers of the Old Testament 1611. Bishop of Coventry and Lichfield (1614) and of Norwich 1618. He was not given to preaching, because *he found he had spoken Latin so long it was troublesome to him to speak English in a continued oration.* Died 1618.]

I KNOW not what he wrote or whether he was any more than a common-prayer Doctor : but most remarqueable by his Wife, who was the greatest Beautie of her time in England. That she was so, I have it attested from the famous Limmer Mr. Hoskins, and other old Painters, besides old Courtiers. She was not more beautifull than she was obligeing and kind, and was so tender-hearted that (truly) she could scarce denie any one. She had (they told me) the loveliest Eies that were ever seen, but wondrous wanton. When she came to Court, or to the Play-house, the Gallants would so flock about her. Richard the Earle of Dorset, and his brother Edward, since Earle, both did mightily adore her. And by their report he must have had a hard heart that did not admire her. Bishop Hall sayeth in his *Meditations* that there is none so old, that a beautifull person loves not ; nor so young, whom a lovely feature moves not.

The good old Deane, notwithstanding he knew well enough that he was horned, loved her infinitely : in so much that he was willing she should enjoy what she had a mind to.

Among others who were charmed by her was Sir John Selby, of Yorkshire. Old Mris. Tyndale (who knew her) remembers a song made of her and Sir John, part whereof was this, viz :—

> *The Deane of Paule's did search for his wife,*
> *and where d'ee thinke he found her ?*
> *Even upon Sir John Selbye's bed,*
> *as flatte as any Flounder.*

Of these two Lovers was made this following copie of Pastorall verses :

Downe lay the Shepherd Swaine
  so sober and demure
Wishing for his wench againe
  so bonny and so pure
With his head on hillock lowe
  and his armes akimboe,
And all was for the losse of his
  hye nonny nonny noe.

His Teares fell as thinne
  as water from the still,
His haire upon his chinne
  grew like Thyme upon a hill,
His cherry cheekes pale as snowe
  did testify his mickle woe
And all was for the losse of his
  hye nonny nonny noe.

Sweet she was, as kind a Love
  as ever fetter'd Swayne ;
Never such a daynty one
  shall man enjoy again.
Sett a thousand on a rowe
  I forbid that any showe
Ever the like of her
  hye nonny nonny noe.

Face she had of Filberd hue
  and bosom'd like a Swan
Back she had of bended Ewe,
  and wasted by a span.
Haire she had as black as Crowe
  from the head unto the toe
Downe downe all over her
  hye nonny nonny noe.

With her Mantle tuck't up high
  she foddered her flock
So bucksome and alluringly
  her knee upheld her smock
So nimbly did she use to goe
  so smooth she danc't on tip-toe,
That all the men were fond of her
  hye nonny nonny noe.

She smiled like a Holy-day,
  she simpred like the Spring,
She pranck't it like a Popingaie,
  and like a Swallow sing :
She trip't it like a barren Doe,
  she strutted like a gor-crowe,
Which made the men so fond of her
  hye nonny nonny noe.

To sport it on the merry downe
  to daunce the Lively Haye ;
To wrastle for a green gowne
  in heate of all the day
Never would she saye me no
  yet me thought I had thô
Never enough of her
  hye nonny nonny noe.

But gonne she is the prettiest Lasse
  that ever trod on plaine.
What ever hath betide of her
  blame not the Shepherd Swayne
For why? she was her owne Foe,
  and gave herselfe the overthrowe
By being so franke of her
  hye nonny nonny noe.

FINIS.

JOHN PELL

[Born 1611. Mathematician. M.A. of Trinity College, Cambridge, 1630. Professor of Mathematics at Amsterdam (1643) and at Breda 1646. Returned to England in 1652 and was employed by Cromwell as a diplomat in Switzerland from 1654 to 1658. Rector of Fobbing 1661–85. Vicar of Laindon 1663–85. D.D. Lambeth 1663. His mathematical reputation was great, but he accomplished little, and left nothing of moment. He died in poverty in 1685.]

JOHN PELL, S. T. Dr., was the son of John, who was the son of John. His father dyed when his son John was but 5 yeares old and six weekes, and left him an excellent Library.

He went to Schoole at the Free-schoole at Stenning, a Burrough towne in Sussex, at the first Founding of the schoole. At 13 yeares and a quarter old he went as good a scholar to Cambridge, to Trinity Colledge, as most Masters of Arts in the University (he understood Latin, Greek, and Hebrew) so that he played not much (one must imagine) with his schoolfellowes, for, when they had play-dayes, or after schoole-time, he spent his time in the Library aforesaid.

Before he went first out of England, he understood these Languages (besides his mother-tongue) viz. Latin, Greek, Hebrue, Arabique, Italian, French, Spanish, High-Dutch, and Low-Dutch.

Anno Domini 1632 he maried Ithamara Reginalds, second daughter to Mr. Henry Reginalds of London. He had by her 4 sonnes and 4 daughters borne in this order S., D., D., S., D., S., D., S.

In the year 1638 Mr. Theodore Haake came first to be acquainted with Mr. Pell by Mr. S. Hartlib's meanes, who having heard of his extraordinarie parts in all kinde of learning, especially the Mathematics, perswaded that the same might be farre more usefully employed and improved for the publick advancement of Learning, he never left soliciting and engaging frends heer to perswade Mr. Pell instead of keeping Scool, as he then did in Sussex, to come up to London, where he soon got into great esteem among the most learned, both Natives and Forreigners, with whom he conversed. But he so minded and followed still the Cultivating of his more abstracting

Studies, and naturally averse from suing or stooping much for what he was worthy of, it was a good while before he obtained any suteable place or settlement.

Mr. Haake recommended him once to my Lord Bishop of Lincoln (*quondam* Lord Keeper of England) who became very desirous to see the Man, inviting them of purpose to dine once with his Lordship for the freer discourse of all sorts of literature and Experiments, to get a touch and taste that satisfaction Mr. Pell could give him . Which proved so pertinent and abundant that my Lord put the question to him whether he would accept of a Benefice which he was ready, glad, and willing to bestow on him for his Encouragement. Mr. Pell thankd his Lordship, saying he was not capacitate for that, as being no Divine and having made the Mathematics his main studie, for the great publick need and usefullnesse therof, which he had in a manner devoted himself to improve and advance to the uttmost of his reach and abilities. Which answer pleased my Lord so well that he replyed, Alasse! what a sad case it is that in this great and opulent kingdome there is no publick encouragement for the excelling in any Profession but that of the Law and Divinity. Were I in place as once I was, I would never give over praying and pressing his Majesty till a noble Stock and Fund might be raised for so fundamentall, universally usefull, and eminent Science as Mathematicks. And therupon his Lordship requested Mr. Pell to befriend him with his visits as often as he could spare time, promising him always a very ·hearty welcome. Yet Mr. Pell who was no Courtier came there no more.

In the mean time he communicated to his friends his excellent *Idea Matheseos* in half a sheet of paper, which got him a great deal of repute, both at home and abroad, but no other special advantage, till Mr. John Morian, a very learned and expert Gentleman, gave Mr. Haake notice that Hortensius, Mathematical Professor at Amsterdam, was deceased, wishing that their friend Mr. Pell might succeed. Sir William Boswell, his Majestie's ambassador in Holland, being here then, Theodore Haake conferred with him about it, who promised all his assistance; and between them, and by these two, a call was procured from Amsterdam for Mr. Pell, in 1643 : and in May 1644 T. H. met him settled there on his return out of Denmarke. Where he was, among others, dearly welcome to Gerardus Joannes Vossius.

And soon after his fame was much augmented by his refuting a large book of Longomontanus *Quadratura,* which caused the Prince of Orange (Henry Frederick) being about to erect an Academie at Breda, to borrow Mr. Pell from the Magistrate of Amsterdam, to grace his new Academe with a man of that fame for a few years. And there being comfortably stayed, the most learned of the then Parliament heer, jealous that others should enjoy a countryman of their own, they never left offers and promises till they got him hither to be—they gave out—Professor Honorarius heer. But the successe prov'd soon deficient, and reduced him to much inconvenience, as having now a charge of a pretty large Family, viz. his wife with 4 or 5 children. And this continued till in 1654 Oliver, Lord Protector, sent him Envoyé to the Protestant Cantons of Switzerland; resided chiefly at Zurich. He was sent out with the Title of Ablegatus, but afterwards he had order to continue there with the Title of Resident.

In 1658 he returned into England and so little before the death of Oliver Cromwell that he never sawe him since he was Protector.

Memorandum that in his Negociation he did no disservice to King Charles II^d, nor to the church, as may appeare by his letters which are in the Secretarie's Office.

Richard Cromwell, Protector, did not fully pay him for his business in Piedmont, wherby he was in some want; and so when King Charles II had been at home ten months, Dr. Sanderson, Bishop of Lincoln, perswaded him to take Holy Orders.

Gilbert Sheldon, Lord Bishop of Lundon, gave Dr. Pell the scurvy Parsonage of Lanedon cum Basseldon in the infamous and unhealthy (aguesh) Hundreds of Essex (they call it Killpriest sarcastically) and King Charles the Second gave him the Parsonage of Fobing, 4 miles distant.

At Fobbing, seven curates dyed within the first ten yeares; in sixteen yeares, six of those that had been his Curates at Laindon are dead; besides those that went away from both places; and the death of his Wife, servants, and grandchildren.

Gilbert Sheldon being made Archbishop of Canterbury, John Pell was made one of his Cambridge Chapleines (He haz 2 Oxford Chaplaines and 2 Cambridge) and complaining one day to his Grace at Lambith of the unhealthinesse of his Benefice as abovesayd, sayd my Lord, I doe not intend that you shall live there. No, sayd Pell, but your Grace does intend that I shall die there.

Lord Brereton was sent to Breda to recieve the Instruction of this worthy Person, by his grandfather (George Goring, the Earle of Norwich) anno 1647, where he became a good proficient, especially in Algebra to which his Genius most inclined him and which he used to his dyeing day, which was 17 March, 1680 : lies buried in St. Martin's church in the Fields.

I cannot mention this Noble Lord but with a great deale of Passion, for a more vertuous person (besides his great learning) I never knew. I have had the honour of his acquaintance since his comeing from Breda into England. Never was there greater love between Master and Scholar then between Dr. Pell and this Scholar of his, whose death hath deprived this worthy Doctor of an ingeniose Companion and a usefull Friend.

Now by this time (1680) you doubt not but this great, learned man, famous both at home and abroad, haz obtained some considerable Dignity in the Church. You ought not in modestie to ghesse at lesse then a Deanery. Why, truly, he is stak't to this poor preferment still! For though the parishes are large, yet (Curates, etc., discharged) he cleares not above 3-score pound per annum (hardly fourscore) and lives in an obscure lodging, three stories high, in Jermyn Street, next to the signe of the Ship, wanting not only bookes but his proper MSS. which are many.

He could not cringe and sneake for preferment though otherwise no man more humble nor more communicative. He was cast into King's Bench prison for Debt Sept 7, 1680.

In March 1682 he was very kindly invited by Daniel Whistler, M.D., to live with him at the Physitians College in London, where he was very kindly entertained ; which the Dr. likt and accepted of, loving good cheer and good liquour, which the other did also ; where eating and drinking too much, was the cause of shortning his daies. About the middle of June he fell extreme sick of a Cold and removed to a grandchild of his maried to one Mr. Hastings in St. Margaret's Churchyard, Westminster, neer the tower, who now (1684) lives in Brownlow Street in Drury Lane, where he was like to have been burnt in his bed by a candle. Nov. 26, fell into convulsion fitts which had almost killed him.

Dr. Pell haz often sayd to me that when he solves a Question, he straines every nerve about him, and that now in his old age it brings him to a Loosenesse.

Dr. J. Pell was the first inventor of that excellent way or method of the marginall working in Algebra. He haz sayd to me that he did believe that he solved some questions *non sine Divino auxilio* [not without divine aid].

Dr. Pell had a brother a Chirurgian and Practitioner in Physick, who purchased an Estate of the Natives of New-York and when he died left it to his Nephew John Pell, only son of the Doctor, who is a Justice of the Peace in New Yorke, and lives well. It is a great estate 8 miles broad and several miles long. Dr. Pell thought to have gonne over to him.

[232]

Both his Parsonages are of the value of two hundred pounds per annum (or so accounted) but the Doctor was a most shiftless man as to worldly affaires, and his Tenants and Relations cousin'd him of the Profits and kept him so indigent that he wanted necessarys, even paper and Inke, and he had not 6d. in his purse when he dyed, and was buried by the Charity of Dr. Richard Busby and Dr. Sharp, Rector of St. Giles-in-the-fields and Dean of Norwich, who ordered his Body to lye in a Vault belonging to the Rector (the price is X pounds).

He dyed of a broaken heart.

WILLIAM PENN

[Born 1644. Quaker and founder of Pennsylvania. Educated at
Christ Church, Oxford, where he became a Quaker and was in consequence expelled from the University. For attacking the doctrines
of the Trinity, the Atonement and Justification by Faith, he was
imprisoned in the Tower in 1668, where he wrote *No Cross, No Crown*.
He was again imprisoned for preaching in 1671 and used his enforced
leisure to write *The Great Cause of Liberty of Conscience,* an able defence
of religious toleration. In 1681 he was granted the territory now
forming the State of Pennsylvania by Charles II, and he determined
to found there a community based upon the principles of toleration.
But his later years were embittered by troubles in Pennsylvania and
by the dishonesty of one of his agents, who nearly ruined him and who
was the cause of his being imprisoned for debt. He died soon after
his release in 1718.]

WILLIAM PENN was the eldest son of Sir William
Penn, Knight, Admirall both of the English Navy
before the Restauration of the King, and commanded
as Captain-Generall under the Duke of York in 1665 against
the Dutch Fleet. His father was .a very good man, but no
Quaker ; was very much against his sonne.

He was mighty lively but with Innocence, and extremely
tender under rebuke ; and very early delighted in retirement ;
much given to reading and meditating of the Scriptures, and
at 14 had marked over the Bible. Oftentimes at 13 or 14 in his
meditations ravisht with joy, and dissolved into teares.

The first Sense he had of God was when he was 11 yeares
old at Chigwell, being retired in a chamber alone ; he was
so suddenly surprized with an inward comfort and (as he
thought) an externall glory in the roome that he has many
times sayd that from thence he had the Seale of divinity and
Immortality, that there was a God and that the Soule of man
was capable of enjoying his divine communications. His
schoolmaster was not of his Perswasion.

About the Plague, growing entirely solitary, was employed
by his father in a Journey into Ireland to the Duke of Ormond's
court : the diversions of which not being able to keepe downe
the stronger motions of his Soule to a more religious and
retired life, upon the hearing of one Thomas Lowe, a Trades-

man, of Oxon at Cork, 1667, was so thoroughly convinced of the simplicity and selfe-deniall of the way of the people called Quakers that from thence he heartily espoused that Judgement and Beliefe.

Since which time he has passed a life of great variety of circumstances, both with respect to good and evill report, divers controversies orall and written, severall Imprisonments ; one in Ireland, one in the Tower, 3rd in Newgate.

Notwithstanding those many odd adventures of his Life, he hath severall times found favour from his Majestie and also the D. Y., with divers of the Nobilitye, and men of Quality and learning in this Kingdome.

Travelled into Germany, Upper and Lower, annis 1671 and 1677, where severall were affected with his way. Did he gaine any to him in France ? *Negat.*

His Majestie owing to his father 10,000 pounds (which, with the interest of it, came not to lesse than 20,000 pounds) did in consideration therof grant to him and his heirs a province in America which his Majesty was pleased to name Pennsylvania, the 4th day of March 1681. His Patent for Transylvania is from the beginning of the 40th degree to 43 degrees in Latitude, and 5 degrees in Longitude from Chisapeak-bay.

August 26, 1682, Saturday. This day about 4 a clock P.M., W. Penne, Esq., went towards Deale to launch for Pensylvania. God send him a prosperous and safe Voyage.

He speaks well the Latin and the French tongues, and his owne with great mastership. He was chosen, *nemine contradicente,* Fellow of the Royal Societie, London, with much respecte. He often declares in the Assemblies of his Friends, and that with much eloquence and fervency of spirit : by which, and his perpetuall attendances on King and Prince for the reliefs of his Friends, he often exposes his health to hazard.

W. Penn, Esq., married Gulielma Maria Springet, daughter of Sir William Springet, of the Springets of the Broyles in Sussex. She was a *posthuma* of her father, a young Gent. of Religion and courage who dyed at the Siege of Arundel. His daughter was his Image in person and qualities, virtuous, generous, wise, humble, plaine ; generally beloved for those good qualities and one more—the great cures she does, having great skill in physic and surgery, which she freely bestows.

She early espoused the same way, about anno 1657. She was a great fortune to her husband, being worth *de claro* above 10,000 pounds. Her fortune, quality, and good humour gave her the importunity of many suitors of extraordinary condition, e.g. Lord Brookes and Lord John Vaughan, etc. ; but valueing the Unity of beliefe and selfe deniall of her profession above the glories of the World, resisted their motions till Providence brought a man of equall condicion and fortune to herself to the syncere embracing of the same Fayth, whose mariage haz been crowned with a continued affection.

Sir William Penn, Knight, his father, was a man of excellent naturall abilities, not equalled in his time for the knowledge of navall affayres : and instrumentall to the raysing of many families. Bred his son religiously ; and, as the times grew loose, would have his sonn of the fashion, and was therfore extreme bitter at his sonne's retirement. But this lasted not alwayes ; for, in the conclusion of his life, he grew not only kind, but fonde ; made him the judge and ruler of his Family ; was sorry he had no more to leave him (and yet, in England and Ireland, he left him 1500 pounds per annum). But, which is most remarkeable, he that opposed his sonne's way because of the crosse that was in it to the world's Latitude, did himselfe embrace this faith, recommending to his son the plainesse and selfe deniall of it, sayeing, *Keep to the plainesse of your way, and you will make an end of the Priests to the ends of the Earth.* And so he deceased, desiring that none but his son William should close his eies (which he did).

SIR WILLIAM PETTY

[Born 1623. Political economist. He went to sea at an early age, but his precocious talents so excited the envy of his fellow-seamen that they deserted him on the coast of France with a broken leg. Instead of returning home, he studied on the Continent. He published economic treatises, the most important of which was entitled *Political Arithmetic* (1690) a term signifying what we now call statistics. He died in 1687.]

HIS father was by profession a clothier, and also did dye his owne cloathes : he left little or no estate to Sir William. About 12 or 13, i.e. before 15, he haz told me, happened to him the most remarkable *accident of life* (which he did not tell me) and which was the foundation of all the rest of his greatnes and acquiring riches. He haz told me that he never gott by Legacies, but only x pounds, which was not payd.

He enformed me that, about 15, in March, he went over into Normandy, to Caen, in a vessell that went hence, with a little stock, and began to play the merchant, and had so good successe that he maintained himselfe, and also educated himselfe ; this I guessed was that most remarkable *accident* that he meant. Here he learn't the French tongue, and perfected himselfe in the Latin (before, but a competent smattering) and had Greeke enough to serve his turne. Here (at Caen) he studied the Arts : he was sometime at La Flesshe in the college of Jesuites. At 18, he was (I have heard him say) a better Mathematician then he is now ; but when occasion is, he knows how to recurre to more mathematicall Knowledge. At Paris he studied Anatomie, and read Vesalius with Mr. Thomas Hobbes, who loved his company. Mr. H. then wrot his *Optiques* ; Sir W. P. then had a fine hand in drawing and limning, and drew Mr. Hobbes Opticall schemes for him, which he was pleased to like. At Paris, one time, it happened that he was driven to a great streight for money, and I have heard him say, that he lived a weeke on two peniworth (or 3, I have forgott which, but I thinke the former) of Walnutts.

He came to Oxon, and entred himselfe of Brasen-nose college. Here he taught Anatomy to the young Scholars. Anatomy was then but little understood by the university, and

I remember he kept a body that he brought by water from Reding a good while to read upon some way soused or pickled. About these times Experimentall Philosophy first budded here and was first cultivated by these Vertuosi in that darke time.

Anno Domini 1650 happened that memorable accident and experiment of the reviving Nan Green a servant maid, who was hang'd in the castle of Oxon for murdering her bastard-child. After she had suffer'd the law, she was cut downe, and carried away in order to be anatomiz'd by some yong physitians, but Dr. William Petty finding life in her, would not venter upon her, only so farr as to recover her life. Which being look'd upon as a great wonder, there was a relation of her recovery printed, and at the end several copies of verses made by the young poets of the Universitie were added.

He was about 1650 elected Professor of Musique at Gresham Colledge, by, and by the Interest of his Friend Captaine John Graunt (who wrote the Observations on the Bills of Mortality) and at that time was worth but fourtie pounds in all the world.

Shortly after, he was recommended to the Parliament to be one of the Surveyors of Ireland, to which employment Capt. John Graunt's interest did also help to give him a Lift, and Edmund Wyld, Esq., also, then a Member of Parliament, and a good fautor of Ingeniose and good men, for meer meritt sake (not being formerly acquainted with him) did him great service, which perhaps he knowes not of.

Severall made offers to the Parliament to survey it (when the Parliament ordered to have it surveyed) for 4000 pounds, 5000 pounds, 6000 pounds ; but Sir William (then Dr.) went *lower* then them all and gott it. Sir Jonas More contemnd it as dangerous, loving to sleepe in a whole skin : he was afrayd of the Tories.

By this Surveying Employment he gott an Estate in Ireland (before the restauration of King Charles II) of 18,000 pounds per annum, the greatest part wherof he was forced afterwards to refund, the former owners being then declared Innocents. He hath yet there 7 or 8000 pounds per annum and can, from the Mount Mangorton in the com. of Kerry, behold 50,000 Acres of his owne land. He hath an Estate in every province of Ireland.

The Kingdome of Ireland he hath surveyed, and that with that exactnesse, that there is no Estate there to the value of threscore pounds per annum but he can shew, to the value, and those that he employed for the Geometricall part were ordinary fellowes, some (perhaps) foot-soldiers, that circumambulated with their *box and needles,* not knowing what they did, which Sir William knew right well how to make use of.

I remember about 1660 there was a great difference between him and Sir Hierome Sanchy, one of Oliver's knights. They printed one against the other : this knight was wont to preach at Dublin. The Knight had been a Soldier, and challenged Sir William to fight with him. Sir William is extremely short sighted, and being the challengee it belonged to him to nominate place and weapon. He nominates, for the place, a darke Cellar, and the weapon to be a great Carpenter's Axe. This turned the knight's challenge into Ridicule, and so it came to nought.

Before he went into Ireland, he sollicited, and no doubt he was an admirable good Sollicitor. I have heard him say that in Solliciting (with the same paines) he could dispatch severall businesses, nay, better than one alone, for by conversing with severall he should gaine the more knowledge, and the greater Interest.

In the time of the Warre with the Dutch, they concluded at the Councell-board at London, to have so many sea men out of Irland (I think 1500). Away to Irland came one with a Commission, and acquaints Sir William with it ; sayes Sir William, You will never rayse this number here. Oh, sayd the other, I warrant you, I will not abate you a man. Now Sir William knew 'twas impossible, for he knew how many Tunne of shipping belongd to Ireland, and the rule is, to so many tunnes so many men. Of these shipps halfe were abroad, and of those at home so many men unfit. In fine, the Commissioner with all his diligence could not possibly rayse above 200 seamen there. So we may see how statesmen may mistake for want of this Politique Arithmetique.

Another time the Councell at Dublin were all in a great racket for the prohibition of Coale from England and Wales, considering that all about Dublin is such a vast quantity of Turfe ; so they would improve their rents, sett poor men on worke, and the City should be served with Fuell cheaper. Sir William prima facie knew that this project could not succeed. Sayd he, If you will make an order to hinder the bringing-in of Coales by foreigne vessells, and bring it in Vessells of your owne, I approve of it very well : But for your supposition of the cheapnesse of the Turfe, 'tis true 'tis cheape on the place, but consider carriage, consider the yards that must contayn such a quantity for respective houses, these yards must be rented ; what will be the chardge ? They supputated, and found that (every thing considered) 'twas much dearer then to fetch coale from Wales, or etc.

Sir W. Petty was a Rota man, and troubled Mr. James Harrington with his Arithmeticall proportions, reducing Politie to Numbers.

Anno 1660 he came into England, and was presently recieved into good grace with his Majestie, who was mightily pleased with his discourse. He can be an excellent Droll (if he haz a mind to it) and will preach *extempore* incomparably, either the Presbyterian way, Independent, Cappucin frier, or Jesuite.

I remember one St. Andrewe's day (which is the day of the Generall Meeting of the Royall Society for Annuall Elections) I sayd, Methought 'twas not so well that we should pitch upon the Patron of Scotland's day, we should rather have taken St. George or St. Isidore (a Philosopher canonized). No, said Sir William, I would rather have had it on St. Thomas day, for he would not beleeve till he had seen and putt his fingers into the Holes, according to the Motto *Nullius in verba* [not bound to swear obedience to any man's dogma].

Anno Domini 1663 he made his double-bottom'd Vessell (launched about New-yeare's tide) of which he gave a Modell to the Royall Societie made with his owne hands, and it is kept in the Repository at Gresham College. It did doe very good service, but happned to be lost in an extraordinary storme in the Irish sea. About 1665 he presented to the Royall Societie a Discourse of his (in manuscript, of about a Quire of paper) of Building of Shippes, which the Lord Brounker (then President) tooke away, and still keepes, saying, 'Twas too great an Arcanum of State to be commonly perused; but Sir William told me that Dr. Robert Wood, M.D. has a copie of it, which he himselfe haz not.

Anno Domini 1667 he maried on Trinity Sunday the relict of Sir Maurice Fenton, of Ireland, Knight, daughter of Sir Hasdras Waller of Ireland, a very beautifull and ingeniose Lady, browne, with glorious Eies, by whom he hath some sonnes and daughters, very lovely children, but all like the Mother. He has a naturall Daughter that much resembles him, no legitimate child so much, that acts at the Duke's Play-house.

He is a proper handsome man, measured six foot high, good head of browne haire, moderately turning up. His eies are a kind of goose-gray, but very short sighted, and, as to aspect, beautifull, and promise sweetnes of nature, and they doe not decieve, for he is a marvellous good-natured person. Eie-browes thick, darke, and straight (horizontall).

He is a person of an admirable inventive head, and practicall parts. He hath told me that he hath read but little, that is to say, not since 25 aetat., and is of Mr. Hobbes his mind, that had he read much, as some men have, he had not known so much as he does, nor should have made such Discoveries and improvements.

He had his patent for Earle of Kilmore and Baron of Shelbrooke, which he stifles during his life to avoyd Envy, but his Sonne will have the benefit of the Precedency. (I expected that his Sonne would have broken-out a Lord or Earle : but it seemes that he had enemies at the Court at Dublin, which out of envy obstructed the passing of his Patent.)

Monday, 20th March, he was affronted by Mr. Vernon : Tuesday following Sir William and his Ladie's brother (Mr. Waller) Hectored Mr. Vernon and caned him.

He has told me, that wheras some men have accidentally come into the way of preferment, by lying at an Inne, and there contracting an Acquaintance ; on the Roade ; or as some others have donne ; he never had any such like opportunity, but hewed out his Fortune himselfe. To be short, he is a person of so great worth and learning, and haz such a prodigious working witt, that he is both fitt for, and an honour to, the highest preferment.

Sir William Petty had a boy that whistled incomparably well. He after wayted on a Lady, a widowe, of good fortune. Every night this boy was to whistle his Lady asleepe. At last shee could hold out no longer, but bids her chamber-mayd withdrawe : bids him come to bed, setts him to worke, and marries him the next day. This is certeyn true.

Sir William Petty died at his house in Peccadilly-street (almost opposite to St. James church) on fryday, 16th day of December, 1687, of a Gangrene in his foot, occasioned by the swelling of the Gowt, and is buried with his father and mother in the church at Rumsey, a little Haven towne in Hampshire.

KATHERINE PHILIPS

[Born 1631. Poet. The daughter of John Fowler, a London merchant, she married James Philips in 1647. She adopted the pseudonym Orinda, to which her contemporaries prefixed the epithet Matchless. Her earliest verses were prefixed to the *Poems of Henry Vaughan* in 1651 and her collected verses appeared in 1667. She instituted a Society of Friendship, a literary salon for the discussion of poetry and similar topics. Her translation of Corneille's *Pompée* was acted in Dublin with great success. Cowley, in an elegy, mourned her death from smallpox in 1664.]

SHE was very religiously devoted when she was young; prayed by herself an hower together, and tooke Sermons verbatim when she was but 10 yeares old. (At the age of nine yeares, Thomas Randolph wrot the History of our Saviour's Incarnation in English verse, which his brother John haz to shew under his owne handwriting—never printed, kept as a Raritie.)

She was when a Child much against the Bishops, and prayd to God to take them to him, but afterwards was reconciled to them. Prayed aloud, as the hypocriticall fashion then was, and was overheared.

From her cosen Blacket, who lived with her from her swadling cloutes to eight, and taught her to read :—when a child she was mighty apt to learne, and she assures me that she had read the Bible thorough before she was full four yeares old ; she could have sayd I know not how many places of Scripture and chapters. She was a frequent Hearer of Sermons ; had an excellent Memory and could have brought away a sermon in her memory. Very good-natured ; not at all high-minded ; pretty fatt ; not tall ; read pumpled face ; wrote out Verses in Innes, or Mottos in windowes, in her table-booke.

Mr. J. Oxenbridge, her uncle, is now Prisoner in the Fleet on her account for a Dept of her husband, bound for him 28 yeares since.

SIR WILLIAM PLATERS

[Born 1590. Knighted 1623. Succeeded to his father's Baronetcy 1638. The loyal and gallant achievements of this gentleman and his son are recorded on his wife's tomb at Dickleburgh in Norfolk— Here under lyeth buried the body of Dame Frances Platers, the daughter and heir of Charles le Grys, of Billingford, in Norff., Esq. She married Sir William Playters, of Sotterley, in Suffolk, Knt. and Bart.; sometimes one of the deputie Lieuetenants and Vice-Admiral of the said countie, and Justice of the Peace and Coram; and Collonel of a regiment of foot, till turn'd out of all by the then rebellious Parliament; and in fine out of that Hous of Parliament, whereof he had the misfortune to be a member. She had issue by him only Thomas, who married with Rebecka, the daughter and co-heir of Tho. Chapman, of Woormly, in the county of Hartford, Esq., which said Sir Tho. was a great traveller before and after marriage, his ladie sometimes beyond the seas with him : a learned schollar; an exact linguist, expert in all arts and knowledge; of rare temper and courage; and of great esteem in most courts in Christendom; High Sheriff for the countie of Suffolk, by commission from His Majestie of blessed memory, 1646, till forc'd by that fatal Parliament to flee to the King at Oxford, where, by commission from his Majesty, he raised a regiment of Hors, wherewith he performed remarkable service, till his Majesties forces were totally ruin'd; and then he departed the Kingdome, arriving in Cicilia, where, by commission from that Viceroy, he had command of a squadron of six shipps against all enemies to the crown of Spain, which being prepared, he put to sea, and performed many gallant services, much to the honour of the Spanish flagg. In July, 1651, he put into the port of Messina with a very rich prize and posted to the court at Palermo, where he met with an honourable reception for the several good services he had performed; but at 4 days end he there fell ill of a violent fever, whereof within 8 days he died, aged about 35 years; and by the Princes ordir had an honourable interment, and much lamented there, but much greater cause at home, leaving no issue, but a sorrowful widow and sad childless parents. Sir William died in 1668.]

SIR WILLIAM PLATER, Knight, was a Cambridgeshire Gentleman. He had a good Estate, about 3000 pounds per annum. He was a very well bred Gentleman, as most was of those times; had travelled France, Italie, etc., and understood well those languages. He was one of the Long Parliament in the time of the late Warres.

He was a merry man in the raigne of the Saints.

He was a great admirer and lover of handsome woemen, and kept severall. Henry Martyn and he were great Cronies, but one time (about 1644) there was some difference between them : H. M. invited him to a Treat, where Sir William fell in love with one of his Misses and slockst her away, and Sir John Berkinhead inserted in his *Mercurius Aulicus* how the Saintes fell out. He was temperate and thriftie as to all other things.

He had onely one Sonne, who was handsome and ingeniose, and whome he cultivated with all imaginable care and Education, and, knowing that he was flesh and bloud, tooke care himselfe to provide sound and agreeable females for him. He allowed his son liberally, but enjoyned him still temperance, and to sett downe his expences.

His Sonne made a very good returne of his Education. He was a Colonel in the King's Army, and was killed in his service, which his father tooke so to heart that he enjoyed not himselfe afterwards.

SIR JOHN POPHAM

[Born 1531. Lawyer. Educated at Balliol College, Oxford. M.P. for Bristol 1571–83. Privy Councillor 1571. He drafted a Bill for preventing idleness by setting the poor to work (1572) and later drafted the Act for transporting vagabonds. Solicitor-General 1579. Speaker of the House of Commons 1580 : on being asked by Queen Elizabeth, shortly after the prorogation of Parliament, what had passed in the House, he replied, If it please your Majesty, seven weeks. Attorney-General 1581. Lord Chief Justice and knighted 1592. He presided at the trials of Essex, Raleigh and the Gunpowder Plotters. He died in 1607.]

HE for severall yeares addicted himselfe but little to the Studie of the Lawes, but profligate company, and was wont to tak a purse with them. His wife considered her and his condition, and at last prevailed with him to lead another life, and to stick to the Studie of the Lawe ; which upon her importunity he did, being then about thirtie yeares old. He spake to his wife to provide a very good Entertainment for his Camerades, to take his Leave of them, and after that day fell extremely hard to his Studie, and profited exceedingly. He was a strong, stout man, and could endure to sit at it day and night, became eminent in his calling, had good practise ; called to be a serjeant, and a Judge.

Sir John Dayrell of Littlecote in Com. Wilts having gott his Ladie's waiting woman with child, when her travell came sent a servant with a horse for a midwife, whom he was to bring hood-winked. She was brought and layd the woman, but as soon as the child was borne, she saw the Knight take the Child and murther it, and burn it in the fire in the chamber. She having donne her businesse was extraordinarily rewarded for her paines, and sent blinfold away. This horrid Action did much run in her mind, and she had a desire to discover it, but knew not where 'twas. She considerd with her selfe the time that she was riding, and how many miles might be rode at that rate in that time, and that it must be some great person's house, for the roome was twelve foot high ; and she could knowe the chamber if she sawe it. She went to a Justice of peace, and search was made. The very chamber found. The Knight was brought to his Tryall, and, to be short, this Judge had this noble Howse, parke and mannor, and (I thinke) more for a Bribe to save his life : Sir John Popham gave Sentence according to Lawe ; but being a Great person, and a Favourite, he procured a *Noli prosequi*.

I have seen his picture ; he was a huge, heavie, ugly man. He left a vast estate to his son, Sir Francis (I thinke ten thousand pounds per annum) he lived like a hog, but his sonne John was a great waster, and dyed in his father's time. He was the greatest Howse-keeper in England ; would have at Littlecote four or five or more Lords at a time. His wife (Harvey) was worth to him I thinke 60,000 pounds, and she was as vaine as he, and she sayd that she had brought such an estate, and she scorned but she would live as high as he did, and in her husband's abscence would have all the woemen of the countrey thither, and feast them and make them drunke ; as she would be herselfe. They both dyed by excesse ; and, by Luxury, and cosonage by their servants, when he dyed there was, I thinke, a hundred thousand pound debt.

Old Sir Francis he lived like a hog at Hownstret in Somerset all this while with a moderate pittance.

Mr. John would say that his wive's estate was ill gott, and that was the reason they prospered no better. She would say that the old Judge gott the estate unjustly, and thus they would twitt one another, and that with matter of trueth.

I remember this Epitaph was made on Mr. John Popham :

> *Here lies he who not long since*
> *Kept a Table like a Prince,*
> *Till Death came, and tooke away.*
> *Then ask't the old man, what's to pay?*

Lord Chief Justice Popham first brought in (i.e. revived) Brick building in London (*scil*. after Lincolne's Inne and St. James's) and first sett-afoote the Plantations, e.g. Virginia, which he stockt or planted out of all the Gaoles of England.

At the Hall in Wellington, in the Countie of Somerset (the ancient seate of the Popham's) and which was this Sir John's, Lord Chiefe Justice, hang Iron Shackells : of which the Tradicion of the Countrey is, that long agoe, one of the Pophams (Lord of this place) was taken and kept a slave by the Turkes, for a good while, and that by his Ladie's great pietie and continuall prayers he was brought to this place by an invisible power with these Shackells on his legges, which were hung-up as a memoriall, and continued till the Howse (being a Garrison) was burn't. All the Countrey people steadfastly beleeve the trueth thereof.

FRANCIS POTTER

[Born 1594. Divine and Mechanician. Master of Arts at Trinity College, Oxford, 1616. Bachelor of Divinity 1625. Rector of Kilmington 1628–78. Fellow of the Royal Society 1663. His book *The Number of the Beast* was commended by Joseph Mead as *a wonderful discovery, the happiest that ever yet came into the world,* and as calculated *to make some of your German speculatives half wild.* Died 1678.]

ANNO AETATIS 15 he went to Trinity Colledge in Oxon, where his brother Hannibal was his Tutor. Here he was a Commoner twenty-seaven yeares, and was senior to all the house, but Dr. Kettle and his brother.

His Genius lay most of all to the Mechanicks; he had an admirable mechanicall Invention, but in that darke time wanted encouragement, and when his father dyed, he succeeded him in the Parsonage of Kilmanton, worth, per annum, about 140 pounds.

Anno Domini 1625, goeing into his chamber, the notion of 25, the roote of 666, for the roote of the number of the Beast in the Revelation, came into his head; so he opposed 25 to 12, the roote of 144.

He published nothing but his *Interpretation of the number* 666, in 4to, printed at Oxford, 1642, which haz been twice translated into Latin, into French, and other languages. Mr. Launcelot Moorhouse, a very learned man, and a solid and profound Mathematician, wrote against Mr. Francis Potter's booke of 666, and falls upon him, for that 25 is not the true roote, but the propinque root; to which Mr. Potter replied with some sharpnes, and that it ought not to be the true roote, for this agrees better with his purpose.

When he tooke his Degree of Batchelaur in Divinity, his Question was, *An Papa sit Anti-Christus?* [Whether the Pope be Anti-Christ?] In his younger yeares he was very apt to fall into a Swoune, and so he did when he was disputing in the Divinity-schoole upon that Question. I remember he told me that one time reading Aristotle *De Natura Animalium,* where he describes how that the Lionesses, when great with young, and neer their time of parturition, doe goe between two trees that growe neer together, and squeeze out their young ones out of their bellies ; he had such a strong Idea of this, and of the paine that the lionesse was in, that he fell into a Swoune.

He was of a very tender constitution, and sickly most of his younger yeares. His manner was, when he was beginning to be sick, to *breath strongly* a good while together, which he sayed did emitt the noxious vapours. As he was never a strong man, so in his later times he had his health best ; only about four or five yeares before his death his eie-sight was bad, and before he dyed quite lost.

He look't the most like a Monk, or one of the Pastours of the old time, that ever I saw one. He was pretty long visagd and pale cleare skin, gray eie. His discourse was admirable, and all new and unvulgar. His house was as undeckt as a Monke's cell ; yet he had there so many ingeniose inventions that it was very delightfull. I never have enjoyed so much pleasure, nor ever was so much pleased with such Philosophicall and heartie Entertainment as from him.

On the buttery-dore in his Parlour he drew his father's picture at length, with his booke (fore-shortned) and on the spectacles in his hand is the reflection of the Gothique South windowe. I mention this picture the rather, because in processe of time it may be mistaken by tradition for his son Francis's picture, author of the booke aforesayd. He was from a Boy given to draweing and painting. The Founder's (Sir Thomas Pope's) picture in Trinity colledge hall is of his copying.

He was alwayes much Contemplative, and had an excellent Philosophicall head. He was no great read man ; he had a competent knowledge in the Latin, Greeke, and Hebrue tongues, but not a Critique. Greeke he learn'd by Montanus's *Interlineary Testament,* after he was a man, without a Grammar, and then he read Homer. He understood only common Arithmetique, and never went farther in Geometrie then the first six bookes of Euclid ; but he had such an inventive head, that with this foundation he was able to doe great matters in the Mechaniques, and to solve *phaenomena* in naturall philosophy. He had but few bookes, which when he dyed were sold for fifty-six shillings, and surely no great bargaine.

He invented and made with his owne handes a paire of beame Compasses, which will divide an inch into a hundred or a thousand parts. I have heard him say that he had never seen a water-house-engine, but that he could invent a better.

At the Epiphanie, 1649, when I was at his house, he then told me his notion of curing diseases, etc., by Transfusion of Bloud out of one man into another, and that the hint came into his head reflecting on Ovid's story of Medea and Jason, and that this was a matter of ten yeares before that time. About a yeare after, he and I went to trye the experiment, but 'twas on a Hen, and the creature to little and our tooles not good : I then sent him a Surgeon's Lancet. Anno 1652, I recieved a letter from him concerning this Subject, which many yeares since I shewed, and was read and entred in the bookes of the Royall Societie, for Dr. Lower would have arrogated the Invention to himselfe, and now one R. Griffith, Dr. of Physique, of Richmond, is publishing a booke of the transfusion of bloud. (Mr. Meredith Lloyd tells me that Libavius speakes of the Transfusion of Bloud, which I dare sweare Mr. F. Potter never sawe in his life.)

In the troublesome times 'twas his happinesse never to bee sequestred. He was once maliciously informed against to the Committee at Wells (a thing very common in those times). When he came before them, one of them (I have forgot his name) gave him a pint of wine, and gave him great prayse, and bade him goe home, and feare nothing.

He haz told me that he had oftentimes dream't that he was at Rome, and being in fright that he should be seised on and brought before the Pope, did wake with the feare. (Pope Innocent IV, against whom Robert Grotest, Bishop of Lincolne, wrote, dreamt that the Bishop of Lincolne came to him, and gave him a great blowe over the face with his Staffe.)

'Twas pitty that such a delicate inventive Witt should be staked to a private preferment in an obscure corner where he wanted ingeniose conversation, from whence men rarely emerge to higher preferment, but contract a mosse on them like an old pale in an Orchard for want of ingeniose conversation, which is a great want even to the deepest thinking men (as Mr. Hobbes haz often sayd to me).

The last time I sawe this honoured friend of mine, Octob. 1674, I had not seen him in 3 yeares before, and his lippitude then was come even to blindnesse, which did much grieve me to behold. He had let his beard be uncutt, which was wont to be but little. I asked him why he did not get some kinswoman or kinsman of his to live with him, and looke to him now in his great age ? He answer'd me that he had tryed that way, and found it not so well ; for they did begrudge what he spent that 'twas too much and went from them, whereas his servants (strangers) were kind to him and tooke care of him.

WILLIAM PRYNNE

[Born 1600. Controversial writer. Educated at Oxford, he studied law at Lincoln's Inn until he became immersed in writing controversial pamphlets, the best known of which was his *Histrio-Mastix, or a Scourge for Stage Players* (1633), a bitter attack on most of the popular amusements of the day. For writing it, Prynne was brought before the Star Chamber, fined £5000, pilloried, and had both his ears cut off, besides being sentenced to imprisonment for life. Undeterred by this, he issued from his prison a fierce attack on Laud and the hierarchy, for which he was again fined, pilloried, and branded on both cheeks with the letters S.L. for Seditious Libeller. Removed to Carnavon Castle, he remained there until liberated in 1641 by the Long Parliament. He soon after became a Member of the House and joined with extreme rancour in the prosecution of Laud. He then turned his attacks onto the Independents, the Army and the Protectorate, and was among those expelled from the House of Commons by Cromwell, whom he had opposed in regard to the execution of the King with such asperity that he again suffered imprisonment, from which he was released in 1652. He supported the Restoration and was by Charles II appointed Keeper of the Records in the Tower, where he did good service by compiling the *Calendar of Parliamentary Writs and Records*. He published altogether about two hundred books and pamphlets, dying in 1669.]

ANNO 1637 he was stigmatized in the Pillorie, and then Banished to Cornet-castle in Guernsey, where he was very civilly treated by the Governour Carteret, a very ancient familie in that Island. His Eares were not quite cutt off, only the upper part, his tippes were visible. Bishop William Lawd, A. B. Cant., was much blamed for being a Spectator, when he was his Judge. Anno 1641 he was, with Burton and Bastwyck, called home by the Parliament, and hundreds mett him and them out of London some miles.

He was a learned man, of immense reading, but is much blamed for his unfaithfull quotations. He was of a strange Saturnine complexion. Sir C. W. sayd once, that he had the countenance of a Witch.

His manner of Studie was thus : he wore a long quilt cap, which came 2 or 3, at least, inches over his eies, which served him as an Umbrella to defend his Eies from the light. About every three houres his man was to bring him a roll and a pott of Ale to refocillate his wasted spirits : so he studied and dranke, and munched some bread ; and this maintained him till night, and then, he made a good Supper : now he did well not to dine, which breakes of one's fancy, which will not presently be regained : and 'tis with Invention as a flux, when once it is flowing, it runnes amaine : if it is checked, flowes but *guttim* : and the like for perspiration, check it, and 'tis spoyled.

He endured severall Imprisonments for the King's cause, and was (really) very instrumentall in his restauracion.

Upon the opening of the Parliament, viz. letting in the Secluded Members, he girt on his old long rustie Sword (longer then ordinary.) Sir William Waller marching behind him (as he went to the Howse) W. Prynne's long sword ranne between Sir William's short legges, and threw him downe, which caused laughter.

ELEANOR RADCLIFFE :
COUNTESS OF SUSSEX

[Wife of Edward Radcliffe, who became the sixth Earl of Sussex on the death of his cousin in 1629. He died without issue in 1641 and his widow died in 1666.]

COUNTESS OF SUSSEX, a great and sad example of the power of Lust and Slavery of it. She was as great a beautie as any in England, and had a good Witt. After her Lord's death (he was jealous) she sends for one (formerly her Footman) and makes him groom of the chamber. He had the Pox and shee knew it ; a damnable Sott. He waz not very handsom, but his body of an exquisite shape (*hinc sagittae*). His Nostrils were stufft and borne out with corkes in which were quills to breath through. About 1666 this Countesse dyed of the Pox.

SIR WALTER RALEIGH

[Born 1552. Military and naval commander and author. He
served as a soldier in France and Ireland. Became a favourite of
Queen Elizabeth, who vastly enriched him. Founded the first
Virginia colony, explored Guiana, led an attack on the Spanish navy
at Cadiz (1596) besides other naval ventures. The death of Elizabeth
in 1603 was the turning-point in Raleigh's fortunes. Thenceforward
disaster clouded his days. He was unjustly sentenced to death for
treason in 1603, and though he was reprieved, spent thirteen years
in the Tower. Released in 1615 he set out on his last voyage to
Guiana, which proved a failure and in which he lost his eldest son.
He returned a broken and dying man, but met with no pity from his
ungenerous King, who, urged, it is believed, by the King of Spain,
had him beheaded on 29th October, 1618.)

IN his youth for several yeares he was under streights for
want of money. I remember that Mr. Thomas Child, of
Worcestershire, told me that Sir Walter borrowed a Gowne
of him when he was at Oxford (they were both of the same
College) which he never restored, nor money for it.

He went into Ireland, where he served in the Warres, and
shewed much courage and conduct, but he would be perpetually
differing with (I thinke) Gray, then Lord Deputy, so that at
last the Hearing was to be at councell table before the Queen,
which was what he desired; where he told his Tale so well,
and with so goode a Grace and Presence, that the Queen tooke
especiall notice of him, and presently preferred him. So that
it must be before this that he served in the French warres.

Queen Elizabeth loved to have all the Servants of her Court
proper men, and as beforesaid Sir W. R.'s gracefull presence
was no meane recommendation to him. I thinke his first preferment at Court was, Captaine of her Majestie's Guard. There
came a countrey gentleman (or sufficient yeoman) up to Towne,
who had severall sonnes, but one an extraordinary proper
handsome fellowe, whom he did hope to have preferred to be
a Yeoman of the Guard. The father (a goodly man himselfe)
comes to Sir Walter Raleigh, a stranger to him, and told him
that he had brought up a boy that he would desire (having many
children) should be one of her Majestie's guard. Quod Sir
Walter Raleigh, had you spake for yourselfe I should readily

have graunted your desire, for your person deserves it, but I putt in no boyes. Said the father, Boy come in. The Son enters, about 18 or 19, but such a goodly proper young Fellow as Sir Walter had not seen the like : He was the tallest of all the Guard. Sir Walter Raleigh sweares him immediately ; and ordered him to carry up the first Dish at Dinner, where the Queen beheld him with admiration, as if a beautiful young Giant had stalked in with the service.

Sir Walter Raleigh was a great Chymist, and amongst some MSS. receipts I have seen some secrets from him. He studied most in his Sea-Voyages, where he carried always a Trunke of Bookes along with him, and had nothing to divert him. He made an excellent Cordiall, good in Feavers, etc. ; Mr. Robert Boyle haz the recipe, and makes it and does great Cures by it.

A person so much immerst in action all along, and in fabrication of his owne Fortunes (till his confinement in the Tower) could have but little time to study but what he could spare in the morning. He was no Slug ; without doubt he had a wonderfull waking spirit, and a great judgment to guide it.

Durham House was a noble palace ; after he came to his greatness he lived there or in some apartment of it. I well remember his study, which was a little turret that looked into and over the Thames, and had the prospect which is pleasant perhaps as any in the World, and which not only refreshes the eie-sight but cheeres the spirits, and (to speake my mind) I beleeve enlarges an ingeniose man's thoughts.

Shirburne castle, parke, mannor, etc., did belong (and still ought to belong) to the Church of Sarum. Sir W. R. begged it as a Bôn from Queen Elizabeth : where he built a delicate Lodge in the Park of Brick ; not big : but very convenient for the bignes, a place to retire from the Court in Summer time, and to contemplate, etc. Upon his attainder it was begged by the favorite Carr, Earl of Somerset, who forfeited it (I thinke) about the poysoning of Sir John Overbury. Then John, Earl of Bristowe, had it given him for his good service in the Ambassade in Spaine, and added two Wings to Sir Walter Raleighs Lodge. In short and indeed, 'tis a most sweet and pleasant place and site as any in the West : perhaps none like it.

He was a tall, handsome and bold man ; but his *naeve* was that he was damnable proud. Old Sir Robert Harley, of Brampton Brian Castle, who knew him, would say it was a great question who was the proudest, Sir Walter or Sir Thomas Overbury, but the difference that was, was judged on Sir Thomas's side.

Old John Long, who then wayted on Sir W. Long, being one time in the Privy-garden with his master, saw the Earle of Nottingham wipe the dust from Sir Walter R.'s shoes with his cloake, in compliment. He was a second to the Earle of Oxford in a Duell. Was acquainted and accepted with all the Hero's of our Nation in his time.

He had a most remarkeable aspect, an exceeding high forehead, long-faced and sour eie-lidded, a kind of pigge-eie. His Beard turnd up naturally.

In the great parlour at Downton, at Mr. Raleghs, is a good piece (an originall) of Sir W. in a white sattin doublet, all embroidered with rich pearles, and a mighty rich chaine of great Pearles about his neck, and the old servants have told me that the pearles were neer as big as the painted ones.

Old Sir Thomas Malett, one of the Justices of the King's bench *tempore Caroli I et II,* knew Sir Walter, and I have heard him say, that notwithstanding his so great Mastership in Style and his conversation with the learnedest and politest persons, yet he spake broad Devonshire to his dying day. His voice was small, as likewise were my schoolfellowes his grand-nephewes.

In his youth his Companions were boysterous blades, but generally those that had witt ; except otherwise uppon designe, to gett them engaged for him, e.g., Sir Charles Snell, of Kington Saint Michael in North Wilts, my good neighbour, an honest young gentleman but kept a perpetuall Sott. He engaged him to build a ship, the *Angel Gabriel,* for the Designe for Guiana, which cost him the mannor of Yatton Keynell, the farme at Easton Piers, Thornhill, and the church-lease of Bishops Cannings ; which ship, upon Sir Walter Raleigh's attainder, was forfeited.

In his youthful time was one Charles Chester, that often kept company with his acquaintance : he was a bold, impertenent fellowe, and they could never be at quiet for him ; a perpetuall talker, and made a noyse like a drumme in a roome. So one time at a taverne, Sir W. R. beates him and seales up his mouth, i.e. his upper and neather beard, with hard wax. From him Ben Jonson takes his Carlo Buffono (i.e. Jester) in *Every Man out of his Humour*.

He loved a wench well ; and one time getting up one of the Mayds of Honour up against a tree in a Wood ('twas his first Lady) who seemed at first boarding to be something fearfull of her Honour, and modest, she cryed, sweet Sir Walter, what doe you me ask ? Will you undoe me ? Nay, sweet Sir Walter ! Sweet Sir Walter ! Sir Walter ! At last, as the danger and the pleasure at the same time grew higher, she cryed in the extasey, Swisser Swatter Swisser Swatter. She proved with child, and I doubt not but this Hero tooke care of them both, as also that the Product was more than an ordinary mortal.

My old friend James Harrington, Esq., was well acquainted with Sir Benjamin Ruddyer, who was an acquaintance of Sir Walter Raleigh's. He told Mr. J. H. that Sir Walter Raleigh, being invited to dinner with some great person, where his son was to goe with him: He sayd to his Son, Thou art such a quarrelsome, affronting creature that I am ashamed to have such a Beare in my Company. Mr. Walt humbled himselfe to his Father, and promised he would behave himselfe mightily mannerly. So away they went, and Sir Benjamin, I thinke, with them. He sate next to his Father and was very demure at leaste halfe dinner time. Then sayd he, I this morning, not having the feare of God before my eies, but by the instigation of the devill, went to a Whore. I was very eager of her, kissed and embraced her, and went to enjoy her, but she thrust me from her, and vowed I should not, *For your father lay with me but an hower ago.* Sir Walt, being so strangely supprized and putt out of his countenance at so great a Table, gives his son a damned blow over the face; his son, as rude as he was, would not strike his father, but strikes over the face of the Gentleman that sate next to him, and sayed, *Box about, 'twill come to my Father anon..* 'Tis now a common used Proverb.

His intimate Acquaintance and Friends were:—Edward de Vere, Earle of Oxford, Sir Francis Vere, Sir Horatio Vere, Sir Francis Drake, Nicholas Hill, Thomas Cavendish, Mr. Thomas Hariot, Sir Walter Long, of Dracot in Wilts, Cavaliero Surff, Ben Johnson, etc.

Sir Walter was the first that brought Tobacco into England and into fashion. In our part of North Wilts, e.g. Malmesbury hundred, it first came into fashion by Sir Walter Long.

I have heard my grandfather Lyte say that one pipe was handed round from man to man about the Table. They had first silver pipes, the ordinary sort made use of a walnute-shell and a strawe.

It was sold then for its wayte in Silver. I have heard some of our old yeomen neighbours say, that when they went to Malmesbury or Chippenham market, they culled out their biggest shillings to lay in the Scales against the Tobacco.

Sir W. R., standing in a Stand at Sir Robert Poyntz parke at Acton (which was built by Sir Robert's Grandfather to keep his Whores in) tooke a pipe of Tobacco, which made the Ladies quitt it till he had donne.

Within these 35 yeares 'twas scandalous for a Divine to take Tobacco. Now, the Customes of it are the greatest his Majestie hath.

I have now forgott whether Sir Walter Raleigh was not for the putting of Mary Queen of Scotts to death ; I thinke, yea : but besides that, at a consultation at Whitehall after Queen Elizabeth's death, how matters were to be ordered and what ought to be donne, Sir Walter Raleigh declared his opinion, 'twas the wisest way for them to keepe the Government in their owne hands and sett up a Commonwealth, and not to be subject to a needy, beggarly nation. It seems there were some of this caball who kept this not so secret but that it came to King James' eare, who, where the English Noblesse mett and received him, being told upon presentment to his Majesty their names, when Sir Walter Raleigh's name was told (Ralegh) said the King, O my soule, mon, I have heard rawly of thee.

It was a most stately sight, the glory of that Reception of his Majesty, where the Nobility and Gentry were in exceeding rich equippage, having enjoyed a long peace under the most excellent of Queens : and the Company was so exceeding numerous that their obedience carried a secret dread with it. King James did not inwardly like it, and, with an inward envy, sayd that he doubted not but that he should have been able on his owne strength (should the English have kept him out) to have dealt with them, and get his Right. Sayd Sir Walter Raleigh to him, Would to God that had been putt to the tryall : Why doe you wish that sayd the King. Because, sayd Sir Walter ; that then you would have known your friends from your foes. But that reason of Sir Walter was never forgotten nor forgiven.

He was such a person (every way) that (as King Charles I sayes of Lord Strafford) a Prince would rather be afrayd of then ashamed of. He had that awfulness and ascendency in his Aspect over other mortalls.

Old Major Stansby of Hants, a most intimate friend and neighbour and coetanean of the late Earle of Southampton (Lord Treasurer) told me from his friend, the Earle, that as to the plott and businesse about the Lord Cobham, he being then Governor of Jersey, would not fully doe things unless they would goe to his island, and there advise and resolve about it ; and that really and indeed Sir Walter's purpose was when he had them there, to have betrayed them and the plott, and to have them delivered up to the King and made his Peace.

As for his noble Design in Guiana ; *vide* a Latin voyage which John, Lord Vaughan, showed me, where is mention of

Captaine North (brother to the Lord North) who went with Sir Walter, where is a large account of these matters. Mr. Edmund Wyld knew him, and sayes he was a learned and sober Gentleman and good Mathematician, but if you happened to speake of Guiana he would be strangely passionate and say 'twas the blessedst countrey under the Sun, etc., reflecting on the spoyling that brave Designe.

Captain Roger North was a most accomplished Gentleman : he was a great Algebrist, which was rare in those dayes ; but he had the acquaintance of his fellow-Traveller Mr. Hariot. He had excellent Collections and Remarques of his Voyages, which were all unfortunately burnt in Fleet Street at the great Conflagration of the City. This Family speakes not well of Sir Walter Raleigh, that Sir Walter designed to breake with the Spanyard, and to make himselfe popular in England. When he came to Guiana, he could not show them where the Mines of Gold were. He would have then gonne to the King of France (Lewis XIII) but his owne men brought him back.

When Sir Walter Raleigh was carried prisoner from the West to London, he lay at Salisbury, where, by his great Skill in Chimistry, he made himself like a Leper : by which meanes he thought he might retard his journey to a Prison : and study his escape. Dr. Heydock was sent for to give his opinion, if the Prisoner might be carried to London without danger of his life. The Dr. feeles Sr. Walters Pulses, and found they did beat well : and so detected the Imposture.

I have heard old Major Cosh say that Sir W. Raleigh did not care to goe on the Thames in a Wherry-boate ; he would rather goe round about over London bridg.

When he was attached by the Officer about the business which cost him his head, he was carried in a whery, I thinke only with two men. King James was wont to say he was a Coward to be so taken and conveyed, for els he might easily have made his escape from so slight a guard.

I have heard my cosen Whitney say that he saw him in the Tower. He had a velvet cap laced, and a rich Gowne and trunke-hose.

He there (besides compiling his *History of the World*) studyed Chymistry. The Earle of Northumberland was prisoner at the same time, who was Patrone to Mr. Harriot and Mr. Warner, two of the best Mathematicians then in the world, as also Mr. Hues, who wrote *De Globis*. Serjeant Hoskins (the Poet) was a prisoner there too : he was Sir Walter's Aristarchus.

At the end of his *History of the World,* he laments the Death of the most noble and most hopefull Prince Henry, whose great

Favorite He was : and who, had he survived his father, would quickly have enlarged him ; with rewards of Honour. So upon the Prince's death ends his first part of his *History of the World*, with a gallant Eulogie of Him, and concludes : *Versa est in Luctum Cithara mea ; at cantus meus invocem flentium* [my lyre is changed into the sound of mourning ; and my song into the voices of people weeping].

His Booke sold very slowly at first, and the Booke-seller complayned of it, and told him that he should be a looser by it, which put Sir W. into a passion, and sayd that since the world did not understand it, they should not have his second part, which he tooke and threw into the fire, and burnt before his face.

He was scandalised with Atheisme ; but he was a bold man, and would venture at discourse which was unpleasant to the Church-men. I remember my Lord Scudamour sayd, 'twas basely sayd of Sir W. R. to talke of the Anagramme of Dog. In his speech on the Scaffold, I have heard my cosen Whitney say (and I thinke 'tis printed) that he spake not one word of Christ, but of the great and incomprehensible God, with much zeale and adoration, so that he concluded that he was an a-christ, not an atheist.

He tooke a pipe of Tobacco a little before he went to the scaffold, which some formall persons were scandalised at, but I thinke 'twas well and properly donne, to settle his spirits.

I remember I heard old father Symonds say that a father was at his execution, and that to his knowledge he dyed with a Lye in his mouth : I have now forgott what 'twas. The time of his Execution was contrived to be on my Lord Mayers day (viz. the day after St. Simon and St. Jude) 1618, that the Pageants and fine shewes might drawe away the people from beholding the Tragoedie of one of the gallants worthies that ever England bred. Buryed privately under the high altar at St. Margaret's Church in Westminster, in which grave (or neer) lies James Harrington, Esq., author of *Oceana*.

Mr. Elias Ashmole told me that his son Carew Ralegh told him that he had his father's Skull ; that some yeares since, upon digging up the grave, his skull and neck bone being viewed, they found the bone of his Neck lapped over, so that he could not have been hanged.

> *Even such is tyme that takes in Trust*
> *Our Youth, our Joyes, our all we have,*
> *And payes us but with Earth and Dust ;*
> *Who, in the darke and silent Grave,*

When we have wandered all our wayes
Shutts up the Story of our Dayes.
But from this Earth, this Grave, this Dust,
My God shall rayse me up I trust.

These Lines Sir Walter Raleigh wrote in his Bible, the night
before he was beheaded, and desired his Relations with these
words, viz. *beg my dead body, which living is denyed you ; and bury
it either in Sherbourne or Exeter Church.* He was somtimes a Poet,
not often.

A Scaffold was erected in the old Palace yard, upon which
after 14 yeares reprivement, his head was cutt off : at which
time, such abundance of bloud issued from his veines, that
shewed he had stock of nature enough left to have continued
him many yeares in life, though now above three score yeares
old, if it had not been taken away by the hand of Violence. And
this was the end of the great Sir Walter Raleigh : great sometimes in the favour of Queen Elizabeth, and next to Sir Francis
Drake, the great Scourge and hate of the Spaniard, who had
many things to be commended in his life, but none more than
his constancy at his death, which he tooke with so undaunted
a resolution that one might perceive that he had a certain
expectation of a better life after it, so far he was from holding
those Atheisticall opinions, an Aspersion whereof some had cast
upon him.

On the famous Sir Walter Rawleigh, who fell a Sacrifice
to Spanish Politicks :

Here lieth, hidden in this Pitt,
The Wonder of the World for Witt.
It to small purpose did him serve ;
His Witt could not his Life preserve.
Hee living, was belov'd of none,
Yet in his death all did him moane.
Heaven hath his Soule, the world his Fame,
The grave his Corps ; Stukley his shame.

MARY RICH : COUNTESS OF WARWICK

[Born 1625. She was the seventh daughter and thirteenth child of Richard Boyle, first Earl of Cork. At the age of fourteen, she expressed *a very high averseness and contradicon* to the suitor chosen for her by her father : *Being refused in marriadge by my unrewly daughter Mary,* the old Earl noted angrily in his Journal, *he departed my hows the second of September to the Bathe.* His daughter later gave her own explanation. *Living so much at my ease,* she said, *I was unwilling to change my condition,* for the Earl of Cork had recently moved to the Savoy and *when we were once settled there, my father living extraordinarily high, drew a very great resort thither.* Amongst other visitors was Charles Rich, second son of the Earl of Warwick, a poverty stricken young man *with £1300 or £1400 a year at the most.* A young man in such straitened circumstances had little hope of gaining the hand of the great Earl's daughter, and yet for two years he proved *a most diligent gallant to me,* Mary reported, *applying himself, when there were no other beholders in the room but my sister, to me ; but if any other person came in he took no more than ordinary notice of me.* However Mary caught measles, when she was sixteen, and Charles Rich's anxiety was so marked that the family's suspicions were at last aroused. Mary Boyle was therefore packed off into the country in disgrace, but not before she had accepted Charles Rich, *so handsome did he express his passion.* After several weeks the Earl of Cork relented and gave his daughter permission to marry and a dowry of £7000 : whereupon Mary Boyle, who had been *always a great enemy to a public marriage,* insisted on eloping. Five years later, her only son, *which I then doated on with great fondness,* fell seriously ill and his mother vowed to God that she would become *a new creature,* if her child recovered. He did get better, and Mary Rich, who had always been *stedfastly set against being a Puritan* and had particularly delighted in *constant crowds of company,* now *began to find in myself a greate desire to go into the country, which I never remember before to have had, thinking it allways the saddest thing that could be when we were to remove.* Her home in Essex thereafter became the resort of pious Puritan ministers and Bishops from London, and her new faith stood her in good stead when her only child finally died of smallpox in his twenty-first year : *I was dumb,* she says, *and held my peace, because God did it.* Her husband became fourth Earl of Warwick on his brother's death, in 1659, and died himself in 1673, leaving his entire estate at his wife's disposal for her lifetime. She became widely known for her charity and died in 1678.]

SHEE needed neither borrowed Shades, nor reflexive Lights, to set her off, being personally great in all naturall Endowments and accomplishments of Soul and Body, Wisdome, Beautie, Favour, and Virtue ;

Great in the honour of her Birth, being born a Lady and a Virtuosa both ;

Great by her Tongue, for never woman used one better, speaking so gracefully, promptly, discreetly, pertinently, holily, that I have often admired the edifying words that proceeded from her mouth ;

Great by her Pen, as you may discover by that little tast of it the world hath been happy in, the hasty fruit of one or two interrupted houres after Supper, which she professed to me, with a little regret, when she was surprised with it's sliding into the world without her knowledge, or allowance, and wholly beside her expectation ;

Great by being the greatest Mistresse and Promotress, not to say the Foundress and Inventress, of a new Science—the Art of obliging ; in which she attain'd that Sovereign Perfection, that she reigned over all their hearts with whom she did converse ;

Great in her nobleness of Living and Hospitality ;

Great in the unparallelld sincerity of constant, faithfull, condescending Friendship, and for that Law of Kindness which dwelt in her Lips and Heart ;

Great in her dexterity of Management ;

Great in her quick apprehension of the difficulties of her Affaires, and where the stress and pinch lay, to untie the Knot, and loose and ease them ;

Great in the conquest of her selfe ;

Great in a thousand things beside, which the world admires as such : but she despised them all, and counted them but loss and dung in comparison of the feare of God, and the excellency of the Knowledge of Christ Jesus.

CHARLES ROBSON

[Born 1598. Divine. Fellow of Queen's College, Oxford, 1620. Owing to his lax habits the College gladly gave him three years' leave of absence in 1623, and he was appointed preacher to the colony of English merchants at Aleppo at a salary of £50 a year. This leave was extended and Robson did not return to England until 1630, when he became a Bachelor of Divinity. However, in 1631, he was deprived of his Fellowship on account of his dissolute haunting of taverns and brothels and his neglect of study and divine worship, and the University appointed him to a vicarage in Cumberland. He died in 1638.]

ROBSON was the first that brought into England the Art of making Venice-glasses, but Sir Edward Zouche (a Courtier and a drolling Favourite of King James) oppressed this poor man Robson, and forc't it from him, by these four verses to King James, which made his Majestie laugh so that he was ready to beshitt his Briggs. The verses are these :—

> Severn, Humber, Trent, and Thames,
> And thy great Ocean, and her Streames,
> Must putt downe Robson, and his Fires
> Or downe goes Zouche and his desires.

The King granted this ingeniose manufacture to Zouch, being tickled as aforesayd with these Rythmes ; and so poor Robson was oppressed and utterly undon : and came to that low degree of Poverty that Mr. Philips told me that he swept the Yard at Whitehall and that he himselfe saw him doe it.

WALTER RUMSEY

[Born 1584. Lawyer. He was called to the Bar in 1608. Judge of Great Sessions for the Counties of Brecknock, Glamorgan and Radnor from 1631 till he was removed by Parliament in 1647. At the Restoration he was made Keeper of the Judicial Seal for the same counties and was nominated to be a Knight of the Royal Oak. He died in 1660.]

H E was so excellent a lawyer, that he was called *The Pick-lock of the Lawe*.

He was an ingeniose man, and had a Philosophicall head ; he was most curious for graffing, inocculating, and planting, and ponds. If he had any old dead plumbe-tree or apple-tree, he lett them stand, and planted Vines at the bottome, and lett them climbe up, and they would beare very well.

He was one of my Councell in my Law-suites in Breconshire about the Entaile : he had a kindnesse for me and invited me to his house, and told me a great many fine things, both naturall and antiquarian.

He was very facetious, and a good Musitian, playd on the organ and lute. He could compose.

He was much troubled with Flegme, and being so one winter at the Court at Ludlowe (where he was one of the councesellors) sitting by the fire, spitting and spawling, he tooke a fine tender sprig and tied a ragge at the end, and conceited he putt it downe his throat and fetch-up the Flegme, and he did so. Afterwards he made this instrument of Whale-bone. I have oftentimes seen him use it. I could never make it goe downe my throat, but for those that can 'tis a most incomparable engine. If troubled with the wind, it cures you immediately, with a blast as when a Bottle is un-stopp't. It makes you vomit without any paine, and besides, the Vomits of Apothecaries have *aliquid veneni* [some poison] in them. He wrote a little booke of this way of medicine, called *Organon Salutis* (An Instrument to cleanse the stomach). I had a young fellow, Marc Collins, that was my servant, that used it incomparably, more easily than the Judge : he made of them. In Wilts, among my things, are some of his making still. The Judge sayd he never sawe any one use it so dexterously in his life. It is no paine, when downe your throate ; he would touch the bottome of his Stomach with it.

THOMAS SACKVILLE : EARL
OF DORSET

[Born 1536. Poet and statesman. He was a cousin of Queen Elizabeth and studied at both Oxford and Cambridge, before removing to the Inner Temple. He was created Lord Buckhurst in 1566. His father had amassed so great a fortune that he was known as *Sir Richard Fill Sack,* but his son was extravagant beyond all bounds and soon fell into considerable difficulties, but he was so humiliated by being kept waiting by one of his creditors that he embraced a *magnificent economy.* Queen Elizabeth sent him on an embassy to Paris in 1570 to treat of the marriage then proposed between herself and the Duke of Anjou ; appointed him one of the Commissioners for the trial of Mary Queen of Scots, and he had to announce to her the sentence of death and to superintend her execution. In 1587 he was imprisoned for a year after a quarrel with Leicester, but in 1588 he was made a Knight of the Garter and, in 1591, he became Chancellor of the University of Oxford. He was selected to negotiate peace with Spain in 1598, and on the death of Burghley, he was appointed Lord High Treasurer, in which office he was confirmed by James I, who created him Earl of Dorset in 1604. At the age of seventy-two he was seriously ill and the King sent him a ring set with twenty diamonds, hoping *that he might live as long as the dyamonds of that ring did endure.* However he died soon after, in 1608, in the presence of the King and *on opening his head, they found in it certain little bags of water, which, falling upon his brain, caused his death.* In his poetry, Sackville is the connecting link between Chaucer and Spenser. In conjunction with Thomas Norton, he wrote *Gorboduc,* the first regular English tragedy, which rid the theatre of the rigid conventions of its infancy and cleared the stage for the genius of Marlowe and Shakespeare.]

EPIGRAM on the Earle of Dorset, who dyed suddenly at the Council-Boord :

> *Uncivil Death ! that would'st not once conferre,*
> *Dispute, or parle with our Treasurer,*
> *Had He been Thee, or of thy fatall Tribe,*
> *He would have spar'd thy life, and ta'ne a Bribe.*
> *He that so often had, with gold and witt,*
> *Injur'd strong Lawe, and almost conquer'd it,*
> *At length, for want of evidence to shewe,*
> *Was forc't himselfe to take a deadly blowe.*

[265]

The Tryall was with this Sir Richard Temple's great Grand-father. The Lord Treasurer had in his Bosome some writings, which as he was pulling-out to give in evidence, sayed *Here is that will strike you dead!* and as soon as he had spoken these words, fell downe starke dead in the place.

Richard, Earle of Dorset, (eldest grandson and heire to the Lord Treasurer) lived in the greatest grandeur of any noble-man of his time in England. He had 30 Gentlemen, and gave to each 50 pounds per annum, besides keeping and his horse. G. Villiers (after Duke of Bucks) was a Petitioner to have had a Gentleman's place under him, and miss't it, and within 12 moneth was a greater man himselfe; but the Duke ever after bore a grudge to the Earl of Dorset. 'Twas he that translated *the Cid* (a French Comoedie) into English, about 1640. His eldest sonne is Richard, Earl of Dorset and Middlesex, a most noble Lord and my most kind friend.

SIR HENRY SAVILE

[Born 1549. Scholar. Fellow of Merton College, Oxford, at the age of sixteen. Lectured in mathematics. Warden of Merton 1585–1622. Translated *Histories of Tacitus* 1591. Secretary of Latin tongue to Queen Elizabeth. Provost of Eton 1596. Knighted 1604. He was one of the scholars commissioned to prepare the authorised translation of the Bible. He assisted Sir Thomas Bodley in founding his library. Founded the Savile Professorships of Geometry and Astronomy at Oxford. Died 1622.]

SIR HENRY SAVILL, Knight was a younger (or son of a younger) brother, not borne to a foot of land.

He was a learned gentleman as most was of his time; he would faine have been thought (I have heard Mr. Hobbes say) to have been as great a scholar as Joseph Scaliger. But as for Mathematiques, I have heard Dr. Wallis say that he look't on him to be as able a Mathematician as any of his time. He was an extraordinary handsome and beautifull man; no lady had a finer complexion.

Queen Elizabeth favoured him much; he read I thinke Greeke and Politiques to her. He was also preferred to be Provost of Eaton colledge.

He was a very severe Governour, the scholars hated him for his austerity. He could not abide Witts: when a young Scholar was recommended to him for a good Witt, *Out upon him, I'le have nothing to doe with him; give me the ploding student. If I would look for witts, I would goe to Newgate: there be the Witts;* and John Earles (afterwards Bishop of Sarum) was the only scholar that ever he tooke as recommended for a Witt, which was from Dr. Goodwyn, of Christ Church.

He was not only a severe Governor, but old Mr. Yates (who was fellow in his time) would make lamentable complaints of him to his dyeing day, that he did oppresse the fellows grievously, and he was so great and a favourite to the Queen, that there was no dealing with him; his *naeve* was that he was too much inflated with his learning and riches.

He was very munificent, as appeares by the two Lectures he has given to Astronomy and Geometry. Bishop Seth Ward, of Sarum, has told me that he first sent for Mr. Gunter, from London (being of Oxford University) to have been his Professor of Geometrie : so he came and brought with him his Sector and Quadrant, and fell to resolving of Triangles and doeing a great many fine things. Said the grave Knight, *Doe you call this reading of Geometrie? This is shewing of tricks, man!* and so dismisst him with scorne, and sent for Henry Briggs, from Cambridge.

I have heard Dr. Wallis say, that Sir H. Savill has sufficiently confuted Joseph Scaliger *de Quadratura Circuli,* in the very margent of the booke : and that sometimes when J. Scaliger sayes AB=CD ex constructione, Sir H. Savill writes sometimes in the margent, *Et Dominatio vestra est Asinus ex constructione* [and your rule is an ass by construction]. One sayes of Jos. Scaliger, that where he erres, he erres so ingeniosely, that one had rather erre with him then hit the mark with Clavius.

He had travelled very well, and had a generall acquaintance with the Learned men abroad ; by which meanes he obtained from beyond sea, out of their Libraries, severall rare Greeke MSS., which he had copied by an excellent Amanuensis for the Greeke character. He gave his Collection of Mathematicall Bookes to a peculiar little Library belonging to the Savilian Professors.

SYLVANUS SCORY

[The son of John Scory, Bishop of Hereford. He fought in the Low Countries. Prebendary of Hereford 1565–69. Member of Parliament for Newton in Hampshire in 1597. Died 1617.]

HE was a very handsome Gentleman, and had an excellent Witt, and his father gave him the best Education, both at home and beyond the Seas, that that age would afford, and loved him so dearly that he fleeced the Church of Hereford to leave him a good estate : and he did let such long and so many leases, that, as Mris. Masters told me, they were not out till about these 60 yeares. To my best remembrance she told me that the estate left him was 1500 pounds per annum, which he reduced to nothing (allowing himselfe the libertie to enjoy all the pleasures of this World) and left his sonne so poor, that when he came among gentlemen, they would fancy a crowne or ten shillings for him.

I have heard Sir John Denham saye that he haz been well enformed that he was the most accomplished Gentleman of his time : 'tis a good testimoniall of his worth, that Mr Benjamin Johnson (who ever scorned an unworthy Patrone) dedicated to him. I have heard Sir John Denham also say, that he was the greatest confident and intimate Favourite of Monsieur of France (brother to the French King) who was a suitor to Queen Elizabeth, and whom her Majestie entirely loved ; and as a Signalle of it, one time at St. Paules church London, openly kissed him in time of divine Service ; and would have had him for her Husband, but only for reasons of State.

When her Majestie dismissed him 'twas donne with all passion and respecte imaginable. She gave him royall presents : he was attended to Dover by the flower of the Court ; among others by this Sparke of whom I now write. When Monsieur tooke his leave of him, he told him that though 'twas so that her Majestie could not marie him (as aforesayd) yet he knew that she so much loved him that she would not deny him any request, wherby he might honour and benefit a Friend : and accordingly writes his love-letter to his Mistresse the Queen of England, and in it only begs that single favour to looke upon Mr. Scorie (the bearer) with a particular and extraordinary grace for his sake : delivered him the letter (and, as I take it, gave him a jewell).

As Sylvanus returned to London through Canterbury, the Mayer there (a Shoemaker) a pragmaticall fellow, examined him, who and whence, etc., and what his business was, and if he had a Passe ? Yes, quod he, I have a Passe, and produces Monsieur's letter, superscribed to her Majestie, which, one would have thought, had been enough to have shewen. The Mayor presently breakes open the Love-letter, and reades it. I know not how, this action happened to take wind; and 'twas brought to Court, and became so ridicule, that Sylvanus Scory was so laughed at and jeer'd that he never delivered the letter to the Queen; which had been the easiest and most honourable step to preferment that mortall man could have desired.

JOHN SELDEN

[Born 1584. Jurist. His first work, written in 1606, was *Analecton Anglo-Britannicon,* a chronological collection of English records down to the Norman invasion. In 1610 appeared a treatise on the *Duello, or Single Combat ;* in 1614 he wrote *Titles of Honour,* which is full of profound learning and is still a high authority ; and three years later he gained a European reputation as a scholar through his book *De Deis Syris* (On the Gods of Syria) an enquiry into Polytheism. He was forced to recant, before the High Commission Court, the doctrines he had put forward in his *History of Tithes* in 1618, and in 1621 he was imprisoned for opposition to James I's prerogative. He was Member of Parliament for Lancaster in 1623 and his moderate views brought him under suspicion from both sides, so that he was imprisoned in the Tower from 1630 until 1634. After the execution of the King, to which he was strongly opposed, he took little part in public affairs and died in 1654.]

HIS father was a yeomanly man, of about fourty pounds per annum, and played well on the violin, in which he tooke delight, and at Christmas time, to please him selfe and his neighbours, he would play to them as they danced.

He was of Hart-hall in Oxon, and Sir Giles Mompesson told me that he was then of that house, and that he was a long scabby-pold boy, but a good student.

Thence he came to the Inner-Temple. He was quickly taken notice of for his learning, and was Sollicitor and Steward to the Earle of Kent, whose Countesse, being an ingeniose woman and loving men, would let him lye with her, and her husband knew it. After the Earle's death he maried her. He did lye with Mris. Williamson (one of my Lady's woemen) a lusty bouncing woman, who robbed him on his death-bed. I remember in 1646, or 1647, they did talk also of my Lady's Shee Blackamore.

I remember my Sadler (who wrought many years to that Family) told me that Mr. Selden had got more by his Prick then he had done by his practise. He was no eminent practiser at Barre.

He never owned the mariage with the Countesse of Kent till after her death, upon some Lawe-account.

He kept a plentifull Table, and was never without learned company : he was temperate in eating and drinking. He had a slight stuffe, or silke, kind of false carpet, to cast over the table where he read and his papers lay, when a stranger came-in, so that he needed not to displace his bookes or papers.

His treatise that Tythes were not *jure divino* drew a great deale of Envy upon him from the Clergie. W. Laud, Archbishop of Canterbury, made him make his Recantation before the High Commission Court. After, he would never forgive the Bishops, but did still in his writings levell them with Presbyterie.

After he had got a *dulce ocium* he chiefly addicted himselfe to his more ingeniose studies and Records. He was one of the Assembly of Divines and was like a Thorne in their sides : he was wont to mock the Assembly-men about their little gilt Bibles, and would baffle and vexe them sadly : sayd he, *I doe consider the original :* for he was able to runne them all downe with his Greeke and Antiquities.

He was very tall, I guesse about 6 foot high, sharp ovall face, head not very big, long nose inclining to one side, full popping Eie (gray). He was a Poet.

In his younger yeares he affected obscurity of style, which, after, he quite left off, and wrote perspicuously. 'Twill be granted that he was one of the greatest Critiques of his time.

Mr. J. Selden writt a 4to booke called *Tabletalke* ; which will not endure the Test of the Presse.

Sir Robert Cotton (the great Antiquary, that collected the Library) was his great Friend, whose son Sir Thomas Cotton was obnoxious to the Parliament and skulked in the Countrey. Mr. Selden had the Key and command of the Library, and preserved it, being then a Parliament-man.

He intended to have given his owne Library to the University of Oxford, but received disobligation from them, for that they would not lend him some MSS. ; wherfore by his Will he left it to the disposall of his Executors (viz. Lord Chiefe Justice Hales, Lord Chief Justice Vaughan, Rowland Jukes, and his flatterer) who gave it to the Bodleian Library, at Oxon.

He would tell his intimate friends, Sir Bennet Hoskyns, etc., that he had no body to make his heire, excepte, it were a Milke-mayd : and that such people did not know what to doe with a great estate. (Bishop Grostest, of Lincoln, told his brother, who asked him to make him a grate man ; Brother, said he, if your Plough is Broken, I'le pay the mending of it ; or if an Oxe is dead, I'le pay for another : but a Plough-man I found you, and a Plough-man I'le leave you.)

He dyed of a Dropsey ; he had his Funerall Scutcheons all ready moneths before he dyed. When he was neer death, the

Minister was comeing to him to assoile him : Mr. Hobbes happened then to be there, sayd he, What, will you that have wrote like a man, now dye like a woman ? So the Minister was not let in.

Mr. Johnson, Minister of the Temple, buryed him, the Directory way, where, amongst other things, he quoted the sayeing of a learned man (he did not name him) that *when a learned man dies, there dyes a great deale of learning with him,* and that *if Learning could have kept a man alive our Brother had not dyed.*

WILLIAM SEYMOUR:
DUKE OF SOMERSET

[Born 1588. Courtier and soldier. There were some doubts about his legitimacy. Against James I's wishes, he secretly married Arabella Stuart in 1610, and when the marriage was discovered he was committed to the Tower. Having made a plan to join Arabella Stuart on the Continent, his barber, Batten, helped him to escape. Batten, who was well known to the guards, presented himself at the Tower completely disguised and asked for Mr. Seymour's barber, whom he professed to know was within. On being admitted, he transferred the disguise to Seymour and then boldly sallied forth with him. The barber was committed to the Tower next day and Seymour fled to the Continent, but his wife was prevented from joining him and, after her death in the Tower in 1615, he made his peace with the King and returned to England. Knight of the Bath 1616. He adopted the title of Baron Beauchamp 1618. On his grandfather's death, he became Earl of Hertford in 1621. Privy Councillor and created Marquis of Hertford 1640. Governor to Charles, Prince of Wales 1641. In the Civil Wars he became a Royalist Commander, capturing Hereford, Cirencester and Bristol and being victorious at Lansdown in 1643. In 1645 he was put in charge of Oxford and, on its surrender next year, he compounded for his estates and attended Charles I during his imprisonment. He joined with the Duke of Richmond and the Earl of Southampton in praying the King's Judges to lay upon them, as Charles's advisers, the exclusive responsibility for his acts, and when this plea failed, he obtained permission to bury the King's body at Windsor. He received the Garter, the Barony of Seymour and the Dukedom of Somerset at the Restoration, but died the same year.]

CONCERNING *Furze-cutters* :—Brianston by Blandford in Dorset was, *tempore Henr*. 8, belonging to Sir John (I thinke) Rocklington : he had a faire Estate, and no child ; and there was a poor cottager whose name was Rogers that had a pretty wife whom this Knight did visit and had a mind to have a child by her. As he did suppose he afterwards had ; and in consideration of affection, etc., settled his whole estate on this young Rogers. William, Lord Marquesse Hartford, Duke of Somerset, was son of the grand-daughter of this Rogers.

This present Lord Roberts of Truro (now Earl of Radnor) his grandfather (or great-grandfather) was a Furze-cutter in Cornwall ; which I have heard old Parson Wodenot of Linkenhorne in Cornwall say many times.

WILLIAM SHAKESPEARE

[Born 1564. Actor, poet and playwright. Died 1616.]

MR. WILLIAM SHAKESPEARE was borne at Stratford upon Avon in the County of Warwick. His father was a Butcher, and I have been told heretofore by some of the neighbours, that when he was a boy he exercised his father's Trade, but when he kill'd a Calfe he would doe it in a high style, and make a Speech. There was at this time another Butcher's son in this Towne that was held not at all inferior to him for a naturall witt, his acquaintance and coetanean, byt dyed young.

This William, being inclined naturally to Poetry and acting, came to London, I guesse about 18 : and was an Actor at one of the Play-houses, and did acte exceedingly well : now B. Johnson was never a good Actor, but an excellent Instructor.

He began early to make essayes at Dramatique Poetry, which at that time was very lowe ; and his Playes tooke well.

He was a handsome, well-shap't man : very good company, and of a very readie and pleasant smoothe Witt.

The Humour of the Constable in Midsomernight's Dreame, he happened to take at Grendon, in Bucks (I thinke it was Midsomer night that he happened to lye there) which is the roade from London to Stratford, and there was living that Constable about 1642, when I first came to Oxon. Ben Johnson and he did gather Humours of men dayly where ever they came. One time as he was at the Tavern at Stratford super Avon, one Combes, an old rich Usurer, was to be buryed. He makes there this extemporary Epitaph :

> Ten in the Hundred the Devill allowes,
> But Combes will have twelve he sweares and vowes :
> If anyone askes who lies in this Tombe,
> Hoh ! quoth the Devill, 'Tis my John o' Combe.

He was wont to goe to his native Countrey once a yeare. I thinke I have been told that he left 2 or 300 pounds per annum there and thereabout to a sister.

I have heard Sir William Davenant and Mr. Thomas Shadwell

(who is counted the best Comoedian we have now) say that he had a most prodigious Witt, and did admire his naturall parts beyond all other Dramaticall writers.

His Comoedies will remaine witt as long as the English tongue is understood, for that he handles *mores hominum* [the ways of mankind]. Now our present writers reflect so much on particular persons and coxcombeities that twenty yeares hence they will not be understood.

Though, as Ben Johnson sayes of him, that he had little Latine and lesse Greek, He understood Latine pretty well: for he had been in his younger yeares a schoolmaster in the countrey.

He was wont to say that he never blotted out a line in his life. Sayd Ben: Johnson, I wish he had blotted-out a thousand.

OLIVE SHERINGTON

[She was the daughter and co-heir of Sir Henry Sherington, who in his turn had succeeded to the vast estates left by his brother, Sir William, whose third wife was the mother of his brother Henry's wife. This Sir William was one of the chief officers of the Mint under Henry VIII and by malpractices, carried to an enormous extent, obtained the means of speculating on a vast scale in the purchase of Abbey lands, but his frauds were discovered in 1548 and he was clapt up in the Tower. On his own confession he was convicted of having counterfeited twelve thousand pounds worth of coinage in a single year, besides having defrauded the King of clippings and shearings of coin to the amount of several thousand pounds more and of having falsified indentures and books : all this to such an extent that he was quite unable to declare the whole amount of his profits. For these offences he was attainted and his lands forfeited. The fact of his confession showed, according to Bishop Latimer, that *he is a chosen man of God, and one of his elected* and, within three years, he had amassed another fortune sufficiently large to enable him to buy back all his estates for £13,000. Olive Sherington, after the death of John Talbot, her first husband, was married to Sir Robert Stapylton of Yorkshire and, after her second widowhood, lived at Lacock Abbey until her death.]

DAME OLAVE, a Daughter and coheir of Sir Henry Sharington of Lacock being in Love with John Talbot (a younger Brother of the Earle of Shrewsbury) and her Father not consenting that she should marry Him : discoursing with Him one night from the Battlements of the Abbey-Church ; said shee, *I will leap downe to you* : her sweet Heart replied, He would catch Her then : but he did not believe she would have done it : she leap't downe and the wind (which was then high) came under her coates : and did something breake the fall : Mr. Talbot caught her in his armes, but she struck him dead ; she cried out for help, and he was with great difficulty brought to life again : her father told her that since she had made such a leap she should e'en marrie him. She was my honoured friend Col. Sharington Talbot's Grand Mother : and died at her house at Lacock about 1651, being about an hundred years old.

SIR PHILIP SIDNEY

[Born 1554. Soldier, statesman and poet. His father was three times Lord Deputy of Ireland and President of Wales. He was at the French Court on the fateful 24th August, 1572, the Massacre of Saint Bartholomew, but left Paris soon after and went to Germany, Poland, Hungary and Italy. On his return he became a friend of Spenser, who dedicated to him his *Shepheard's Calendar*. In 1580 he lost the favour of the Queen by remonstrating against her proposed marriage with the Duke of Anjou, and in 1583 he was married himself to the daughter of Sir Francis Walsingham. His writings consist of his famous pastoral romance of *Arcadia*, his sonnets *Astrophel and Stella*, and his *Defence of Poesie*. Sidney has always been considered as the type of English chivalry ; and his extraordinary contemporary reputation, resting on his personal qualities of nobility and generosity (for none of his works were published in his lifetime) is shown by the inscription on the tomb of Fulke Greville, Lord Brooke : *Here lies the body of Sir Fulke Grevile, Knight, Servant to Queen Elizabeth, Counsellor to King James, and Friend to Sir Philip Sidney.* In 1585 Sidney was engaged in the war in the Low Countries and was fatally wounded at Zutphen.]

SIR PHILIP SYDNEY, Knight, whose Fame will never dye, whilest Poetrie lives, was the most accomplished Cavalier of his time. He was not only of an excellent witt, but extremely beautifull : he much resembled his sister, but his Haire was not red, but a little inclining, viz. a darke ambor colour. If I were to find a fault in it, methinkes 'tis not masculine enough ; yett he was a person of great courage.

He travelled France, Italie Germany ; he was in the Poland warres, and at that time he had to his Page (and as an excellent accomplishment) Henry Danvers (afterwards Earle of Danby) then second son of Sir John Danvers of Dantesey in Wilts, who accounted himselfe happy that his son was so bestowed. He makes mention, in his *Art of Poesie,* of his being in Hungarie (I remember).

He was a reviver of Poetry in those darke times, which was then at a very low ebbe : there is not 3 lines but there is *by God,* or *by God's wounds.*

He was much at Wilton with his sister, and at Ivy-church (which adjoyns to the parke pale of Clarindon Parke) situated on a hill that overlookes all the Country westwards, and North over Sarum and the plaines, and into that delicious parke (which was accounted the best of England) Eastwards. It was anciently a pleasant Monasterie (the Cloysters remayne still).

My great Uncle Mr. Thomas Browne remembred him; and sayd that he was wont, as he was hunting on our pleasant plaines, to take his Table booke out of his pocket, and write downe his notions as they came into his head, when he was writing his *Arcadia* (which was never finished by him): he made it young, and Diying desired his folies might be burnt. These Romancy Plaines, and Boscages did no doubt conduce to the heightening of Sir Philip Sidneys Phansie.

He was of a very munificent spirit, and liberall to all Lovers of Learning, and to those that pretended to any acquaintance with Parnassus: in so much that he was cloyed and surfeited with the Poetasters of those dayes. Among others, Mr. Edmund Spenser made his addresse to him, and brought his *Faery Queen*. Sir Philip was busy at his Study, and his servant delivered Mr. Spencer's booke to his master, who layd it by, thinking it might be such kind of Stuffe as he was frequently troubled with. Mr. Spencer stayed so long that his patience was wearied, and went his way discontented, and never intended to come again. When Sir Philip perused it, he was so exceedingly delighted with it that he was extremely sorry he was gonne, and where to send for him he knew not. After much enquiry he learned his lodgeing, and sent for him, mightily caressed him, and ordered his servant to give him so many pounds in gold. His servant sayd that that was too much. No, sayd Sir Philip, and ordered an addition. From this time there was a great friendship between them, to his dying day.

Tilting was much used at Wilton in the times of Henry Earle of Pembroke, and Sir Philip Sydney. At the Solemniza-tion of the great Wedding of William the 2ᵈ Earle of Pembroke to one of the Co-heires of the Earle of Shrewsbury, here was an extraordinary Shew: at which time a great many of the Nobility, and Gentry, exercised: and they had Shields of Past-board painted with their Devices, and Emblemes: which were very pretty and ingenious: and I believe they were most of them contrived by Sir Philip Sidney. There are some of them hanging in some houses at Wilton to this day; but I did remember many more. Most (or all of them) had some relation to Marriage. One (I remember) was a Hawke lett of the hand, with her Leashes hanging at her Legges, which might hang her wher 'ere she pitch't: And is an Embleme of Youth, that is apt to be ensnared by their own too plentiful Estates.

I have heard Dr. Pell say, that he haz been told by ancient

gentlemen of those dayes of Sir Philip, so famous for men at Armes, that 'twas then held as a great disgrace for a young Cavalier to be seen riding in the street in a Coach, as it would now for such a one to be seen in the streetes in a Petticoate and Wastcoate. So much in the fashion of the times nowe altered.

He maried the daughter of Sir Francis Walsingham, Principall Secretary of Estate (I thinke his only child) whom he loved very well : in so much that having received some shott or wound in the Warres in the Lowe-countreys (where he had command of the Ramikins, I thinke) he would not (contrary to the injunction of his Physitians and chirurgions) forbeare his carnall knowledge of her, which cost him his life ; upon which occasion there were some roguish verses made.

His body was putt in a leaden coffin (which, after the firing of Paule's, I myselfe sawe) and with wonderful greate state was caried to St. Paules church, where he was buried in our Ladie's Chapell. There solempnized this Funerall all the Nobility and great Officers of Court ; all the Judges and Serjeants at Lawe ; all the Soldiers and Commanders and Gentry that were in London ; the Lord Mayer and Aldermen, and Liverymen. His body was borne on men's shoulders (perhaps 'twas a false coffin).

When I was a boy 9 yeares old, I was with my father at one Mr. Singleton's an Alderman and Wollen-draper in Glocester, who had in his parlour over the Chimney, the whole description of the Funerall, engraved and printed on papers pasted together, which at length was, I beleeve, the length of the room at least ; but he had contrived it to be turned upon two Pinnes, that turning one of them made the figures march all in order. It did make such a strong impression on my tender Phantasy that I remember it as if it were but yesterday. I could never see it elsewhere. The house is in the great long street, over against the high steeple, and 'tis likely it remaines there still. 'Tis pitty it is not re-donne.

SIR HENRY SPELMAN

[Born 1562. Historian and antiquary. He wrote many valuable works on legal and ecclesiastical antiquities, including *A History of Sacrilege* (published 1698); *Glossarium Archaeologicum,* a dictionary of obsolete law terms, which landed him in trouble with Archbishop Laud for including Magna Charta and Magnum Consilium Regis under the M's (1626); *A History of the English Councils* (1639) and *Tenures by Knight-Service* (1641). He sat in Parliament and on various Commissions, as a reward for which he was voted a grant of £300. He died in 1641.]

WHEN he was about 10 or 12 he went to schoole to a curs't Schoolmaster, to whom he had an Antipathie. His Master would discountenance him, and was very severe to him, and to a dull boy he would say, *as very a dunce as H. Spelman.* He was a boy of great spirit, and would not learne there. He was (upon his importunity) sent to another Schoolmaster and profited very well. I have heard his grandson say, that the Spelmans' Witts open late : Sir Henry did not understand Latin perfectly till he was fourty years old.

He was much perplexed with Lawe-suites and worldly troubles, so that he was about 40 before he could settle himselfe to make any great progresse in learning, which when he did, we find what great Monuments of Antiquarian knowledge he haz left to the World.

When his daughter-in-lawe (Sir John's wife) returned home from visitting her Neighbours, he would alwaies aske her what of Antiquity she had heard or observed, and if she brought home no such account, he would chide her (jestingly). He said to Sir William Dugdale, We are beholding to Mr. Speed and Stowe for *stitching up* for us our English History. It seemes they were both Taylers.

He was a handsome Gentleman (as appeares by his picture in *Bibliotheca Cottoniana*) strong and valiant, and wore allwayes his Sword, till he was about 70 or more, when, finding his legges to faulter through feebleness as he was walking, *Now,* said he, *'tis time to leave off my Sword.*

EDMUND SPENSER

[Born 1552. Poet. He was educated at Merchant Taylors School, then newly opened, and at Pembroke Hall, Cambridge. Through his college friend, Gabriel Harvey, he obtained in 1578 a place in the Earl of Leicester's household and became acquainted with Sir Philip Sidney, with whom he formed a literary club styled the *Areopagus*, chiefly for the purpose of naturalizing the classical metres in English verse. In 1579 he began *The Faerie Queen* and published his *Shepheard's Calender*, which was enthusiastically received. In 1580 he was appointed secretary to Lord Grey de Wilton, then going to Ireland as Lord Deputy. Spenser acquired Kilcolman Castle in County Cork, a former possession of the Earls of Desmond, with three thousand acres attached. Here he settled, and occupied himself with literary work, writing his elegy *Astrophel* on Sir Philip Sidney, and preparing *The Faerie Queen* for the press, three books of which he entrusted to the printer on his visit to London in 1589, during which Sir Walter Raleigh presented him to Queen Elizabeth, who awarded him a pension of fifty pounds. He reluctantly returned to Kilcolman, which he regarded as a place of exile, in 1591, and wrote *Colin Clouts come home againe*. In 1594 Spenser celebrated his marriage to Elizabeth Boyle in his splendid *Epithalamion*, and two years later published the second part of *The Faerie Queen*. His castle of Kilcolman was burnt in October 1598, in a sudden insurrection, and his youngest child perished in the flames. Spenser and his wife escaped with difficulty and he died in destitution in London in 1599 and was buried near Chaucer in Westminster Abbey.]

MR. BEESTON sayes, he was a little man, wore short haire, little band and little cuffs.

Mr. Edmund Spencer was of Pembroke-hall in Cambridge; he misst the Fellowship there, which Bishop Andrewes gott. He was an acquaintance and frequenter of Sir Erasmus Dreyden : His Mistris Rosalind was a kinswoman of Sir Erasmus Ladys. The chamber there at Sir Erasmus' is still called Mr. Spencers chamber. Lately, at the college takeing-downe the Wainscot of his chamber, they found an abundance of Cards, with stanzas of the *Faerie Queen* written on them.

Mr. Samuel Woodford (the Poet who paraphras'd the Psalmes) lives in Hampshire neer Alton, and he told me that Mr. Spenser lived sometime in these parts, in this delicate sweet ayre : where he enjoyed his Muse : and writt good part of his Verses. He had lived some time in Ireland, and made a description of it, which is printed.

I have said before that Sir Philip Sidney, and Sir Walter Ralegh were his acquaintance. Sir John Denham told me, that ABp. Usher, Lord Primate of Armagh, was acquainted with him; by this token: when Sir William Davenant's *Gondibert* came forth, Sir John askt the Lord Primate if he had seen it. Said the Primate, Out upon him, with his vaunting Preface, he speakes against my old friend Edmund Spenser.

In the South crosse-aisle of Westminster abbey, next the Dore, is this Inscription:

Heare lies (expecting the second comeing of our Saviour Christ Jesus) the body of Edmund Spencer, the Prince of Poets of his tyme, whose divine spirit needs no other witnesse, then the workes which he left behind him. He was borne in London, in the yeare 1510, and dyed in the yeare 1596.

THOMAS STREET

[Born in Ireland 1622. Astronomer. He was a clerk in the Excise Office. He published *Astronomia Carolina* 1661 ; *The Planetary Systeme* 1670 ; and *The Tables of the Moon and Mercury* ; besides carrying forward the study of Trigonometry. He died in 1689.]

ANNO 1661 he printed that excellent piece of *Astronomia Carolina,* which he dedicated to King Charles II, and also presented it well bound to Prince Rupert and the Duke of Monmouth ; but never had a farthing of any of them.

He had the true motion of the Moon by which he could discover and demonstrate the never yet discovered Art and Science of finding the true Longitude, yet 2 of his familiar acquaintance tell me that he did not committ this Discovery to paper : so it is dead with him.

He made attempts to be introduced to King Charles II and also to King James II, but Courtiers would not doe it without a good gratuitie.

He was of a rough and cholerique humour. Discoursing with Prince Rupert, his Highnesse affirmed something that was not according to Art : sayd Mr. Street, Whoever affirmes that, is no Mathematician. So they would point at him afterwards at Court and say *there's the man that huff't Prince Rupert.*

He dyed in Chanon-row at Westminster, the 17th of August 1689, and is buried in the church yard of the New Chapell there towards the East window of the Chancel, within twenty or 30 foot of the wall. His acquaintance talke of clubbing towards an Inscription. No man living haz deserved so well of Astronomie.

THOMAS STUMP

[Born 1616. Soldier. His great-great-grandfather *Stump, was a wealthy Cloathier at Malmesbury, tempore Henrici VIII : at the Dissolution of the Abbeys he bought a great deal of the Abbey lands thereabout.* When King Henry 8ᵗʰ hunted in Bradon forest, he gave his Majesty and the Court a great entertainment at his House (the Abbey). *The King told him, He was afraid he had undone himself, he replied, that his own Servants should only want their supper for it.* His eldest son, Sir James Stump, was High Sheriff and from him *are descended severall of our greatest Nobility, the Earles of Suffolk and Lincoln, etc.*]

CAPTAIN THOMAS STUMP of Malmesbury. 'Tis pity the strange Adventures of Him should be forgotten. He was the eldest Sonn of Mr. Will: Stump, Rector of Yatton Keynell : was a Boy of most daring Spirit ; he would climb Towers and Trees most dangerously : nay he would walke on the Battlements of the Tower there.

He had too much Spirit to be a Scholar, and about at 16 went in a Voyage with his Uncle (since Sir Thomas) Ivy to Guyana in Anno 1633, or 1632. When the Ship put in somewhere there 4 or 5 of them straggled into the Countrey too far : and in the interim the wind served, and the Sailes were hoist, and the Stragglers left behind.

It was not long before the wild People seized on them, and stript them : and those that had beards, they knocked their braines out : And (as I remember) did eat them : but the Queen saved T. Stump and the other boy. T. Stump threw himself into the River (Oronoque) to have drowned himself, but could not sinke ; he is very full chested. The other youth shortly after died. Thomas Stump lived with them till 1636 or 1637.

His Narrations are very strange and pleasant ; but so many yeares have made me almost forgett all. He sayes there is incomparable Fruits there : and that it may be termed the Paradise of the World. He says that the Spondyles of the back-bones of the huge Serpents there are used, to sit on, as our Women sitt upon Butts. He taught them to build Hovills : and to thatch and wattle. I wish I had a good account of his abode there : He is *fide dignus* [worthy of belief]. I never heard of any man that lived so long among those Salvages.

[285]

A Ship then sayling by (a Portughese) He swam to it; they took him up and made use of him for a Sea-boy. As he was sayling near Cornwall, he stole out of a Port-hole, and swam to shore ; and so beg'd to his Fathers in Wiltshire. When he came home, no body knew him : and they would not own him : only Jo. Harris the Carpenter knew him : At last he recounted so many Circumstances, that he was owned, and in 1642 had a Commission for a Captain of Foot in King Charles Ist army.

SIR JOHN SUCKLING

[Born 1609. Poet. His father was Secretary of State and Comp-
troller of the Household to James I. After travelling on the Continent,
he served for a short time under Gustavus Adolphus and, on his
return to England, he was knighted and went to Court, where his
wealth, generosity and wit made him a general favourite. He became
a leader of the Royalist party in the early troubles, but he got into
trouble in connection with a plot to rescue Strafford from the Tower
and fled to the Continent. He wrote four plays : *Aglaura,* which he
provided with two fifth acts, one tragic, the other not ; *Brennoralt* ;
The Goblins ; and *The Sad One* ; but his chief fame rests on his songs
and ballads. He also wrote *The Session of the Poets* which is mainly of
antiquarian interest. Died 1642.)

I HAVE heard Mris. Bond say that Sir John's father was but
a dull fellow (her husband Mr. Thomas Bond knew him)
the witt came by the mother.

By 18 he had well travelled France and Italie, and part of
Germany, and (I thinke also) of Spaine.

He returned to England an extraordinary accomplished
Gent., grew famous at Court for his readie sparkling witt ;
which was envyed, and he was (Sir William Davenant sayd) the
Bull that was bayted. He was incomparably readie at repartying,
and his Witt most sparkling when most sett-upon and provoked.

He was the greatest gallant of his time, and the greatest
Gamester, both for Bowling and Cards, so that no Shop-
keeper would trust him for 6d, as today, for instance, he might,
by winning, be worth 200 pounds, and the next day he might
not be worth half so much, or perhaps sometimes be *minus
nihilo*. He was one of the best Bowlers of his time in England.
He played at Cards rarely well, and did use to practise by
himselfe a-bed, and there studyed how the best way of managing
the cards could be. His Sisters would come to the Peccadillo-
bowling-green, crying for feare he should loose all their Portions.

Sir John Suckling invented the game of Cribbidge. He
sent his Cards to all Gameing places in the countrey, which
were marked with private markes of his ; he gott twenty
thousand pounds by this way.

Sir William Davenant (who was his intimate friend and
loved him intirely) would say that Sir John, when he was at

his lowest ebbe in gameing, I meane when unfortunate, then would make himselfe most glorious in apparell, and sayd that it exalted his spirits, and that he had then best Luck when he was most gallant, and his Spirits were highest.

Sir William would say that he did not much care for a Lord's converse, for they were in those dayes damnably Proud and arrogant, and the French would say that *My Lord d'Angleterre look't comme un Mastif-dog*. But now the age is more refined, and much by the example of his gracious Majestie who is the Patterne of Courtesie.

There happened, unluckily, a difference between Sir John Suckling and Sir John Digby (brother to Sir Kenelme) about a Mistresse or Gameing, I have now forgott. Sir John was but a slight timberd man, and of midling stature ; Sir John Digby was a proper person of great strength and courage answerable, and yielded to be the best swordsman of his time. Sir John, with two or three of his party, assaults Sir John Digby goeing into a Play-house. Sir J. D. had only his Lacquey with him, but Sir J. D. flew on them like a Tigre, and made them run. 'Twas pitty that this accident brought the blemish of Cowardise to such an ingeniose young Sparke. Sir J. D. was such a Hero that there were very few but he would have served in like manner.

Mr. Snowdon tells me that after Sir John's unluckie rencounter, or Quarrel with Sir John Digby, wherin he was baffled, 'twas strange to see the envie and ill-nature of people to trample, and Scoffe at, and deject one in disgrace ; inhumane as well as unchristian. The Lady Moray had made an entertainment for severall persons of quality at Ashley, in Surrey, near Chertsey, whereat Mr. Snowdon then was. There was the Countess of Middlesexe, whom Sir John had highly courted, and had spent on her, and in treating her, some thousands of pounds. At this entertainment she could not forbeare, but was so severe and ingrate as to upbraid Sir John of his late recieved Baffle ; and some other Ladys had their flirts. The Lady Moray (who invited them) seeing Sir John out of Countenance, for whose worth she alwaies had a respect : Well, sayd shee, I am a merry Wench, and will never forsake an old friend in disgrace, so come, sitt downe by me, Sir John (said she) and seated him on her right hand, and countenanced him. This raysed Sir John's dejected spirites that he threw his Reparties about the Table with so much sparklingnesse and Gentilenes of Witt, to the admiration of them all.

When the Expedition was into Scotland, Sir John Suckling, at his owne chardge raysed a Troope of 100 very handsome young proper men, whom he clad in white doubletts and scarlett breeches, and scarlet Coates, hatts, and feathers, well horsed and armed. They say 'twas one of the finest sights in those days. But Sir John Menis made a Lampoon of it :—

> *The Ladies opened the Windows to see,*
> *So fine and goodly a sight-a . . .* etc.

I thinke the Lampoon sayes he made an inglorious chardge against the Scotts.

He was of middle stature and slight strength, brisque round eie, reddish fac't and red nose (ill liver) his head not very big, his hayre a kind of sand colour, his beard turnd-up naturally, so that he had a briske and gracefull looke. He died a Batchelour.

He made a magnificent entertainment in London for a great number of Ladies of Quality, all beauties and young, which cost him many hundreds of poundes, where were all the rarities that this part of the world could afford, and the last service of all was Silk Stockings and Garters, and I thinke also Gloves.

Anno Domini 1637, Sir John Suckling, William Davenant, Poet Laureate (not then knighted) and Jack Young, came to Bathe. Sir John came like a young Prince for all manner of Equipage and convenience, and Sir W. Davenant told me that he had a Cart-load of Bookes carried downe ; and 'twas there, at Bath, that he writt the little Tract in his Booke about Socinianism. 'Twas as pleasant a journey as ever men had ; in the height of a long Peace and luxury, and in the Venison Season. The second night they lay at Marlborough, and walking on the delicate fine downes at the Backside of the Towne, whilest supper was making ready, the maydes were drying of cloathes on the bushes. Jack Young had espied a very pretty young Girle, and had gott her consent for an assignation, which was about midnight, which they happened to overheare on the other side of the hedge, and were resolved to frustrate his designe. They were wont every night to play at Cards after supper a good while : but Jack Young pretended wearinesse, etc., and must needes goe to Bed, not to be perswaded by any meanes to the contrary. They had their landlady at supper with them ; said they to her, Observe this poor Gentleman, how he yawnes : now is his mad fit comeing uppon him. We beseech you that you make fast his doores, and gett somebody to watch and looke to him, for about midnight he will fall to be most outragious. Gett the Hostler, or some strong fellow, to stay-up, and we will well content him, for he is our worthy friend, and a very honest Gent., only, perhaps, twice in a yeare he falls into these fitts.

Jack Young slept not, but was ready to goe out as the clocke struck to the houre of appointment, and then going to open the Dore he was disappointed, knocks, bounces, stampes, calls *Tapster! Chamberlayne! Hostler!* sweares and curses dreadfully ; nobody would come to him. Sir John and W. Davenant were expectant all this time, and ready to dye with laughter. I know not how, he happened to gett open the Dore, and was comeing downe the stayres. The Hostler, a huge lusty fellow, fell upon him, and held him, and cryed, Good Sir, take God in your mind, you shall not goe out to destroy yourself. J. Young struggled and strived, insomuch that at last he was quite spent and dispirited, and was faine to goe to bed to rest himselfe.

In the morning the Landlady of the House came to see how he did, and brought him a Cawdle ; Oh, Sir, sayd she, You had a heavy fitt last night ; pray, Sir, be pleased to take some of this to comfort your heart. Jack Young thought the woman had been mad, and being exceedingly vexed, flirted the porrenger of Cawdle in her face. The next day his Camerades told him all the plott, how they crosse-bitt him. That night they went to Bronham House, Sir Edward Baynton's (then a noble seate, since burnt in the Civill Warres) where they were nobly entertained severall dayes. From thence, they went to West Kington to Parson Davenant, Sir William's eldest brother, where they stayd a weeke—mirth, witt and good cheer flowing. From thence to Bath, six or seven miles.

My Ladye Southcott, whose husband hanged himselfe, was Sir John Suckling's sister. At her house in Bishopsgate-Street, London, is an originall of her brother Sir John of Sir Anthony van-Dyke, all at length, leaning against a rock, with a play-booke, contemplating. It is a piece of great value.

When his *Aglaura* was put on, he bought all the Cloathes himselfe, which were very rich ; no tinsell, all the lace pure gold and silver, which cost him . . . I have now forgott. He had some scaenes to it, which in those dayes were only used at Masques.

He went into France, where after sometime, being come to the bottome of his Found, reflecting on the miserable and despicable condition he should be reduced to, having nothing left to maintaine him, he (having a convenience for that purpose, lyeing at an apothecarie's house in Paris) tooke poyson, which killed him miserably with vomiting. He was buryed in the Protestants Churchyard. This was (to the best of my remembrance) 1646.

His Picture, which is like him, before his Poemes, says that he was about 28 yeares old when he dyed.

THOMAS SUTTON

[Born 1532. Usurer. Student of Lincoln's Inn. Surveyor of the Ordnance in the Northern Parts 1570. Obtained leases of land rich in coal in Durham and made an enormous fortune, which was further increased by his marriage with Elizabeth, widow of John Dudley. He settled in London 1580. Purchased the Charterhouse (1611), where he established a hospital of eighty inmates and a school of forty boys. He was estimated the richest commoner in England, his estates being reckoned at £5000 a year and his personalty at £60,410. Died 1611.]

THOMAS SUTTON, Founder of the Hospitall, was first a Garrison-soldier at Barwick. He was a lusty, healthy, handsome fellowe, and there was a very rich Brewer that brewed to the Navy, etc., who was ancient and he had maried a young buxome wife, who enjoyed the embraces of this more able performer as to that point. The old brewer doted on his desirable wife and dies and left her all his Estate, which was great.

Sutton was a man of good understanding, and improved it admirably well : But the particular wayes by which he did it I have now forgott. But he was much upon mortgages, and fed severall with hopes of being his Heire. The Earle of Dorset (I thinke Richard) mightily courted him and presented him, hoping to have been his Heire ; and so did severall other great persons.

The later end of his dayes he lived in Fleetstreet at a Wollen draper's shop, opposite to Fetter-lane ; where he had so many great Chests full of money, that his chamber was ready to groane under it ; and Mr. Tyndale, who knew him and I thinke had money of him on mortgage during his Lawe-suite, was afrayd the roome would fall. He lived to establish his Hospitall, and was Governor there himselfe.

'Twas from him that B. Johnson tooke his hint of the Fox : and by Seigneur Volpone is meant Sutton.

SILAS TAYLOR

[Born 1624. Historian. Educated at Westminster School and New Inn Hall, Oxford. Captain in the Parliamentary Army. Commissary for Ammunition under Sir Edward Harley at Dunkirk 1660. He published *The History of the Gavelkind* (1663) and left in manuscript a collection for *The History of Herefordshire*. He died in 1678.)

HE was a Captaine in the Parliamentary Army, under Col. Massey. He was a Sequestrator in Herefordshire : and had in those times great power : which power he used civilly and obligeingly, that he was beloved by all the King's party.

He was very musicall, and hath composed many things, and I have heard Anthemes of his sang before his Majestie, in his Chapell, and the King told him he liked them. He had a very fine chamber organ in those un-musicall dayes.

His father left him a pretty good estate, but he bought Church Lands and had the moeity of the Bishop's palace, at Hereford, where he leyd out much money in building and altering. The times turning, he was faine to disgorge all he had gott, and was ruined, but Sir Paul Neile got for him the Keeper of the King's Stores at Harwich, worth about 1000 pounds per annum.

He was a great lover of Antiquities, and ransackt the MSS. of the Church of Hereford (there were a great many that lay uncouth and unkiss).

He had severall MSS. by him of great Antiquity : one thin 4to. of the Philosopher's Stone, in Hieroglyphicks, with some few Latin verses underneath ; the most curiously limned that ever I sawe. His Majesty offered him 100 pounds for it, but he would not accept it.

Capt. Tayler searched the Records in the Tower, and retrived some Privileges that the Borough of Harwich had lost, for which the Borough ought ever to have his remembrance in esteeme : and tho' he dyed above 100 pounds in their debt, yet the Towne lost not by him, for the reason aforesaid.

The History or Collection of this Ancient Borough he pawned a little before his death to Mr. Baker, the Print-seller by the Old Exchange, for 4 pounds 15s. I acquainted Sir Philip

Parker, whom the Borough uses to choose for their Burghesse, to buy it for his Borough. He would not lay out so much money, which would doe them more service then all his roast-beefe, wine, and ale at an Election.

He also garbled the Library of the Church of Worcester, and Evidences, where he had the originall Grant of King Edgar (θαλασσιαρχης) whence the Kings of England derive their right to the Soveraignty of the Sea. 'Tis printed in Mr. Selden's *Mare Clausum*. I have seen it many times, and it is as legible as but newly written (Roman character). He offered it to the King for 120 pounds but his Majesty would not give so much. Since his death, I acquainted the Secretary of Estate that he dyed in debt and his Creditors seised on his goods and papers. He told me that it did of right belong to Worcester Church. I told one of their Prebends, and they cared not for such things. I beleeve it haz wrapt Herings by this time.

JOHN TOMBES

[Born 1603. Divine. Educated at Magdalen Hall, Oxford. Being a Presbyterian, he refused to baptize infants and appealed to the Westminster Assembly on the subject and published tracts. Master of the Temple 1645–47. In 1646 he had an interview with Cromwell. He organised the Baptist Church and wrote tracts against Paedobaptists, Quakers and Papists. Died 1676.]

HE was a great Master of the Greeke Tongue, and the Hebrue he understood well. He alwaies carried a little Greeke Testament about with him : he had it almost *memoriter*.

He was soon taken notice of for his curious, searching, piercing witt : he preached somewhere Eastwards from Oxon, and had a Sect followed him ; and 'twas predicted he would doe a great deale of mischiefe to the Church of England, reflecting that the greatest Witts have donne the most mischiefe to the Church, introducing new opinions, etc.

He was Vicar of a market-towne in Herefordshire, where he was very well beloved by his parish, and Sir William Croftes, eldest brother to the now Bishop of Hereford, built a house at Leominster, to live there, to heare him preach.

Then he went into his owne country, to Beaudley a market Towne, at which time Mr. Baxter, his Antagonist, preacht at Kitterminster, the next market towne, two miles distant. They preacht against one another's Doctrines, and printed against each other. Mr. Tombes was the Coryphaeus of the Anabaptists : both had great audience ; they went severall miles on foot to each Doctor. Once (I thinke oftner) they disputed face to face ; and the followers were like two armies, about 1500 of a party ; and truly, at last they fell by the eares, hurt was donne, and the civill magistrats had much adoe to quiet them.

About Anno 1664 he came to the Act at Oxford, and did there *in Vesperiis* sett up a Challenge to maintaine *contra omnes gentes* [against all comers] the Anabaptisticall doctrine ; but not a man would grapple with him. Now, though *primâ facie* this might seeme very bold to challenge a whole University, 'twas not so strange neither, for he came throughly prepared,

[294]

after 30 yeares' study and thoughts, and most of them surprised.

He was thought to be as great a Divine as most we had after Bishop Sanderson dyed. I remember he never, or seldome, was wont to say Our Saviour Christ, but *my Lord Christ*. He seemed to be a very pious and zealous Christian. Putting aside his Anabaptisticall positions, he was comfortable enough to the Church of England.

I have heard him say (though he was much opposite to the Romish Religion) that truly, for his part, should he see a poor zealous Friar goeing to preach, he should pay him respect.

NICHOLAS TOWES

TO one Mr. Towes, who had been School-fellow with Sir George Villers, the Father of the first Duke of Buckingham (and was his Friend and Neighbour) as he lay in his bed awake (and it was Day-light) there came into his Chamber the Phantome of his dear Friend Sir George Villers : Said Mr. Towes to him, Why, you are Dead, what make you here ? Said the Knight, I am Dead, but cannot rest in peace for the Wickedness and Abomination of my Son George at Court. I do appear to you, to tell him of it, and to advise and dehort him from his Evil ways. Said Mr. Tows, the Duke will not believe me, but will say, that I am Mad, or Doat. Said Sir George, Go to him from me, and tell him by such a Token (some Mole) that he had in some secret place, which none but himself knew of. Accordingly Mr. Towes went to the Duke, who Laugh'd at his Message. At his return home, the Phantome appeared again ; and told him, that the Duke would be Stab'd (he drew out a Dagger) a quarter of a Year after : And you shall outlive him half a Year ; and the Warning that you shall have of your Death will be, that your Nose will fall a-bleeding : All which accordingly fell out so.

This Account I have had (in the main) from two, or three ; but Sir William Dugdale affirms what I have here taken from him to be true, and that the Apparition told him of several things to come, which proved true, e.g. of a Prisoner in the Tower, that should be honourably delivered. This Mr. Towes had so often the Ghost of his old Friend appear to him, that it was not at all terrible to him. He was Surveyor of the Works at Windsor (by the favour of the Duke) : Being then sitting in the Hall, he cried out, The Duke of Buckingham is stabb'd : He was stabb'd that very moment.

Sir William Dugdale did farther inform me that Major General Middleton (since Lord) went into the Highlands of Scotland, to endeavour to make a Party for King Charles the First. An Old Gentleman (that was second-sighted) came and told him that his endeavour was good ; but he would be unsuccessful, and moreover, That they would put the King to Death : and that several other Attempts would be made, but all in vain : But that his Son would come in, but not Reign ; but at last would be Restored.

[296]

This Lord Middleton had a great Friendship with the Laird Bocconi, and they had made a Sacrament, That the first of them that Died should appear to the other in extremity. The Lord Middleton was taken Prisoner at Worcester Fight, and was Prisoner in the Tower of London under Three Locks. Lying in his Bed pensive, Bocconi appeared to him ; my Lord Middleton asked him if he were dead or alive ? He said, Dead, and that he was a Ghost, and told him, that within Three Days he should escape, and he did so in his Wive's Cloaths. When he had done his Message, he gave a Frisk, and said,

> *Givenni givanni 'tis very strange,*
> *In the World to see so sudden a Change.*

And then gathered up and vanished.

Anno 1670, not far from Cyrencester, was an Apparition : Being demanded, whether a good Spirit, or a bad ? returned no answer, but disappeared with a curious Perfume and most melodious Twang. Mr. W. Lilly believes it was a Farie.

THOMAS TRIPLETT

[Born 1603. Divine. Educated at St. Paul's School and Christ Church, Oxford. Vicar of Woodburn, Northumberland, 1630 ; Rector of Whitburn in Durham 1631 ; and of Washington in the same county 1640. Canon of York 1641 ; collated to Canonries at Salisbury (1645) and Durham (1649), but he was sequestered by Parliament and was not installed till 1660. Sub-Dean and Canon of Westminster 1662. In his will he left £20 a year *in trust for Foure of the most worthy Schollers of the Free Schoole of Westminster that want means to subsist att the university.* He died in 1670.]

H E went to schoole to Dr. Gill, as appears by his Ballad, which will last longer than any Sermon that ever he made.

Dr. Gill was a very ingeniose person, as may appeare by his Writings. Notwithstanding, he had moodes and humours, as particularly his whipping fitts :

> *As Paedants out of the schoole-boies breeches*
> *doe clawe and curry their owne itches.*

This Dr. Gill whipt Sir John Duncomb (who was not long after a Colonel of Dragoons at Edgehill-fight) taken pissing against the wall. He had his sword by his side, but the boyes surprized him : somebody had throwen a stone in at the windowe ; and they seised on the first man they lighted on. He would have cutt the Doctor, but he never went abroad but to church, and then his army went with him. He complained to the Councill, but it became ridicule, and so his revenge sank.

Dr. Triplet came to give his Master a Visit, and He whip't him. The Dr. gott Pitcher of Oxford, who had a strong and sweet Base, to sing this Song under the schoole windowes, and gott a good guard to secure him with swords, etc., and he was preserved from the examen of the little myrmidons which issued-out to attach him ; but he was so frighted that he beshitt him-selfe most fearfully :

> *A French man voyd of English*
> *Enquiring for Paul's steeple*
> *His Pardonnez-moy*
> *He counted a toy,*
> *For he whip't him before all the people.*

For a piece of Beef and Turnip,
Neglected, with a Cabbage,
He took up the Pillion
Of his bouncing Mayd Jillian,
And sowc't her like a Baggage.

After his Sequestration, Dr. Triplett kept a Schoole at Dublyn, when the King was beheaded. Afterwards at Hayes, Surrey, 12 miles from London. 'Twas here our common friend George Ent went to schoole to him, who told me that he had forgott the smart of his old master Gill. He was very severe.

I'le tell you a story of our old friend. His Master Triplett was a great lover of Honey, and one of his Schoole-fellowe's mothers having sent a pott of honey to the Doctor, G. Ent putt his schoole-fellow to beg a little of his Master, and he had gott a manchet and so they would have a *Regalio*. The Doctor was in his study; and the boy takes the confidence to approach with his *Quaeso, Praeceptor, da mihi Mel* [Please, Sir, give me some Honey]. G. Ent was sneaking behind. Quoth the disturbed doctor, You audacious raskall, and gave him a good cuff on the eare, How dare you be thus impudent? Sirrah, who putt you on? The boy answered, whiningly, G. Ent. The enraged Doctor flies out of his study (he was a very strong man) gives poor George a kick in the breech, and made him fly downe a flight of 7 or 8 staires to the landing place, where his head first came to. He was stunn'd, but 'twas well his neck was not broken. 'Twas a most cruel and inhumane act to use a poore child so. It so happened that a day or two before G. E. had shaled a Tooth. He writes a letter to his father (now Sir George Ent) and incloses the tooth in it; relates the story, and that he lost the tooth by that meanes. The next day the grave and learned Dr. Ent comes to Hayes (the fame of whose learning and Testimonie did give great credit and reputation to this schoole) expostulates with the Doctor about his sonne. To be short, tooke him away, and placed him with Mr. William Radford (an honest sequestred fellow of Trinity College, Oxon, and an excellent schoolmaster, having been bred at Thame under Dr. Birt and afterwards sent to Winton). This accident well-nigh did breake Dr. Triplett's schoole. But shortly after this time, happened the Restauration of his Majestie, and then he was also restored to his former preferments.

WILLIAM TWISSE

[Born 1578. Puritan divine. Probationer Fellow of New College, Oxford 1596. Chaplain to Elizabeth, Queen of Bohemia, at Heidelberg 1613. Rector of Newington Longueville 1613. Vicar of Newbury 1620. He then refused all further preferment, as *lacking music in singing and rhetoric for the preaching, and not skilled to stroke a cathedral beard canonically*. He became Prolocutor of the Westminster Assembly in 1643, but was opposed to the alienation of Church property. He died in 1646 and was buried in Westminster Abbey, but in 1661, his remains were, by royal command, disinterred and thrown into a common pit in St. Margaret's Churchyard.]

HIS sonne Dr. Twisse, Minister of the New-church neer Tothill-street Westminster, told me, that he had heard his father say, that when he was a schoole-boy at Winton-colledge, that he was a rakell ; and that one of his Schoole-fellowes and camerades (as wild as himselfe) dyed there ; and that, his father goeing in the night to the House of office, the phantome or Ghost of his dead schoolefellow appeared to him, and told him *I am damn'd* : and that this was the Beginning of his Conversion.

Memorandum :—the Dr. had a melancholique and Hypo-condriaque temperament.

THOMAS TYNDALE

[Born 1588. Son of Thomas Tyndale of Eastwood Park, Thorn-
bury, by Oriane, sister and co-heir of Claudius le Bon, Seigneur de
Fourneau in Normandy. In 1620 he married Dorothy, the daughter
of William Stafford, author of *A Brief Concert of English Polity,* who
had, in 1587, revealed a plot against Queen Elizabeth, only to find
himself implicated, for which he was imprisoned in the Tower.
Thomas Tyndale sold Eastwood Park in 1619 and bought the site and
demesne of the Priory of Kington St. Michael, where he lived until
his death in 1672. His widow told Aubrey many of the more scandalous
stories about the Elizabethan Court.]

THOMAS TYNDALE, an old Gentleman that remembers
Queen Elizabeth's raigne and Court, one of true Gravity
and prudence, not one that depends upon the grave
cutt of his beard to be thought so. He hath seen much in his
time both at home and abroade ; and with much choler inveighes
against things now :—Alas ! O' God's will ! Now-a-dayes
every one, forsooth ! must have coaches, forsooth ! In those
dayes Gentlemen kept horses for a man-at-Armes, besides their
Hackney and hunting horses. This made the Gentry robust
and hardy and fitt for service ; were able to be their owne
guides in case of a rout or so, when occasion should so require.
Our Gentry forsooth in these dayes are so effeminated that they
know not how to ride on horseback.

The advantage that King Charles I had : Gentlemen tho
[then] kept good horses, and many horses for a man-at-Armes,
and men that could ride them ; hunting horses. Now we are
come all to our Coaches forsooth ! Now young men are so
farre from managing good horses, they know not how to ride
a hunting nag or handle their weapons. So God help the King
if, etc.

In Sir Philip Sydney's time 'twas as much disgrace for a
Cavalier to be seen in London rideing in a Coach in the street
as now 'twould be to be seen in a petticoate and wastcoate.
In those days when a Senator went to the Parliament-house
a-foote, or a horse-back with his rich Footcloath, he had at his
heeles ½ a dozen or 10 tall fellowes with blew coates and badges
and long basket-hilt swords. Now forsooth only a laquey
and a little spitt-pig.

Tho when the Gentry mett, it was not at a poor blind sordid alehouse, to drinke up a barrell of drinke and lie drunke there two or three dayes together; fall together by the eares. They mett tho in the fields, well-appointed, with their Hounds or their Hawkes; kept up good Hospitality; and kept a good retinue, that would venture that bloud and spirit that filled their vaines which their Masters tables nourisht; kept their Tenants in due respect of them. We had no depopulacion in those dayes.

You see in me the Ruines of Time. The day is almost at end with me, and truly I am glad of it: I desire not to live in this corrupt age. I foresawe and foretold the late changes, and now easily foresee what will follow after. Alas! O' God's will! It was not so in Queen Elizabeth's time: then youth bare Respect to old Age.

Tho the elders and better sort of the Parish sate and beheld the pastimes of the young men, as wrastling, shooting at Butts, bowling, and dancing. All this is now lost; and pride, whoreing, wantonnesses, and drunkennesses. Their servants like clownes too, drunkards too: breeches of one sort, Doublet of another, drabled with the teares of the Tankard and greasie. Dick Pawlet built an alehouse for his Servants, without the Gate, for convenience sake, because the servants should be within call.

In those dayes Hunting and Falconery were at the height. Good cheere was then much in use; but to be wiser then one's neighbours, scandalous and to be envyed at. And the Nobility and Gentry were, in that soft peace, damnable prowd and insolent.

HENRY AND THOMAS VAUGHAN

[Born 1622. Poets and physicians. Henry was known as the *Silurist* because of his love for the County of Brecknockshire, the county of his birth, which was anciently inhabited by the Silures. He was at Jesus College, Oxford, and studied law in London, before settling as a physician at Brecon and Newton-by-Usk. In his youth he was a decided Royalist and, along with his twin brother Thomas, was imprisoned. His first book, which appeared in 1646, was *Poems, with the Tenth Satire of Juvenal Englished*. *Olor Iscanus* (The Swan of Usk), a collection of poems and translations, was surreptitiously published in 1651. About this time he had a serious illness which led to deep spiritual impressions, and thereafter his writings were almost entirely religious. *Silex Scintillans* (Sparks from the Flint) is his best known work and contains the magnificent *They are all gone into the world of light*. *Flores Solitudinis* (Flowers of Solitude) and *The Mount of Olives* are devout meditations in prose. The two brothers were joint authors of *Thalia Rediviva : the Pastimes and Diversions of a Country Muse* (1678), a collection of translations and original poems. Thomas Vaughan died in 1666 and Henry in 1695.]

THERE were two Vaughans (Twinnes) both very in-geniose, and writers. One writt a Poeme called *Olor Iscanus* (Henry Vaughan, the first-borne) and another booke of divine meditations. He is ingeniose, but prowd and humorous. His brother wrote severall Treatises, whose names I have now forgott, but names himself *Eugenius Philalethes*.

They were borne at Llansanfraid in Brecknockshire, by the river Uske (Isca). Their grandmother was an Aubrey : their father, a coxcombe and no honester then he should be— he cosèned me of 50s. once.

Eugenius Philalethes was of Jesus College. Whither Henry was I have forgotten ; but he was a Clarke sometime to Judge Sir Marmaduke Lloyd.

This Account I had from Mr. Henry Vaughan, whose handwriting it is :

Honoured Cousin.

Yours of the 10th. June I received att Breckon, where I am still attendinge our Bishops Lady in a tertian feaver, and cannot as yet have the leasure to step home; butt lest my delayings of tyme here should bringe the account (you expect) too late into your hands : I shall now in part give you the best I can, and be more exact in my next.

My brother and I were borne att Newtin, in Brecknockshire, in the parish of St. Bridget's, in the year 1621.

I stayed not att Oxford to take my degree, butt was sent to London, beinge then designed by my father for the study of the Law, which the sudden eruption of our late civil warres wholie frustrated.

My brother continued there for 10 or 12 yeares, and I thinke he could be noe lesse than Master of Arts. He died upon an imployment for his majesty, within 5 or 6 miles of Oxford, in the yeare that the last great plague visited London. He was buried by Sir Robert Murrey, his great friend (and then Secretary of Estate for the Kingdome of Scotland) to whom he gave his bookes and MSS.

My brothers imployment was in physic and Chymistrie : he was ordayned minister by bishop Mainwaringe and presented to the Rectorie of St. Brigets by his kinsman, Sir George Vaughan.

My profession allso is physic, which I have practised now for many years with good successe (I thanke god!) and a repute big enough for a person of greater parts than my selfe.

My brother died in the seaven and fortieth year of his age, upon the 27th of Februarie in the yeare 1666, and was buried upon the first of March.

Dear Sir, I am highly obliged to you that you would be pleased to remember and reflect upon such low and forgotten thinges as my brother and my selfe. I shall be ever ready to acknowledge the honour you have done us, and if you have any Concerne in these parts that I may be serviceable in : I humblie beg, that you would call upon and Command,

Honoured Cousin,
Your most affectionate and most faithfull humble servant. H: Vaughan.
June the 15th —73.

Sir Robert Moray the morning he dyed told me he buryed my cosen Thomas Vaughan at Albery neer Ricot within three miles of Oxford. He dyed at Mr. Kem's howse, the minister.

EDWARD DE VERE:
EARL OF OXFORD

[Born 1550. He was a courtier of Queen Elizabeth, who lost his friends by his insolence and pride, and his fortune by his extravagance. He married a daughter of Lord Burghley, who had to support his family after her death. He had some reputation as a writer of short pieces, many of which are in *The Paradise of Dainty Devices*. He was the seventeenth holder of the title and died in 1604.]

THIS Earle of Oxford, making of his low obeisance to Queen Elizabeth, happened to let a Fart, at which he was so abashed and ashamed that he went to Travell, 7 yeares. On his returne the Queen welcomed him home, and sayd, My Lord, I had forgott the Fart.

Mr. Nicholas Hill was one of the most learned men of his Time : a great Mathematician and Philosopher, and a Poet and Traveller. But no writer (that I ever heard of) or, if he was, his writings had the usuall fate of those not printed in the Author's life-time. He was (or leaning) a Roman Catholiq. He was so eminent for knowledge, that he was the favourite of the great Earle of Oxford, who had him to accompanie him in his Travells (he was his Steward) which were so splendid and sumptuous, that he lived at Florence in more grandeur than the Duke of Tuscany. This Earle spent fourty thousand pounds per annum in seaven yeares Travell.

In his Travells with his Lord (I forget whither Italy or Germany, but I thinke the former) a poor man begged him to give him a penny. A penny ! said Mr. Hill, what dost say to ten pound ? Ah ! ten pound ! said the Beggar, that would make a man happy. N. Hill gave him immediately 10 pounds and putt it downe upon account—Item, to a Beggar ten pounds, to make him happy, which his Lordship allowed and was well pleased at it.

As I have heard, it was that great Antiquary King Charles the First his observation, that the three ancientist Families of Europe for Nobility, were the *Veres* in England, Earls of Oxford, and the *Fitz-Geralds* in Ireland, Earls of Kildare, and *Momorancy* in France.

Surlinesse and inurbanitie too common in England :
Chastise these very severely. A better instance of a squeamish
and disobligeing, slighting, insolent, proud fellow, perhaps
cannot be found then in Gwin, the Earle of Oxford's Secretary.
No reason satisfies him, but he overweenes and cutts some sower
faces that would turne the milke in a faire ladie's breast.

WILLIAM DE VISSCHER

[Born 1595. Merchant. His family came from Emden, where he was born, which was then a Hanseatic Port and so one of the main trading centres in Europe. He died in 1668.]

AT two yeares old was brought into England by his father, an eminent Merchant; lived 55 yeares in one house at St. Mary Hill, and dyed in the 74th yeare of his age. He lived there till the Fire of London; he dyed about 3 yeares after—he did not enjoy himselfe afterwards.

In the last great Dearth of Corne in England, when there was a great complaint and Cry of the Poore, he bade them bee of good comfort for they should not starve, for he would give them his labour and the use of his Estate for that yeare. He (being a man of vast Credit) gave his Factors order that what corne they could buy at such and such rates beyond sea, to hire flye-boates and send them over to the Port of London, of which he bought in one yeare two thousand five hundred sayle. The Corne that cost him 12s. per bushell beyond sea, he sold here for 14s.; and some of the places from whence he had corne (they selling it by reason of the greatnesse of the price) afterwards wanted it themselves and were faine to be supplied from hence; for which they were faine to pay halfe value more then the first cost, or els must have starved.

Many Disasters happened to many of the Shippes that were bound for London (some that never arrived were destroyed by foule weather; some wind-bound so long till their Corne fired for want of ayering, and was faine to be throwne overboard) that in the whole matter, after all the adventures runne, he did not gaine five and twenty hundred pounds. The Fly-boates caryed 800 tunne, and some more.

He was a very eminent Merchant, as most was of his time; and was valued by common reputation (when he maried his daughter) to be worth sixscore thousand pounds.

He stayed in London during the whole time of the Plague, and had not all that time one sick in his family. He was a temperate man, and had his house very cleanly kept.

EDMUND WALLER

[Born 1606. Poet. He belonged to an old and wealthy family, and though he was related to John Hampden and was distantly connected with Oliver Cromwell, he was a staunch Royalist. At the age of sixteen he became a Member of Parliament, in which he sat for various constituencies for the rest of his life. In 1631 he added still further to his fortune by marrying Anne Banks, a London heiress, who died three years later. In 1643 he was detected in a Royalist plot and was expelled from the House, fined £10,000, and banished. On this occasion he showed cowardice and treachery, humiliating himself in the most abject manner and betraying all his associates. Returning to England by permission in 1652, he addressed some laudatory verses to Cromwell. Nevertheless, at the Restoration he was ready with a congratulatory address to Charles II, and when the King pointed out its inferiority to the Ode on Cromwell, Waller replied, *Poets, Sire, succeed better in fiction than in truth*. The poem, however, succeeded in its object, and the poet became a favourite at court and sat in Parliament until his death in 1687.]

I HAVE heard Mr. Thomas Bigge, of Wickham, say (who was his schoole-fellow, and of the same forme) that he little thought then he would have been so rare a Poet; he was wont to make his Exercise for him.

About 23, or between that and 30, he grew (upon I know not what occasion) mad; but 'twas (I thinke) not long ere he was cured. He was proud: to such, a Check often gives that distemper. He was passionately in love with Dorothea, the eldest daughter of the Earle of Leicester, whom he haz eternized in his Poems: and the Earle loved him, and would have been contented that he should have had one of the youngest daughters; perhaps *this* might be the Check.

One of the first refiners of our English language and poetrey. When he was a brisque young sparke, and first studyed Poetry; me thought, sayd he, I never sawe a good copie of English verses; they want smoothness; then I began to essay. I have severall times heard him say that he cannot versify when he will: but when the Fitt comes upon him, he does it easily, i.e. in plaine terms, when his Mercurius and Venus are well aspected.

He told me he was not acquainted with Ben Johnson (who

dyed about 1638) but familiarly with Lucius, Lord Falkland, Sydney Godolphin, Mr. Hobbes, etc.

I have heard Mr. Edmund Waller say that the Lord Marquisse of Newcastle was a great Patron to Dr. Gassendi, and M. DesCartes, as well as Mr. Hobbes, and that he hath dined with them all three at the Marquiss's Table at Paris.

He was very much admired at Court before the late Civill Warres. 1643, he being then a Member of the house of Commons, he was committed prisoner to the Tower for the Plott with Tomkins (his cosen germane) and Chaloner, for firing the City of London and delivering the Parliament, etc., to the King's partie. He had much adoe then to save his life, and in order to do it, sold his Estate in Bedfordshire, about 1300 pounds per annum, to Dr. Wright, M.D., for about 10,000 pounds (much under value) which was procured in 24 hours time or els he had been hanged : With which money he Bribed the whole House, which was the first time a house of Commons was ever bribed. His excellent rhetoricall speech to the House to save his life, as also his Panegyrique to Oliver, Lord Protector, he would not suffer to be inserted in the edition of his *Poems* since the restauration of King Charles II.

When King Charles II returned, he received Mr. Waller very kindly, and no man's conversation is more esteemed at Court now then his. The Dutches of Yorke (daughter to the Duke of Modena) very much delights in his company, and hath layd her commands on him to write, which he hath dedicated to her Highnes.

His Intellectuals are very good yet (1680) and he makes verses, but he growes feeble. He wrote verses of the Bermudas 50 yeares since, upon the information of one who had been there ; walking in his fine woods the poetique spirit came upon him.

He is of somewhat above a middle stature, thin body, not at all robust ; fine thin skin, his face somewhat of an olivaster, his hayre frizzd, of a brownish colour ; full eye, popping out and working ; ovall faced, his forehead high and full of wrinckles : his head but small, braine very hott, and apt to be cholerique. He is something magisteriall, and haz a great mastership of the English Language. He is of admirable and gracefull Elocution and exceeding ready.

He has spent most of his time in London ; especially in Winter ; but oftentimes in the Summer he enjoyes his Muse at Beconsfield in Bucks, which is incomparable Aire, and where are delicious walkes in the woods. Now I speake of Woods, I remember he told us there, that he cutt downe and grubbed-up a Beech wood of his, at Beconsfield in Bucks, and without soweing, but naturally, there sprang up a wood all of Birch.

He haz but a tender weake body, but was alwayes very temperate. They made him damnable drunke at Somerset-house, where, at the water stayres, he fell downe, and had a cruell fall. 'Twas pitty to use such a sweet swan so inhumanely.

I have heard him say that he so much admired Mr. Thomas Hobbes booke *De Cive,* when it came forth, that he was very desirous to have it donne into English, and Mr. Hobbes was most willing it should be done by Mr. Waller's hand, for that he was so great a Master of our English language. Mr. Waller freely promised him to doe it, but first he would desire Mr. Hobbes to make an Essaye; he (T. H.) did the first booke, and did it so extremely well, that Mr. Waller would not meddle with it, for that nobody els could doe it so well.

Mr. Christopher Wase repeating to him the bitter satyricall verses made on Sir Carre Scroop, viz :

> *Thy Brother murdred, and thy Sister whor'd,*
> *Thy Mother too, and yet thy Penne's thy Sword ;*

Mr. Waller replyed sur le champ, That men write ill things well, and good things ill ; that Satyricall writing was downe-hill, most easie and naturall ; that at Billingsgate one might hear great heights of such witt ; that the cursed earth naturally produces briars and thornes and weeds, but roses and fine flowers require cultivation. All his writings are free from offence.

Mr. Edm: Waller sayd to Eliz: Countess of Thanet, That Poetrie was abused, when 'twas turned to any other way, than hymnes.

He hath a great memory : and remembers a History best when read to him : yet, notwithstanding his great Witt and mastership in rhetorique, he will oftentimes be guilty of mispelling in English. He writes a lamentably poor hand, as bad as the scratching of a hen.

He was borne in the parish of Agmundesham, in Buckinghamshire, at a place called Winchmore-hill, which was sold by his father, and which he had a very great desire to have bought again, not long before his death, but the Owner would not sell it. Said he, to his cosen Hamden, *A Stagge, when he is hunted, and neer spent, alwayes returnes home.*

He made some verses of his owne dyeing, but a fortnight, or a little more before his Decease. He dyed at 83, and his Witt was as florid then as at any time of his Life. He derived his Poetick witt from the Hamdens ; severall of them have been Poets.

SETH WARD

[Born 1617. Divine. At Cambridge he was *Terrae filius,* that is, he had to make a satirical speech at the Act, but his contribution was so alarmingly witty that he nearly lost his degree. Prebendary (1660), Dean (1661) and Bishop (1662) of Exeter. Translated to Salisbury 1667. Chancellor of the Garter 1671. He was extremely severe with dissenters. He published his sermons and some theological and mathematical treatises. Died 1689.]

SETH WARD, Lord Bishop of Sarum, was borne at Huntingford, a small market-towne in Hartfordshire, anno Domini 1618 (when the great blazing Starre appeared). His Father was an Attorney there, and of very honest repute. (Dr. Guydos, physician of Bath, says that anciently there was but One Attorney in Somerset, and he was so poor, that he went a foot to London; and now, 1689, they swarme there like Locusts : they go to Market and breed Contention.) His father taught him common arithmetique, and his Genius lay much to the Mathematiques, which being naturall to him, he quickly and easily attained.

At sixteen yeares old he went to Sydney colledge in Cambridge ; he was Servitour to Dr. Ward (Master of the Colledge, and Professor of Divinity) who being much taken with his ingenuity and industry, as also with his suavity of nature, quickly made him Scholar of the Howse, and after, Fellowe. Though he was of his name, he was not at all akinne to him (which most men imagined because of the great kindnesse to him) but the consimility of their dispositions was a greater tye of Friendship then that of blood, which signifies but little, as to that point.

Sir Charles Scarborough, M.D. (then an ingeniose young student, and Fellowe of Caius Colledge in Cambridge) was his great acquaintance ; both students in mathematiques ; which the better to perfect, they went to Mr. William Oughtred, at Albury in Surrey, to be enformed by him in his *Clavis Mathematica,* which was then a booke of *Aenigmata.* Mr. Oughtred treated them with exceeding humanity, being pleased at his heart when an ingeniose young man came to him that would ply his Algebra hard. When they returned to Cambridge, they read the *Clavis Mathematica* to their Pupills, which was the first time that that booke was ever read in a University. Mr.

Laurence Rooke, a good mathematician and algebrist (and I thinke had also been Mr. Oughtred's disciple) was his great acquaintance.

Anno Domini 1644, at the breaking out of the Civill-warres, he was a Prisoner, together with Dr. Ward, Dr. Collins, Sir Thomas Hatton, &c. for the King's Cause, in St. John's Colledge in Cambridge, and was put out of his Fellowship at Sydney Colledge. Being gott out of Prison, he was very civilly and kindly received by his friend and neighbour, Ralph Freeman, of Apsten, Esq., a vertuous and hospitable Gentleman.

Anno Domini 1648 the Visitation of the Parliament was Oxford, and turned out a great many Professors and Fellowes. The Astronomy Reader, Dr. Greaves, being sure to be ejected, was unwilling to be turned out of his place, but desired to resigne it rather to some worthy person, wherupon Dr. Charles Scarborough and William Holder, D.D. recommended to Dr. Greaves, their common friend, Mr. Seth Ward. Seth Ward, A.M. was invited to succeed him, and came from Mr. Freeman's to Oxford, had the Astronomy Professor's place, and lived at Wadham Colledge, where he conversed with the Warden, Dr. John Wilkins.

Anno Domini 1656, he had from Brownrigg, Bishop of Exon, the grant of the Chantor's place of the Church of Exon (which then signified nothing).

Anno Domini 1659, William Hawes, then President of Trinity Colledge in Oxford, having broken in his lunges a vein (which was not curable) Mr. Ward being very well acquainted and beloved in that colledge ; by the consent of all the Fellowes, William Hawes resigned up his Presidentship to him, and dyed some few days after. Anno 1660, upon the restauration of King Charles II, Dr. Hannibal Potter (the President sequestred by the Parliamentary Visitors) re-enjoyed the Presidentship again.

He then enjoyed his Chanters place at Excester, and, I thinke, was certainly minister of St. Laurence church in London.

Anno Domini 1661, the Deane of Exon dyed, and then it was his right to step-in next to the Deanry.

Anno Domini 1663, the Bishop of Exon dyed : Dr. Ward, the Deane, was in Devonshire at that time, at a Visitation, where were a great number of the Gentrey of the Countrey. Deane Ward was very well knowne to the Gentry, and his learning, prudence, and Comity had wonne them all to be his Friends. The newes of the death of the Bishop being brought to them, who were all very merry and rejoycing with good entertainment, with great Alacrity the Gentlemen cryed all, *uno uno*, Wee will have Mr. Deane to be our Bishop. This was at that criticall time when the House of Commons were the King's darlings. The Deane told them that for his part he had no interest or acquaintance at Court; but intimated to them how much the King esteemed the Members of Parliament (and a great many Parliament men were then there) and that his Majestie would deny them nothing. If 'tis so, Gentlemen (sayd Mr. Deane) that you will needes have me to be your bishop, if some of you will make your addresse to his Majestie, 'twill be donne. With that they dranke the other Glasse, a health to the King, and another to their wished-for Bishop; had their horses presently made ready, putt foot in Stirrup, and away they rode merrily to London; went to the King, and he immediately graunted them their request. This is the first time that ever a Bishop was made by the House of Commons.

Now, though Envy cannot deny, that this worthy Person was very well worthy any Preferment could be conferred on him, Yet the old Bishops were exceedingly disgruntled at it, to see a briske young Bishop that could see through all their formall gravity, but 40 yeares old, not come in at the right dore but leape over the pale. It went to their very hearts. Well, Bishop of Excester he was, to the great joy of all the Diocese. Being Bishop he had then free accesse to his Majestie, who is a lover of ingenuity and a discerner of ingeniose men, and quickly tooke a liking to him.

He is (without all manner of flattery) so prudent, learned, and good a man, that he honours his Preferment as much as the Preferment does him: and is such a one that cannot be advanced too high. My Lord (Lucius) Falkland was wont to say that he never knew any one that a paire of Lawne sleeves had not altered from himselfe, but only Bishop Juxon; had he knowne this excellent Prelate, he would have sayd he had knowne one more. As he is the pattern of humility and courtesie, so he knowes when to be severe and austere; and he is not one to be trampled or worked upon. He is a Batchelour, and of a most magnificent and munificent mind.

He hath been a Benefactor to the Royall Societie (of which he was one of the first Members and Institutors: the beginning of Philosophical Experiments was at Oxon, 1649, by Dr. Wilkins, Seth Ward, Ralph Bathurst, &c.) He also gave a noble pendulum Clock to the Royall Societie (which goes a weeke) to perpetuate the memory of his deare and learned friend, Mr. Laurence Rooke, who tooke his sicknesse of which he dyed by setting up so often for Astronomicall Observations. He haz perused all the Records of the Church of Sarum, which, with long lyeing, had been conglutinated together; read them all over, and taken abridgements of them, which haz not been donne by any of his predecessors I beleeve for some hundreds of yeares.

Anno 1669, Dr. Christopher Wren was invited by the Bishop of Sarum (Seth Ward) where he made a particular Survey of the Cathedrall Church. He was at least a weeke about it, and a curious discourse it was : it was not above two sheetes. Upon my writing *The Natural History of Wilts,* I had occasion to insert it there : I asked the Bishop for it, and he told me he had lent it, to whome he could not tell, and had no copy of it. 'Tis great pity the paines of so great an artist should be lost. Sir Christopher tells me he hath no copie of it neither.

The black malice of the Deane of Sarum—he printed sarcasticall Pamphletts against him—was the cause of his disturbd spirit, wherby at length, he quite lost his memorie. For about a moneth before he dyed he tooke very little Sustenance, but lived on the Stock, and died a Skeleton.

I searcht all Seth, Episcopus Sarum's, papers that were at his house at Knightsbridge neer London where he dyed. The custome is, when the Bishop of Sarum dies, that the Deane and Chapter lock-up his Studie and put a Seale on it. His scatterd papers I rescued from being used by the Cooke since his death ; which was destinated with other good papers and letters to be put under pies.

WALTER WARNER

[While William Harvey may have read Warner's manuscript treatise about the circulation of the blood, it is obvious that Warner's views were based on the current knowledge of the period, correct in certain details, but ignorant of the implications of the whole. Professor Rolleston said in the Harveian Oration of 1873 : What was left for Harvey to discover was nothing less than *the circulation itself*. His predecessors had but impinged, and that by guesswork, upon different segments of the circle, and then gone off at a tangent into outer darkness, whilst he worked and proved and demonstrated round its entire periphery. Warner died in 1640.]

THIS Walter Warner was both Mathematician and Philosopher, and 'twas he that putt-out Thomas Hariot's *Algebra,* though he mentions it not.

Walter had but one hand (borne so) : Dr. John Pell thinks a right hand ; his mother was frighted, which caused this deformity, so that instead of a left hand, he had only a Stump with five warts upon it, instead of a hand and fingers. He wore a cuffe on it like a pockett. The Doctor never sawe his stump, but Mr. Warner's man told him so.

This account I received from Mr. Isaac Walton : this is his owne hand writing—Mr. Warner did long and constantly lodg nere the Water-stares or market in Woolstable (Woolstable is a place or lane not far from Charing Crosse, and nerer to Northumberland howse). My Lord of Winchester tells me he knew him, and that he saide he first fownd out the cerculation of the blood, and discover'd it to Do^r Harvie (who said that 'twas he (himselfe) that found it) for which he is so memorably famose.

Mr. Warner did tell Dr. Pell, that when Dr. Harvey came out with his *Circulation of the Blood,* he did wonder whence Dr. Harvey had it : but comeing one day to the Earle of Leicester, he found Dr. Harvey in the Hall, talking very familiarly with Mr. Prothero, to whom Mr. Warner had discoursed concerning this Exercitation of his *De Circulatione Sanguinis,* and made no question but Dr. Harvey had his Hint from Prothero. Dr. Pell sayes that Mr. Warner rationated demonstratively by Beates of the Pulses that there must be a Circulation of the Blood.

Warnei nad a pention of 40 pounds a yeare from that Earle
of Northumberland that lay so long a prisner in the Towre,
and som alowance from Sir Tho. Alesbery with whome he
usually spent his sumer in Windesor park, and was welcom, for
he was harmless and quet. His winter was spent at the
Wolstable, where he dyed in the time of the Parliament of 1640,
of which, or whome, he was no louer.

Mr. Walter Warner made an Inverted Logarithmicall
Table, i.e. whereas Briggs' table fills his Margin with Numbers
encreasing by Unites, and over-against them setts their
Logarithms, which because of incommensurability must needs
be either abundant or deficient; Mr. Warner (like a Dictionary
of the Latine before the English) fills the Margin with
Logarithmes encreasing by Unites, and setts to every one of
them so many continuall meane proportionalls between one
and 10, and they for the same reason must also have the last
figure incompleat. These, which, before Mr. John Pell grew
acquainted with Mr. Warner, were ten thousand, and at Mr.
Warner's request were by Mr. Pell's hands, or direction, made
a hundred-thousand.

Quaere Dr. Pell, what is the use of those Inverted
Logarithmes ? for W. Warner would not doe such a thing in
vaine.

JOHN WHITSON

[Born 1557. Merchant adventurer. When Philip II of Spain laid an embargo on English ships in 1585, Whitson fitted out the *Mayflower* to make reprisals. He took an active part in the early voyages for the settlement of North America. He was four times married and was John Aubrey's godfather. Died 1629.]

JOHN WHITSON, Alderman of the City of Bristol, was borne at Cover in the Forest of Deane in the Countie of Gloucester: he went to schoole at Bristow, where he made a good proficience in the Latin tongue. He was bound Apprentice to Alderman Vawr, a Spanish Merchant of this City. He was a handsome young fellow; and his old Master (the Alderman) being dead, his Mistress one day called him into the Wine-cellar and bad him broach the best Butt in the Cellar for her; and truly he broach't his Mistrisse, who after maried him. This story will last perhaps as long as Bristol is a City.

He had a very good healthy constitution, and was an early Riser; wrote all his Letters and dispatched his businesse betime in the Morning. He had a good naturall Witt, and gaind by the Spanish trade a fair Estate.

He lived nobly; kept a plentifull Table; and was the most popular magistrate in the City, alwaies chosen a Member of Parliament. He kept a noble house, and did entertain and treat the Peers and great Persons that came to the City. He kept his Hawkes.

He was charitable in his Life in breeding-up of poor Scholars: I remember five that had been bred-up under him, but not one of them came to good, they lived so luxuriously.

His second Wife was a very beautifull Dame, as by her picture (at length) in the Dining rome, doeth appear. By her he had a Daughter, his only child, who was counted the Flower of Bristol, who was maried to Sir Thomas Trenchard of Dorset-shire. His beloved and only Daughter dyeing (together with her child) Richard Wheeler, his Nephew, who was bred a Merchant under him with others, was his Heir; but he proving a Sott and a capricious Coxcombe, he setled all his Estate upon the City of Bristow for pious Uses, and was, I doe believe, the greatest Benefactor that ever the City had.

He dyed about the seaventy-sixth yeare of his age by a
fall from his horse ; his head pitching on a nail that stood on
its head by a Smyth's shop.   He was buried very honourably ;
besides all his Relations in mourning, he had as many poor old
men and woemen as he was yeares old in mourning gownes
and hoodes, the Mayor and Aldermen in Mourning ; all the
Trained Band (he was their Colonel) attended the Funerall and
their Pikes had black Ribons and Drummes were covered with
Black cloath.

JOHN WILKINS

[Born 1614. Divine. Though he had been private chaplain to Charles I's nephew, the Prince Palatine, he adhered to the Parliamentary side in the Civil War and took the Covenant. Warden of Wadham College, Oxford, 1648. Master of Trinity College, Cambridge, 1659. Deprived of the Mastership at the Restoration, he became a Prebendary of York. First Secretary of the Royal Society 1662. Dean of Ripon 1663. Bishop of Chester 1668. Died 1672.]

HIS father was a Goldsmith in Oxford. Mr. Francis Potter knew him very well, and was wont to say that he was a very ingeniose man, and had a very Mechanicall head. He was much for Trying of Experiments, and his head ran much upon the *perpetuall motion*. He maryed a daughter of Mr. John Dod (who wrote on the Commandments) at whose house, at Fawlsley, she laye-in with her son John, of whome we are now to speake.

He had his Grammar learning in Oxford (I thinke from Mr. Sylvester, over the meadowes). He was admitted of Magdalen-hall in Oxford, 1627; his Tutor there was the learned Mr. John Tombs (Coryphaeus of the Anabaptists).

He has sayd oftentimes that the first rise, or hint of his Rising, was from goeing accidentally a courseing of a Hare: where an ingeniose Gentleman of good quality falling into discourse with him, and finding him to have very good partes, told him that he would never gett any considerable preferment by continuing in the University; and that his best way was to betake himselfe to some Lord's or great persons' House that had good Benefices to conferre. Sayd Mr. J. Wilkins, I am not knowne in the world; I know not to whom to address myselfe upon such a designe. The Gentleman replied, I will recommend you myselfe, and did so, to (as I thinke) Lord Viscount Say and Seale, where he stayed with very good likeing till the late Civill warres, and then he was Chaplain to his Highnesse Charles Louis, Prince Elector Palatine of the Rhine, with whom he went (after the Peace concluded in Germany) and was well preferred there by his Highnesse.

After the Visitation at Oxon by the Parliament, he gott to be Warden of Wadham Colledge. Anno 1656 he maried to Robina, the Relict of Dr. French, Canon of Christchurch, Oxon, and sister to Oliver, (then) Lord Protector, who made him Master of Trinity colledge in Cambridge (in which place he revived Learning by strickt examinations at elections : he was much honoured there, and heartily loved by all) where he continued till 1660 (the Restauration of his Majestie). Then he was Minister of Saint Laurence church in London. His friend, Seth Ward, D.D., being made Bishop of Excester, he was made there Deane, and anno 1668 by the favour of George, Duke of Buckingham, was made Bishop of Chester ; and was extremely well beloved in his Diocese. Anno Domini 1672 he dyed of the stone.

He left a Legacy of four hundred pounds to the Royall Society, and had he been able would have given more. He was no great read man ; but one of much and deepe thinking, and of a working head ; and a prudent man as well as ingeniose. He was one of Seth, Lord Bishop of Sarum's most intimate Friends. He was a lustie, strong growne, well sett, broad shoulderd person, cheerfull, and hospitable.

He was the principall Reviver of Experimentall Philosophy at Oxford, where he had weekely an experimentall philosophicall Clubbe, which began 1649, and was the *Incunabula* of the Royall Society. When he came to London, they mett at the Bull-head taverne in Cheapside (e.g. 1658, 1659, and after) till it grew to big for a Clubb. The first beginning of the Royal Society (where they putt discourse in paper and brought it to use) was in the Chamber of William Ball, Esqr., eldest son of Sir Peter Ball of Devon, in the Middle Temple. They had meetings at Taverns before, but 'twas here where it formally and in good earnest sett up : and so they came to Gresham Colledge parlour.

Scripsit :—*The Discovery of a World in the Moone* (long since) ; *A Discourse tending to prove that 'tis probable our Earth is one of the Planets ; Art of Praying and Preaching ; Mathematicall Magique,* dedicated to the Prince Elector ; *Reall Character*—This last was his Darling, and nothing troubled him so much when he dyed, as that he had not compleated it ; which will now in a yeare more be donne by the care and studies of Mr. Robert Hooke, of Gresham College ; Mr. Andrew Paschall, B.D. of Chedzoy, in com. Somerset ; Mr. Francis Lodwyck, of London, merchant ; Mr. John Ray, R.S.S., of Essex ; and Mr. Thomas Pigott, M.A. (Wadham College).

JOHN WILMOT :
EARL OF ROCHESTER

[Born 1647. Poet and libertine. Master of Arts at Oxford when little more than fourteen. He travelled abroad and, on his return, he identified himself with the most dissolute set of Charles II's Courtiers, soon excelling them all in profligacy. In 1666 he was made a Gentleman of the King's Bedchamber and, in 1674, he received a special mark of the royal favour by being appointed Keeper of Wood-stock Park. Towards the end of his life he declared that he was under the influence of drink for five consecutive years. At the same time he cultivated a brilliant faculty for amorous lyrics, obscene rhymes and mordant satires in verse, which more than once caused his dismissal from Court. However he was always taken back into favour and although he quickly ruined his physical health by his excesses, his intellect retained all its vivacity until his death in 1680.]

ABOUT 18, he stole his Lady, Elizabeth Malet, a daughter and heir, a great fortune ; for which I remember I sawe him a Prisoner in the Tower about 1662.

His youthly spirit and oppulent fortune did sometimes make him doe extravagant actions, but in the country he was generally civill enough. He was wont to say that when he came to Brentford the Devill entred into him and never left him till he came into the Country again.

He was Raunger of Woodstock-parke and lived often at the Lodge at the west end, a very delightfull place and noble prospect westwards. Here his Lordship had severall lascivious Pictures drawen.

His Lordship read all manner of bookes. Mr. Andrew Marvell (who was a good Judge of Witt) was wont to say that he was the best English Satyrist and had the right veine. 'Twas pitty Death tooke him off so soon.

In his last sicknesse he was exceedingly paenitent and wrote a letter of his repentance to Dr. Burnet, which is printed.

He sent for all his servants, even the piggard-boy, to come and hear his Palinode.

THOMAS WOLSEY

[Born 1475. Cardinal and statesman. Rector of Lymington : Prebendary of Lincoln and Hereford : Canon of Windsor : Dean of Lincoln, Hereford, York and St. Stephen's, Westminster : Precentor of London : Bishop of Tournay, Lincoln, Bath and Wells, Durham and Winchester : Archbishop of York : Cardinal. Chaplain to Henry VII 1507. Almoner to Henry VIII 1509. Lord Chancellor 1515. He accompanied Henry VIII to the Field of the Cloth of Gold in 1520. Wolsey displayed on a colossal scale the pride and power of the mediæval Church and was almost as rich a man as the King himself. For his natural son he obtained four arch-deaconries, a deanery, five prebends and two rectories. Wolsey supported Henry in his divorce from Catherine of Aragon 1527. Owing to the delay in the divorce proceedings, he incurred the dislike of Anne Boleyn, who influenced the King against him, with the result that a Bill of Indictment was preferred against him in 1530. After receiving a General Pardon, he retired to Cawood, but he was again arrested for High Treason on information given by his physician Dr. Agostini, who accused the Cardinal of bringing *the King's Majesty into marvellous danger, for knowing himself to have the foul and contagious disease of the great pox, broken out upon him in divers parts of his body, he had come daily to His Grace, blowing upon him with his perilous and infective breath.* He died at Leicester on his way to London to answer these charges in 1530.]

THOMAS WOLSEY, Cardinal, was a Butcher's son, of Ipswych, in Suffolke. He was Baccalaur of Arts so young, that he was called the Boy-Bacchalaur.

He was a Fellowe of Magdalen Colledge in Oxford, where he was Tutor to a young Gentleman of Limmington, near Ilchester, in whose guift the presentation of that church is, worth the better part of 200 pounds per annum, which he gave to his Tutor Wolsey. He had committed hereabout some debauchery (I thinke, drunke : no doubt he was of a high rough spirit) and spake derogatorily of Sir Amias Paulet (a Justice of Peace in the neighbourhood) who putt him into the Stockes, which, when he came to be Cardinall, he did not forget ; he layed a Fine upon Sir Amias to build the Gate of the Middle Temple.

His Rise was his quick and prudent dispatch of a message to Paris for Henry 8.

He had a most magnificent spirit.

He was a great Builder, as appeares by White-hall, Hampton-Court. Eshur, in Surrey, a noble house, built of the best burn't brick (perhaps) that ever I sawe; stately gate-house and hall. This stately house (a fitt Pallace for a Prince) was bought about 1666 by a Vintner of London, who is since broke, and the house is sold, and pulled downe to the ground, about 1678. He built the stately tower at Magdalen Colledge in Oxford, and that stately Palace at Winchester (where he was Bishop) called Wolsey-house; I remember it pretty well, standing 1647. Now, I thinke, it is most pulled downe.

His noble foundation of his Colledge of Christ-church in Oxford, where the stately hall was only perfected by him. There were designed (as yet may appeare by the building) most magnificent Cloysters (the brave designe wherof Dr. John Fell hath deteriorated with his new device) to an extraordinary spacious Quadrangle, to the entrance whereof was carrying up a Tower (a Gate-house) of extraordinary rich and noble Gothique building. When the present Great-Duke of Tuscany was at Oxford, he was more taken with that, then all the rest of the Buildings he sawe there, and tooke a second viewe of it.

It should not be forgotten what a noble foundation there was for the Chapell, which did runne from the Colledge, along the street as far as the Blew-boare Inne; which was about 7 foot or more high, and adorned with a very rich Gothique Water-table. It was pulled downe by Dr. John Fell (the Deane) about 1670, to use the stones about the Colledge.

William Fenshaw Esq. told me, that he had seen a letter writt by Cardinal Wolsey to this purpose viz:—My Lord, I understand that there is a Reformation in Religion intended by the Parliament; and I wish that severall things were reformed; but let me tell you that when you have reformed, that others will come, and refine upon you, and others again upon them; *et sic deinceps,* that at last there will be no Religion left, but Atheisme will spring up. The Mysteries of Religion are to be let alone; they will not beare an examination.

The Silver Cross that was wont to be carried before Cardinal Wolsey, fell out of its Socket, and was like to have knock'd one of the Bishops' Servants' Brains out. A very little while after, came in a Messenger, and arrested the Cardinal, before he could get out of the House.

Returning to London from Yorke, he died at Leicester,

where he lies buried (to the shame of Christ-church men) yet without any monument.

> And though, from his owne store, Wolsey might have
> A Palace or a Colledge for his Grave,
> Yet here he lies interr'd, as if that all
> Of him to be remembred were his Fall.
> If thou art thus neglected, what shall wee
> Hope after Death that are but Shreds of thee?

FINIS

INDEX

THE spelling of the names in this Index is not always identical with that in the text; the nearest approximation to Aubrey's many variations has been given.

Aubrey's habit of numbering peers by their Christian names has been corrected.

Bishops are listed under their surnames, peers under their titles, and queens under their Christian names. Unless wives are specifically mentioned by name, they are not listed separately from their husbands. Books are included under their authors.

Biblical and mythical characters are not included in this Index, nor are the publishers of Aubrey's works.

[325]